ARMENIAN APOCRYPHA
FROM ADAM TO DANIEL

EARLY JUDAISM AND ITS LITERATURE

Rodney A. Werline, Editor

Editorial Board:
Randall D. Chesnutt
Kelley N. Coblentz Bautch
Maxine L. Grossman
Carol Newsom

Number 55

ARMENIAN APOCRYPHA
FROM ADAM TO DANIEL

BY

MICHAEL E. STONE

Atlanta

Copyright © 2021 by Michael E. Stone

All rights reserved. No part of this work may be reproduced or transmitted in any form or by any means, electronic or mechanical, including photocopying and recording, or by means of any information storage or retrieval system, except as may be expressly permitted by the 1976 Copyright Act or in writing from the publisher. Requests for permission should be addressed in writing to the Rights and Permissions Office, SBL Press, 825 Houston Mill Road, Atlanta, GA 30329 USA.

Library of Congress Control Number: 2021948769

Table of Contents

Preface	xi
Texts Published in This Book	xiii
Manuscript Sources of Texts Published Within	xv
Procedures	xvii
Critical Signs	xviii
Abbreviations	xix
Published Armenian Apocryphal and Associated Works Mentioned	xxiii

Part 1. Heaven and Hell, Angels and Demons

1.	Concerning Heaven: How Many Heavens Are There?	3
	Introductory Remarks	3
	Text	4
	Translation	5
2.	Concerning Hell And Its Most Bitter Punishment	8
	Introductory Remarks	8
	Text	9
	Translation	11
3.	Angels and the Demon	15
	Introductory Remarks	15
	Text	16
	Translation	17
4.	Classes of Angels	19
	Introductory Remarks	19
	4.1. The Nine Archangels and Their Names	20
	4.2. The Praises Sung by the Nine Classes of Angels	22
	4.3. Origen and the Classes of Angels	24
5.	Numbers and Ranks of the Angels	26
	Introductory Remarks	26

Text	27
Translation	27

6. **PRAYER TO THE ARCHANGELS** — 29
    Introductory Remarks — 29
    Text — 31
    Translation — 33

PART 2. ADAM TO ABRAHAM

7. **CREATION OF EVE AND DISOBEDIENCE** — 41
    Introductory Remarks — 41
    Text — 42
    Translation — 43

8. **THE FORM AND STRUCTURE OF NOAH'S ARK** — 45
    Introductory Remarks — 45
    Text — 47
    Translation — 48

9. **TOWER OF BABEL AND THE CONFUSION OF THE LANGUAGES** — 52
    9.1. Concerning the Tower 1 — 52
        Introductory Remarks — 52
        Texts — 54
        Translations — 56
    9.2. Concerning the Tower 2 — 59
        Introductory Remarks — 59
        Text — 59
        Translation — 61
    9.3. Second Question: Adam's Language — 64
        Introductory Remarks — 64
        Text — 64
        Translation — 65
    9.4. Tower Text 3: The Division of the Earth, and the Tower — 67
        Introductory Remarks — 67
        Text — 68
        Translation — 68
    9.5. Appendix: Other Related Textual Fragments — 69
        9.5.1. The Tower — 69
        9.5.2. On the Tower 129v — 70

CONTENTS vii

  9.5.3. The Story of Noah   70
  9.5.4. The Teaching of St. Gregory   71

Part 3. Abraham to Jacob

10. Abraham, John the Baptist, and Solomon   75
  Introductory Remarks   75
  10.1. Abraham and the Idols   75
    Introductory Remarks   75
    Text and Translation   76
  10.2. John the Baptist's Food   77
    Introductory Remarks   77
    Text and Translation   77
  10.3. Solomon's Saying   78
    Text and Translation   78

11. From Abraham to Jacob   79
  Introductory Remarks   79
  Text   81
  Translation   96

Part 4. Moses to Daniel

12. Of Moses and Aaron   121
  Introductory Remarks   121
  Excursus: Moses in Ethiopia, *by Oren Ableman*   122
  Text   134
  Translation   142

13. Question concerning Moses's Countenance   154
  Introductory Remarks   154
  Text   155
  Translation   157

14. Joshua b. Nun: Text 9   159
  Introductory Remarks   159
  Text   159
  Translation   160

15. Eli the Priest   164
  Introductory Remarks   164

Text	164
Translation	165
16. ELISHA	166
Introductory Remarks	166
Text	167
Translation	168
17. JONAH	170
17.1. Jonah 1	170
Introductory Remarks	170
Text	171
Translation	177
17.2. Jonah 2	187
Introductory Remarks	187
Text	189
Translation	190
17.3. The Preaching of the Prophet Jonah in Nineveh	193
Introductory Remarks	193
Translation	193
18. JOB THE RIGHTEOUS	199
Introductory Remarks	199
Text	199
Translation	204
19. DANIEL EPITOME, PART 2	211
Introductory Remarks	211
19.1. Coda to Daniel Epitome, Part 1	211
Text	211
Translation	211
19.2. Coda to Daniel Epitome, Part 2	212
Text	212
Translation	214
20. DANIEL THE PROPHET AND THE THREE YOUNG MEN	220
Introductory Remarks	220
Text	223
Translation	229

21. THE HISTORY OF THE THREE YOUNG MEN	238
Introductory Remarks	238
Text	239
Translation	242

PART 5. THE SIBYL AND KING SOLOMON

22. CONCERNING THE SIBYL, A WOMAN PHILOSOPHER	251
Introductory Remarks	251
Regarding the Armenian Text, *by Lorenzo DiTommaso*	252
Text	254
Translation	254
23. QUESTIONS AND ANSWERS FROM HOLY BOOKS	255
Introductory Remarks	255
23.1. The Long Recension	259
Text	259
Translation	272
23.2. Manuscript M1405, the Short Recension	286
Text	286
Translation	289
24. THREE TALES: SOLOMON, NOAH, AND SATAN	293
Introductory Remarks	293
24.1. Solomon Text 8	294
24.2. Noah	295
24.3. Satan	296
Bibliography	299
Index of Subjects	309
Index of Ancient Sources	327
Index of Manuscripts	339

Preface

This is the sixth volume of the series Armenian Apocrypha that I have published since the appearance of *Armenian Apocrypha Relating to Patriarchs and Prophets* in 1982. It does not exhaust the unpublished apocryphal texts known to me today, *a fortiori* works still lying undiscovered in Armenian manuscripts, awaiting the eager student.

The process of location of the documents to be included in these volumes has been a lengthy but pleasant task, as it is to express thanks to those who helped me on this way. To the unfailing graciousness and encouragement of the authorities of the Mashtots Matenadaran Institute of Ancient Manuscripts in Erevan, Armenia I am in profound debt. The director, Dr. Vahan Ter-Ghevondyan, and the keeper of manuscripts, Dr. Gēorg Ter-Vardanyan, have supported me and my work there over the years in every way possible. The late former directors of Matenadaran, Dr. Sen Arevshatyan and Dr. Hrachea Tamrazian were equally supportive and helpful. The young scholars of the Matenadaran, a group of learned and energetic folk, have given me hope for the future of Armenian textual studies and philology as well as tactful and gracious support. My dear friends, Aram Topchyan and Gohar Muradyan have done all that one could imagine learned and affectionate friends doing to help me in my research. Many others, too, have turned my research visits to Erevan into the most delightful of experiences.

The staff at Oxford's great Bodleian Library were unfailingly gracious and helpful in multiple ways. I am glad to be able to publish some of their treasures here. The image on p. 30 is published by permission of that library. The publishers of this book, the SBL Press, have shown every courtesy and highly professional expertise in the course of production of this book.

To all of these I am indebted as I am to my assistants in Jerusalem: Dr. Oren Ableman, Dr. Dina Blokland, Yuval Pollak, Anita Shtrubel, Maria Ushakova, and Matthew Wilson for their unfailing care and diligence over the years. Theo van Lint and Abraham Terian have, as always, freely shared the sweet fruit of their learning with me. Ani Arakelyan of the Matenadaran most carefully checked my collations. Thanks to her, many errors have been avoided.

The book was supported by grant 1592/18 of the Israel Science Foundation. That Foundation has also supported others of my projects over decades. My deep thanks are expressed to ISF hereby.

Michael E. Stone
Jerusalem
Summer 2020

Texts Published in This Book

Text Number and Title	MS No.	Fols	Date
1. Concerning Heaven: How Many Heavens Are There?	M10561	75v–76v	17th cent.
2. Concerning Hell and Its Most Bitter Punishment	Bod Marsh 467	359r–360v	17th cent.
3. Angels and the Demon	M1386	180r–180v	17th cent.
4.1. Classes of Angels	M10561	146r–146v	17th cent.
4.2. Praises Sung by the Classes of Angels	M10561	146v	17th cent.
4.3. Origen and the Classes of Angels	M10561	147r	17th cent.
5. Numbers and Ranks of the Angels	M2245	148r–148v	1689
6. Prayer to the Archangels	Bod arm g4		1706–1707
7. Creation of Eve and Disobedience	M1386	183v	17th cent.
8. Form and Structure of Noah's Ark	M4618	53r	1675–1706
9.1a. Concerning the Tower 1	M8531	82r–82v	15th cent.
9.1b. Concerning the Tower 1	M2939	422v	18th cent.
9.1c. Concerning the Tower 1	M1495	158r	1684
9.2a. Tower Text 2	M4618	43r	1675–1706
9.2b. Tower Text 2	M10561	148r–149r	17th cent.
9.4. Tower Text 3	M5571	206v	1657–1659
10. Abraham, John the Baptist, and Solomon	M4618	131v	1675–1706
11. From Abraham to Jacob	M1137	13r–19v	15th cent.
12a. Of Moses and Aaron	Bod Marsh 438	55r–57r	1482
12b. Of Moses and Aaron	M1099	177v–182r	17th cent.

13. Question concerning Moses's Countenance	M1134	152r–152v	1695
14. Joshua b. Nun 9 (olim 2)	Bod Marsh 438	32v	1482
15. Eli the Priest	Bod Marsh 438	450r	1482
16. Elisha	Bod Marsh 438	510v–513r	1482
17.1. Jonah 1	M1099	202r–207v	15th cent.
17.2. Jonah 2	Bod Marsh 438	61r–61v	1482
17.3. Preaching of the Prophet Jonah in Nineveh	V1541	pp. 195–200	1627
18. Job the Righteous	Bod Marsh 438	454v–456r	1482
19. Daniel Epitome, Part 2	M1134	84r–86v	1695
20. Daniel and the Three Young Men	M1099	183v–188r	17th cent.
21. The History of the Three Young Men	Bod ms arm f11	179v–182v	1651–1655
22. Concerning the Sibyl: A Woman Philosopher	M101	104v	1740
23.1. Questions and Answers from the Holy Books	M1654	189v–197v	1336
23.1. Questions and Answers from the Holy Books	M1254	156v–159v	17th cent.
23.2. Questions and Answers from the Holy Books	M1405	146r–148v	18th cent.
24. Three Tales: Solomon, Noah, and Satan	M2188	265r–266v	15th cent.

Manuscript Sources of Texts Published Within

MS No.	Text Number and Title	Fols	Date
Bod arm g4	6. Prayer to the Archangels		1706–1707
Bod Marsh 438	12a. Of Moses and Aaron	55r–57r	1482
Bod Marsh 438	14. Joshua b. Nun 9 (olim 2)	32v	1482
Bod Marsh 438	15. Eli the Priest	450r	1482
Bod Marsh 438	16. Elisha	510v–513r	1482
Bod Marsh 438	17.2. Jonah 2	61r–61v	1482
Bod Marsh 438	18. Job the Righteous	454v–456r	1482
Bod Marsh 467	2. Concerning Hell and Its Most Bitter Punishment	359r–360v	17th cent.
Bod ms arm f11	21. The History of the Three Young Men	179v–182v	1651–1655
M101	22. Concerning the Sibyl: A Woman Philosopher	104v	1740
M10561	1. Concerning Heaven: How Many Heavens Are There?	75v–76v	17th cent.
M10561	4.1. Classes of Angels	146r–146v	17th cent.
M10561	4.2. Praises Sung by the Classes of Angels	146v	17th cent.
M10561	4.3. Origen and the Classes of Angels	147r	17th cent.
M10561	9.2b. Tower Text 2	148r–149r	17th cent.
M1099	12b. Of Moses and Aaron	177v–182r	17th cent.
M1099	17.1. Jonah 1	202r–207v	15th cent.
M1099	20. Daniel and the Three Young Men	183v–188r	17th cent.
M1134	13. Question concerning Moses's Countenance	152r–152v	1695
M1134	19. Daniel Epitome, Part 2	84r–86v	1695
M1137	11. From Abraham to Jacob	13r–19v	15th cent.

M1254	23.1. Questions and Answers from the Holy Books	156v–159v	17th cent.
M1386	3. Angels and the Demon	180r–180v	17th cent.
M1386	7. Creation of Eve and Disobedience	183v	17th cent.
M1495	9.1c. Concerning the Tower 1	158r	1684
M1405	23.2. Questions and Answers from the Holy Books	146r–148v	18th cent.
M1654	23.1. Questions and Answers from the Holy Books	189v–197v	1336
M2188	24. Three Tales: Solomon, Noah and Satan	265r–266v	15th cent.
M2245	5. Numbers and Ranks of the Angels	148r–148v	1689
M2939	9.1b. Concerning the Tower 1	422v	18th cent.
M4618	8. Form and Structure of Noah's Ark	53r	1675–1706
M4618	9.2a. Tower Text 2	43r	1675–1706
M4618	10. Abraham, John the Baptist and Solomon	131v	1675–1706
M5571	9.3. Tower Text 3	206v	1657–1659
M8531	9.1a. Concerning the Tower 1	82r–82v	15th cent.
V1541	17.3. The Preaching of the Prophet Jonah in Nineveh	pp. 343–348	1627

Procedures

1. The quotations of the English Bible are taken from NRSV unless otherwise noted.

2. The titles or chapter and verse numbering of certain biblical books differ in the Hebrew and Armenian versions. In these cases, Hebrew references are given first and then the Armenian references in parentheses.

3. Armenian is transliterated according the system used by the *Revue des études arméniennes*. Sigla of manuscripts to which reference is made follow the system of the Association internationale des études arméniennes.

4. Many little-known Armenian pseudepigrapha are cited. An alphabetical list of these, with relevant primary references is given following the abbreviations. Moreover, the names of these Armenian Pseudepigrapha are capitalized in the text. In the Index of Subjects, Persons, and Places, they are all characterized as "works."

Critical Signs

§	section number
( )	word/s added by the editor to the translation for stylistic reasons
< >	word/s added from another source than the text, including word/s emended
{ }	corruption
[ ]	physical lacuna in the manuscript; letters and words within these brackets are supplied by the editor
∞	transposition
. . .	illegible or incomprehensible letters or words

In the apparatuses, all text following a colon (:) is introduced by the editor.

Abbreviations

Arm	preceding "Bible" or the name of a biblical book means the Armenian version of said work
bis	following a variant indicates that it occurs twice in the same section or word
cent.	century
fol, fols	folio, folios
inc.	indicates the beginning of a section, usually in an apparatus, when a word is added at the beginning
l. ll.	line, lines
LXX	Septuagint
marg.	margin
MT	Masoretic text
p., pp.	page, pages
p.m., s.m., etc.	prima manu, secunda manu, etc.
pers.	person (grammatical)
plur.	plural
r, v	following a numeral, designates the two sides of a folio, recto and verso
sing.	singular
s.v.	sub vocem
transl.	translated
v., vv.	verse, verses

Cited Catalogues of Manuscripts

Bodleian Catalogue
> Sukias Baronian and Frederick C. Conybeare, *Catalogue of the Armenian Manuscripts in the Bodleian Library.* Oxford: Clarendon, 1918.

General Catalogue 4
> A. Kʻeōškerean, K. Sukʻiasean, and Y. Kʻeosēean, *General Catalogue of Armenian Manuscripts of the Maštocʻ Matenadaran*

(Մայր ցուցակ հայերէն ձեռագրաց Մաշտոցի անուան Մատենադարանի), vol. 4. Erevan: Nairi, 2008.

General Catalogue 7
: Gēorg Tēr Vardanyan, Մայր ցուցակ հայերէն ձեռագրաց Մաշտոցի անուան Մատենադարանի [General Catalogue of Armenian Manuscripts of the Maštocʻ Matenadaran], vol. 7. Erevan: Nairi, 2012.

General Catalogue 9
: Gēorg Tēr Vardanyan, *General Catalogue of Armenian Manuscripts of the Maštocʻ Matenadaran* (Մայր ցուցակ հայերէն ձեռագրաց Մաշտոցի անուան Մատենադարանի), vol. 9. Erevan: Nairi, 2017.

Short Catalogue 1, 2
: O. Eganyan, A. Zeytʻunyan, and Pʻ. Antʻabyan. *Catalogue of Manuscripts of the Maštocʻ Matenadaran* (Ցուցակ ձեռագրաց Մաշտոցի անուան Մատենադարանի), vols. 1, 2. Erevan: Academy of Sciences, 1965–1966.

Short Catalogue 3
: Armen Malxasyan, *Catalogue of Manuscripts of the Maštocʻ Matenadaran* (Ցուցակ ձեռագրաց Մաշտոցի անուան Մատենադարանի), vol. 3. Erevan: Erevan State University Press, 2007.

OTHER BIBLIOGRAPHIC ABBREVIATIONS

AB	Anchor Bible
ABR	*Australian Biblical Review*
CSCO	Corpus Scriptorum Christianorum Orientaliuman
EJL	Early Judaism and Its Literature
HATS	Harvard Armenian Texts and Studies
HTR	*Harvard Theological Review*
HUAS	Hebrew University Armenian Series
IDB	*Interpreter's Dictionary of the Bible*. Edited by George A. Buttrick. 4 vols. New York: Abingdon, 1962
JSJ	*Journal for the Study of Judaism in the Persian, Hellenistic, and Roman Periods*
JSJSup	Journal for the Study of Judaism in the Persian, Hellenistic, and Roman Periods, Supplements
JSP	*Journal for the Study of Pseudepigrapha*
JTS	*Journal of Theological Studies (New Series)*

ABBREVIATIONS   xxi

MH 5   [n.a.]. *Armenian Classical Authors* (Մատենագիրք հայոց, Ճ. դար), vol. 5.1. Antelias: Armenian Catholicossate of Cilicia, 2005.
MOTP 1   Bauckham, R., James R. Davila, and Alexander Panayotov. *Old Testament Pseudepigrapha: More Noncanonical Scriptures*. Grand Rapids: Eerdmans, 2013.
NBHL   G. Awetikʻean, X. Siwrmēlean, and M. Awkʻerean, *New Dictionary of the Armenian Language* (*n Նոր բառգիրք հայկազեան լեզուի*). 2 vols. Venice: St. Lazzaro, 1837.
OED   Oxford English Dictionary
OLA   Orientalia Lovaniensia Analecta
PhA   Philosophia Antiqua
PVTG   Pseudepigrapha Veteris Testamenti Graece
REArm   *Revue des études arméniennes*
SBLDS   Society of Biblical Literature Dissertation Series
SBLTT   Society of Biblical Literature Texts and Translations Pseudepigrapha Series
SVTP   Studia in Veteris Testamenti Pseudepigrapha
TU   Texte und Untersuchungen zur Geschichte der altchristlichen Literatur
UPATS   University of Pennsylvania Armenian Texts and Studies
WUNT   Wissenschaftliche Untersuchungen zum Neuen Testament

Abbreviations for Ancient Sources

A.J.   Josephus, *Jewish Antiquities*
ALD   Aramaic Levi Document
Apoc. Ab.   Apocalypse of Abraham
Apoc. Sedr.   Apocalypse of Sedrach
3 Bar.   3 Baruch (Greek Apocalypse)
b. B. Bat.   Baba Batra
Deut. Rab.   Deuteronomy Rabbah
1 En.   1 Enoch (Ethiopic Apocalypse)
2 En.   2 Enoch (Slavonic Apocalypse)
b. ʻErub.   Erubin
2 Esd   2 Esdras
Death Adam   Death of Adam
Exod. Rab.   Exodus Rabbah
Gen. Rab.   Genesis Rabbah
Hist. Rech.   History of the Rechabites

Jos. Asen.	Joseph and Aseneth
Jub.	Jubilees
LAB	Liber antiquitatum biblicarum (Pseudo-Philo)
LAE	Life of Adam and Eve
1 Macc	1 Maccabees
Num. Rab.	Numbers Rabbah
Odes Sol.	Odes of Solomon
Pr Azar	Prayer of Azariah
Pr. Man.	Prayer of Manasseh
1QapGen ar	Genesis Apocryphon
1QH	Thanksgiving Hymns
4Q464	Exposition on the Patriarchs
Ques. Ezra	Questions of Ezra
Ques. Greg.	Questions of Gregory
b. Sanh.	Sanhedrin
Sib. Or.	Sibylline Oracles
Sipre Deut.	Sipre Deuteronomy
Sipre Num.	Sipre Numbers
Sir	Sirach
Syr. Men.	Syriac Menander
Tanḥ. Beshalaḥ	Tanḥuma Beshalaḥ
Tanḥ. Exod.	Tanḥuma Exodus
m. Tanḥ. Vayakhel	Tanḥuma Vayakhel
Tg. Ps.-J.	Targum Pseudo-Jonathan
T. Job	Testament of Job
T. Jos.	Testament of Joseph
T. Levi	Testament of Levi

Published Armenian Apocryphal and Associated Works Mentioned

The notes refer only to a source where the work may be found.

Abraham and the Idols[1]
Abraham, Isaac and Jacob, Stories of[2]
Abraham, Story of Father.[3]
Abraham, Synaxarium entry for[4]
Abraham; The Ten Trials of[5]
Adam and his Grandsons, History of[6]
Adam, The Twelve Gifts Lost by[7]
Adam's Language, Questions concerning[8]
Ahiqar, History and Discourses of[9]
Angels Praise of the[10]
Angels, The Number and the Twelve Classes of[11]
Archangels, Question concerning the[12]

---

1. M4618, 131v: Michael E. Stone, *Armenian Apocrypha Relating to Biblical Heroes*, EJL 49 (Atlanta: SBL Press, 2019), 20–23.

2. Michael E. Stone, *Armenian Apocrypha Relating to Abraham*, EJL 37 (Atlanta: Society of Biblical Literature, 2012), 101–21; M8532.

3. Stone, *Abraham*, 37–50; M10561 133v–135r; M4618 53v–55r.

4. Stone, *Abraham*, 236–37.

5. Stone, *Abraham*, 204–5.

6. Michael E. Stone, *Armenian Apocrypha Relating to Adam and Eve*, SVTP 14 (Leiden: Brill, 1996), 80–98; M4618 1r–6v.

7. Stone, *Biblical Heroes*, 10–16.

8. See p. 53. M4618 43r.

9. M1495 13r–17r; M10561 60v–67r; A. A. Mardirosean, *The Story and Councels of Xikar the Wise*, 2 vols. (Erevan: Academy of Sciences, 1969) [Armenian].

10. Michael E. Stone, *Armenian Apocrypha: Relating to Angels and Biblical Heroes*, EJL 45 (Atlanta: SBL Press, 2016), 77–85.

11. Stone, *Biblical Heroes*, 1–3.

12. M2245 114v–115v; Stone, *Angels and Heroes*, 72–75.

Biblical Paraphrases[13]
Cain and Abel, Adam's sons History of[14]
Ezra, Questions of, and Answers of the Angel[15]
Fifteen Signs of Doomsday[16]
Flood, Sermon Concerning the[17]
Forefathers, Adam His Sons and Grandsons, History of the[18]
Forefathers, History of the[19]
Gems, Names and Colors of[20]
Gems, Names of the Twelve[21]
Hezekiah and Manasseh[22]
Holy Books, Questions and Answers from the[23]
Hours of the Day and Night, Concerning the Names of the Twenty-Four[24]
Hours of the Night, Concerning the Twelve[25]
Joseph, The Third Story of[26]
Joshua bin Nun, The Story of[27]
Joshua, Brief History of[28]

---

13. Michael E. Stone, *Armenian Apocrypha Relating to Patriarchs and Prophets* (Jerusalem: Israel Academy of Sciences, 1982), 81–126.

14. M4618, 138r–140r (p. 78); W. Lowndes Lipscomb, *The Armenian Apocryphal Adam Literature*, UPATS 8 (Atlanta: Scholars Press, 1990), 108–27.

15. Michael E. Stone, "A New Edition and Translation of the Questions of Ezra," in *Solving Riddles and Untying Knots: Biblical, Epigraphic, and Semitic Studies in Honor of Jonas C. Greenfield*, ed. Ziony Zevit, Seymour Gitin, and Michael Sokoloff (Winona Lake, IN: Eisenbrauns, 1995), 293–316; Sargis Yovsēpʻeanc, *Uncanonical Books of the Old Testament* (Անկանոն Գիրք Հին Կտակարանաց), (Venice: Mekhitarist, 1896), 300–306.

16. M2939 441v–442r; Michael E. Stone, *Signs of the Judgement, Onomastica Sacra, and the Generations from Adam*, UPATS 3 (Chico, CA: Scholars Press, 1981).

17. M2245 fols 4r–18r; Stone, *Adam and Eve*, 174–200.

18. Stone, *Adam and Eve*, 180–200.

19. M2245 279r–281r (p. 63).

20. Oxford Bod Marsh 467 372v–374r; Stone, *Adam and Eve*, 180–200.

21. M1495 162r; Stone, *Angels and Heroes*, 22–24; compare Felix Albrecht, and Arthur Manukyan. *Epiphanius von Salamis: Über die Zwölf Steine im hohepriesterlichen Brustchild (De Duodecim Gemmis Rationalis)*, Gorgias Eastern Christian Studies 37 (Piscataway, NJ: Gorgias, 2014).

22. M4618, fols 142r–143v; *Biblical Heroes*, 180–96

23. Edited below.

24. Stone, *Angels and Heroes*, 1–4.

25. Stone, *Angels and Heroes*, 1.

26. M2245 330r–349v; Stone, *Angels and Heroes*, 176–228.

27. Stone, *Patriarchs and Prophets*, 117–20.

28. M4618 fols 146v–148v; Stone, *Biblical Heroes* 57–108.

Languages, Seventy-Two[29]
Matriarchs; Names of the Four[30]
Men of Sodom and Gomorra, Supplication concerning[31]
Moses, Armenian Life of[32]
Nathan, a work on[33]
Noah, Generations of the Sons of[34]
Noah, Story of in Biblical Paraphrases[35]
Noah's Ark, Concerning[36]
Patriarchs, Names of the[37]
Prophets' Names, Lists of[38]
Questions and Answers from the Holy Books[39]
Questions of the Queen[40]
Seth, Concerning the Birth of[41]
Seth, Concerning the Good Tidings of[42]
Seventy-Two Translators[43]
Signs and Wonders of the Temple[44]

---

29. Stone, *Adam and Eve*, 158–63; Stone, *Angels and Heroes*, 161. The oldest form of this material is to be found in the Chronography of Philo of Tikor, MH, 5.897–970. The chief ideas embodied in it already occur in Ełiše, *Commentary on Genesis*, on Gen 11:1–28. See the critical edition of this text in L. Xač'ikyan, Y. Kēosēeyan and M. Papazian, eds., *Commentary of Genesis by Eghishe* [Armenian] (Erevan: Magharat, 2004), 106–9.
30. Stone, *Adam and Eve*, 167.
31. Stone, *Biblical Heroes*, 24–56.
32. Stone, *Patriarchs and Prophets*, 154–55.
33. Stone, *Angels and Heroes*, 163–65.
34. Stone, *Signs of the Judgement*.
35. Stone, *Patriarchs and Prophets*, 88–101.
36. M8513; M4618 fols. 53r-v; published in this volume (p. 52).
37. W. Lowndes Lipscomb, "A Tradition from the Book of Jubilees in Armenian," *JJS* 29 (1978): 149–63; Stone, *Adam and Eve*, 174–75.
38. Stone, *Adam and Eve*, 174–75, four lists.
39. Published in this volume, pp. 255–92.
40. Yovsēp'eanc' 1896, 229–31, Sebastian P. Brock. "The Queen of Sheba's Questions to Solomon: A Syriac Version," *Le Muséon* 92 (1979): 331–45.
41. M4618, fols140r-142r; Lipscomb, *Armenian Apocryphal Adam Literature*, 173–205.
42. See Yovsēp'eanc' 1896, 213–324; Lipscomb, *Armenian Apocryphal Adam Literature*.
43. Michael E. Stone and Roberta R. Ervine, *The Armenian Texts of Epiphanius of Salamis De mensuris et ponderibus*, CSCO 583; CSCO Subsidia 105 (Leuven: Peeters, 2000), 69 and 92.
44. M4618, 109v (p. 46); Stone, *Biblical Heroes*, 137–42.

Solomon and the Bubu Bird[45]
Solomon Text 2[46]
Solomon, Concerning the Writings of[47]
Solomon's Ring[48]
Solomon's Temple, Concerning the Wonders of[49] also called Signs and Wonders of Solomon's Temple[50]
Sons of Noah, Peoples of the[51]
St. Gregory, Questions of[52]
The Tower[53]
Tower, Concerning the, 1 and 2[54]
Tower, Questions concerning the[55]
Twelve Literate Peoples[56]
Two Stone Tablets in the Ark[57]
Wives of the Forefathers and Patriarchs; Names of the[58]

---

45. M4618 fol. 133r; Stone, *Biblical Heroes* 167–70; Armenuhi Srapyan, *Medieval Armenian Tales* (Հայ միջնադարեան զրոյցներ) (Erevan: Academy, 1969), 318–19.
46. Stone, *Biblical Heroes*, 149–61.
47. M10561 90r–91r (p. 3).Yovsēpʻeancʻ, 232–34; Stone, *Biblical Heroes*, 159–62.
48. M4618 (p. 46); *Biblical Heroes* 152–66.
49. Stone, *Biblical Heroes*, 136–42.
50. Stone, *Biblical Heroes*, 137–42.
51. Stone, *Patriarchs and Prophets*, 221–27.
52. Michael E. Stone, "The Armenian Questions of St. Gregory: A Text Descended from 4 Ezra: Edition of Recension I," *Le Muséon* 131 (2018): 141–72. M4618, fol. 9r–10v (p. 45); M2245 235r–238v (p. 26).
53. Published in this volume, pp. 69–70.
54. Edited pp. 52–64; M4618 fols. 43r–44r (pp. 59–63); 53v; M8531 82r–82v; p. 54.
55. Edited below, pp. 55–57.
56. Stone, *Adam and Eve*, 163.
57. M3929 340r.
58. See p. 255.

PART 1

HEAVEN AND HELL, ANGELS AND DEMONS

1. Concerning Heaven: How Many Heavens Are There?

Introductory Remarks

M10561 is a seventeenth-century miscellany of unknown provenance. It has very rich and varied contents: As well as the present work, it contains such writings as The Sayings of Ahiqar (Hikar) the Wise (60v–67r);[1] The Epistle That God Gave to Adam at the Time of the Expulsion (80r–81r); Concerning the Writings of Solomon (90r–91r);[2] The Story of Joshua Son of Nun (122r–124r); and The Story of Father Abraham (133v–135r), all of which are significant works in the tradition of Armenian pseudepigraphical literature. It is notable that on fols 98v–100v of the same manuscript, there is a copy of Abraham Text 14, which I had reprinted from the Constantinople Synaxarium printing of 1730.[3] This rich lode of texts is worthy of further mining.[4]

The document that I present here occurs in M10561 on fols 75v–76v and it is a brief statement about the constitution of the heavens and the earth. It illustrates some cosmogonic and cosmological views held by the Armenians in the seventeenth century at least and it contains several points of interest. For one thing, it is quite often stated, as it is here, that creation was through wisdom; see for an ancient example, Agatʻangełos §274.[5] The idea of creation

---

1. See A. A. Martirosean, *The Story and Counsels of Xikar the Wise*, 2 vols. (Erevan: Academy of Sciences, 1969), in Armenian. This work is also named Ahiqar, History and Discourses of. An earlier edition of the text is Frederick C. Conybeare, J. Rendel Harris, and Agnes Lewis Smith, *The Story of Aḥiḳar from the Aramaic, Syriac, Arabic, Armenian, Ethiopic, Old Turkish, Greek and Slavonic Versions* (Cambridge: Cambridge University Press, 1913).
2. This is published in Stone, *Angels and Heroes*, 146–47, 159–62.
3. See Stone, *Abraham*, 206–12, Text 14.
4. *Short Catalogue* 3.115–18.
5. See also Michael E. Stone, *Adam and Eve in the Armenian Traditions: Fifth through Seventeenth Centuries*, EJL 38 (Atlanta: Society of Biblical Literature, 2013), 199. For earlier sources, see Michael E. Stone, *Fourth Ezra: A Commentary on the Book of Fourth Ezra*, Hermeneia (Minneapolis: Fortress, 1990), 184, and also 2 En. 30.8.

from nothing may also be observed in *Agatʻangełos* §276; *Yačaxapatum Čaṙkʻ* 33,[6] Frik;[7] Simēon Aparancʻi, *Epic on the Pahlavuni House* §2, and other sources covering most centuries of Armenian literacy.[8]

Text

1/M10561 / fol 75v / Յաղագս երկնի, թէ քանի են երկինք եւ որպէս իմաստութեամբ յանգոյից եղեն Աստուծոյ:

Արարիչն Աստուած իմաստութեամբ եւ զօրութեամբ արար զաշխարհի ամենայն, եւ երեւի զօրութիւն նորա, զի յոչրնչէ արար զամենայն արարածս, եւ տեսանի իմաստութիւն, զի գեղեցիկ արուեստիւ յօրինեաց զերկինս եւ զերկիր:

2/ Չորս նիւթ արար Աստուած ի պէտս շինութեան յաշխարհի. հուր եւ հողմ, ջուր եւ հող: Եւ սոքա սկզբունք եւ արմատք են ամենայն զոյիցս եւ են հակառակ միմեանց:

Իսկ այլ արարածքս ծայրք եւ ծնունդք ի սոցանէ յառաջ եկեալ եւ խառնեալ ընդ միմեանս, յորմէ ստեղ/ fol 76r /ծան եղականքս բուսականք եւ կենդանիք: Եւ պիտոյ էր այս չորք տարերքս, զի առանց հողոյ ոչ լինէր թանձր մարմին, եւ ոչ առանց ջրոյ շարժումն եւ միաւութիւն, եւ առանց աղոյ, որ է հողմն, շարժումն ոչ լինէր, եւ ոչ առանց հրոյ գոյնն երեւումն:

3/ Վասն որոյ ստեղծ զամենայն զզալի եւ նիւթական եղեալքս ի հողոյ եւ դալարացոյց ջրովն, ետ շարժումն ի յաղդոյն, եւ երեւումն եւ գոյն ի հրոյն: Եւ այս է, զոր ասէ մեծ մարգարէն Մովսէս. «Ի սկզբանէ արար Աստուած զերկինս եւ զերկիր»:

4/ Չի երկինքն երկու իրք է՛ հող եւ ջուր. եւ յորժամ ստեղծ զայս չորք տարերքս, արուեստ իմաստութեան Աստուծոյ երեւեցաւ ի ստեղծուածն իւր, զի հողն ծանր էր, զներքին վայրն էառ, եւ ջուրն ի վերայ հողին զի տեղեցաւ, եւ աղն,[9] որ թեթեւ էր քան զջուրն, ի վերայ ջրոյն կայացաւ, եւ հուրն, որ առաւել թեթեւ էր քան զաղն, ի վերոյ քան զնա սահմանեցաւ: Եւ քեզ օրինակ բանիս. թէ առնուս աւազ եւ ջուր, եւ ձէթ, եւ արկանես ամման մի խեցեղէն, աւազն յատակն նրստի, ջուրն ի վերոյ գայ, եւ ձէթն ի վերոյ քան զջուրն, եւ խեցեղէն ամանն զամենայնն ի ներքոյ իւր ունի: Ըստ այնմ նմանութեանս եւ չորք տարերքս / fol 76v / դասեցան.

---

6. Stone, *Traditions*, 282.
7. Stone, *Traditions*, 460.
8. Stone, *Traditions*, 640.
9. I read աւթ as աւղ.

1. CONCERNING HEAVEN

5/ հուրն, զի թեթեւ է բնութեամբ եւ շարժումն ի վեր ունի, եւ զնդածեւ[10] շրջապատեաց զայլ Գ. (3) տարերքն:

Եւ զի հողմն ի ներքո անցեալ փչեաց, փետեկտեաց ի վեց կողմն՝ ի վեր եւ ի վ<տ>այր, եւ Դ. (4) կողմ յաշխարհի. եւ զհետ հրեղէն երկնի ձեւացաւ եւ հողմն, կարգեցաւ ի ծոց նորա, որպէս աման արկեալ: Եւ երկիրս, որ է հողն եւ ջուրն, ի միջոցի երկնից կառուցաւ:

6/ Ահա այս է հրեղէն երկինքն, զոր արար Աստուած առաջին աւուր արարչութեան, որ բաժանեցաւ յերկուս կիսագունդ. զի որպէս ի վերոյ երկրի կամարածեւ է եւ բոլոր, նոյնպէս է եւ ի ներքո երկրի, քանզի հեռի է երկրէս ի վեց կողմանէ ի վերոյ երկրի, որպէս տեսանես զմիջոցս զայս, որ ի վեր է երկինքն երկրէս. նոյնպէս եւ այս չափովս ի ներքս երկրի, ներ ի փորուածն եւ ծոցն, այնպէս ընդ արեւելս, եւ ընդ արեւմուտս, եւ ի հիւսուս, եւ ի հարաւ հեռի է երկինքն յերկրէ:

Translation

1/ Concerning heaven: How many heavens are there, and how did they come into being from the nonexistent through God's wisdom?

The Creator, God, through wisdom and power made the whole world and his power (thus) was evident. For he made all the creations from nothing and thus (his) wisdom is visible.[11] For he created the heavens and the earth with beautiful artistry.[12]

2/ God made four elements[13] for the needs of construction in the world: fire and wind, water and earth.[14] And these are the beginnings and roots of all existent things and they are opposed to one another.

The other creations, then, are the end and the outcome that came forth from these, and they are mixed[15] with one another from which[16] the sorts of flora and fauna were created. And it was necessary (to have) these four ele-

---

10. Read this word as զնդածեւ (A. Arakelyan).
11. This is an idea drawn ultimately from the Hellenistic world, but a commonplace in Armenian texts.
12. Or: "beautiful through (his) artistry."
13. նիւթ translates ὕλη but may also mean "element." տարր, used further on in the text, means only "element." The same view, which integrates Greek ideas into a biblically based cosmology is already found in the Yačaxapatum Čaṙk‘ 3, a sixth-century composition. See Stone, *Traditions*, 42 (index), s.v. "elements" for a number of further instances.
14. Note the deep penetration of the Greek idea of four elements into Armenian creation accounts: Stone, *Traditions*, 42–43.
15. Here a participle is used as finite verb.
16. That is, mixing.

ments, for without earth the heavy body would not have come into being, and without water—movement and cohesion,[17] and without air, which is wind, movement would not come into being,[18] nor without fire would there be color (and) appearance.[19]

3/ On account of this Christ created all sensible and material beings from earth, and he greened (it) through water. He gave movement through the air, and appearance and color through the fire. And this is what the great prophet Moses says: "In the beginning God made the heavens and the earth."[20]

4/ For the heaven is (of) two things,[21] earth and water. And when the artisanship of the wisdom of God created these four elements, it was made evident in its creation.[22] Because the earth was heavy, it took the inner place; and the water (is) above the earth, for it rained;[23] and the air which was lighter than the water took its position above the water; and the fire, which was even lighter than the air, set its boundaries above it. And an example of this thing[24] for you: if you take sand and water and oil and you cast them into a pottery vessel, the sand sits on the bottom, the water comes above (it), and the oil above the water. And the pottery vessel holds all in its inside. According to this likeness,[25] the four elements were set in order.

5/ The fire, because it is by nature light and movement, also has upward movement; it both surrounds and girdles the other three elements. And because the wind passes by, it blows underneath and is split into six directions: from above, from below[26] and the four directions of (in) the world. And it was formed after the fiery heaven[27] and the wind was regulated from

---

17. Here I read միաւութիւն as միաւորութիւն.
18. Movement is mentioned twice, once as generated by water and again by air.
19. Fire is often connected with light and, therefore, with vision: see §5, below.
20. Gen 1:1. On God Incarnated as creator, see Stone, *Traditions*, 129, 156.
21. The manuscript's word-division makes no sense. The phrase is better read as: երկու իրք է "is (of) two things."
22. Here the text recaps §1 and interprets the word սկզբանէ "beginning" of Gen 1:1 as if it were սկզբունք "beginnings, first principles."
23. See Gen 2:5. The next phrase is an interpretation of Gen 1:2.
24. Or: matter.
25. Or: parable.
26. This word is not in the dictionaries. Its context requires the meaning "below," suggesting that it might be a corruption of վայր.
27. Heavens made of fire: Mxit'ar Ayrivanec'i, apud Stone, *Traditions*, 138; Samuel Anec'i, apud Stone, *Traditions*, 446; Grigor Tat'ewac'i apud Stone, *Traditions*, 533. Compare ps.-Zeno 1.1.2 (Michael E. Stone and M. E. Shirinian, *Pseudo-Zeno, Anonymous Philosophical Treatise*, PhA 83 [Leiden: Brill, 2000], 127).

its bosom just as if cast into a vessel.[28] And the earth which is wind and water was constructed in the midst of the heavens.

6/ Behold this is the fiery heavens which God made on the first day of creation[29] on which it was divided into two hemispheres. For just as it is above the whole earth, arched and round, thus also[30] it is also beneath the earth, for it is distant from this earth, from the six directions above the earth. Just as you see this interval that the heavens (are) from this earth, in the same way it also is below this earth by this measure, within the hollow and the bosom. Thus (it is also) to the east and to the west, to the north and to the south. (To this same measure) the heaven is distant from the earth.[31]

---

28. The idea that the wind's blowing is regulated in the celestial region is discussed in Michael E. Stone, "Lists of Revealed Things in the Apocalyptic Literature," in *Magnalia Dei, the Mighty Acts of God: Essays on the Bible and Archaeology in Memory of G. Ernest Wright*, ed. Frank M. Cross, Werner E. Lemke, and Patrick D. Miller (New York: Doubleday, 1976), 414–54, and the actual weighing is described on p. 432; see 1 En. 41.4, 60.12. No weighing is described in 1 En. 40.11.

29. According to Gen 1:3–5 the heavens were not created on the first day. That is inferred from Gen 2:4 and in this statement that verse is combined with Gen 1:6–11, the other version of the creation of the heavens.

30. That is, there is a hemisphere.

31. This distance was of interest to Armenian savants. See, as an example, the writing called The Height of the Heavens in Michael E. Stone, "Some Armenian Angelological and Uranographical Texts," *Le Muséon* 105 (1992): 156–57; repr. in Michael E. Stone, ed., *Apocrypha, Pseudepigrapha and Armenian Studies*, 2 vols. (Leuven: Peeters, 2006), 1:424–25.

2. Concerning Hell and Its Most Bitter Punishment

Introductory Remarks

There exist a number of unpublished texts in Armenian containing descriptions of hell or various aspects of the underworld. In addition to these texts about hell in general, there are also texts about the unsleeping worm and the unquenchable fire, denizens of the underworld that developed from consideration of the last verse of the book of Isaiah (66:24).[1] The text about hell published here is from Bodleian Library MS Marsh 467, a miscellany of religious texts, fols 359r–360v.[2] The script is notrgir and the catalogue dates it to the seventeenth century.[3]

This text is an example of the very varied documents relating to the underworld and eschatological punishments.[4] This whole topic deserves a

---

1. In the course of studies in manuscript libraries, in addition to the work published here, I have noted the following titles. It is unclear how many different works these titles represent: Concerning Hell—M2177, 269v-275r; Concerning the Places of Hell—M4618, 146r-v; Concerning the Divisions of Hell—M6340, 146r; Concerning Hell and the Unsleeping Worm—M6712, 139v; Discourse Concerning Hell—M7054, 148v-153v; M10945; Story of Hell—OXLArm f10, 99r-111. More copies of these and other such works undoubtedly exist. Copies of what appears to be another, different work or works dealing with the unsleeping worm have also been observed in the following manuscripts: M2177, 266r-269v; M2782, 44r-46v; M2890, 80v-85r; M2939, 592r-595v; M6712; M8130; M9532; M10429, fols. 134v-139v; NOJ427, 150r-159r; NOJ428, item ՃԴ. Again, observe that these titles, although they resemble one another, may designate different works.

2. Bodleian Catalogue, 81–88, No. 40.

3. Bodleian Catalogue, 81.

4. Among texts dealing with aspects of the underworld, observe also the published text, drawn from Latin, on the idea of Limbo: Michael E. Stone, "Three Apocryphal Fragments from Armenian Manuscripts," in *A Teacher for All Generations: Essays in Honor of James C. Vanderkam*, ed. Eric F. Mason et al. (Leiden: Brill, 2012), 939–46. In addition, the work entitled Questions of St. Gregory includes many details relating to postmortem punishment and its locations: See Michael E. Stone, "The Armenian Questions of St. Gregory: A Text Descended from 4 Ezra: Edition of Recension I," *Le Muséon* 131 (2018): 141–72.

thorough investigation, the texts should be published, and their role in medieval Armenian thought should be considered.⁵ I hope that this first publication will whet the appetite of others to investigate this rich literature.

As will become evident from the notes below, this text shares many concepts and also specific details of its description of postmortem punishment with other Armenian treatments of the same subject, as are evident in Questions of Ezra, Aṙakʻel Siwnecʻi's *Adamgirkʻ*, and similar sources. This indicates that a whole realm of medieval Armenian thought most probably is hidden still in many or all of the numerous unpublished manuscript texts mentioned above, and others.

In addition to the text published here, that manuscript contains a number of texts of pseudepigraphical interest. These include: *Canon List of Anania of Širak* (371r–372v),⁶ *Names and Colors of the Gems* by the same author (372v–374r);⁷ *On Weights and Measures* (374r–377r).⁸ All three works are related to Anania's metrological and scientific interests.

Text

0/ Bodleian Library MS Marsh 467 / fol 359r / Վասն դժոխոցն եւ դառնագոյն տանջանաց նորա

1/ Չար է անուն դժոխոց ի լսելիս մարդկան, եւ անբարի է յիշատակ նորա ի լսելիս որդւոց Ադամայ։ Վա՛յ, զի մեղաւորք անդարձք անարգեն զնա եւ զայն, որ արար զնա։

2/ Եւ երանի՛, զի անարատ արդարք գնծայլով խնդան, զի ոչ երկնչին ի դառն տանջանաց դժոխոց եւ ափնաբանեն զայն, որ արար զնա։ Քանզի որպէս պղղովատ երկսայրի սրով, նովաւ սաստեն մեզ աստուածեղէն զիրք։

3/ Եւ արդ՝ սովորութիւն է աստուածեղէն գրոց, որ զամենայն տեղի, որ նեղ եւ խաւար լինի, զայն դժոխք կոչեն։

---

5. On descriptions of hell or Hades in earlier times, see Martha Himmelfarb, *Tours of Hell: An Apocalyptic Form in Jewish and Christian Literature* (Philadelphia: University of Pennsylvania, 1983). Michael E. Stone and John Strugnell, *The Books of Elijah*, Parts 1 and 2, SBLTT 5 (Missoula, MT: Scholars Press, 1979), 14–26 also published some older descriptions extant in early Jewish literature.

6. Michael E. Stone, "Armenian Canon Lists II: The Stichometry of Anania of Shirak (ca. 615–ca. 690 C.E.)," *HTR* 68 (1975), 253–60.

7. See also Michael E. Stone, "An Armenian Epitome of Epiphanius' *de Gemmis*," *HTR* 82 (1982), 467–76. Epiphanius's work has recently been issued in a new edition: Albrecht and Manukyan, *Epiphanius von Salamis*.

8. Stone and Ervine, *Armenian Texts of Epiphanius of Salamis*.

4/ Եւ սովորութեամբ գմահապարտաց բանտս, զոր թագաւորք շինեցին, եւ գտուն խաւարամած, դժոխք կոչեն:

5/ Ասի դժոխք եւ տուն կապլուտ: Ասի դժոխք եւ խաւար գիշեր, որ լինի հողմով եւ անձրեւով: Ասի դժոխք եւ նեղ ճանապարհի, չար եւ մացառուտ:

6/ Իսկ աստուածեղ/ fol 360r /<էն>քն, որ աննաւագնաց է եւ ի մէջ ահագին լերանց բարձրագունից ի խորագոյնն: եւ թէ անդ խառնակին պիղծ եւ զարշելի դեւքն ընդ դաժանագոյն եւ չարահոտ վիշապան,

7/ եւ ժահահոտ զարշելի գոլորշից նոցա ելեալ տարածանի յայդս եւ բերէ մահաշունչ ցաւք⁹ մարդկան եւ անասնց: Իսկ մարդիքն զԲաբելովն եւ զԵգիպտոս դժոխք կոչեցի<ն>¹⁰ Իսրայելի, զի դառնագոյն տանջէին զնոսա:

8/ Իսկ կենարար Տէրն մեր Յիսուս Քրիստոս ի սուրբ Աւետարանին՝ թանձրամած խաւար ասաց գդժոխքն, որպէս այն, որ եղեւ յԵգիպտոս հրամանաւ Աստուծոյ ի ձեռն Մովսեսի՝ թանձր խաւար իբրեւ զորմ:

9/ Եւ է նա արտաքոյ աշխարհիս, տեղի ահագին, դառնագոյն եւ յոյժ խոր, անհուն մինչեւ յանդունդս ներքինս, լի հրախառն խաւարաւ եւ ծծմբով, եւ չարակսկիծ սառնամանեաւք լցեալ:

10/ Այրեցող եւ յոյժ մորմոք աղեւան¹¹ մահ. աւր խօսել ոչ կարեն մեղաւորքն, այղ միայն լան, եւ ի սաստիկ այրեցմանէն գատամունս կրճեն, որպէս եւ Տէր մեր հրամայէ, թէ՝ «Հանէք գնոսա ի խաւարն արտաքին, ուր լալ աչաց է եւ կրճել ատամանց / fol 360r / էն»:

11/ Գիրք կոչեն դժոխք եւ զայս աշխարհս, որ առ դրախտին փափկութիւնն եւ հեշտ հանգիստն, քանզի որպէս մահապարտ ձգեցաւ Ադամ յայս աշխարհի անիծից: Կոչեն դժոխք աստուածաշունչ գիրք եւ զգերեզմանս,

12/ Չի չար եւ դառնագոյն է տեսել նորա եւ անախորժելի, րստ այնմ. «Ոչ թէ որ ի դժոխս են, խոստովան առնիցին քեզ»: Եւ թէ. Ո՛վ է մարդ, որ փրկեսցէ զանձն իւր ի ձեռաց դժոխոց, որ է գերեզման:

13/ Եւ դարձեալ ասի բան, թէ՛ դժոխս յայսմ աշխարհի է տեղի խաւարամած, արհաւրաց եւ դողձմանց վայր, եւ սահման ահագին եւ ոսկալի, նեղ եւ խորագոյն յոյժ ի մէջ քարակարկատ, ահագնատես

---
9. An accusative would be expected.
10. Editor's emendation.
11. This word is not in the dictionaries, nor is any orthographic variant that occurs to me.

2. CONCERNING HELL

վիմաց բարձրագունից. եւ ասի, թէ անդ ունէր սատանայ¹² զհոգիսն մինչեւ յամէնաւրինեալ զալուստն Քրիստոսի Աստուծոյ մերոյ:

14/ Եւ դարձեալ ասի բան, թէ՛ ի սանդարամետս անդնդոց է դժոխքն, ի ներքոյ աշխարհի, լի չարաչար կապար<ան>աւք, եւս առաւել տանջանարանաւք, ուր էջ եւ իջանելոց է սատանայ պիղծ եւ անմաքուր դիւաւք իւրովք եւ անգէոշ մեղաւորաւք:

15/ Եւ դարձեալ ասի բան, թէ՛ ի մէջ դառնագոյն անդնդական ծովուց է դժոխ / fol 360v / քանզի եւ այս աշխարհի դրախտանայ եւ տուն Աստուծոյ լինի, եւ արքայութիւն: Եւ չէ աւրէն զմահապարտ ի տան թագաւորի սպանանել, այդ արտաքոյ քաղաքի:

16/ Նաեւ մեծ առաքեալն Պաւղոս ասէ վասն դժոխոցն, թէ՛ Կայցեն ի նմա մեղաւորքն յաւիտեան անմահ, բայց այնպէս կացցեն, որպէս թէ ոք ի հուր մտեալ այրեցոյ յոյժ սաստիկ եւ ոչ մեռանիցի:

17/ Եւ մարգարէն ասէ վասն մեղաւորացն ի դժոխքն, թէ՛ Որդն նոցա ոչ մեռանի եւ հուրն ոչ շիջանի: Յորում փրկեսցէ զմեզ Քրիստոս, եւ նմա փառք յաւիտեանս. ամէն:

Translation

0/ Concerning hell and its most bitter punishments

1/ The name of hell is evil in men's hearing and mention of it is bad in the hearing of sons of Adam. Woe, for irrevocable sinners despise it and that one who made it.[13]

2/ And it is a blessing, since the immaculately righteous rejoice joyously, for they do not fear the bitter torments of hell, and they praise Him who made it, because the divine Book[14] reproaches us with it as with a two-edged steel sword.[15]

3/ And now, it is the custom of the divine Book to call every place which is narrow and dark, hell.

---

12. An arc is written under սատանա as is common with this name.
13. The meaning is that God created hell; see further §2 below. However, this is not the only view known in Armenian literature and quite often Satan is said to have built hell; see Stone, *Traditions*, 179, citing Yoav Loeff, "Four Texts from the Oldest Known Armenian Amulet Scroll: Matenadaran 115 (1428) with Introduction, Translation" (MA thesis (Hebrew University of Jerusalem, 2002).
14. That is, the Bible, which is often called Աստուածաշունչ "the God-Inspired," the term also occurs in §11 of this text.
15. See Wis 18:16 where the divine word carries a sword, and even closer is Heb 4:12 "Indeed, the word of God is living and active, sharper than any two-edged sword." That is the source used here.

4/ And customarily, they also call prisons of those condemned to death which kings built, also the gloomy house, hell.

5/ Hell is also called[16] a house of reprimand; hell is also called a dark night, which comes with wind and rain; hell is also called a narrow way, bad and (through) a thicket is called hell.

6/ But the divine things,[17] which are without a captain and amidst fearsome mountains, from the highest to the deepest. And there, abominable and revolting demons have union with most rough and stinking dragons,[18]

7/ Then their evil, revolting odor of their exhalations issues forth and is spread in the atmosphere and brings death-breathing pains to men and beasts. Moreover, men called Babylon and Egypt "the hell of Israel," for they were tormenting them most bitterly.[19]

8/ But our vivifying Lord Jesus Christ said in the holy Gospel, that hell is thick darkness, like that which took place in Egypt by God's command, by the hand of Moses, thick darkness like a wall.[20]

---

16. The text is, literally, "is said," and so throughout this paragraph.

17. The meaning is unclear, for the rest of the sentence continues the description of hell, saying եւ թէ անդ "and there...."

18. Dragons or *višaps* are legendary water-monsters of Armenia. They were introduced into the Armenian Bible in such contexts as Gen 1:21 and the book of Jonah. On *višaps*, see Ł. Alishan, *Ancient and Pagan Religion of the Armenians* (Հին հաւատք կամ հեթանոսական կրօնք հայոց) (Venice: Mechitarist, 1910), 162–70; James R. Russell, *Zoroastrianism in Armenia*, Harvard Iranian Series 5 (Cambridge: Harvard University, Department of Near Eastern Languages and Civilizations, 1987), 205–13; Russell, *Armenian and Iranian Studies*, Harvard Armenian Texts and Studies 9 (Cambridge: Harvard University Press and Armenian Heritage Press, 2004), 373 and elsewhere. See most recently: A. Bobokhyan, Alexandra Gilibert, and Pavel Hnila, eds., *The Vishap on the Borderline of Fairy Tale and Reality* (Վիշապը հեքիաթի եվ իրականության սահմանին) (Erevan: Institute of Archeology, 2019).

19. This expression is not found in the Bible.

20. The gospels contain no reference to the darkness of Egypt. Matthew refers on a number of occasions to the sinners being cast into the outer darkness: see 8:12, 22:13, and 25:30. There are further uses of the phrase "outer darkness" in 2 Esd 5:5, Ques. Ezra A3, and also Aṙakʻel Siwnecʻi, *Adamgirkʻ* (transl. Michael E. Stone), 2, 68, 116, 124–60; and let these few examples stand for many. The phrase "thick darkness" occurs nineteen times in the Hebrew Bible, none of which is in a negative context. Darkness is not compared to a wall in the whole of biblical literature. "Wall" serves as an image for the accumulated waters of the divided Red Sea in Exod 14:22, 29.

2. CONCERNING HELL

9/ And it (hell) is outside this world,[21] a frightful place—most bitter and very deep, inaccessible down to the abyss below, full of darkness mixed with fire[22] and bitumen, and full of oppressive icy cold.[23]

10/ Death is a burning and very distressful <unknown word>, a day (on which) sinners cannot speak but they only weep; and from the frightful conflagration they gnash their teeth, just as our Lord commands, that "you shall cast them out to the outer darkness where there is weeping of eyes and gnashing of teeth."[24]

11/ Scripture also calls this world hell, which is against the delight of the Garden and the pleasurable repose. For just as Adam was condemned to death, (so) he was cast into this world of curses.[25]

The divinely inspired Book also calls graves, hell.[26]

12/ For it is bad and most bitter to see it, and unappetizing, according to that (saying):[27] "Not that those who are in hell will confess to you," and "Who is a man who will save his own soul from the power of hell, which is a tomb?"

13/ And again the word is said[28] that hell is a place of thick darkness in this world, an area of terrors, and of groaning; and a fearsome and terrible region, narrow and most deep in the midst of the hail of stones, of very high rocks of frightening aspect, and it is said that there Satan holds the souls until the all-blessed coming of Christ our God.[29]

---

21. See "outer darkness" mentioned in the preceding note.
22. This idea is not biblical.
23. Cold as a punishment appears in Armenian sources, such as Ques. Ezra A16. It is repeatedly mentioned by Aṙakʻel Siwnecʻi in this context in the *Adamgirkʻ*: see Michael E. Stone, *Adamgirkʻ: The Adam Book of Aṙakʻel of Siwnikʻ* (Oxford: Oxford University Press, 2007), 10, 118, 121, 123–26, 175, 261.
24. Matt 8:12, 22:13, 25:30.
25. That is implied from Gen 3:23, where Adam is expelled from the Garden and immediately enters this world.
26. This world as hell is not found in the Genesis story. For the grave, compare Ps 16(15):10, 28(27):1.
27. This is followed by two quotations, but I have not been able to find their direct sources. The first might be based on Ps 115:17 (113:25).
28. That is, it is said, people say.
29. In its piling up of attributes this section closely resembles Ques. Ezra A16. Moreover, a number of the attributes are similar in the two sources. Satan's imprisonment of the souls in the air is also to be found in Ques. Ezra A31, B11–12. Ques. Ezra A16 reads: "He takes the soul, brings it through the east: they pass through frost, through snow, through darkness, through hail, through ice, through storm, through hosts of Satan, through streams, and through the wind of terrible rains, through the fearsome and wondrous paths,

14/ And again the word is said[30] that hell is in the deep caverns of the abyss underneath the world, full of cruel <chains> and even more with instruments of torture. Where Satan descended and will descend with his abominable and unclean demons and with unrepentant sinners?

15/ And again the word is said that hell is in the midst of the bitterest infernal seas, because this world both becomes paradisiacal and becomes the house of God and (his) kingdom. And it is not customary to kill the one condemned to death within a king's house, but outside a city.

16/ The great apostle Paul also says concerning hell, that the sinners will remain in it for ever, undying.[31] But they will remain thus, as is one who, having entered a fire, will be burned very terribly and will not die.

17/ And a prophet[32] says concerning the sinners in hell, that "their worm does not die and (their) fire is not extinguished."[33] From which Christ will save us and glory to Him forever.

---

through narrow defiles, and through high mountains. See Michael E. Stone, "Sadayēl's Fall from Heaven," forthcoming, n. 10.

30. That is: it is said. Similarly also §15.
31. The source referred to is unclear; perhaps it relates to Rom 11:10.
32. That is, Isaiah.
33. This is a citation of Isa 66:24.

3. Angels and the Demon

Introductory Remarks

The text being published here is composed of three questions and answers relating to angels and demons. They occur within a more extensive document of questions and answers; following these questions relating to angels and the demon, the document continues with a discussion of the senses. It is found in manuscript M1386, a miscellany copied in the seventeenth century, on fols 180r–180v.[1] Its questions deal with angelological subjects that also occur in other documents, a number of which were published in Stone, *Angels and Heroes*, 65–111.[2]

When the text comes to answer the question posed at the beginning of §1, "How many classes of angels (are there)?" it lists the nine ranks (դասք) of angels and divides them into three groups. The nine names, usually starting from Thrones and concluding with Angels, are commonplace and the idea that there were nine classes of angels derives from The Heavenly Hierarchy of Pseudo-Dionysius. The text here, however, though it says there are nine classes, also lists a tenth one. This tenth class is ecclesiastics, also called "strayed sheep." There is no precise parallel to this particular in any other Armenian list known to date, though a tenth class constituted of humans is known from a number of texts.[3]

Various orderings of the traditional classes of angels are to be found, sometimes differing greatly. Some examples are set forth in table 1.

My appreciation is expressed to Abraham Terian who kindly helped me resolve issues raised by this somewhat enigmatic text.

1. The manuscript is discussed in more detail in connection with Creation of Eve and Disobedience, Text 7 below.

2. A number of these questions are also discussed in M682, which will be published in an additional volume of this series.

3. This is discussed in detail in a note in a future volume.

Table 1

M1386	*Angels & Heroes* 3.5	*Angels & Heroes* 3.6	*Angels & Heroes* 3.7
Thrones	Thrones	Cherubs	Thrones
Cherubs	Cherubs	Seraphs	Seraphs
Seraphs	Seraphs	Princedoms	Cherubs
Dominions	Dominions	Powers	Dominions
Powers	Powers	Principalities	Powers
Princedoms	Princedoms	Dominions	Princedoms (Rulers)
Principalities	Principalities	Thrones	Principalities
Archangels	Archangels	Archangels	Archangels
Angels	Angels	Angels	Angels
Orders			

The second section of the text is composed of the names of the archangels, with their onomastic explanations. This type of list is not unusual. The angelic names vary greatly in orthography in different sources and the etymological explanations given here are paralleled in other onomastic lists. Stone, *Angels and Heroes*, text no. 3.2 is another copy of the same list and it is annotated there. In the present edition, we give just the text and translation for completeness' sake. The third question and answer are somewhat lapidary in their formulation. The answer describes Satan's fall as due to pride and narcissism, and his enmity to humans as due to jealousy.[4] This subject occurs elsewhere and an example is also published in Stone, *Angels and Heroes*, text no. 3.2, referred to directly above.

Text

1/ M1386 / fol 180r / Հարց: Որքա՞ն դասք հրեշտակաց:

Պատասխանի: Թ. (9). ասացին: Առաջինն է՝ աթոռք, քերովբէք եւ սերովբէք, քահանայապետութիւնք. դաս առաջին:

Երկրորդ՝ տերութիւնք, զօրութիւնք, իշխանութիւնք, որ են միջակ դասք:

Երրորդ՝ պետութիւնք, հրեշտակապետք եւ հրեշտակք,
եւ վերջին՝ կարգաւորութիւնք:

---

4. The subject of the fall of Satan(a)ēl is discussed extensively in Stone, "Sadayēl's Fall," forthcoming.

3. ANGELS AND THE DEMON

Եւ է առաջինքն իմացական, եւ միջինքն՝ իմանալիք, եւ վերջինքն՝ իմացականք եւ իմանալիք։ Թ. (9) ասացին. մի դասուք[5] չափ անկեալ Ժ. (10) դաս ասելն. մինն մարդա մոլորակ ոչխարին ասացին։

2/ Վասն անուանց հրեշտակաց.
Առաջին՝ Գաբրիէլ, որ է պատկեր Աստուծոյ։
Բ.րդ՝ Միքայէլ- հզօր։
Գ.րդ՝ Ռաքայէլ- բժշկութիւն։
Դ.րդ՝ Անայէլ- լրումն Աստուծոյ։
Ե.րդ՝ Ուրիէլ- տեսումն Աստուծոյ։
Զ.րդ՝ Դակուէլ- ինքն աստուածային։
Է.րդ՝ Բարագուէլ- սկիզբն աստուածայնոյ։
Ը.րդ՝ Ադոնիէլ- Տեառն իմոյ Աստուծոյ։
Թ.րդ՝ Փանուէլ- յայտնութիւն Աստուծոյ։

3/ Հարց. Անկումն դիւաց.
Պատասխանի. Պատճառ հպարտութեան ոչ ժամի եկաց Ճշմարտութեան շուոտով ուռացեալ, իւր լոյսն տեսանելով, ոչ ետ փառս Աստուծոյ, փառաբանութիւն յափշտակեաց առ զինքն, առժամայն խաւար դարձաւ, անկաւ։ Թէպէտ լուսոյ կերպարանի, այլ ինքն ոչ տեսանէ լուսն։ Վասն այն չարի առ մարդն տե/ fol 180v / սանելով զփառս մարդկանս։

Translation

1/ Question: How many classes of angels (are there)?
Answer: They said, nine. The first is: Thrones, Cherubs, and Seraphs[6]—high priests, the first classes.
Second: Dominions, Powers, Princedoms, which are the middle classes.
Third: Principalities, Archangels, and Angels, and the last, orders.[7]
And the first ones are intellective, and the middle ones are intelligible, and the last ones are intellective and intelligible. They said, nine (classes). The quantity of one class[8] having fallen, they said that (there are) ten class(es). That one, they said, is human beings, called strayed sheep.[9]

---

5. For this use of the plural, see text no. 4, n. 25.
6. In Stone, *Angels and Heroes*, Text 3.6, where the ranking is given, Seraphs precede Cherubs. In Text 3.5 and elsewhere, the order found in the present text prevails. See also table 1 above.
7. That is, of ecclesiastics.
8. Literally: one quantity by classes.
9. Ps 119(118):176, Isa 53:6, Jer 50:6, 1 Pet 2:25.

2/ Concerning the names of angels.
The first is Gabriel, which is "image of God."[10]
Second—Michael, "might."
Third—Raphael, "healing."
Fourth—Anayel, "God's fullness."
Fifth—Uriel, "seeing of God."
Sixth—Daguel, "himself the divine."
Seventh—Baraguel,[11] "of the divine."
Eighth—Adoniel, "of my Lord God."
Ninth—Phanuel, "revelation of God."
3/ Question: The fall of demons?
Answer: The reason, pride; he did not stand at the hour (of prayer); he denounced truth quickly; seeing his own light, he did not glorify God;[12] he appropriated the glorification to himself, at which time he turned to darkness (and) he fell. Although he still had the form of light, he did not see the light. On account of that (he is) evil towards men, seeing the glory of men.

---

10. See Text 4.2, n. 15 on "Michael."
11. That is, Barak'iel.
12. The idea that Satan who fell was luminous derives, of course, from Isa 14:12. Hybris is commonly said to be the reason for his fall. See Stone, "Sadayēl's Fall from Heaven," forthcoming.

4. Classes of Angels

Introductory Remarks

This text is a combination of smaller textual units that do not appear as a single whole in the material gathered in Stone, *Angels and Heroes*. However, this text partakes of general ideas and terminology of many of the documents published there.[1]

The text occurs in Matenadaran manuscript M10561 fols 146r–146v, which is described in detail in the introductory remarks to Concerning the Heavens.[2] The writing is composed of three parts. Part 1 is a list of the nine angelic classes in descending order of importance. Another catalogue of nine angelic classes follows, with an onomastic list giving the putative meanings of their names. This list is similar to those in Part 1, having nine classes, and its order and its onomastic explanations resemble other lists that circulated as separate documents, of which some examples have been published.[3]

The second part is a catalogue of the laudatory verses sung by each of these angelic classes. This strongly resembles the previously published text, Praise of the Angels, but is more abbreviated than it.[4]

The third part of the writing is an anti-Origenic discussion on beliefs about angels and it has not previously been published.

---

1. In addition to Stone, *Angels and Heroes*, a number of studies dealing with angelology have been published. Prominent among these are material contained in Sargis Harut'yunyan, *Armenian Incantations and Folk Prayers* (Հայ հմայական եւ ժողովրդական աղոթքներ) (Erevan: Erevan State University Press, 2006); Frédéric Feydit, *Amulettes de l'Arménie chrétienne*, Bibliothèque arménienne de la Fondation Calouste Gulbenkian (Venice: St. Lazare, 1986); Stone, "Some Armenian Angelological and Uranographical Texts," 147–57; Stone, "Further Angelological Texts" in *Apocrypha, Pseudepigrapha and Armenian Studies: Collected Papers*, OLA 144 (Leuven: Peeters, 2006), 1:427–35.

2. See pp. 3–4 above.

3. See M537 and M286 (Stone, *Angels and Heroes*, 66, 70–71); those texts are very close to the present document.

4. See Stone, *Angels and Heroes*, 77–85.

4.1. The Nine Archangels and Their Names

Text

1/ M10561 / fol 146r / <Հարց>:[5] Որքա՞ն է դասք հրեշտակաց:
Պատասխանի: Թ. (9) դաս, երիս երիս երրեակս որոշեալ թըվոց, որոց առաջինք՝ աթոռք, սերովբէք, քերովբէք,
եւ է առաջին դաս[6] քահանայապետութիւն:
Երկրորդ՝ տերութիւնք, զօրութի<ւն>ք, իշխանութի<ւն>ք, որք են մէջի դաս:
Երրորդ՝ պետութիւնք, հրեշտակապետք եւ հրեշտակ:[7]
2/ <Հարց>:[8] Եւ քանի՞ հրեշտակապետ ասի կամ մեկնի:
Պատասխանի: Թ. (9):
Առաջինն՝ Գաբրիէլ, որ է պատկեր Աստուծոյ:
Երկրորդ՝ Միքայէլ, որպէս զԱստուած կամ հզաւր:
Երրորդ՝ Ռայֆայէլ, որ է բժշկութիւն:
Չորրորդ՝ Անայէլ - լրումն Աստուծոյ:
Հինգերրորդ՝ Ուրիէլ - տեսումն Աստուծոյ:
Վեցերրորդ՝ Դակուէլ - յինքն աստուածային: / fol 146v /
Եւթներրորդ՝ Բարաքիէլ - սկիզբն աստուածայնոյ:
Ութերրորդ՝ Ադոնիէլ - Տէառն իմոյ Աստուծոյ:
Իններրորդ՝ Փանուէլ - յայտնութիւն Աստուծոյ:

Translation

1/ <Question:> How many classes of angels are there?
Answer: Nine classes;[9] the numbers (are) divided threefold into three threes.

---

5. The tag, "Question" seems to have been lost. The order of the nine classes should be compared with table 1 above.

6. Observe that here դաս may be taken as a *pluralis tantum*. This phenomenon occurs elsewhere in these lists of angelic classes.

7. Note the loss of -ք in the combination -կք. See Michael E. Stone and Vered Hillel, "Index of Variants," in *The Armenian Version of the Testaments of the Twelve Patriarchs: Edition, Apparatus, Translation and Commentary*, HUAS 11 (Leuven: Peeters, 2012), no. 333.

8. The tag, "Question" seems to have been lost. A text very similar to §2 here is to be found in Stone, *Angels and Heroes*, 71. It, too, is formulated as a question and answer. There are slight variants in certain names and also in the etymologies offered. These are noted below.

9. See the discussion in Stone, *Angels and Heroes*, 66.

4. CLASSES OF ANGELS

Of these, the first (are): Thrones, Seraphs, Cherubs. And the first class is high priesthood.[10]

The second (are): Dominions, Powers, Rulers, which are the middle class. Third: Principalities, Archangels, and Angels.[11]

2/ <Question:> And how are archangel(s) spoken of or interpreted.[12]

Answer: nine.

The first, Gabriel, which is "image of God."[13]
The second, Michael, "like God"[14] or "mighty."[15]
The third, Rayphael,[16] which is "healing."
The fourth, Anayel—"God's fullness."[17]
The fifth, Uriel—"seeing of God."
The sixth, Dakuel[18]—"to his divine."
The seventh, Barakiel, "beginning of divine."[19]
The eighth, Adoniel—"of the Lord my God."

---

10. The division of the nine classes of angels into three groups is not common, but not surprising. The number seven for angelic classes is also widespread (see, e.g., Stone, *Angels and Heroes*, 67), and the nine classes are associated with pseudo-Dionysius the Areopagite. The characterization of the first class here as "high priests" is also to be observed in Stone, *Angels and Heroes*, 81, text no. 3.5 §12. There, the Thrones are equated with high priests. Naturally, one chief role of the angels was considered to be the conduct of the liturgy in the heavenly temple. However, this is not carried through angelological texts systematically.

11. Note that this group is not characterized.

12. That is, given pseudo-etymological explanations. For such explanations, see Franz Xavier Wutz, *Onomastica Sacra: Untersuchungen zum Liber Interpretationis Nominum Hebraeorum des Hl. Hieronymous*, Texte und Untersuchungen 41/2 (Leipzig: Hinrichs, 1915) and Stone, *Signs of the Judgement*.

13. This "etymology" is not of Michael; see n. 92 below.

14. M535 has կատ hqop. This explanation of Michael is an amalgam of the usual explanation of Gabriel as "power of God," and Michael, "who is like God." In Armenian texts, Gabriel is often first in the list.

15. "Like God" is a reasonable etymology of the Hebrew name: "mighty" is odd, but can also be observed in Text 3, section 2. It might have migrated from "Gabriel," while the present explanation of Gabriel might have originated with Michael.

16. A variant spelling of Raphael.

17. This is inexplicable as it stands. However, լրութիւ "fullness" might be corrupt for the similar լսութիւ "listening," parsing Anayel from Hebrew ענ"י "respond." No other, even remote etymology comes to mind.

18. In Stone, *Angels and Heroes*, 72, M537 reads Daksiel. Both Dokiel and Daksiel are known angelic names in Armenian.

19. Conceivably connected with Hebrew בר"א "create."

The ninth, Phanuel—"revelation of God."[20]

4.2. The Praises Sung by the Nine Classes of Angels[21]

Text

/ fol 146v /

3/ Եւ փառաբանութիւն է նոցա այսպէս.[22]
ներքին դասն, որ է հրեշտակաց, որք են պատգամաբերք եւ հրամանատարք, եւ փառաբանութիւն է նոցա այսպէս. «Փառք ի բարձունս Աստուծոյ», զոր լուան հովիւքն:

4/ Երկրորդ դասք հրեշտակապետաց, եւ փառաբանութիւն է նոցա. «Ողորմեա՛, Տէ՛ր, քո արարածոց», զոր լուաւ Զաքարիաս, երէ. «Մինչեւ յէ՞րբ ոչ ողորմեցիս Երուսաղեմի եւ քաղաքաց Յուդա»:

5/ Երրորդ դասք պետութեանց, եւ փառաբանութիւն է նոցա. «Դու ես քահանա<յ> յաւիտեան, ըստ կարգին Մելքիսեդեկի»:

6/ Չորրորդ դասք իշխանութեանց, եւ ասեն. «Տուան քեզ հեթանոսք իշխանութիւն եւ ժառանգութիւն»:

7/ Հինգերրորդ դասք զօրութեանց, եւ ասեն. «Տէր հզօր զօրութեամբ իւրով, Տէր կարող:

8/ Վեցերրորդ տերութեանց, եւ ասէ.[23] «Արքայութիւն քո արքայութիւն եղիցի եւ տերութիւն»:

9/ Եւթերրորդ սերովբէից, եւ ասեն. «Սուրբ, սուրբ, սուրբ Տէր զօրութեանց, լի են երկինք եւ երկիր»:

10/ Ութերրորդ՚ սերովբէից, որք են վարս հրեղէնք, եւ ասեն. «Աւրհնեալ է փառք Տեառն ի տեղոջն իւրում»:

11/ Իններրորդ / fol 147r / դասք աթոռք, եւ ասեն. «Աթոռ քո, Աստուած, յաւիտեանս յաւիտենից»:

---

20. Either derived exegetically from Gen 32:30 and, anyway, etymologically from "God's face." Alternatively, it could be taken secondarily as a hybrid Greek-Hebrew φαίνω + 'el.

21. This unit of text is extracted from a document overall resembling those published in Stone, *Angels and Heroes*, 77–85, text no. 3.5.

22. This section is based on a text like Stone, *Angels and Heroes*, text no. 3.6, but the order of the classes and a number of other details differ. *Angels and Heroes*, text no. 3.5 also has a similar text, but it presents the angels in the reverse of the order found in the present document.

23. On the analogy of the other classes of angels, a plur. verb would be expected.

4. CLASSES OF ANGELS

Translation

3/ And their praise is thus:
The lowest class, which is of the Angels, who are carriers of messages and givers of commands, and their praise is thus: "Glory to God on high," which the shepherds heard.[24]

4/ The second class[25] (is) of the Archangels and their praise is: "Have mercy, Lord, on your creatures," which Zacharias heard, "Until when will you not pity Jerusalem and the cities of Judah?"[26]

5/ The third class (is) of the Dominions[27] and their praise is, "You are a priest forever according to the order of Melchizedek."[28]

6/ The fourth class is of the Princedoms[29] and they say, "The heathen are given to you for princedoms and inheritance."[30]

7/ The fifth class (is) of the Powers[31] and they say, "The Lord is mighty through his power, the Lord is strong."[32]

8/ The sixth (is) of the Dominions and it says, "Your kingdom will be a[33] kingdom and a dominion."[34]

9/ The seventh is of the Seraphs and they say, "Holy, Holy, Holy the Lord of Hosts, the heavens and earth are full …"[35]

---

24. Luke 2:14.
25. Here and throughout the word ṇuup is plural in form but singular in meaning, being treated as a plurale tantum. See text no. 3, n. 25.
26. Zech 1:12.
27. The Dominions are fourth in Stone, *Angels and Heroes*, text no. 3.6.
28. Ps 110(109):4.
29. The Princedoms are seventh in *Angels and Heroes*, text no. 3.6.
30. Based on Ps 2:8.
31. The Powers are sixth in *Angels and Heroes*, text no. 3.6.
32. Ps 24(23):8. The quotation here is a few words longer than in *Angels and Heroes*, text no. 3.6.
33. The word "eternal" has been lost.
34. The Dominions are sixth in *Angels and Heroes*, text no. 3.6. The quotation is from Ps 145(144):13.
35. The Seraphs are eighth in *Angels and Heroes*, text no. 3.6. They praise with Isa 6:3 as reformulated in the Sanctus prayer. The form "heaven and earth" is taken from the Sanctus prayer, and replaces "all the earth" in Isa 6:3.

10/ The eighth (are) {Seraphs}[36] who are fiery conduct,[37] and they say, "Blessed is the glory of the Lord in his place."[38]

11/ The ninth class (is) Thrones, "God, forever and ever."[39]

4.3. Origen and the Classes of Angels

Text

12/ / fol 147r / Այս են Թ. (9) թաւք[40] հրեշտակաց, եւ քան զայս աւելի մի ինչ թվեցցուք եւ իմասցուք, որպէս եղկելին Որոգինէս, աւելի քան զգրեալն իմանալով, կործանեցաւ անկանգնելի.

13/ զապիրատութիւն ի բարձունս խորհեցաւ, զայս ասելով, թէ՛ մարդիկ ոչ տեսանեն զհրեշտակս, եւ ոչ հրեշտակ մարդկան զհոգիսն։ Եւ Հոգին Սուրբ ոչ տեսանէ զՈրդին, եւ սուրբ Որդին ոչ տեսանէ զՀայր սուրբ։

14/ Բայց մեզ քաւ եւ մի լիցի բանս, քանզի եւ Մովսէս այլ ոչ ինչ ասաց, բայց միայն զեռականս
վասն հրեշտակաց։

Translation

12/ These are the nine classes of angels and we shall not reckon and apprehend any more than these. Just as miserable Origen by apprehending more than are written, perished and could not be reestablished.[41]

---

36. This should read "Cherubs," who are the ninth class in *Angels and Heroes*, text no. 3.6.

37. This is odd. Could there be a corruption of *կատ > վարս? Only here does *Angels and Heroes*, text no. 3.6 differ substantially when it says, որ լսին վարք իմաստութեան Աստուծոյ "who heard the conduct of God's wisdom." Of course, "Seraph," Hebrew שרף, could be understood as deriving from Hebrew שׂר"פ, which root means "to burn."

38. Ps 72(71):19.

39. The Thrones are third in *Angels and Heroes*, text no. 3.6. The words, աթոռք քո "your thrones (are)" have been lost by haplography. The praise is drawn from Ps 45:5(44:7).

40. Orthographic error for դասք.

41. The question whether Origen could be saved and, indeed, the deep ambiguity of attitudes towards him are succinctly presented by Henry Chadwick, *Early Christian Thought and the Classical Tradition: Studies in Justin, Clement, and Origen* (Oxford: Clarendon, 1966), 95–98.

4. CLASSES OF ANGELS

13/ He thought wickedness[42] (about things) on high by saying this—that men do not see angels, and angels (do not see) the spirits of men, and the Holy Spirit does not see the Son, and the holy Son does not see the holy Father.

14/ But, Heaven forefend, and let not this thing happen to us, because even Moses says only general things about angels.

---

42. That is, wickedness about things on high. The views attributed to Origen are, in fact, misrepresented. The chief passage that was subject to misinterpretation is Origen, *On First Principles* 1.1.8 and the misrepresentation goes back to Epiphanius in his Panarion 64.4.3–4, which text reads rather like ours: "4.3 For Origen claims, and at once dares, if you please, to say first that the Only-begotten Son cannot see the Father, and neither can the Spirit behold the Son; and angels surely cannot behold the Spirit, nor men the angels. 4. And this is his first downfall." Quoted from Frank Williams, *The Panarion of Epiphanius of Salamis: Books II and III (Sects 47–80 De Fide)*, Nag Hammadi and Manichaean Studies 36 (Leiden: Brill, 1994), 137. The absurdity of Epiphanius's polemic is discussed in Henri Crouzel, *Origen* (Edinburgh: T&T Clark, 1989), 102–3.

5. Numbers and Ranks of the Angels

Introductory Remarks

Interest in the angelic world is to be found throughout medieval Armenian literature. Texts dealing with angels often occur in scholastic manuscripts and are widespread also in apotropaic and magical manuscripts. A number of documents have been published previously, and the angelological texts edited in the present work join them.[1]

The short piece being edited here occurs in M2245 on fols 148r–148v and is not noted in the *General Catalogue*.[2] The manuscript is a miscellany very rich in texts of pseudepigraphical interest, including: Sermon Concerning the Flood, 4r–18r;[3] Sermon concerning the Sodomites, 18r–31v; Sermon concerning the Three Young Men, 87r–97v; Question concerning the Archangels, 114v–115r;[4] Fall of the Angels I and II, 114v–116r; The Number and the Twelve Classes of Angels, 148r–v;[5] Questions of St. Gregory, 235r–238v;[6] History of the Forefathers, 279r–281;[7] Question concerning Angels, 286v–296v;

---

1. See, in addition to the documents published in the present volume, Stone, *Angels and Heroes*, 65–111; Stone, "Some Armenian Angelological and Uranographical Texts"; Stone, "Further Angelological Texts." The texts of many apotropaic and magical documents mentioning angels are published in Feydit, *Amulettes* and Sargis Harut'yunyan, *Armenian Incantations*.

2. *General Catalogue* 7:619–28. See also on this manuscript, Stone, *Biblical Heroes*, 1.

3. Published from M5571 in Stone, *Adam and Eve*, 174–200. The title "Sermon" is sometimes given to texts that are basically narrative with little or no homiletics. See, for instance, *Sermon concerning the Flood* in Stone, *Adam and Eve*, 174–179 and *Sermon concerning the Sodomites*, in Stone, *Abraham*, 178–203, as well as the texts listed in this paragraph.

4. Edited and published in Stone, *Angels and Heroes*, 72–75.

5. Stone, *Biblical Heroes*, 1–3.

6. I am preparing an edition of this text, of which the first recension has been published in Stone, "Questions of St. Gregory."

7. Stone, *Adam and Eve*, 180–200.

5. NUMBERS AND RANKS OF THE ANGELS

Concerning the Numbers of the Angels, 260v; The Third Story of Joseph, 330r–349v.[8]

The intent of the text being presented here is unclear compared with the numerous lists of angelic ranks and classes that I have published previously.[9] Thus, Angels text no. 2 is clearly apotropaic and Angels text no. 5 deals with the heavenly liturgy and the correspondence of heavenly and earthly hierarchies. In addition, Numbers and Ranks of Angels seems to know two traditions of angelic classes, one of nine classes and the other of twelve. In the manuscript this text is followed by a short list of the four types of wood of which the cross was constructed. The two documents are not related.

Text

0/ M2245 / fol 148r / Յաղագս հրեշտակաց թւոյն եւ դասուց բաժանմանցն:

1/ Բայց մեք վերցացեալպս ի թուոց նոցա, եւ ի բարձրութենէ, եւ ի պայծառութենէ, զի. Թ. (9) դասք են նորա, եւ ամենայն դասք ԲԺ.ն (12) զունդք, զոր առաքեալքն նահապետութեան ասէ. Եւ ամենայն զունդք հազարք հազարաց եւ բիւր բիւրոց:

2/ Բարձր, քան զմիմեանս, որպէս երկինք քան զերկիր, պայծառ քան զմիմեանս որպէս արեգակ, քան զլուսին: Եւ մեկ / fol 148v / դասն շատ է, քան զամենայն մարդկութիւնս, եւ զօրագոյնք են, քան զամենայն արըս, որպէս հրեշտակք, քան զմարդ:

3/ Եւ են անդի խոնարհ աթոռք, քերովբէք, սերովբէք, տերութիւնք, զօրութիւնք, իշխանութիւնք, պետութիւնք, հրեշտակապետք, հրեշտակք:[10]

Translation

0/ Concerning the Number of Angels and the Division of (their) Classes

1/ Then we abandon their numbers and elevation and brightness. For their classes are nine and each class is composed of twelve hosts, (of) which the emissaries of the Leader says,[11] "and each host thousands of thousands, and myriads of myriads."[12]

---

8. Stone, *Angels and Heroes*, 176–229.
9. Stone, *Angels and Heroes*, 67–110.
10. This is the standard list of nine angelic classes, widespread in Armenian literature. See Stone, *Angels and Heroes*, 81–90 and in many other sources.
11. Unclear. առաքեալքն is plur. and the verb ասէ is singular.
12. Dan 7:10.

2/ (They are) higher than one another as the heavens are (higher) than the earth;[13] brighter than one another as the sun is (brighter) than the moon. And one[14] class is more numerous than all mankind, and they are stronger than all humans, just as the angels (are stronger) than a human.

3/ And from there, descending, they are: Thrones, Cherubs, Seraphs, Dominions, Powers, Rulers, Archangels, Angels.

---

13. See on the height of the heavens, Stone, "Some Armenian Angelological and Uranographical Texts," text no. 5.
14. That is: a single.

6. Prayer to the Archangels

Introductory Remarks

This text occurs in an amulet scroll of the years 1706–1707 in the Bodleian Library, Oxford, numbered arm g 4. The particular prayer that I am editing here follows the image of an angel and it is an invocation of specific angels for help in various enumerated quandaries that it sets forth. In Stone, *Angels and Heroes*, text nos. 3.1–3.2 other prayers of the same type are published.[1] A very similar prayer, indeed apparently another form of the same underlying text, was published by Feydit.[2] Each angel is mentioned with its specific ability, which can be invoked. In the notes, I give the functions of various of the angels in a number of different lists. There is a fair amount of consistency of names and functions between these lists, though, as is natural with names of this sort, various orthographic variants occur, as well as apocopation at the beginning.[3]

Such invocations of angels are rather common. They appear not only in amulet rolls, but in some codices, and sometimes the manuscripts containing them are actually more hagiographical than magical. After all, there are feasts of various archangels on the church calendar. The amulet is a nice specimen of the rather numerous members of this genre. It is written by hand on a long strip of paper. The amulet and its contents are described by Baronian and Conybeare.[4]

---

1. On such apotropaic prayers, see Stone, *Angels and Heroes*, 69.
2. See Feydit, *Amulettes*, 222–24. Feydit has taken it from amulet 257 of the Bibliothèque nationale de France. It does not seem to be included in Harut'yunyan, *Armenian Incantations*.
3. It would be of great service if a list of the angelic names found in all published apotropaic and magical texts were to be assembled. For the present, no such catalogue exists.
4. Bodleian Catalogue, 73–75.

Picture of an archangel, Bodleian arm g 6. Published by permission of the Bodleian Library.

6. PRAYER TO THE ARCHANGELS

Text

Bodleian arm g6/ Title/ Մաղթանք առ սուրբ հրեշտա[կա]պետացն[5] Գաբրիէլի եւ Միքայէլի, եւ ամենայն երկնային զաւրացն. եղիցի պահպանութիւն ծառայիս Աստուծոյ. [ա]մէն:

1/ Անըսկիզբն Աստուած, Հայր սուրբ, Որդիդ միածին, Սուրբ Հոգիդ Ճշմարիտ, բազմութիւն սերովբէից եւ քերովբէից, որ են անուանքն այսոքիկ Միքայէլ, Գաբրիէլ, Ուրիէլ, Սաղաթիէլ. սրբայ են, որ շուրջ կան զաթոռովն Աստուծոյ, եւ ունին իշխանութիւն բժշկել զախտս եւ զհիւանդութիւնս:

2/ Եւ եթէ մարդ ոք ի սատանայական ախտից վշտացեալ է եւ կարդասցէ առ Հռափայէլ հրեշտակն, ոչ ինչ լինի նմա չար:

3/ Եւ որ ի վերայ լերանց ունի իշխանութիւն, Հռափէլ կոչի անուն նորա. սա դարմանիչ է անասնոց, խնդութիւն հովուաց, առաջադէմ երրնջոց, բազմութիւն կաթին պահէ առողջութեամբ: Եւ որ կարդան զանուն նորա, ըշտեմարանք նոցա աճին եւ բազմանան առողջութեամբ: Եւ երինջք նոցա ծնընդեամբ դիեցուցանեն զորդիս իւրեանց:

4/ Եւ որ ի վերայ ջրոյն ունին[6] իշխանութիւն, Մեղբոս կոչի անուն նորա: Եւ յորժամ ըմպես ջուր, կարդայ զանուն նորա, զի սայ աղիճնեաց զաղբիւրս ջրոց: Սայ է յօդս եւ ճայն բարբառոյ յանապատի: Սայ էջ ի յերկնից եւ աղիճնեաց գՅորդանան եւ Տէր մեր Յիսուս Քրիստոս լոյս աշխարհի, որ լուսաւորէ զազգս որդւոց մարդկան եւ զարթուցանէ ի բարաբանութիւն[7] Աստուծոյ:

5/ Եւ որ ի վերայ քնոյ ունի իշխանութիւն, Յովիէլ կոչի անուն նորա: Սայ է ճրագ, որ լուսաւորէ զազգս մարդկան, եւ որ զգեցեալ ունի զանուն նորա, փրկի ի խաւարէ:

6/ Եւ որ ի վերայ ծննդոց ունի իշխանութիւն, Սարաբինէլ կոչի անուն նորա: Որ յիշէ զանուն նորա, ոչ վնասի ի ծննդոց, եւ որ կարդան զանուն նորա, ոչ անկանին ի մեղս, այլ ապաշխարութեան արժանի լինին:

7/ Եւ որ ի վերայ մանկանց ունի իշխանութիւն, Նաթանայէլ կոչի անուն նորա: Որ կարդան զանուն նորա, ազատին ի մեղաց: Եւ

---

5. One would expect an accusative case in standard Ancient Armenian. This is apparently a dative.

6. The final ն is either a third pers. plur. ending or it is a demonstrative. The subject is in the singular.

7. ռ over բ, p.m. This is presumably a misspelling of փառաբանութիւն "glorification."

մանկանց տղայոց օգնական է. սա ընկալաւ զտղայս ի Հերովդիէ, սա լուսաւոր արար զտղայսն անձեռագործ տաճարն:

8/ Եւ որ ի վերայ ջերման ունի իշխանութիւն, Սուքայէլ կոչի անուն նորա։ Եւ որ յիշէ զանուն նորա, ոչ մերձենա ի նա ջերմն:

9/ Եւ որ ի վերայ մայրեաց ունի իշխանութիւն, Մաղանիէլ կոչի անուն նորա: Սայ է սահմանիչ մայրեաց եւ հաստատիչ տանց, պահէ զաղքատս եւ մեծացուցանէ:

10/ Եւ որ ի վերայ հիմանց ունի իշխանութիւն. Թովբան, Ազզբան, Սուքայէլ՝ հաստատիչ ամենայն տիեզերաց եւ բժշկութիւն ամենայն ախտից, որք անկանին ի չարիս:

11/ Եւ որ ի վերայ երկուց լուսաւորացն ունին իշխանութիւն, Կոճդիոս կոչի անուն նորա: Սայ է, որ վարէ զլուսին եւ զարեգակն, սայ է, որ կա առաջի Աստուծոյ, յորժամ բարբառեն սերովբէքն՝ ասելով՝ Սուրբ, սուրբ, սուրբ Տէր զաւրութեանց, լի են երկինք եւ երկիր փառօք քո:⁸

12/ Անանիայ, առաջի<ն> հրեշտակապետն Միքայէլ,⁹ Բարէզեւ, Փութիէլ,¹⁰ Թերուքէլ, Քարիբէն, Թովբենիմինէլ, Բէլի, Սաղագին, Կեպիմէլ, Մուսիէլ, Խթիէլ: Ձայս անուանքս¹¹ ով որ ունի եւ պահէ սրբութեամբ, եղիցի վշտաց օգնական, ղիւաց հալածումն, ախտաժետաց առողջութիւն, հոգոց եւ մա[ր]մնոց փրկութիւն ի Քրիստոս Յիսուս ի Տէր մեր, որում փառք, իշխանութիւն եւ պատիւ, այժմ եւ միշտ եւ յաւիտեանս յաւիտենից. ամէն:

Apparatus

The text is Bodleian arm g 4; the variants are from Feydit, *Amulettes*, Text LXIX, 222–24.

Title/ omit
1/ անսկիզբն | Որդիղ | Հոգիղ| | սերովբէից| որ] որ[ոց] | անուանք | սրա | զհիւանդութիւնս

---

8. This form of "Holy, holy, holy" is found in the Sanctus prayer, which draws the formula from Isa 6:3.

9. Feydit has Անանիայ առաջի հրեշտակապետն Միքայէլ "Devant Ananie, l'archange Michel." Whichever option one chooses, it is ungrammatical without emendation. See n. 169 below.

10. Note Stone, *Angels and Heroes*, 69, which has Butayēl (an archangel).

11. The ք is anomalous.

3/ Հռաքիէլ | դարմանիչն | անասնոց] +եւ | առաջադէմ երրնշոց] առաջնորդ է մեր ընչուց | որ2°] որ[բ] | շտեմարանք/ | ծննդեամբ] սննդեամբ : Feydit's emendation | դիացուցանեն | գորդիսն] գորբու : Feydit's emendation

4/ ջ[ր]ոյս | | ունի | -եւ յորժամ] յորժամ | կարդա | զի սայ] սա | օրհնեաց | զադբերս | չրոյ | սա | յաւդս | սա | օրհնեաց | Տէր] [զ]Տէրն | որդ[ւ]ոց | եւ զարթուցանէ ի բարաբանութիւն Աստուծոյ] om

5/ բնդն | սա | մարդկան] + [եւ զարթուցանէ ի փառաբանութիւն Աստուծոյ] om

7/ Աթանայէլ | աղնակաեն | գտդայսն ի Հերովդիսէ | [յ] անձերագործ տաճարն

8/ մերձենայ | չերմ

9/ Մադանայէլ | սա

10/ ունի[ն] իշխանութիւն] + այս են անուանք հրեշտակացն : Ազգրուն | preferable | որք] եւ որք

11/ ունի | սա | վարէ զարեգակն եւ զլուսինն | սա | կայ | բարբարին | սերովբէք եւ քերովբէք | գօրութեանց

12/ առաջի | Բարեքսա | Թովբենի, Մինէլ | Կեպիմիէլ | Խթիէլ] + Յակիէլ | որ ունին | պահեն | | աղնական | ախտաժետաց | հոգւոյ | մարմնոյ | իշխանութիւն] --- յաւիտեանս. ամէն

Translation

Title/ Prayer to the Holy Archangels Gabriel and Michael[12] and all the heavenly hosts. May it be protection for me, a servant of God. [A]men.

1/ God without beginning—holy Father, only-born Son, true Holy Spirit, multitude of Seraphs and Cherubs, who(se) names are these: Michael, Gabriel, Uriel, Salathiel. These are (those) who stand around God's throne[13] and have the power to heal afflictions and illnesses.

---

12. These two names are standard in lists of the four or seven archangels. Gabriel and Michael are commonly paired, as may be seen in the list in Stone, "Some Armenian Angelological and Uranographical Texts," 111 and elsewhere. There is a feast dedicated to these two archangels together in the calendar of saints of the Armenian Church on 10 November.

13. This list of four angels is similar to the lists of seven and nine angels discussed in Stone, *Angels and Heroes*, 66. There the fourth is Zitʻayel, while here it is Salathiel. Salathiel is not mentioned in the published sources that contain apotropaic prayers. There was a person called Salathiel father of Zerubbabel, mentioned in 1 Chr 3:17; Ezra 3:8; 5:2; Neh 12:1; Hag 1:1, 12, 14; 2:2, 23; Matt 1:12; and Luke 3:27. In 4 Ezra, Shealtiel (Salathiel) is another name for Ezra: see the discussion in Stone, *4 Ezra*, 55–56. Feydit, *Amulettes*, 212–19 prints a number of texts that open with similar, but not identical, lists of angelic

2/ And if any man is suffering from Satanic afflictions and he calls on the angel Raphael,[14] no evil will befall him.[15]

3/ And he who has power over mountains, his name is called Hṙakʻēl.[16] He is the restorer of animals, the delight of shepherds, the preceder[17] of heifers. He preserves a large quantity of milk[18] through health.[19] And those who call his name—their store rooms will increase and multiply healthily and their heifers on calving give suck to their offspring.

4/ And he who has authority over the water, his name is called Mełkʻos.[20] And when you drink water, call out his name for he blessed the springs of

---

names. Usually the angels around the Throne of God are four in number and those called angels of the presence are seven. Older Jewish tradition speaks of four angels around the divine throne: Michael, Gabriel, Raphael, and Uriel. Angels of the Presence are those who "see God's face," that is, who enter the immediate environs of the Deity.

14. On Raphael, see Stone, "Some Armenian Angelological and Uranographical Texts," 154, where he delivers "from pain and sadness." In Stone, *Angels and Heroes*, 76, invoking his name keeps one "unharmed by distress." Moreover, his name is effective against "pains and sadness" (111). In Jewish tradition Raphael was one of the most important archangels; see the preceding note.

15. Observe the same content with different wording in Feydit, *Amulettes*, LXVIII.

16. This angelic name is the same as the Armenian form of "Rachel," Jacob's wife's name. However, we have transliterated it here because it seems as likely to be a corruption as that the angel was called "Rachel." It is a transliteration of a Greek name starting with ρ, which regularly appears in Armenian as *hṙ*. Text LXIX printed by Feydit reads Հռաքէլ, that is Hṙakʻiēl. Notably, even though his name is made from the Hebrew rood רפא "to heal," Raphael is not found in the text at this point. In addition, it is interesting to observe that Feydit, *Amulettes*, 213 does list an angel Սառա "Sarah," and some other personal names familiar from the Bible appear elsewhere as names of angels in lists. So, it remains possible that, despite my doubts, this angel was called "Rachel." Were the matriarchs Sarah and Rachel transmuted into apotropaic angels? In a different context, Andrei Orlov has written about heavenly doubles of earthly patriarchs; see Andrei Orlov, "Moses' Heavenly Counterpart in the Book of Jubilees and the Exagoge of Ezekiel the Tragedian," *Biblica* 88 (2007): 153–73, and Orlov, "The Face as the Heavenly Counterpart of the Visionary in the Slavonic Ladder of Jacob," in *Of Scribes and Sages: Early Jewish Interpretation and Transmission of Scripture*, ed. Craig A. Evans, 2 vols., Studies in Scripture in Early Judaism and Christianity 9 (London: T&T Clark, 2004), 2:59–76.

17. Perhaps this means "the one who stands before."

18. That is, he guarantees the abundance of the milk yielded by heifers.

19. Or: healthily.

20. In Stone, "Some Armenian Angelological and Uranographical Texts," 151 and Stone, *Angels and Heroes*, 70, the angel over waters is Mełkʻisn, a graphic variant of the form here: See Stone and Hillel, "Index of Variants," item 46 for the variant u/n. Melkʻos is also over the sea. In Stone, *Angels and Heroes*, 111 the name is apocopated to Ełkʻos.

waters. He is in the air[21] and (he is) the voice of speech in the desert.[22] He descended from heaven and blessed the Jordan and our Lord Jesus Christ, light of the world,[23] who illumines this race of the children of men and arouses (them) to the praising of God.

5/ And he who has authority over sleep, his name is called Yoviēl.[24] This one is a lantern that illuminates the races of men, and he who has put on[25] (and) has his name is saved from darkness.[26]

6/ And he who has authority over births, his name is called Sarakʻiēl.[27] He who remembers his name is not hurt by births. And those who call his name do not fall into sin but become worthy of repentance.[28]

7/ And he who has authority over children, his name is called Natʻanayēl. Those who call his name are freed from sins. And he is a helper of male chil-

---

21. The idea of spirits, demons, and souls in the air is found in other Armenian texts. See p. 13 n. 29.

22. This seems to allude to John the Baptist, dependent on Matt 3:3, Mark 1:3, Luke 3:4, and John 1:23. The gospels, of course, draw the phrase from Isa 40:3.

23. See Matt 5:14; John 8:12, 12:46.

24. In Stone, "Some Armenian Angelological and Uranographical Texts," 151, 154 and Stone, *Angels and Heroes*, 70 the same angel is over sleep. On p. 111 of Stone, *Angels and Heroes*, it says that if he is invoked, "demons and demonic magic will be put to flight." These are preeminently nocturnal threats and in Hours of the Day and Night, demons praise God in the first watch of the night (see Stone, *Adam and Eve*, 68–69).

25. Is this a reference to an amulet inscribed with the angel's name? The Armenian զգեցեալ is the word for putting on a garment. See Stone, "Some Armenian Angelological and Uranographical Texts," 419 where the same expression զգեցեալ նևիք occurs. There I translated it as "having put on (the magical object with the angel's name), holds onto his name." This may well be correct, and perhaps the known custom of wearing hmayil scrolls on the body confirms it. Also note the practice discussed in Meir Bar-Ilan. "Magic Seals on the Body Among Jews in the First Centuries C.E.," *Tarbiz* 57 (1988): 37–50 [Hebrew].

26. Presumably either the darkness that is seen when one is unable to sleep or Hades, which is sometimes called "darkness"; Michael E. Stone and Edda Vardanyan, "Jacob and the Man at the Ford of Jabbok: A Biblical Subject in the Vine Scroll Frieze of the Church of the Holy Cross at Ałtʻamar," in *Armenia through the Lens of Time: Multidisciplinary Studies in Honour of Theo Maarten van Lint*, ed. Frederico Alpi, Robin Meyer, Irene Tinti, and David Zakarian (Leiden: Brill, forthcoming) dealing with darkness.

27. In Stone, "Some Armenian Angelological and Uranographical Texts," 153, this angel (there the name is spelt Saragiēl) is invoked to avoid "every straitness." On p. 111, this name occurs twice in one and the same list. In §2 Saragiēl saves "from every distress," while in §8, like here, he is over births.

28. In Stone, *Angels and Heroes*, 70 this function is attributed to Azariēl.

dren: He received the boys from Herod.[29] He made luminous the children (of, in) the temple not made with hands.[30]

8/ And he who has authority over fever, his name is called Sukʻayēl.[31] He who remembers his name, fever does not come close to him (them).

9/ And he who has authority over forests,[32] his name is called Małaniēl.[33] He the one who limits[34] woods and constructs houses.[35] He cares for the poor and makes (them) great.

10/ And he who has authority over foundations (is) Tʻovban, Asgban.[36]

Sukʻayēl (is) founder of all universes[37] and healing of all afflictions that fall upon the wicked.

---

29. That is, the male children under two years of age whom Herod killed. See Matt 2:13–16. These are the children referred to in the next phrase, who are in the luminous heavenly temple.

30. The expression "temple not made with hands" designates the heavenly or eschatological temple: see Mark 14:58, cf. 2 Cor 5:1, Heb 9:11. The luminous or shining nature of the heavenly righteous is widely encountered. See 4 Ezra 7:97, 125 and further, Aṙakʻel Siwnecʻi, *Adamgirkʻ* 1.24.69 (Stone, *Adamgirkʻ*, 247). In 4 Ezra 13:36 a mountain "carved out without hands" symbolized "Zion … prepared and built." Strangely, in 4 Ezra 13:5 the man arising from the sea, the redeemer, is said to have "carved out for himself a great mountain."

31. In Stone, "Some Armenian Angelological and Uranographical Texts," 151 the authority over fever is in the hands of Sokʻayēl, a variant of the name here; similarly, see p. 70, where it is spelt Sukʻiēl. This angel is also mentioned in §8 of the present text.

32. Feydit translates: *tanières* "lair, den."

33. In Stone, "Some Armenian Angelological and Uranographical Texts," 152 the angel with this function is called Sałamanos. This is probably a variant of the name here. According to that text, the woods are feared because they might contain "enemies, visible and invisible." Here it seems to be the encroachment of forests onto settled land that is the object of the invocation, as becomes clear in the latter part of this section.

34. Literally: limiter of.

35. Which would otherwise be threatened by the encroachment of forests.

36. "Tʻovban, Asgban" are mysterious names. Feydit, *Amulettes*, Text LXIX precedes these names with the explanatory words, "the names of the angels are" which accords with the formula used in the preceding sections. Sukʻayēl was already mentioned above in no. 8 and it should be observed that there is a functional overlap between the "healer of all afflictions" and the one "whose name prevents fevers."

37. This function is quite unusual. The word աշխարհք "universe(s)" is a *pluralis tantum* in Armenian and so we cannot tell whether one should translate "universe" or "universes."

6. PRAYER TO THE ARCHANGELS

11/ And he who has[38] authority over the two luminaries,[39] his name is called Kr̄etios.[40] He it is that directs the moon and the sun. He it is who stands before God when the Seraphs praise saying, "Holy, Holy, Holy is the Lord of Powers (Hosts), heaven and earth are full of thy glory."[41]

12/ Anania, the firs<t>[42] archangel Michael, Barēgēs, P'ut'iēl, T'eruk'ēl, K'ariben, T'ovbeniminēl,[43] Bēli, Sadagin, Kepimēl, Musiēl, Xt'iēl.[44] Whoever has these names, and preserves (them) with sanctity, that will be an assistance in difficulties, an expulsion of demons, a healing of the infirm, a redemption of souls and bodies; in Christ Jesus, in our Lord to whom glory, authority, and honor, now and always and forever and ever.[45] Amen.

---

38. The verb is in the plural, strictly "have," but the next phrase makes it quite clear that a singular is demanded.

39. See Stone, "Some Armenian Angelological and Uranographical Texts," 148, 153–54; *Angels and Heroes*, 70–73. None of these texts makes him founder of all universes, as is the case here. That appellation is found in Feydit, *Amulettes*, 225, text LXI.

40. This is exactly parallel to Feydit, *Amulettes*, text LXIX.

41. This is a variant form of Isa 6:3 that is found in Christian liturgical use in the Sanctus prayer. What is described here is the heaven liturgy of angelic song, and that song is identified as the praise sung by the angels in Isa 6. This feature is common to Jewish and Christian descriptions of the angelic liturgy. For further examples, see Stone, *Angels and Heroes*, 81, 82, 84, etc., and p. 32 n. 8.

42. Observe that in Stone, "Further Angelological Texts," 430–31, in a list of archangels we read: "Առաջին Գաբրիէլ First – Gabriēl." He is the first archangel, like Michael here. So, we think that Feydit's word division and translation as "Devant Ananie, l'archange Michel" is less probable than the emendations.

43. This might be two names, T'ovbeni and Minēl as Feydit in his Armenian and French texts suggests: *Amulettes*, 225. Alternatively, it can be divided into T'ovi Benimin-ēl, the middle element then resembling Benjamin. The name(s) are unusual.

44. Feydit, *Amulettes*, 225 has one further name, Yakiēl.

45. The doxology is shorter in Feydit, *Amulettes*, 225.

PART 2

ADAM TO ABRAHAM

7. Creation of Eve and Disobedience

Introductory Remarks

In manuscript M1386, a miscellany of the seventeenth century, on fol 183v writing in a new hand starts.[1] It is very cursive in style and begins under a horizontal line that separates the end of the previous text from the new document. The composition found on this page bears no title, and I have designated it Creation of Eve and Disobedience. This small fragment deals with Adam, the creation of Eve, and God's command not to eat the fruit of the tree. It does not occur in any of the Adam texts I have studied so far.[2]

It is worth noting that this text seeks to soften the biblical narrative. Although Eve is to be subordinate to Adam, nonetheless her centrality for a man is stressed. Equally, Adam and Eve's eating the fruit is compared to the dangers cattle may encounter when eating poisonous plants along with grass. This differs from the usual Armenian attitude to that event, which is to view it as wicked disobedience. The serpent is quite absent from this description. Another text in the same hand follows, dealing with creation and cosmogony.

The document is quite unusual in that it attempts to reduce the impact of a number of obtrusive points in the usual interpretation of the biblical text. To do this, in §§1–4 the author accepts a series of particular interpretations of various issues connected with the creation of Eve. Adam's deep sleep (Gen 2:21), he asserts, was a visionary trance (§1); Eve was created from Adam's rib so that the two of them will be one limb and care for one another (§2); the rib, a central part of Adam, was chosen because it shows the central role of the

---

1. See *General Catalogue* 4:1129–1134.
2. For the main published Adam texts and references see: Yovsēpʻeanc, 24–26, 307–32; W. Lowndes Lipscomb, *The Armenian Apocryphal Adam Literature*, UPATS 8 (Atlanta: Scholars Press, 1990); Michael E. Stone, "The Death of Adam: An Armenian Adam Book," *HTR* 59 (1966): 283–91; Stone, *The Penitence of Adam*, CSCO 429–430; SerArm 13–14 (Leuven: Peeters, 1981); Stone, *Patriarchs and Prophets*; Stone, *Adam and Eve*; Stone, *Traditions*; Stone, *Noncanonical Books and Traditions* (Պարականոն գիրքեր եւ աւանդութիւններ) (Erevan: Matenadaran, 2015).

woman (§3); they were astounded by the glory of the garden, which resembled the vision of God's glory (§4). Finally, the commandment that God gave resembled advice from a friend, and its contravention was an error in judgment by Adam and is compared to a beast that made an error (§5).

The first four of these interpretations are also to be found in the works of Grigor Tat'ewac'i (1344?–1409).[3] This is in itself very striking, and it is an observation that is reinforced by similarity of phrasing and word choice. This tends to indicate a date in or around the fourteenth century for the composition of the document. A further point, however, is to be noted. Grigor in his works very often, indeed mostly, offers a series of (frequently ten) responses to difficulties he raised or of answers to questions he poses. From among Grigor's multiple options, as it were, the author of Eve and Disobedience has chosen those that show the role of Eve in the most positive way. In §5, dealing with the prohibition to eat of the tree and its transgression, all implications of blame to be imputed to Eve and Adam are rejected, asserting that this was an error, just like a grazing ruminant that ate a poisonous plant by mistake. This is a very striking comparison.

These attitudes contrast strongly with other interpretations of the creation of Eve from Adam's rib and other readings of the responsibility for and the nature of the sin in the garden.[4] Moreover, Satan is omitted from this text. Take, for example, another interpretation of the rib in Grigor Tat'ewac'i, in the same passage on which, it seems, §3 was based (Stone, *Traditions*, 577–78):

> Sixth, the rib has a shining surface and there is sediment inside, likewise the woman exhibits beauty in the face, but has a heart full of deceit, for one thing is on (her) tongue and another in (her) heart…. and the passage continues in this vein.

This highlights the distinctiveness, not of each element of this text in itself, but of their selection and collocation.

Text

1/ M1386 / fol 183v / Վասն Ադամայ ոչ բնոյ թմրութեան, այլ որպէս ափշումն զարմացման անպատմելի փառացն, Տէր էառ կողից նորա, վասն սակաւ ցաւուն

---

3. See the notes on the text of these sections given below.
4. For the ideas discussed here, see Stone, *Traditions*, 59–60, 103–4, 143–44, etc.

2/ «Այվայ» ասաց, որ է՝ Եւայ. հնազանդեցէ զլխոյն Ադամայ, զի մի օտար երեւեցէ⁵ այլ ի նմանէ կողիցն: Վասն որոյ երկոքեանն մի անդամ եղիցի, մի անգուշ, այլ զուշ տարցեն միմեանց:

3/ Վասն է՞ր կողիցն էառ, որ է ձախ կողն: Մարդոյս ձախ կողն մինն պակաս է: Վասն միջասահման լինելոյ, ոչ որպէս գլուխ, եւ ոչ որպէս ոտք խոնարհի, այլ միջոյ սահման պահել կինն:

4/ Վասն որոյ պշուցեալ հայէին գեղեցկութիւն դրախտին, ընդ ծառս, պտուղս, անթառամ ծաղիկս, տերեւս, տեսին Աստուծոյ:

5/ Ոչ թէ Աստուած պատուիրեաց / fol 184r / Ադամայ, որպէս տէր ծառայի, կամ թագաւոր նախարարաց իւրոց, կամ յօրէնս եդ, այլ որպէս հայր որդոյ, կամ բարեկամ բարեկամի, սիրելաբար. «Ամենայն ծառոց ուտիցես, բայց միոյ ծառոյն, որ է ի մէջ դրախտին»: Այլ ընտրողութեամբ մի վատթարն, որ է մահ, որպէս անասուն երբեմն ուտէ մահացու խոտ, սպանանէ զինքն:

TRANSLATION

1/ Because Adam's was not deep slumber, but like astonishment at the wondering at indescribable glory, to lessen the pain—(for) God took one of his ribs.⁶

2/ He said "Ayvay" which is Eve.⁷ She will be obedient to the head, to Adam; for she will not appear as a stranger, but from his ribs.⁸ Therefore, the two of them will be one limb,⁹ not uncaring, but having care for one another.¹⁰

3/ Why did he take one of (his) ribs, which is on the left side?¹¹ One left rib of this man was missing. (This was) on account of its being a middle area,

---

5. եր written below the line.

6. This resembles strikingly a passage in Grigor Tat'ewac', *Book of Sermons Called Summer Volume* (Գիրք քարոզութեան, որ կոչի Ամառան հատոր) (Constantinople, 1741; repr., Jerusalem: St. James, 1998) quoted in Stone, *Traditions*, 575, "It is not a natural sleep … but it is a rapture of the mind risen to God through the spirit of prophecy.…"

7. This etymology is not encountered elsewhere.

8. Literally: "from him, from ribs."

9. Or: (bodily) member.

10. This mutual care of man and woman, here given as the only explanation of Eve's creation from a rib, is an uncommon feature. In the course of his ten solutions of the conundrum, "Why was Eve made from Adam's Rib?" Grigor Tat'ewac'i says: "But (she was made) of Adam's body, so that man would love his wife like his own body and they would be sharers of each other's pain"; see Stone, *Traditions*, 576. As well as similar conceptions, a number of lexemes are shared by the present text and Tat'ewac'i; see nn. 12 and 13 below.

11. See Stone, *Traditions*, 578.

unlike the head and not humble like the feet, but the woman is to be kept in a middle area.[12]

4/ On account of this, they were amazed when they regarded the beauty of the garden, with trees, fruit, unfading flowers, leaves—the vision of God![13]

5/ (It is) not that God commanded Adam as a master does a servant, or a king his nobles, or (as if) he set it into a law, but (he spoke) like a father to a son, or a friend to a friend, lovingly, "You shall eat of all the trees; except of the one which is in the midst of the garden." But (Adam ate of it) by a bad choice, which is death, just as a beast sometimes eats deadly grass, (and) kills itself.

---

12. That is, he is to give her a central position. A similar idea is present in Grigor Tatʻewacʻi, *Summer Volume*, which passage reads: "Fourth, because the rib is an intermediary place: it shows that the woman's honor is not equal to the head, nor is it trodden underfoot and dishonorable, but receiving the middle, love is for her." This translation is taken from in Stone, *Traditions*, 577.

13. Once more, there is a close parallel to the sentiment and language of this section in Grigor Tatʻewacʻi, but this time in *Book of Questions* (Գիրք Հարցմանց) (Constantinople, 1729; repr. Jerusalem: St. James, 1993), 278, which reads: "Fourth, because they were amazed at the trees of the garden and unfading flowers and very variegated fruits." The expression "vision of God" is not in the relevant text of the *Book of Questions*.

8. THE FORM AND STRUCTURE OF NOAH'S ARK

INTRODUCTORY REMARKS

M4618 contains a number of texts published in this and the preceding volumes of Armenian apocrypha.[1] A partial account of the manuscript, including references to pseudepigraphical and associated books it contains, was given in that connection.[2] Since M4618 is such a rich repository of pseudepigraphical and parabiblical texts, here we shall give a fuller description.[3] The manuscript was copied in Van 1675–1706 by different scribes: Ignatios of Amida (1–78v); Grigor (79r–93r); and Anonymous (162v–167v) on behalf of a merchant David of Tʿoxatʿ and Rev. Mxitʿar. As for the leaves not mentioned above in the description, they are unprovenanced and their scribes unidentified. M4618 contains a cornucopia of works of interest to pseudepigrapha research:

1r–6r	History of Adam and Eve: another copy of Lipscomb, *Armenian Apocryphal Adam Literature*, 128–141
9r–10v	Questions of St Gregory: another copy of Stone, "Armenian Questions of St. Gregory," 141–72
43r–44r	Concerning the Tower 2: published below pp. 59–63
53r–v	Noah's Ark: published in full below pp. 45–50[4]

---

1. See Stone, *Angels and Heroes*, 34–38; Stone, *Biblical Heroes*, 35–36. In the present volume, I publish a further three works drawn from this manuscript. These are: Concerning Adam's Language from fol. 43r, Text 9.2 Concerning the Tower 2 published on pp. 59–64 below, and the present composition.

2. Stone, *Biblical Heroes*, 35.

3. For the description of this manuscript I have drawn upon a full description made available to me by Dr. Gēorg Ter-Vardanian, keeper of manuscripts of the Matenadaran, whose support has contributed greatly to all my research on Matenadaran manuscripts, and in the present matter too.

4. Published in part in *Biblical Heroes* 7–14 ; this work partly draws on Grigor Tatʿewacʿi, *Book of Questions*, 293, but has other elements as well.

-45-

53v	Concerning the Tower: variants published below, see pp. 59–63
53v–55r	Story concerning Abraham: another copy of Stone, *Abraham*, 36–50
109v	Signs and Wonders of the Temple: another copy the text published in *Biblical Heroes*, 137–42
131v	Abraham and the Idols: published in Stone, *Biblical Heroes*, 20–23
132v–133r	King Solomon's Ring: published in Stone, *Biblical Heroes*, 152–66
133r	Solomon and the Bubu Bird: published in Stone, *Biblical Heroes*, 167–70[5]
133v–138r	The Fall of Satanel and Adam
138r–140r	History of Cain and Abel, Adam's Sons: Lipscomb, *Armenian Adam Literature*, 108–27
140r–142r	Concerning the Birth of Seth: Lipscomb, *Armenian Adam Literature*, 173–205
142r–143v	Hezekiah and Manasseh: published in Stone, *Biblical Heroes* 180–96
146r–v	Concerning the Places of Hell
146v–148v	Brief History of Joshua: published in Stone, *Biblical Heroes* 57–108
158r–159r	Concerning the Seven Divisions of the Earth
178r–198v	Calendar of Months and of the Moon by Daniel including Syriac Month Names

This list gives an overview of the relevant material and includes a number of texts still to be published.

The erotapokritic writing being presented here is a Question and Answer that occur on fol 53r of the manuscript and it is included in the list above. In *Biblical Heroes*, a short excerpt from this document was published under the title The Construction of Noah's Ark. Now it has become possible to publish a full text of this Question and Answer, adding quite a lot of information to that already presented in *Biblical Heroes*.[6]

---

5. The text is also printed in Armenuhi Srapyan, *Medieval Armenian Tales* (Հայ միջնադարեան զրոյցներ) (Erevan: Academy: 1969), 318–19.

6. The edition here incorporates all the information from the previous, partial edition.

8. THE FORM AND STRUCTURE OF NOAH'S ARK

Text

1/ M4618 / fol 53r / Թէ որպէ՞ս է Նոյեան տապանին ձեւն եւ շէնքն

2/ Ասէ գիրն, թէ՛ չորեք անկիւնի. ներքոյ եւ արտաքոյ նաւթիւ ծեփեալ, որ է կուպրն, զի մի վնասեցի:

3/ Երկայն ՅՃ. (300) կանգուն, եւ լայն Ծ. (50), եւ բարձր Լ. (30), ԺԵ. (15) կանգուն հաւասար բարձրացոյց եւ ի ԺԵ.ն. (15)- նրբեցոյց, զի չուրն վիժեցի. նման է սագաշէն եկեղեցւոյ:

4/ Եւ դուռն յետուստ կողմանէ, զի դիւրաւ մտցեն կենդանիքն: Եւ արուեստաւորին անունն Ներսեւ է: Այնքան ողջախոհ էր Նոյ, որ Լ. (30) ամն մի անգամ մերձենայր ի կինն:[7]

5/ Եւ ի Ճ. (100) ամն Գ. (3) որդի ծնաւ՝ ՍԵմ, Քամ, Յաբեդ, եւ ապա սկսաւ շինել զտապանն, Ճ. (100) ամն կատարեցաւ: Հարցին գնա, թէ զի՞նչ գործես, եւ նա ասէր, թէ՛ ձեր մեղացն բարկացեալ է Աստուած, չրհեղեղ կու տայ: Տրտմէին եւ տարակուսէին, բայց սովորական[8] յաղթէր: Կատակ արարեալ ծիծաղէին, ուտէին ըմպէին, կանայս առնէին եւ արանց լինէին:

6/ Եւ ասէ Տէրն ցՆոյ, թէ՛ ես որ յական թօթափելն զաշխարհս արարի, կարող չե՞մ քեզ փայտէ տուն մի շինել, այլ վասն այնորիկ Ճ. (100) ամ աշխատ[9] արարի զքեզ, զի նոքա հարցցեն զպատճառն շինութեան, եւ դու պատմես նոցա, թերեւս զղջացեալ ապաշխարեսցեն: Եւ եմուտ Նոյ ի տապանն, եւ որդիք իւր, եւ կին իւր, եւ կանայք որդւոցն ընդ նմա:

7/ Որպէ՞ս ժողովեցան կենդանիքն ի դուռն տապանին: Գիտելի է, զի ի փայտէ կոշնակ կազմեաց Նոյ եւ ահար գայն: Եւ ընդ ձայնի կոշնակին կենաց հոտ բուրեաց ի տապանէն, ի ձայնէ կոշնակին եւ անոյշ հոտոյն՝ ի Դ. (4) կողմ աշխարհէս գնաց Բ.-Բ. (երկու-երկու) արու եւ էգ: Եւ Նոյ էառ զամենեսեան ի տապանն:

8/ ՃԾ. (150) օր բարձրացաւ չուրն եւ յետոյ ՃԾ. (150) օր գածացաւ, որ լինի Ժ. (10) ամիս: Քան զբարձրագոյն լերինս ԺԵ. (15) կանգուն բարձրացաւ, ի Մասիս լեառն արգելեալ: Եւ յետ Ժ. (10) ամսեան եւ Խ. (40) աւուր երաց Նոյ զպատուհան տապանին եւ արձակեաց զագռաւն. էլել եւ ոչ դարձաւ: Եւ արձակեաց զաղաւնին զմիամիտ թռչունն. չգտեալ հանգիստ ուտիցն եւ դարձաւ:

---

7. ՛Գ --- զտապանն is in the marg. p.m.
8. A word may be missing from the text. I have supplied "their" in the translation.
9. See in Sodomites §30 in Stone, *Biblical Heroes*.

9/ Եւ յետ է. (7) աւուր դարձեալ արձակեաց զաղաւնին. ընդ երեկո դարձաւ՝ ունելով տերեւ ձիթենոյ ի բերանն, զաւետիս սպասատմանն երկրի։ Եւ յետ աւուրս է. (7) դարձեալ արձակեաց զաղաւնին, այլ ոչ դարձաւ առ ինքն։ Իար ամսոյ ի ԻԷ. (27) մտին ի տապանն, եւ ի նոյնքան ամսոյն ելին։ Կերակուր ժողովեաց եւ ոչ կերին, մնացին որպէս մանուկ յարգանդի մօրն։

Translation

1/ Of[10] what form and construction is Noah's ark?

2/ Scripture says that it was four-cornered. It was plastered inside and outside with pitch,[11] which is bitumen, so that it would not be damaged.

3/ It was three hundred cubits long and fifty cubits wide and it was thirty (that is: cubits) high.[12] He raised it to a level of fifteen cubits and at fifteen cubits, he narrowed (it), so that the water would fall off.[13] It is like a gable of a church.[14]

---

10. The text opens with the conjunction թէ "if, so that, or," which is far from usual and indicates that this is an extract from a text or a crystallized oral retelling. In fact, it opens, as we have noted, with a quotation of Grigor Tatʻewacʻi's *Book of Questions*. This section is a question to which the answer is given starting in §2. It lacks the usual tags, հարց "question" and պատասխանի "answer." A second Question and Answer pair are found in §7 which also lacks the tags. It has the interrogative որպէ՞ս "In which fashion?" and the answer formula գիտելի է "It is to be known that": observe the usage in Michael E. Stone with additional annotations by Shlomi Efrati, *The Genesis Commentary by Stepʻanos of Siwnikʻ*, CSCO 695 (Leuven: Peeters, forthcoming), 13–15. An extensive note on the Question and Answer genre may be found in Stone, *Biblical Heroes*, 72.

11. Genesis 6:14 relates that Noah is to cover the ark with pitch. Genesis does not describe it as a rectangular box, but this is its shape in certain early Christian representations of it; see Ruth A. Clements, "A Shelter amid the Flood: Noah's Ark in Early Jewish and Christian Art," in *Noah and His Books*, ed. Michael E. Stone, Aryeh Amihay, and Vered Hillel, EJL 28 (Atlanta: Society of Biblical Literature, 2010), 277–99 and particularly 278–87.

12. These are the measurements given in Gen 6:15.

13. I.e., drain off.

14. Exactly what is intended in Gen 6:16 by "finish it to a cubit above" is unclear, but regardless, it does not mention a change of dimensions after the height of fifteen cubits was reached.

8. THE FORM AND STRUCTURE OF NOAH'S ARK

4/ And the door (was) from the stern, so that the animals might enter easily. And the craftsman's name is Nersēs.[15] Noah was so chaste that he approached his wife only once in thirty years.[16]

5/ And in the one hundredth year he begot three sons, Shem, Ham, Japheth. And then he began to build the ark and in the one hundredth year it was completed.[17] They asked him, "What are you doing?" and he said, "God is wrath at your sins; He will bring a Flood." They were sad and doubted, but (their) habitude won out.[18] Making sport (of him), they mocked (him).[19] They ate, they drank, they took women and they were with men.[20]

6/ And the Lord said to Noah, "I, who made this world in the blink of an eye, could I not have built you a house of wood?[21] But for that (reason) I put you to work for a hundred years, so that they would ask the reason for building, and you would tell them. Perhaps regretting (their actions), they would

---

15. Nersēs is also mentioned in one other document, Noah and the Cheirograph 3; see Michael E. Stone, "Hidden in Crannies in Noah's Ark," in *Festschrift in Honor of Levon Ter Petrossian's 75th Anniversary* (Erevan: Matenadaran, 2021), 333–57.

16. The Armenian tradition makes much of Noah's chastity, which is how the phrase "walked with God" (Gen 6:9) is understood in a Christian reading. See in Sodomites §30 and Concerning the Good Tidings of Seth §§29–33 (Lipscomb, *Armenian Adam Literature*, 196–97). The period of thirty years between births is to be found in many apocryphal stories. Some striking instances occur, such as History of Adam and His Grandsons §§1–12 which sets at a space of thirty years between each of the following events: Adam's first intercourse with Eve and the birth of Cain, the begetting of Abel, and the killing of Abel. In Stone, *Adam and Eve*, 92, there is an extensive note on this topic. Noah's age when Shem was born is not given in Genesis. Jubilees, which revels in dates, in 4:33 gives two years between the births of each of Noah's three sons. In a number of texts, Noah is said to have been celibate for five hundred years, until the birth of Shem, which is a Christian reading of Gen 5:32.

17. According to Gen 5:31, Noah begat his three sons at the age of five hundred. This likely means that his oldest son was born when he was five hundred. The Bible does not give separate dates for the birth of the second and third sons. Our text assumes that they were not triplets but were born at intervals. Then the flood came when he was six hundred years old (Gen 7:6). This is the chronology reflected in §5 of our text here. The first one hundredth year is surely corrupt for five hundredth, see Gen 5:32. That the ark was one hundred years in the building is inferred from Gen 7:6.

18. The idea of his contemporaries mocking Noah is in part derived from Gen 6:9, which says that Noah "was blameless in his generation." His contemporaries, clearly, were blameworthy because of their mocking.

19. See Good Tidings of Seth §38c.

20. արանց is a genitive/dative of այր and so this means "they were to men," that is, they were promiscuous both with men and with women.

21. Which would float upon the water.

repent."²² And Noah entered the ark and his sons and his wife and the wives of his sons with him.²³

7/ How did he gather the animals into the ark? It is to be known that Noah fashioned a wooden semantron,²⁴ and hit it. And at the sound of the semantron the fragrance of life wafted from the ark. And at the sound of the semantron and the sweet smell, from the four corners of the earth, two by two, male and female came.²⁵ Noah took all of them into the ark.

8/ The water rose for one hundred and fifty days and then, for a hundred and fifty days it receded, which were ten months.²⁶ It rose to fifteen cubits above the highest mountains.²⁷ It stopped at Mt. Masis.²⁸ And after ten months and forty days,²⁹ Noah opened the window of the ark and despatched the raven; it went forth and did not return. And he sent the dove, the faithful³⁰ bird. It found no rest for its feet and returned.³¹

---

22. The argument adduced in this explanation resembles the common Armenian exegesis of God's question, "Where are you?" in Gen 3:9. The purpose of the divine action is to elicit repentance.

23. His wife was named Noyem Zara according to History of Adam and His Grandsons §97 and according to Good Tidings of Seth §33 she was called Noemzara, an orthographic variant of that. These forms are the same name as is found in Jub. 4:33; see Michael E. Stone, *Ancient Judaism: New Visions and Views* (Grand Rapids: Eerdmans, 2011), 58.

24. A suspended wooden or metal board that is struck rhythmically to summon worshippers to church. The fragrance of life is, so the text implies, that of the garden of Eden. On fragrance typical of Eden, see Stone, *Adamgirkʻ*, 90, 92, 166, 167, 270; see also Jos. Asen. 56:17 and numerous other sources.

25. This verb is aorist 3 pers. sing. and it is unclear how it is to be construed.

26. Genesis 7:24 of the swelling of the flood; the receding for one hundred and and fifty days is not mentioned. Ten months totaling one hundred and fifty days clearly implies ten months of thirty days, which is the length of the month in the old Armenian calendar. See for an outline of the Armenian reckoning: Avedis K. Sanjian, *Colophons of Armenian Manuscripts 1301–1480*, Harvard Armenian Texts and Studies 2 (Cambridge: Harvard University Press, 1969), 36–37; the matter is discussed in further detail in Michael E. Stone, "The Months of the Hebrews," *Le Muséon* 101 (1988), 5–12: repr. in Michael E. Stone, ed., *Apocrypha, Pseudepigrapha and Armenian Studies*, 2 vols. (Leuven: Peeters, 2006), 1:437–44.

27. Gen 7:19.

28. The Armenian name of Mt. Ararat. On identification of biblical Mt. Ararat, see Michael E. Stone and Aram Topchyan, *Studies in the History of the Jews in Armenia*, forthcoming, chapter 1.

29. Gen 8:5–6.

30. Or: innocent.

31. Gen 8:9.

8. THE FORM AND STRUCTURE OF NOAH'S ARK

9/ And after seven days, he again sent the dove.[32] Towards evening it returned holding leaves of an olive tree in its beak, the good news of the drying of the earth. And after seven days, he sent the dove again, but it returned no more to him.

On the 27th of Iyyar[33] they entered the ark, and on the same day of the month they came forth. He gathered food and they did not eat, like a child in its mother's womb.[34]

---

32. Genesis 8:8–11 relates that the dove was sent out thrice. The text above only mentions the dove's second, successful mission. The drying of the earth is confirmed by its third dispatch; see Gen 8:12.

33. This Syriac month name may well indicate a Syriac source of this tradition. The Hebrew Bible here has "in the first (month) on the first of the month" (Gen 8:13). The date of their entry into the ark" is "in the second month, on the seventeenth day of the month," Gen 7:11. This does not equal 28 Iyyar. Iyyar is the second month in a year starting with the month of Nisan.

34. Note that in Concerning the Tower §4 the ark is likened to a womb, just as here.

9. Tower of Babel and the Confusion of the Languages

In this section of the book a number of texts are presented containing narratives concerning the tower of Babel and the consequent confusion of tongues. As happens with regard to other themes, here the gathering together of various short and seemingly inconsequential texts helps show forth a whole tradition complex.

9.1. Concerning the Tower 1

Introductory Remarks

Recension 1a. This short text was published in Stone, *Angels and Heroes* from fols 82r–82v of M8531, a miscellany of the fifteenth century.[1] This manuscript contains a number of further texts of apocryphal interest, such as Story Concerning Adam and Eve, Concerning Noah's Ark (fol. 82v), Concerning the Tower I (82r–82v),[2] The Ark of the Covenant, and Story of Father Abraham.[3] The text's wording is close to that of other Tower texts already published or being edited in the present section. For convenience's sake we have also reprinted this short document here. We have added to it the few variants occurring in a second, very similar copy of it newly found in M4618, fol.

---

1. See Stone, *Angels and Heroes*, 113–14. See *Short Catalogue*, 2.766. Note that in Stone, *Angels and Heroes*, 113 a typographical error is present in line 3 of the text, where (յ)213 should have been (յ)ե1և.

2. Published in Stone, *Angels and Heroes*, 113–14.

3. This Abraham work was published in Stone, *Abraham*, 37–50.

9. TOWER OF BABEL AND THE CONFUSION OF THE LANGUAGES 53

53v.[4] Among others, the document contains parallels to the Story of Noah §9[5] and to Tower Text 2: Questions Concerning the Tower and Adam's Language, which are published below.

Recension 1b. Another recension of this text was found in M2939, fol 422v. This manuscript is a miscellany written between 1778 and 1799. It is mainly composed of homilies and the works of pseudepigraphical interest in it include Concerning the Tortures of Hell (fol 132r); Concerning Solomon's Seeing of a Vision (fol 340r); The Two Stone Tablets in the Ark (fol 340r); Story of Our Holy Father Abraham, His Son Isaac, and Melchizedek the Priest (fols 388r–394r); The Story of Adam and Eve, Gog and Magog, and the Antichrist (fols 403r–404r); Concerning Elijah and Enoch (fol 404v); The Praise of Solomon's Temple (fols 438v–439r); The Fifteen Signs of Doomsday (fols 441v–442r); and Concerning the Unsleeping Worm (fols 592r–595v).[6] Although certain of these have been edited, more remain to be studied and their contents compared with those of other, cognate, published documents.

I call this second copy of Tower Text, Recension 1b. It is more expansive than Recension 1a in M8531 and M4618 and I publish this fuller text for the first time here. Much of the text found in Recension 1b and not in Recension 1a (M8531, M4618), is also to be found in Tower Text 2.[7] The manuscript miscellany is composed of several distinct parts, all of the eighteenth century.[8] It has certain spelling peculiarities: It introduces ը in many cases where conventional orthography would leave it unwritten; it also confuses ձ and գ; and on one occasion բ/պ: see հարձում for հարցում, պարցրացութին for բարձրացութին, etc.[9]

Recension 1c. A third copy occurs in M1495, fol 158r. This is another seventeenth-century miscellany, copied in 1684.[10] It includes the following texts of pseudepigraphical interest, in addition to Concerning the Tower: Ahiqar (Xikar, fols 13r–17r); Questions and Answers from the Holy Books

---

4. A description of M4618 is to be found on pp. 45–46 above. It was H. Anasyan who noted the existence of this short text, many years ago, see: H. S. Anasyan, *Armenian Bibliology, 5–18th Centuries* (Հայկական մատենագիտութիւն (Ե-Ժ դդ.) (Erevan: Academy of Sciences, 1959), 1:138, no. 2; my own field notes also mention this title in connection with Venice, V290, 93v, but I have not been able to verify that this is a copy of the same work.

5. Stone, *Patriarchs and Prophets*, 91–92.

6. *General Catalogue* 9:1613–62.

7. M2939's recension, in fact, contains little unique information and all its additional elements are discussed in connection with their appearance in Tower Text 2.

8. *General Catalogue* 9:1613–62.

9. Insignificant, orthographic anomalies are not pointed out.

10. *General Catalogue* 4:1431–42.

(fols 85r–86r);[11] Concerning the Seventy-Two Translators (fols 132r–132v);[12] These are the Names of the Gems (fols 150r–150v); The Names of the Twelve Gems (fol 162r); Dates from Adam to the Flood (fol 169v). It is very close indeed to Text 1b from M2939. It has, however, one section of text not found in that document and that section is given in its place in the text published below. The other variants are to be found in the apparatus that follows the text. On the basis of the data known at present, more cannot be said about the literary relations of these Tower works.

Texts

Recension 1a
Վասն աշտարակին

M8531 / fol 82r /1/ Եւ ՀԲ. (72) տանուտէրք միաբանեցան եւ սկսան շինել թրծեալ աղիւսին ընդդէմ հրոյ եւ կուպրն ի շաղախի տեղ ընդդէմ ջրոյ.

2/ Եւ բարձրացուցին Ժ. (10) ամոյ ճանապարհի ընդ էլն եւ ընդ էջն, թանձրութիւն պարսպին Ղ. (90) կանկուն, մէջն Ծ. (50) կանկուն:

3/ Խ. (40) ամն շինեցին ամառն եւ ձմեռն: Եւ իշխանք վերակացու գործոյն՝ Լամսուր ի Սեմա ազգէն, Հայկն՝ Յաբեդի եւ Բէլն ի Քամա:

4/ Եւ յետ ՇԻԵ. (525) ամաց չհետեղդին էր սկիզբն շինուածոյ աշտարակին եւ յաշխարհին Բաբիլոնի, / fol 82v / ի դաշտին Քաղանէ:

Recension 1a Apparatus

1/ տանուտէրքն | տեղին 2/ պարսպին 3/ սեմայ | քամայ 4/ էր] om

---

11. Published below in this volume, pp. 255–92.

12. This is presumably another copy of the text of the same name published in Stone and Ervine, *Armenian Texts of Epiphanius of Salamis*, 69 and 92.

Recension 1b
ՎԱՍՆ ԱՇՏԱՐԱԿԻ ՀԱՐՑՈՒՄ[13]

M2939 / fol 422v / Եօթանասուն եւ Բ. (72) տանուտեարքն միաբանեցան ի չարն եւ ասեն. «Գործ զշրիեղեղին ունիմք, երկրնչիմք, զի պատուհասէ զմեզ»:

2/ Եւ խրնդրեցին ղղրախստրն, թէ՛ անդ գերծանիմք, եւ ոչ զրտին, զի ծովք եւ շամանդաղք պատեալ էին. եւ խրնդրեցին գտապանն եւ գնայ ոչ զրտին:

3/ Եւ րսկրսան շինել թրծեալ ադիւսրն ի տեղի քարի րնդդեմ հրրոյ, եւ կուպրը ի շաղախի տեղ ընդ<դեմ> {ամենայն}[14] ջրոյ: Եւ պարցրացուցին[15] ոզժ. (10) ամսոյ ճանապարի ընդ ելն եւ ընդ էջրն, զոր ումանք Լ. (30) սղատիր ասեն, զբարձրութիւնն եւ զլայնութիւնն շուրջանակի ԽԴՌ. (44,000) քայլ, այսինքն՛ ԽԴ. (44) մրդոն ձգեալ ասի, եւ թանձրութիւնն պարրսապին Ղ. (90) կանկուն, եւ երկու երեսին մէջը Ծ. (50) կանգնոյ լայնութիւնն:

4/ Եւ զԽ. (40) ամրն շինեցին ամառն, ձրմեռն.

5/ Եւ իշխանք վերակացուք գործոյն՝ Լամսուր՝ ի Սեմայ ազգէն, Հայկրն՝ Յաբեթի եւ Բէլ՝ ի Քամայ, որսորղ նցայ: Եւ յետ Շ. եւ ԻԵ. (525) ամաց ջրիեղեղին էր ըսկիսբըն շինուածոյ աշտարակին ի աշխարհին Բաբիլոնի ի դաշտին Քաղանէ:

Recension 1c

M1495 / fol 158r / Վասն աշտարակի շինութեանն

1/ Եւ գիտելի է, որ ՀԲ. (72) տանուտէրքն միաբանեցան ի չարն եւ ասեն. «Զգործ ջրիեղեղին ունիմք, երկնչիմք, զի պատուհասէ զմեզ»,

2/ Եւ խնդրեցին ղղրախտոն, թէ՛ անդ գնամք եւ գերծանիմք, եւ ոչ գտին, զի ծովք եւ շամանդաղք պատեալ են, եւ խնդրեցին գտապանն եւ գնա ոչ եւս գտին: Եւ գնացեալ ի լայնանիստ դաշտին Քաղանէ՝ յաշխարհին Բաբելոնի,

3/ եւ սկսան շինել աշտարակ՝ թրծեալ ադիւսն ի տեղ քարի րնդդեմ հրոյ եւ կույրն ի շաղախի տեղ րնդդեմ ջրոյ: Եւ բարձրացուցին գժ. (10) ամսոյ ճանապարի ընդ ելն եւ ընդ էջն, որոց ումանք Լ. (30) ստադիր ասեն, զբարձրութիւնն եւ զլայնութիւնն

---

13. Orthographic error for հարցում.
14. րնդ<դեմ>: the manuscript has ամ which, though it can be an abbreviation of ամենայն "all" here may have arisen from the corruption of դեմ to ամ.
15. This is an orthographic variant of բարձրացուցին.

շուրջանակի Խ. եւ ԴՌ. (44000) բայլ, այսինքն՝ ԽԴ. (44) մղոն ձգեալ ասի, եւ թանձրութիւն պարսպին Ղ. (90) կանգուն, եւ Բ. երեսին մէջն Ծ. (50) կանգնոյ լայնութիւն:

4/ Եւ զԽ. (40) ամն շինեցին ամառն եւ ձմեռն:

5/ Եւ իշխանք վերակացու գործոյն՝ Լամուր ի Սեմա ազգէն, Հայքն՝ Յաբեթի եւ Բէլ ի Քամա, <որսորդ>¹⁶ նոցա: Եւ յետ ԵՃ. եւ ԻԵ. (525) ամաց շրիեղեղին էր ըսկիզբն շինուածոյ աշտարակին:

TRANSLATIONS

Recension 1a
Concerning the Tower

1/ And seventy-two[17] family heads agreed and began to build with baked brick (as a protection) against fire and with pitch in the place of mortar (as a protection against) water.[18]

2/ And they elevated it to the height of ten months' travel in ascent and descent. The thickness of the walls was 90 cubits and their middle (was) fifty cubits.

3/ They built for 40 years in summer and in winter. And the princes supervising the work (were) Lamur of the family of Shem, Hayk of Japheth, and Bēl of Ham.[19]

4/ And five hundred and twenty-five years after the Flood was the commencement of building the tower, and (it was) in the land of Babylon, in the plain of Kʻałanē (Calne).[20]

---

16. The manuscript reads որդոց "of the sons" which is a corruption of որսորդ "hunter."

17. See p. 66 n. 80 below for a discussion of the variation of seventy/seventy-two.

18. As to the materials: the Bible refers to baked bricks and bitumen (Gen 11:3). These are correlated with the expected two floods, one of water and the other of fire. See History of the Forefathers §41; see also 9.2 Tower Text 2 in M4618 below, pp. 59–64.

19. These names occur also in other variant tellings of this tale below. They are not known in these roles elsewhere. Hayk is, of course, the eponymous ancestor of the Armenians. Bel, according to Movēs Xorenacʻi, was Hayk's opponent in Mesopotamia (1.10–11).

20. See Gen 10:10 and Amos 6:2; cf. Isa 10:9.

9. TOWER OF BABEL AND THE CONFUSION OF THE LANGUAGES   57

Recension 1b
Question concerning the Tower

1/ And seventy-two family heads agreed upon evil and said, "We have work for the flood.[21] We fear that He punishes us."

2/ And[22] they looked for the garden, "there we shall live luxuriously" and they did not find (it), for the seas and fogs surrounded it.[23] And they looked for the ark, and did not find it.[24]

3/ And they began to build—baked brick in place of stone (as a protection) against fire and pitch in the place of mortar (as a protection against) water.[25] And they elevated it to the height of ten months' travel, in ascent and descent, which some say is thirty stades in height.[26] And (they say that) in the breadth around about was forty-four thousand paces, that is, forty-four miles. And the thickness of the wall was ninety cubits and between its two faces was fifty cubits width.

4/ They built for forty years in summer (and) in winter.

5/ And the princes supervising the work (were) Lamur of the family of Shem, Hayk of Japheth, and Bēl of Ham, their hunter. And five hundred and twenty-five years after the Flood was the beginning of the building of the tower in the land of Babylon, in the plain of Calneh.

Recension 1c
Concerning the Building of the Tower

1/ And it is to be known[27] that seventy-two family heads agreed upon evil and said, "We have work for the Flood.[28] We fear that He (will) punish us."

---

21. That is: let us work in order to avoid a future flood.
22. Compare Tower Text 2, §3.
23. Searches for paradise were quite common in medieval literature and art. The fog surrounding the garden is reminiscent of the cloud that obscures the Land of the Blessed in Hist. Rech. 2:8. The idea of an ideal, remote land in the sea is to be found in many sources, such as the Greek idea of the Isles of the Blessed. This phrase recurs in Recension 1b, and in Tower Text 2.
24. This material reflects the same tradition as Tower Text 2, §§2–3, and is not found in Tower Text 1a.
25. See Gen 11:3.
26. An ancient measure of length equivalent to a Roman stadium.
27. On this formula, see p. 67 n. 27 above.
28. That is: let us work in order to avoid being punished in a future flood.

2/ And[29] they looked for the garden, "there we shall go there and we shall live luxuriously" and they did not find (it), for the seas and fogs surrounded it.[30] And they looked for the ark, and did not find it any more.[31] And they went to the spacious plain of Kʻałanē (Calne) in the land of Babylon.

3/ And they began to build a tower—baked brick in place of stone (as a protection) against fire and pitch in the place of mortar (as a protection against) water.[32] And they elevated it to the height of ten months' travel in ascent and descent, which some say is thirty stades in height.[33] And (they say that) the breadth around extended for about forty-four thousand paces, that is, forty-four miles. And the thickness of the wall was ninety cubits and between its two faces was fifty cubits width.

4/ They built for forty years in summer and in winter.

5/ And the princes supervising the work (were) Lamur of the family of Shem, Hayk of Japheth, and Bēl of Ham, their <hunter>. And the beginning of the building of the tower was five hundred and twenty-five years after the flood.

---

29. Compare Tower Text 2, §3.

30. See p. 62 n. 50.

31. This material reflects the same tradition as Tower Text 2, §§2–3, and is not found in Tower Text 1a. They expected a flood to come in punishment for their sins and for that reason they sought paradise and Noah's ark. Paradise was thought to be on a mountain or a height, a location particularly stressed in Syriac tradition: see Sebastian P. Brock, "Clothing Metaphors as a Means of Theological Expression in Syriac Tradition," in *Typus, Symbol, Allegorie bei den östlichen Vätern und ihren Parallelen im Mittelalter*, ed. Margot Schmidt in collaboration with C. F. Geyer (Regensburg: Pustet, 1982), 12; Matthias Henze, "Nebuchadnezzar's Madness (Daniel 4) in Syriac Literature," in *The Book of Daniel: Composition and Reception*, ed. John J. Collins and Peter W. Flint (Leiden: Brill, 2001), 558–59 n. 20; Ephrem on Gen 4:8; Ephrem, *Hymns of Paradise* 13, 2–3; Robert Murray, *Symbols of Church and Kingdom: A Study in Early Syriac Tradition* (Cambridge: Cambridge University Press, 1975), 306–10; and Cave of Treasures 18:13 in MOTP 1:554. See also the much earlier writing, the Genesis Apocryphon (1QapGen 2.23). The search for paradise was thus to enable them to be in it, higher than the waters of the flood. Similarly, they sought the ark so as to embark on it when the expected flood arrived and thus to be delivered. The text here also implies that previously they knew where the ark was but now, when they sought protection from a possible flood, it had disappeared. It is not inconceivable that this is connected with some so-far unknown traditions relating to the ark.

32. See Gen 11:3.

33. An ancient measure of length equivalent to a Roman stadium. "Some say" often introduces a tradition from another source.

9. TOWER OF BABEL AND THE CONFUSION OF THE LANGUAGES

9.2. Concerning the Tower 2

Introductory Remarks

This document is formulated as a Question with a very long Answer about the tower of Babel. It is followed by similar Questions and extended Answers about Adam's language.[34] Here I publish two questions with their answers, since they are most closely related to Tower Text 1. Two copies of this document are known, of which one is in M4618, a miscellany composed of several parts, each written at a different date between 1569 and 1714.[35] Fol 43r of this manuscript preserves a notably better text than the other available copy, which in a miscellany, M10561 of the seventeenth century, fols. 148r–149r.[36] Indeed, the text of M10561 is quite corrupt and no instance was found in which it preserves a preferable reading. It does, however, have a number of lines of text at the end that are not preserved in M4618. Here we give the text of M4618 and discuss significant variants of M10561 in the annotations. The additional text that is found in M10561 is given at the end of the text drawn from M4618. A shorter form of this document, omitting a quite considerable amount of material, was published previously, but now the present edition must replace it.[37]

The first question and answer in this text is related to Tower Text 1, discussed immediately above. Next in M4618 fol 43r is a question with an extended answer relating to Adam's language. After all, if the tower explained the multiple human languages, then it follows that before the tower, one language was spoken by humans. Moreover, it seemed most natural to assume that that single language was the one spoken by Adam and Eve.

Text

M4618 / fol 43r / Վասն աշտարակին հարց է:

1/ [Հարց]: Զաշտարակն որպիսի՞ մտօք շինեին:

Պատասխանի: Նախ՝ զի ատէին զԱստուած եւ երկնչէին ի պատժոց, եւ հակառակ էին Աստուծոյ:

---

34. The Armenian Question and Answer texts are discussed in the introductory remarks to *Questions and Answers from the Holy Books*, pp. 255–57 below.
35. On this manuscript, see *Short Catalogue* 1.1247–1248. It is described in detail on pp. 45–46 above.
36. See the description of manuscript M10561 on p. 3 of the present volume.
37. See Stone, *Angels and Heroes*, 113–15.

2/ Եւ որպէս եւթն³⁸ է գործիք ձայնին, որ է՝ թօքն, խռափողն, մակալեզուն, բերանն, լեզուն, ատամունքն եւ շրթունքն,³⁹ միաբանին ի խօսքն,⁴⁰ նոյնպէս եւ Հ. (70) տանուտէրքն միաբանեցան ի չարն եւ ասեն. «Զգործս ջրհեղեղին ունիմք։ Երկնչիմք, զի պատուհասէ զմեզ»։

3/ Եւ խնդրեցին զդրախտն, թէ՛ անդ գերծանիմք, եւ ոչ գտին, զի ծովք եւ շամանդաղ պատեալ են։ Եւ յորժամ խնդրեցին զտապանն եւ զնա ոչ գտին, զի ոչ է հրաման Աստուծոյ, որ մարդ զարգանդ մօր իւրոյ տեսցէ։ Եւ զի մարդիկ ի պատճառս նորա {ան}մերք⁴¹ գործեսցեն, վասն որոյ ոչ կարեն տեսանել զտապանն։

4/ Ապայ ասեն. «Շինեցուք բարձր աշտարակ, զի մի ջրհեղեղ զմեզ կորուսցէ»։ Եւ էր թրծեալ ադիւսն ի տեղի քարի, եւ կուպրն ի շաղախի, թրծեալ ադիւսն ընդդէմ հրոյ, եւ կուպրն ընդդէմ ջրոյ։

5/ Եւ սկսան շինել հաստահիմն, լայնամիջոց, աստիճանաձեւ ելիւք եւ իջիւք, եւ բարձրացուցին Ժ. (10) ամսոյ ճանապարհի ընդ ելն եւ ընդ էջն,⁴² որչափ բարձրացաւ ջուրն, ՃԾ. (150) օր դարձեալ իջաւ, զոր ումանք Լ. (30) ստադիոն ասեն զբարձրութիւնն, եւ զլայնութիւն շուրջանակի ԽԴՌ. (44,000) քայլք, այսինքն՝ մղոն ձգեալ ասի, եւ թանձրութիւն պարսպին Ղ. (90) կանգուն եւ յերկու երեսին մէջն Ծ. (50) կանգնոյ լայնութիւն։

6/ Եւ զի Խ. (40) ամ շինեցին ամառն եւ ձմեռն, վասն բարեխառնութեան տեղւոյն, մինչեւ հասին յոր կծկկուտ օդն, թանձրացեալ ի գլորշեաց եւ ջերմացեալ յարեւու։

7/ Եւ իշխանք վերակացուք գործօն՝ Լամսուր՝ ի Սեմայ ազգէն, Հայկն՝ Յաբեթի, եւ Բէլ՝ ի Քամայ ազգէն, որսորդ նոցա։ Եւ յետ ՇԻԵ. (525) ամաց ջրհեղեղին, էր սկիզբն շինուածոյ ամբարտակին ի աշխարհին⁴³ Բաբելոնի, (ի դաշտին Քաղանէ)։

---

38. Note that M10561 has գործք "works, deeds," which is secondary for գործիք "tools, instruments." Furthermore, M10561 omits թոք "lungs" and consequently only six elements occur in the list it preserves, even though the number seven is mentioned in the text.

39. In M10561 this noun is, for an unclear reason, in the instrumental case.

40. It is not clear why this word is in the nominative plural. This is one of the strange uses of -ք in medieval Armenian texts.

41. The privative ան- precedes this word, but that does not make sense. We regard it as a corruption.

42. ընդ ելանելն եւ իջանելն M10561.

43. Preceding աշխարհին, the inseparable preposition յ- and not ի would be expected.

9. TOWER OF BABEL AND THE CONFUSION OF THE LANGUAGES 61

Only in 2b: M10561:

8/ / fol 148v/ Եւ ասէ Աստուած. «Եկայք իջցուք եւ խառնակեսցուք զլեզուս նոցա». Հայր առ Որդի եւ Հոգին ասաց: Իսկ խառնակելն ոչ շփոթելն ասէ, որ անլուր էին միմեանց լեզուի, այլ խառնումն ի բաժանմանէն ասաց:

9/ Եւ այսմանէ գրու/fol 149r /եաց Աստուած զաշտարակն, նախ՝ զի մի միաբանեալ ի չարն անզեղջապէս գործեցեն, Բ. (2)՝ զի մի վասն աշտարակին ի անդ⁴⁴ մրնասցեն, եւ ամենայն աշխարհի ալեր մնասցէ. ԳԺ. (30) ամոյ ճանապարհի շինել էին, Ե. (5) ելանելն եւ իջանելն:

Translation

Title/ It is a question concerning the tower.

1/ <Question>[45] With which sort of intent did they build (the tower)?

Answer: First, because they hated God and were afraid of punishments, and they were opposed to[46] God.

2/ And just as there are seven instruments of sound (voice), which are the lungs, the larynx, the epiglottis, the mouth, the tongue, the teeth, and the lips (and) they join together for[47] speech. In the same way seventy[48] family heads agreed upon evil and said, "We have works for[49] the flood. We fear that (he will) punish us."

---

44. The preposition has not taken its inseparable form preceding a vowel, as would be expected. This is a locative of անդ "field."

45. As sometimes happens, the tag has been omitted. The second one, "answer" is present.

46. Or simply, "and opposed."

47. Or: in.

48. In M8531 Concerning the Tower 1 (see above) seventy-two householders are mentioned. In The Story of Noah seventy-two princes are mentioned in connection with this incident (Stone, *Patriarchs and Prophets*, 91). The variation of seventy (10 x 7) and seventy-two (12 x 6) is common. Presumably, the number here is derived from or related to the traditional number of the nations set forth in the Tabula Gentium in Gen 10. The seventy or seventy-two households were scattered after the fall of the tower and spoke different tongues. That idea is also reflected in the list, The Seventy-Two Languages, that survives in quite numerous copies: see Stone, *Adam and Eve*, 158–63.

49. That is: deserving of. M10561 reads "thought and works." Originality cannot be determined in this instance, though in all recensions of Tower Text 1 this sentence does not have "thought and."

3/ And they looked for the garden, "so that there we might live luxuriously" and they did not find it, for the seas and fog surrounded (it).[50] And when they sought the ark, they did not find it either,[51] for it is not God's command that man see the womb of his mother.[52] Moreover, because men would commit sins because of it,[53] on that account they were unable to see the ark.

4/ Then they said to one another, "Let us build[54] a high tower, so that a flood will not destroy us."[55] And there was baked brick in place of stone, and bitumen—of mortar;[56] baked brick against fire and bitumen against water.

5/ And they began to build (it) with a firm[57] foundation, broad width, step-formed,[58] with ascent and descent. They made it the height of ten months' travel,[59] ascending and descending according to the rising of the waters, which rose for one hundred and fifty days,[60] which height some say is

---

50. See p. 58 n. 30.
51. See the further explanation of this on p. 57 n. 23.
52. That is, both the garden and the ark are likened to wombs, from which humans emerge. Compare the idea Moses and Jonah had multiple births, which appears in texts published here, pp. 151 n. 122 and 178 n. 12.
53. That is, if they had the ark as a potential way escaping from punishment in the form of a flood, they would commit sins. This oddly contrasts with Gen 9:13–16 where God promises never again to bring a flood. The passage here makes the impression of being taken from a longer apocryphal narrative.
54. Compare Gen 11:4.
55. When they could not find either paradise or the ark, they drew this conclusion.
56. This is, of course, based on the biblical verse Gen 11:3. However, the formulation of the latter part of the section clearly refers to the idea of two floods, one of fire and the other of water. This expectation was well-known and goes back to early texts: for a flood of fire, see already Jub 36:10 and 1 En. 102.1. The two floods are mentioned together in LAE 49:3. See also Josephus, *A.J.* 1:70–71. One Armenian example among many is History of the Forefathers §41 (Stone, *Adam and Eve*, 199). In M10561, Section 4 is corrupt.
57. Or: thick.
58. Is this a reminiscence of the Babylonian ziggurat, which was a stepped / staged tower? The ziggurat has often been seen as influencing the biblical story of the tower of Babel: see *IDB* 1.334. Here the Armenian document introduces the stepped construction of the tower of Babel, which is not to be found in Genesis. M10561 has ճան, which on its own means "ossicle" but is, in fact, in this instance, a remnant of աստիճան "step," the reading of M4618.
59. Literally: "way, road, path."
60. The waters referred to are those of the flood. The Bible gives two numbers for the days of the flood: forty in Gen 7:17 and one hundred and fifty in Gen 7:24. The five months of each of ascent and descent perhaps derive from the one hundred and fifty days, which is five thirty-day months. See also Form and Structure of Noah's Ark, §8.

9. TOWER OF BABEL AND THE CONFUSION OF THE LANGUAGES 63

thirty stadia.[61] And the breadth around was forty-four thousand paces. That is, it is said, extending for a mile.[62] The thickness of the wall was ninety cubits, and between its two faces[63] is a middle area with a breadth of fifty cubits.[64]

6/ And[65] they built for forty years in summer and in winter because of the moderate climate of the site, until they came to the place where the air was thin, (since) being heavy, it evaporated and was heated by the sun.

7/ And the princes appointed to conduct the work (were) Lamsur of the family of Shem,[66] Hayk of the family of Japheth, and Bēl of the family of Ham,[67] their hunter.[68] And after five hundred and twenty-five years from the Flood, there was the beginning of the building of the tower in the land of the Babylonians, in the field of Kʻaɫabē (Calneh).[69]

Only in 2b: M10561:

8/ M10561 / And God said, "Come let us, descend and disorder their languages." The Father said (this) to the Son and the Spirit.[70] Indeed, it says "disorder" not "to blend," so that they were unable to understand one another's language; rather it said "disorder" (that is) through division.[71]

9/ And for this (reason) God scattered the tower:
First, lest they band together for evil (and) act unforgivably.

---

61. Observe the scholastic formula "some say / others say." Such citation of authorities (quite often anonymous) is a feature of school tradition. The text of this section is very similar to Tower Text 1a, 1b, and 1c.
62. The Roman mile, from which the measurement comes, was one thousand paces. The origin of the figure given in the text is unclear.
63. This is describing a wall of two stone faces with fill between them.
64. This sentence is somewhat different in the other version.
65. qh follows this word and is difficult to construe. Perhaps it is an instance of the common variant q- / qh: see Stone and Hillel, "Index," no. 251.
66. This individual is unknown from any other context. These same names are also found in a very similar sentence in Tower Text 1.
67. Hayk is the eponymous ancestor of the Armenians, while Bēl is his giant opponent, who bears the name of the heathen deity Bel (Baal). They play roles in early Armenian legendary history. The claim for Japhetic descent is a crucial feature of Armenian Christianization of the story of their national origins; see Michael E. Stone, "The Armenian Embroidered Bible," *JSP* 29 (2019): 3–11 on the function of this splicing of the Armenians into biblical geneaology.
68. In the Bible, it is Nimrod who is characterized as a hunter (Gen 10:9). Here, Bēl is the hunter who will bring them food.
69. See Gen 10:10 and Amos 6:2; cf. Isa 10:9.
70. This exegesis is intended to explain the plural in Gen 11:7, "Let us do down …"
71. Into different peoples speaking different languages.

Second, so that they should not remain in the field on account of the tower and (thus) all the world would not remain ruined. They had built a road of thirty months, five ascending and descending.[72]

9.3. Second Question: Adam's Language

Introductory Remarks

See the introductory remarks to 9.2.

Text

M4618 / fol 43r / Հարց: Եւ թէ ո՞ր է Ադամայ լեզուն:

Պատասխանի: Ասեմք, եթէ քաղդեացին, որ է արապն, զի մնաց առ երեր եւ ոչ խառնեցաւ:

2/ Հարց: Եւ թէ որպէ՞ս բաժանեցաւ:

Պատասխանի: Ասեն վարդապետք, եթէ հողմն շնչեաց եւ գրուեաց զաշտարակն, զի մի փլուցեալ վնասեցէ զմարդիկ: Եւ ի հողմոյն յայնմանէ հոտ անուշութեան բուրեաց ի նոսա, եւ տեսիլ իմանալի տեսին, եւ լուր իմանալի լուան, եւ յայնմանէ մոռացան զառաջինն: Եւ որպէս ի քնոյ զարթուցեալք՝ ոչ լսէին զլեզու միմեանց, եւ որպէս անդ Հոգին ի նմանութիւն հողմոյ եկեալ՝ զմինն յՀԲ. (72) բաժանեաց, եւ առաքելօքն զՀԲ.ն (72) ի մի հաւաքեաց: / fol 43v /

3/ Եւ յայնմանէ երեքի բազում բարութիւն.

նախ՝ զի յայնմանէ ճանաչեցան, զի անյաղթ եւ ամենայաղթ է զօրութիւն Աստուծոյ:

Երկրորդ՝ զի մի միաբանեալ ի չարն անզղջապէս գործեցեն:

Եւ {եւ} երրորդ՝ զի մի վասն աշտարակին ի նոյն տեղիս մնասցեն, եւ աշխարհի ամենայն ալերակ կացցէ: Վասն որոյ աւրհնութեամբ գրուեաց զնոսա ի վերայ երկրի, զի աճեցեն եւ բազմասցին, եւ լցցեն զերկիր ձեռնոզօք եւ շինութեամբ, եւ բարեզործութեամբ:

ի փառս ամենասուրբ Երրորդութեանն. ամէն:

M10561 has a fragment corresponding to the preceding §3 and dealing only with the tower:

---

72. The last sentence is unclear in its context here. See Tower Text 2 §5, above for the ten months.

4/ / fol 148v / Եւ այսմանէ գրու/ fol 149r /եաց Աստուած զաշտարակն,

նախ՝ զի մի միաբանեալ ի չարն անզեղջապէս գործեսցեն,

Բ. (2)՝ զի մի վասն աշտարակին ի անդ մնասցեն, եւ ամենայն աշխարհի ալեր մնասցէ. ԳԺ. (30) ամսոյ ճանապարհի շինել էին, Ե. (5) ելանելն եւ իջանելն։

Translation

1/ Question: And which is Adam's language?

Answer: We say that (it is) Chaldean, which is Arab. For it remained with Eber and was not mixed.[73]

2/ Question: How was it divided?

---

73. "Arab": This is clearly a late (mis)identification or an error for Aramaic. That Chaldean (Syriac) was the primordial tongue is a view forwarded in many Syriac sources and came into Armenian literature from such sources. Thus, Cave of Treasures promotes Syriac's role and denies the claim of Hebrew: See Carl Bezold, *Die Schatzhöhle, Syrisch und Deutsch herausgegeben* (Leipzig: Hinrichs, 1888), 1:29 and MOTP 1:558. The question of Syriac as the primordial language is dealt with in detail by Sergey Minov, "The Cave of Treasures and the Formation of Syriac Christian Identity in Late Antique Mesopotamia: Between Tradition and Innovation," in *Between Personal and Institutional Religion: Self, Doctrine, and Practice in Late Antique Eastern Christianity*, ed. Brouria Bitton-Ashkelony and Lorenzo Perrone, Cultural Encounters in Late Antiquity and the Middle Ages 15 (Tournhout: Brepols, 2013), 165–77. It is also the subject of an article by Andy Hilkens, "Language, Literacy and Historical Apologetics: Hippolytus of Rome's Lists of Literate Peoples in the Syriac Tradition," *JECS* 72 (2020): 1–32. The text published by Abraham Levene (*The Early Syrian Fathers on Genesis from a Syriac Ms. on the Pentateuch in the Mignana Collection* [London: Taylor's Foreign Press, 1951], 86) has a similar discussion, there claiming that God spoke with the angels in a heavenly language, and with humans in Syriac. Again, an anti-Hebrew polemic is present. The idea of an eschatological holy language is to be observed in 4Q464 and see Esther Eshel and Michael E. Stone, "The Eschatological Holy Tongue in Light of a Fragment from Qumran," *Tarbiz* 62 (1993): 169–77 (Hebrew). On the role of Hebrew, see Milka Rubin, "The Language of Creation or the Primordial Language: A Case of Cultural Polemics in Antiquity," *JJS* 49 (1998): 306–33, especially 306–17. The corruption of the primordial language is claimed with a connection to Enosh and without any specific relationship with the tower, in *History of the Forefathers* §§42–43 (Stone, *Adam and Eve*, 199–200). In the Armenian translation of the Chronography of Michael the Syrian, it is claimed that the Adamic language was preserved by Eber, "which now the Jews have, and not the Chaldeans, they are the Syrians." There is a long editor's note on this identification in Michael the Syrian, *Chronicle of Rev. Michael, Patriarch of the Syrians* (Jerusalem: St. James, 1871), 14.

Answer:[74] The doctors[75] say that the wind blew (and) scattered the tower, lest falling, it hurt humans. And from that wind, a smell of sweetness[76] spread its odor among them. And they saw an intelligible[77] vision and they heard an intelligible sound, and from that, they forgot the former thing.[78] And like those awakened from sleep they did not comprehend one another's languages; and as if the Spirit[79] came there in the likeness of wind and in one time divided the one into seventy-two.[80] And by the Apostles, it gathered the seventy-two into one.[81]

3/ And from that many good things were seen:[82]

First, that through that they recognized that the power of God is invincible and vanquishes all.

And second, lest they band together for evil (and) act unforgivably.

---

74. The traditions in this section, the sweet odor of the wind and its function in the confusion of tongues are not to be found in any other source we examined.

75. That is, *vardapets*. The specific reference has not yet been located. Note that this expression betrays the scholastic background of the material, which is anyway evident from the eratoapokritic form.

76. The Armenian Life of Moses speaks of smelling sweetness, and then exclaims, "Oh, for these heavenly things are sweeter than honeycomb" (Stone, *Patriarchs and Prophets*, 154–55). Reference is made to God's sweetness in "The *Sermo Asceticus* of Stephen the Theban in Sahidic Coptic" A8 published by Alain Suciu in JTS 69 (2018), 665 and in other early Christian sources. I discussed the special sweet odor of paradise above on p. 50 n. 24.

77. The word "intelligible" is a common attribute of supra-worldly entities and states. See in Stone, *Adamgirkʻ*, 1.21.6; 3.4.17, and in the present volume in Question concerning Moses's Countenance, 159 (text no. 13) and in Angels and the Demon 17 (text no. 3 above).

78. Or: state.

79. Apparently, the Holy Spirit.

80. Seventy-two languages are mentioned in the seventh-century Armenian Chronography of Philo of Tikor in MH 5, 906 §57. See also the rather later *Chronography of Rev. Michael, Patriarch of the Syrians*, 13. The languages are seventy-two in number according to *Biblical Paraphrases* (Stone, *Patriarchs and Prophets*, 92) and they are coordinated with the seventy-two princes (93). Agatʻangełos §297 correlates the number of languages with the number of the sons of God in Deut 32:8, but does not give the specific figure of seventy-two. Indeed, while the chronographies bear an overall likeness to the apocryphal Tower texts, Agatʻangełos is less similar to them. The seventy-two languages are also discussed also on p. 61 n. 48 and on p. 68.

81. The Apostles united all the seventy-two languages or nations into one Christian people, see John 11:52 and Rev 7:9.

82. That is: issued, became evident.

9. TOWER OF BABEL AND THE CONFUSION OF THE LANGUAGES

And third, lest they remain in the same place because of the tower, and the whole earth would be desolate. On account of this, through[83] a blessing, he scattered them upon the earth so that they might increase and multiply and fill the earth[84] with offspring and building and good deeds.[85] And glory to the All-Holy Trinity. Amen.

M10561 has a fragment corresponding to the preceding §3 and dealing only with the tower:

4/ And due to this God scattered the tower:
First, lest they band together for evil (and) act unforgivably.
Second, lest they should not remain in the field (plain) on account of the tower and all the world would remain ruined. They had built a road of thirty months, five ascending and descending.[86]

9.4. Tower Text 3: The Division of the Earth, and the Tower

Introductory Remarks

This fragment is embedded at the beginning of the text entitled Supplication concerning the Men of Sodom and Gomorra, and occurs in M5571 on fol 206v.[87] A description of the manuscript is to be found in connection with the publication of that text.[88] Suffice it here to note that the manuscript is a miscellany, copied in 1657–1659.[89] The same text also occurs in M2242, 18r and its variants are recorded in Stone, *Abraham*, 188.

In M5571 this fragment opens with a rubricated letter and, following it, the next body of text has similar rubrication. From a literary perspective, it has no inherent connection with the text of the homily that follows. It is a

---

83. Or: with. The blessing given in Gen 1:28, including the words: "Be fruitful and multiply, and fill the earth."
84. This phrase is also from God's blessings on creatures in Gen 1:22, 28.
85. This fits with the Christian interpretation of the tower incident, according to which the scattering did not just serve as a punishment, but also brought in its wake the possibility of redemption, when the apostles spread Christianity throughout the whole world. See Robert W. Thomson, *Teaching of St. Gregory*, rev. ed., Avant 1 (New Rochelle: St. Nersess Armenian Seminary, 2001), 198–202.
86. The last sentence is unclear in its context here, but refers to the ten months mentioned above (Tower Text 2, §5). The "thirty months" remain obscure.
87. This text was first published in Stone, *Abraham*, 178–203.
88. Stone, *Abraham*, 8–9.
89. See *Short Catalogue*, 2.136.

self-contained literary unit and its publication anew here is undertaken for its contribution to the discourse about the tower of Babel.

The chief point of interest in this section of text is the number twelve for the dispersed peoples and tongues. Above, we noted the number seventy-two for the princes who led the building of the tower, and then for the many tongues after the dispersion. This was observed to correlate with the list of seventy-two languages or peoples that circulated widely as an independent work and was also introduced into chronographies and similar works.[90] In the text being presented here, the number is twelve, and I regard this connected with the list of Twelve Literate Nations that is often found in manuscripts following the list of Seventy-Two Languages.[91]

Text

M5571 / fol 206v / [3]որժամ ելՆոյ ի տապանէն եւ բաժանեաց Գ. (3) բաժին աշխարհս ի վերայ երից որդոցն, զԱսիայ, զԵլպիա եւ զԼիբիա, եւ Շխ. (540) ամն լցաւ աշխարհս ծնընդոք նոցա, եւ ապա շինեցին քաշտարակն հերկիւղէ[92] քրիեղեղին, եւ յետ կործանման աշտարակին երկուտասան լեզուացն մոլորեցան մարդիկք եւ անկան ի կռապաշտութիւն:

Translation

1/ When Noah went forth from the ark and divided this world into three divisions, upon (according to) the three sons—Asia, Elpia, and Lybia.[93] And

---

90. Of course, it may have been drawn originally from a chronicle, too.

91. I published this document some years ago in Stone, *Adam and Eve*, 163. I have since discovered that it occurs in numerous copies, far more than were at my disposal when I edited it. A very early form of it is to be found in the seventh-century *Chronography* of Philo of Tikor (MH, 5. §101–105). That document is preserved in M2679 fol 36v of the year 981 CE. I have noted further copies in the following manuscripts: M268, fol 152v; M537, 233v–234r; M605, 135; M8494, 215r; P0121, 149r–151r. Undoubtedly still further copies exist. The list of Twelve Literate Nations is to be found in non-Armenian sources as well; see Hilkens, "Language, Literacy and Historical Apologetics."

92. Orthographic error for յերկիւղէ.

93. Traditionally, this should be Asia, Europe, and Africa, but it is unclear how this name Elpia might signify or derive from "Europe." See, e.g., the various texts on the division of the earth, such as Peoples of the Sons of Noah in Stone, *Signs of the Judgment*, 221–27. See Jub 8.10–9.15 for a detailed, early description of this. Further, see James M. Scott, "The Division of the Earth in Jubilees 8:10–9:15 and Early Christian Chronography," in *Studies in the Book of Jubilees*, ed. Matthias Albani, Jörg Frey, and Armin Lange (Tübingen:

9. TOWER OF BABEL AND THE CONFUSION OF THE LANGUAGES 69

for five hundred and forty years this world was filled with their descendants.[94] And then they built the tower from fear of the flood[95] and after the destruction of the tower, men of twelve tongues[96] wandered and fell into idol worship.

9.5. Appendix: Other Related Textual Fragments

9.5.1. The Tower

M10200 / fol 193r / Չկնի փլման աշտարակին ժէ. (17) դարուն, Նեփրովք յառաջ Թադ եդ ի Բաբելոն եւ ի Պարս երթեալ՝ զհուրն պաշտել ետ նոցա. այս Ռագաւա ժամանակն է։

In the seventeenth century after the destruction of the tower, Nepʻrovtʻ[97] first placed Tʻad in Babylon and went to Persia. He caused them to worship fire.[98] This is the time of Reʻu.

Mohr Siebeck, 1997), 370 n. 8. The relevant biblical verses are in Gen 10. See also Robert H. Charles, *The Book of Jubilees or the Little Genesis* (London: Black, 1902), 68 and Esther Eshel, "The Imago Mundi of the Genesis Apocryphon," in *Heavenly Tablets: Interpretation, Identity and Tradition in Ancient Judaism*, ed. Lynn LiDonnici and Andrea Lieber, JSJSup 119 (Leiden: Brill, 2007), 111–31. In another form this division occurs in Charles J. F. Dowsett, *The History of the Caucasian Albanians by Movses Dasxurancʻi*, London Oriental Series 8 (London: Oxford University Press, 1961), 1–2 and in Matenadaran M2679 of 981 CE, fol 31r.

94. According to both Jubilees and biblical chronology the period is significantly shorter.

95. This differs from the biblical motive for building the tower; see Gen 11:4, which says: "Then they said, 'Come, let us build ourselves a city, and a tower with its top in the heavens, and let us make a name for ourselves; otherwise we shall be scattered abroad upon the face of the whole earth.'" The ignoring of the hybristic purpose is shared, however, by the preceding Tower texts.

96. This may refer to the same tradition as the list of Twelve Literate Peoples published by Stone, *Adam and Eve*, 159. The text already occurs in Matenadaran M2679 of 981 CE, 32r. In the Tower texts above, there are seventy-two languages, not twelve. See also p. 66 above.

97. I.e., Nimrod.

98. To be Zoroastrians. Here Nimrod's connection with fire is related to the legend of his trial of Abraham and Nahor by fire. The identity of Tʻad is unknown to me.

9.5.2. On the Tower 129v

/ M609 / Իսկ ի փլանել աշտարակին խառնեցան լեզուքն: Եւ բաժանեաց Աստուած զմի լեզուն ՀԲ. (72), ԵԺ. (15) լեզու արարին ազգն Յաբեթի, ԼԲ. (32)՝ ազգն Քամա, ԻԵ.՝ (25) ազգն Սեմայ:

Then, in the falling of the tower, the languages were mixed up. God divided the one language into seventy-two: the family of Japheth made fifteen languages; the family of Ham, thirty-two; and the family of Shem, twenty-five.[99]

9.5.3. The Story of Noah

This text, part of a larger work called Biblical Paraphrases, was published from two manuscripts M3854 (1471)and M4231 (fifteenth century).[100] One of the subdivisions of this text is entitled Story of Noah. Here we reproduce §9 of Story of Noah, a passage that is parallel in content to the documents published above.[101]

9/ / p. 91 / Եւ բազմացան որդիք Նոյի եւ գնացին ի յարեւելս եւ գտին դաշտ, եւ ասեն ընդ իրար եւթանասուն եւ երկու իշխանքն. «Եկայք արկցուք ադիւս եւ թրծեսքուք[102] հրով, այն լիցի քարի տեղ, եւ կուպր ի կրի տեղ, եւ շինեցուք մեզ քաղաքս եւ աշտարակս, որ գլուխն հասանի մինչեւ յերկինս, եւ ստասցուք մեզ անուն!: / p. 92 / Եւ արարին այնպէս եւ շինեցին: Եւ գնաց Տէր ի տեսանել զաշտարակն եւ ասէ Տէր Աստուած. «Ահա ազգ մի եւ լեզու մի ամենայն երկիրս, եւ զայդ սկսան գործել: Եւ գնացից եւ խառնակեցից զլեզուս նոցա, եւ գրուեցից գնոսա ընդ երկիր, զի մի լուիցեն զխաւսս միմեանց»: Եւ անդ խառնակեաց Տէր զլեզուս ամենայն երկրի. եւթանասուն եւ երկու լեզուս բաժանեցաւ, եւ ինքեանք պակեցին զաշտարակն, եւ պատառեաց երկիր, եւ եկուլ զքաղաքն եւ զաշտարակն, եւ գրուեաց զնոսա ընդ երկիր:

---

99. Together, these make seventy-two. This division of the seventy-two languages was known traditionally, see p. 65 above.

100. Biblical Paraphrases was published in Stone, *Patriarchs and Prophets*, 81–126.

101. Story of Noah is in Stone, *Patriarchs and Prophets*, 91–93. The punctuation of the edition, which followed the base manuscript, has been preserved, but for very few instances where it might have led to confusion.

102. Orthograpic error for թրծեսցուք.

9. TOWER OF BABEL AND THE CONFUSION OF THE LANGUAGES

9/ And the sons of Noah increased, and they went to the east, and they found a plain, and the seventy-two princes said to one another, "Come, let us make[103] bricks and burn[104] them (in) fire; that will be instead of stone, and pitch instead of mortar (lime). And let us build for ourselves this city and this tower, whose top reaches to the heavens, and let us make a name for ourselves."[105] And they did thus, and they built. And the Lord went to see the tower. And the Lord God said, "Behold, all this earth is one people and one tongue,[106] and they have started to do this. And I will go and I will scatter them over the earth, so that they shall not understand one another's speech." And there the Lord confused the tongues of all the earth. And he separated seventy-two tongues. And they destroyed the tower, and the earth split open and swallowed up the city and the tower, and he scattered them over the earth.[107]

9.5.4. The Teaching of St. Gregory

Agat'angełos' *Teaching of St. Gregory*, dating from the fifth century, is one of the oldest and most influential sources discussing the tower of Babel. Agat'angełos' text is given here and then the translation by Robert Thomson.[108] Notable here is the correlation, which we have already seen above, of the number of languages and the seventy-two nations. This goes back to the LXX's[109] and Arm Bible's reading in Deut 32:8 "according to the number of the angels of God." The idea of seventy or seventy-two nations originates in calculations in the Tabula Gentium in Gen. 10.[110] It will be observed, however, that Agat'angełos' text does not show striking similarities with the later retellings of this story, and features common to Agat'angełos and the other retellings published here, for the most part, go back to Genesis.

---

103. Literally: cast.
104. Or: bake.
105. See Gen 11:3–4.
106. See Gen 11:1.
107. See Gen 11:7–9. This passage is annotated in Stone, *Patriarchs and Prophets*, 91–92.
108. Thomson, *Teaching of St. Gregory*, 40. Agat'angełos, *History of the Armenians* (Պատմութիւն Հայոց), Loukasean Library 15 (Tbilisi: Ałanean, 1914).
109. The New Testament reads "the children of Israel" for "the angels of God."
110. See the old but still useful article, Kaufman Kohler and Isaac Broydé, "Nations and Languages, The Seventy," *Jewish Encyclopedia* 9:188–90.

§297 Բայց ապա միատոհմ միալեզու ազգին բազմացելոյ
խորհուրդ առեալ աշխարհագունդ՝ երկնաբերձ աշտարակ
շինելոյ, անուանակիր առ ի յիշատակ մշտնջենաւոր, փոխանակ
յաւիտենականին Աստուծոյ, որոյ պատմի անուն յաւիտենից
յաւիտեանս եւ յիշատակ ազգաց յազգս։ Որոյ բարձրագոյն
ազդեցութեամբ ցուցեալ զաստուածագործ գիտութիւնն ի
խառնակելն, յամբոխելն, եւ զմիասնունդ ազգն ի բազում ազգս
այլալեզուս օտարածայնս անձանօթս միմեանց ընդ երեսս երկրի
սփռեր, զի մի կամայական սահման անձանց արկանիցեն, այլ
յաւիտենադիր սահմանացն Աստուծոյ հնազանդեալ գնասցեն։
Որ ի բաժանել ազգացն եւ ի խառնակել լեզուացն, եւ ի ցանել
որդւոցն Ադամայ՝ կարգեաց սահմանս ամենայն ազգաց ըստ թուոյ
հրեշտակացն Աստուծոյ։

§279 But then the race which was one family and of one language (Gen 11:1–9) multiplied, and they took counsel to build a round tower reaching to the heavens, celebrated to eternal memory in the place of the eternal God whose "name is told from age to age and whose memory from people to people (Ps 135[134]:13)." Who as a warning from on high showed his divine knowledge in confusing and dividing the race which had been brought up as one into many races, speaking tongues unknown to each other, and scattered them over the face of the earth, that they might not fix a self-willed limit for themselves, but might walk in obedience to the eternally ordained limits of God. In dividing the races and confusing the tongues and scattering the sons of Adam, He set limits to all races according to the number of the angels of God (Deut 32:8).

PART 3

ABRAHAM TO JACOB

10. Abraham, John the Baptist, and Solomon

Introductory Remarks

This brief document is preserved in M4618 on fol 131v.[1] It is a filler, written by another hand to that of the scribe of this part of the manuscript. Two further passages follow it, each also written by a different scribe.[2] Thus, this page of writing is composed of three units of text dealing with details of biblical and parabiblical narrative copied by three different individuals. Moreover, the first unit of text that is published here is itself composed three fragmentary pieces. The first fragment is about Abraham and the sale of idols. The second fragment deals with John the Baptist's food, and the third with King Solomon.[3] The provenance of these fragmentary texts remains unknown and I am publishing the first fragment here.

The second and third units of text on the page are lacunose, for the left-hand part of the page has been torn off. The second passage deals with Satan and his son; the third is List of Twelve Literate Nations.[4] None of them draws an explicit moral or has any homiletic features.

10.1. Abraham and the Idols

Introductory Remarks

In my study of the Armenian Abraham Saga[5] I dealt with the three chief narratives about Abraham's recognition of God. The number of variants of these

---

1. On the manuscript, see the introductory remarks to text 9, pp. 45–46 above.
2. This is clear from the image. The manuscript is described briefly in *Short Catalogue* 1.1247–48 and see above pp. 45–46.
3. On Solomon texts in general, see the introductory remarks to M 2188 Three Tales: Solomon, Noah, and Satan on pp. 295–96 below. See further Stone, *Biblical Heroes*, 143–45.
4. See on the Twelve Literate Nations the data assembled on pp. 65, 68–69 above.
5. Stone, *Abraham*.

traditions is, however, very large indeed and they should be studied in a dedicated monograph.

One of these narratives is the story God's saving Terah's field from the depredations of the ravens.[6] The second relates Abraham's discovery of God through the contemplation of the heavens.[7] This idea is widespread in Jewish and Christian texts,[8] as in Stone, *Abraham*, text no. 2.3 and it is sometimes combined with either the story of the ravens or that of Terah, idol maker.[9] A third, less commonly encountered narrative says that God's saving of Lot brought Abraham to recognize Him. This is found in The Story of Terah and of Father Abraham §31.[10]

The text I am publishing here presents another variant of the "idols" story. The present document relates an incident highlighting the idols' impotence, as do other texts. Here Abraham and the Idols describes how Terah, Abraham's father, was involved in the manufacture and sale of idols. It relates their falling into filth and Abraham's subsequent realization of their powerlessness. This is a good example of such stories.[11]

Text and Translation

1/ M4618 / fol 131v / Թարա՝ հայրն Աբրահամու, կուռք կու շինէր, եւ Աբրահամ ծախէր։ Եւ օր մի տարաւ ի շուկայն իշարեր մի

---

6. Birds: Stone, *Abraham*, 18–19, 43, 51–53, 148, 193. For further relevant references in that book to various stories of Abraham's discovery of God, its index may be consulted. The origins of the "bird" story are also discussed there.

7. Astronomical: Stone, *Abraham*, 51–53, 148, 193; see also Louis Ginzberg, *The Legends of the Jews*, 7 vols. (Philadelphia: Jewish Publication Society of America, 1909–1938), 5:210 n. 6.

8. See Ginzberg, *Legends of the Jews*. See Stone, *Abraham* 8.5, 11.2, and 15.2; compare Gen. Rab. 38:28. For different versions of the story of Abraham and the idols, see Bernhard Beer, *Leben Abrahams nach Auffassung der jüdischen Sagen* (Leipzig: Oskar Leiner, 1859), 9–11; cf. Tanḥ. Lek Leka 2.2: see also Apoc. Ab. 1–3. See further, Stone, *Abraham*, 112 and 238.

9. Discussed below, pp. 77, 90.

10. Lot: Stone, *Abraham*, 156. The position of the incident in this text is also unusual. To maintain that Abraham only recognized God at the time of the Sodom incident raises narrative difficulties, when set alongside the biblical text.

11. Idols: See discussion in Stone, *Abraham*, 147 and index s.v., and Ginzberg, *Legends of the Jews*, 5.215–218.

կուրք, եւ յանկարծակի անկաւ էշն ի չամուրն,¹² եւ կուռքն ամենայն չարդեցան, եւ Աբրահամ փախեաւ ի հօրէն:

1/ Terah, Abraham's father, built idols and Abraham sold (them). And one day he was bringing a donkey-load of idols to the market. And suddenly the donkey fell in the dirt and all the idols were broken into pieces and Abraham fled from his father.¹³

10.2. John the Baptist's Food

Introductory Remarks

This brief text deals with John the Baptist's food. The "locusts and wild honey" of Matt 3:4 and Mark 1:6 apparently interested the author and he attempts to explain them. His explanation does not reflect any geographical or botanical knowledge.

Text and Translation

2/ M4618 / fol 131v / Սուրբն Յովհաննէս Մկրտիչն ի տեղին ուր բնակէր, Փառան կոչի, որպէս ասի, եւ կերակուր նորա՝ մարախ եւ մեղր վայրենի: Մարախն խոտ է, ի Հրէաստան յոլով լինի. ամառն զծիլն ուտէր եւ զձմեռն զտակն: Եւ մեղրն վայրենի՝ պիծակի մեղրն է:

2/ St. John the Baptist, in the place where he dwelt, it was called Pharan¹⁴ as is related. And his food (was) locusts¹⁵ and wild honey. The locust is a sort

---

12. In preparing my preliminary edition of this document published in Stone, *Abraham*, 238, I could not identify this word. It eventuates that it is actually the Turkish word *čamur*, which means "dirt, filth."

13. This is part of one of the stories of Abraham's discovery of God: I have already published the text on Abraham with a translation in Stone, *Abraham*, 238.

14. This is apparently the wilderness of Paran, mentioned in Gen 21:21, Num 10:12, 13:13, etc.

15. John's diet is mentioned in Matt 3:4 and Mark 1:6 as "locusts and wild honey." The Greek for "locusts" is ἀκρίδες in those verses, which designates the insect. The Armenian author, worried apparently by John's eating the insects, explains that the word մարախ "locust" means a sort of grass. NBHL notes occasional equivalence with մատռւտակ, "a sweet root." By what seems to be a strange coincidence, "locust" in English may also designate both the insect and a number of sorts of tree, including the carob: see OED, s.v. In fact, in Middle Eastern diets, as well as carob pods, locusts (the insects) were eaten, notably by Bedouin, and they are regarded as a permitted food by the Rabbis.

of grass; it is in all Judea. In the summer he ate the buds, and in winter, the lower part. and wild honey is wasp honey.

10.3. Solomon's Saying

Text and Translation

3/ M4618 / fol 131v / [Զ]ի՞նչ է, որ ասէ Սողոմոն, թէ Ռ. (1000) ծով՝ մէջ մէկ նաւի:
Պատասխանի: Սուրբ [Աստուա]ծածինն է:[16]
Ձգայլու ձագն յուսումն տվին եւ ասէին, թէ՝ այբ, բեն, գիմ: Եւ նա ասէր այծ բուծ գառն:

What is that which Solomon said, "A thousand sea(s) in one ship"?[17]
Answer: It is the holy Theotokos.
They gave a wolf cub to be taught: and they were saying, "ayb, ben, gim"; and it (the cub) said, "goat, ewe lamb, lamb."[18]

---

16. A tear has carried away the first part of this word, adding to the obscurity of the preceding.

17. The meaning and the source of this Solomonic saying are not evident. It is not drawn from any of the biblical Books of Solomon, or from Questions of the Queen, which exists in Armenian; see Yovsēp'eanc', 220–31 and Sebastian P. Brock, "The Queen of Sheba's Questions to Solomon: A Syriac Version," *Le Muséon* 92 (1979): 331–45. On the various traditions about Solomon, see Pablo Torijano Morales, *Solomon the Esoteric King: From King to Magus, Development of a Tradition*, JSJSup 72 (Leiden: Brill, 2002).

18. This is a wisdom saying the import of which is the following: on being taught the first three letters ayb, ben, gim, the wolf cub responds with the names of three beasts on which wolves prey, whose names start with these three letters. One might summarize the meaning as "a wolf in sheep's clothing is still a wolf." This is a clearly parabolic story.

11. From Abraham to Jacob

Introductory Remarks

This document is found in M1137, a fifteenth-century miscellany of religious texts. The document published here commences on fol 13r but is incomplete at the start, and it continues down to fol 19v.[1] It presents biblical history from Abraham to the death of Jacob and it is comprised in Vardan's *Commentary on Genesis*, which takes up the first 57 folios of the manuscript. I have assigned the title to it.

Stone, *Abraham* includes other works covering the same span of history. From Abraham to Jacob differs from them in a very significant respect: those works were written to instruct and, perhaps, do it interestingly. They very often forward an agenda, such as to present an overall understanding of the *Heilsgeschichte*.

In contrast to them, the present work is basically a summary of biblical events, tendentious in very few respects and marked by features of learned, scholarly writing, a number of instances of which are signaled in the notes below.[2] Instead of telling a tale, embroidered with apocryphal tendrils, this author makes clear that he is dependent on "Moses," that is, the Pentateuch, which he is summarizing. This is explicit; see §37 and §60.

The first sentence of §37 relates Abraham's death and his disposal of his goods among his children. This addition, the author feels, is needed to complete Abraham's story. Then he remarks,

> Moses relates concerning Ishmael and speaks of his children, and then[3] he returns to Isaac, who went to Abimelech's place to escape the famine, and this was on account of his wife, that she would be a sister. And nonetheless, no one drew near to her, etc.

---

1. *General Catalogue* 4:406–410.
2. See nn. 4, 98, 169, 193, 207, 284, etc.
3. Literally: thus.

This is a summary by a scholar who does not wish to omit part of the evidence but, on the other hand, avoids setting it out in detail by referring to his source, the Pentateuch, referenced by its author's name: "Moses relates." Moreover, even the words եւ այլն "etc." are to be found in the Armenian text, another indication of its learned character.⁴

Similarly, in §37 the text omits the listing of Ishmael's sons and, moreover, Esau's sons are omitted from §60, with due notice given. The passage reads: "Esau had two wives and many sons, and he was called Edom and Sēir. Moses recounts his offspring and those of his children and of his grandchildren. And thus, he leaves this matter and says where they dwelt." This summary statement is followed directly by the beginning of the Joseph romance.

In both these instances, From Abraham to Jacob omits lists of names and refers the reader to the Bible.⁵ In the annotations, a good number of other points bearing the stamp of school transmission are to be observed. The document is a summary of biblical verses, prepared in a scholarly context. However, very few instances of the adducing of alternative exegeses and previous authorities are to be found.⁶ Such discussions of alternative exegesis are not infrequent elsewhere in the extensive Armenian apocryphal literature of scholastic character. From Abraham to Jacob is apparently governed by its character as a biblical epitome.

One particular point is shared with many Armenian texts relating the patriarchal events. That is that, despite §6, which says Abraham received զերկիրն աւետեաց "the promised land," From Abraham to Jacob in fact downplays and omits God's promises of the land (§7). Other texts similarly pass over such promises to Abraham in silence, as has been noted previously.⁷

In addition to the procedures followed throughout this volume, the following additional special features have been observed in the edition of this text:

1. Quite often the manuscript has o for աւ as a sort of abbreviation, even in positions where standard spelling would demand աւ. This usage is preserved and no notation is made.

2. Misspellings and careless errors can be observed, such as ուդ for ուդա; նմաւ for նմա; ամպ for ամ, etc. There are many erasures.

---

4. Observe the use of եւ այլն "etc." in citing a biblical verse by catch-phrase, §3. That passage also contains an explicit exegetical remark. Another such instance of եւ այլն, this time mentioning different views of a certain matter, may be seen at the end of §33.

5. See also §14 where another list of names is omitted, though in this instance "Moses" is not referred to.

6. See, e.g., §4.

7. See Stone, *Abraham*, 95.

11. FROM ABRAHAM TO JACOB

Text

1 M1137 / fol 13r / . . .Աբրահամ, Արամ եւ Նաքովր։ Արամ ծնո զՂովտ եւ երկուս դստերս՝ զՍարա եւ զՄելքայ։ Մեռաւ Արամ, Աբրահամ առ զՍարայ, եւ Նաքովր՝ զՄելքայ։

2/ Յայնմ ժամանակի պաշտեցին եգիպտացիքն զհուռ, եւ վասն զի Աբրահամ եւ Նաքովր ոչ կամէին պաշտել, ընկեցին զնոսա ի հուր։ Մեռաւ Նաքովր, եւ զերծաւ Աբրահամ։ Յաղագս Թարայի անյայտ է, թէ պաշտէր։

3/ Եւ մնացին Աբրամ եւ Ղովտ. եւ հօրն Աբրամու ազդ եղեւ յԱստուծոյ ելանել յերկրէն։ Եւ ել եւ եկն ի Խառան, ուր վախճանեցաւ Թարայ։ Եւ անդ ասացաւ նմա. «Ե՛լ յերկրէ քումմէ » եւ այլն։ Այնուհետեւ ելեալ էր։ Ել այսինքն՝ մի՛ ունիցիս կամս առ ի դառնալ։ Եւ եկին յերկիրն Քանանու։

4/ Եղեւ սով սաստիկ, չուեցին յԵգիպտոս, ուր առատութիւն էր յոյժ։ Եւ մինչդեռ երթային, ասէ ցկինն իւր. «Մի՛ ասասցես, աղաչեմ, թէ կին իցես իմ, այլ քոյր»։ Պատմեցո թագաւորին վասն նորա, առ զնա եւ կալաւ։ Բայց ասեն սուրբք, թէ ոչ մերձեցաւ ի նա, քանզի կրօնք էր նոցա պահել զկանայս ամ մի, եւ ապայ գիտելն զնոսա ի բաղանիսն։

5/ Հարաւ յարուածով[8] մեծաւ եւ այնպէս պատմեցաւ նմա, թէ կին իցէ նորա։ Եւ ասէ. «Ընդէ՞ր խաբեցեր զիս»։ Եւ ասէ. « Երկեա, թէ սպանցես զիս վասն նորա, թէ ասիցեմ, թէ կին իցէ»։ Եւ դարձոյց զնա բազում ընծայիւք, եւ դարձ..ք յերկիրն աւետեաց։

6/ Հովիւքն Ղովտայ կագել սկսան ընդ հովիւս նորա, վասն այնորիկ ասաց գնա. «Հայեաց յարեւելս եւ կալ զկողմն ցայն, եւ ապայ թէ ոչ յարեւմուտս եւ ես՝ զմիւսն»։ Հայեցաւ անդրէն ի մերձակայն եւ առ զՍոդոմ եւ զԳոմոր, եւ Աբրահամ՝ զերկիրն[9] աւետեաց։

7/ Եւ ասացաւ նմա. «Յարեւելից եւ յարեւմտից քեզ տաց եւ զոսկի քում», բայց ոչ տուաւ նմա, այլ զաւակի նորա։ Շինեաց անդ սեղան եւ մատոյց պատարագ։

8/ Յայնմ ժամանակի չորք թագաւորք յարեան ի վերայ Ե.-ից (5) թագաւորացն, որք բնակէին ի Սոդոմ եւ ի Գոմոր, ի Սեգովր, ի Սեմէի, եւ յԱդամէ։ Ընդէ՞ր. զի Ե. (5) թագաւորքն այնոքիկ տուեալ էին հարկս քոդող[ո]գոմորայ, որ էր աւագ չորիցն այնոցիկ զամ{պ}ս[10] ԲԺ.ան

---

8. Orthographic anomaly for հարուած.
9. This word has been corrected p.m.
10. This is to be understood as ամ "year" spelled with a superfluous պ and not as ամպ "cloud." I have thus translated "years."

(12): Եւ յԳԺ. (13)-ան ամի երորդի[11] արգելին, եւ ի ԴԺ.աներորդին (14) զումարեցին[12] ի վերայ նոցա եւ աւերեցին զաւանս եւ զդդեակս նոցա։ Եւ սոքա ելեալք ընդդէմ նոցա պարտեցան։ Եւ Ղովտ, զի բնակէր ընդ նոքաւք, գերեցօ հանդերձ ամենայն ստացուածովք։

9/ Պատմեցաւ / fol 13v / Աբրահամու վասն եղբաւրորդոյն իւրոյ, որ էր ի գերութեանն։ Կոչեաց զԳԾ. եւ զԺԸ. (318) ընդօծինս իւր եւ պնդեցաւ զհետ նոցա. զՂովտ ազատեաց եւ զաւարն ամենայն դարձոյց։

10/ Ի դառնառն[13] նորա, Մելքիսեդեկ քահանայ Աստուծոյ բարձրելոյ ընդ առաջ եղեւ նմա, մատուցեալ հաց եւ գինի ի կերակուր մանկություն։ Եւ նա նմա մատոյց տասանորդս յամենայնէ, զոր առեալն էր։ Թագօորն Սոդոմայ լուաւ գյաղթութենէ նորա, ընդ յառաջ եկն նմա եւ ասէ. «Ամենայն, զոր առեր, ի ձեռին քո են»։ Եւ ասէ Աբրահամ. «Ամբառնամ զձեռս իմ յերկինս, զի ոչ ինչ յայնցանէ, զորս յափշտակեցից ի նոցանէ, կալայց, բայց ի կերակրոյ, որով ընդ յիս են եւ թէ առին մասն ինչ։

11/ Յայնժամ պատմեցաւ նմա ի հրեշտակէն. «Մի՛ երկնչիր, զի արարից զքեզ ազգ մեծ»։ Եւ ասէ. «Զիա՞րդ կարասցէ այս լինել, զի ես ծեր եմ եւ որդի ոչ ունիմ»։ Ասէ ցնա. «Ունիցիս որդի»։ Ասէ Աբրահամ. «Ո՞չ աւանիկ Եղիազար Դամասկացի որդի ընդօծնի վերակացու ի տան իմոյ, նա ժառանգեցէ զիս»։

12/ Պատասխանի ետ հրեշտակն. «Ոչ, այլ ունիցիս որդի»։ Եւ ասէ. «Զի՞նչ եղիցի նշան»։ «Ա՛ռ երինչ երեմեան, եւ այծ երեմեան, եւ խոյ երեմեա[ն],[14] եւ աղաւնի, եւ տատրակ, եւ յօշեցես ընդ մէջ, եւ զհօսն ոչ»։ Եւ արար այնպես, եւ գային թռչունք, եւ ստուցանէր զնոսա։ Ընդ երեկս եկն հուր յերկնից, եւ ծախեաց։ Եւ ասէ. «Այս եղիցի նշան»։

13/ Եւ յետ այնորիկ ասէ ցնա Սարա. «Մո՛ւտ առ աղախին իմ, զի ունիցիս որդի»։ Եմուտ առ Ագար հարճ իւր, եւ յղացաւ։ Իսկ նա աբացաւ ընդդէմ տիկնոջ իւրոյ, ուստի նա սրտմտեալ ասէ ցԱբրահամ. «Բուռն առնես ինձ»։ Եւ ասէ Աբրամ. «Ի ձեռին քոյ է, արա՛ զինչ եւ կամիս»։

14/ Եւ նա սկսաւ հարկանել զնա եւ զանիք տանջել, ուստի նա ելեալ յուղի փախչեր։ Պատահել նմա հրեշտակ, ասէ. «Յո՞ երթաս,

---

11. An erased letter follows ր1°.
12. Գումարեցին p.m. with a correction mark and ս in the marg. p.m.
13. The word դառնառն does not appear in the dictionaries, and it might be corrupt for դառնալն. Regardless, fom the context one may learn that it clearly means "return."
14. The final letter is lost in a lacuna, and I have restored it.

11. FROM ABRAHAM TO JACOB

Ազա՛րը», եւ ասէ. «Յերեսաց տիկնոջ իմոյ փախեալ եմ»: Եւ ասէ հրեշտակն. «Դարձի՛ր առ նա,- եւ խոնարհեաց ընդ նովաւ,- եւ ունիցիս որդի, ուստի երկոժ.ան (12) ժողովուրդք ելցեն»: Դարձեալ նմա ի տուն, ծնաւ զԻսմայէլ, որ եւ ի նմանէ եղեն ԲԺ.-ան (12) իշխանք, եւ ի նոցանէ՝ ԲԺ.-ան (12) ժողովուրդք:

15/ Յայնժամ ասացաւ Աբրահամու թլփատել զմարմին անթլփատութեան իւրոյ եւ ընդոծնաց իւրոց: Իսկ որ ոչ թլփատեցի, կո<րի>/ fol 14r /գէ[15] անձն այն ի ժողովրդենէ իմմէ: Այսինքն նա կորիցէ: Եւ ասացաւ նմա, թէ ազգ նորա լինելոց է յԵգիպտոս գշորեքձ. (400) ամս, եւ թէ որպէս փրկելոց էին, եւ վասն հարուածոցն Եգիպտոսի, եւ պատառման Կարմիր ծովուն:

16/ Յայնմ ժամանակի եկին Գ. (3) հրեշտակք առ նա ի կերպարանս մարդկան: Երիս եւտես եւ միոյ երկրպագեաց, զի մին ի նոցանէ մեծագոյն թուէր: Եւ պատրաստեաց խրախութիւնս, այսինքն՝ որթ, նկանակ հաց, եւ այլս: Ընդ երեկս ասէ մին. «Ո՛ւր է Սառա կին քո», եւ ասէ. «Տէ՛ր, ի խորանին է»: Եւ ասէ հրեշտակն. «Ունիցի Սառա որդի»: Եւ նա լուեալ ծիծաղեցաւ յետոյ դրանն: Եւ ասէ. «Ընդէ՞ր ծիծաղեցար», եւ ասէ. «Տէ՛ր, ոչ ծիծաղեցա»: Եւ ասէ. «Մի՛ երկնչիր, Սարայ, վասն զի ուղղեկցելով կենաց, դարձայց առ քեզ ի միւս ամի: Եւ եղիցի Սարայի որդի»,- խօսէր մարդկաւրէն:

17/ Յայնժամ փոխեցաւ անունն Աբրահամու եւ Սառայի: Նախ կոչիւր Աբրամ, որ է՝ հայր բարձր, եւ յետ այնորիկ կոչեցաւ Աբրահամ, որ է՝ հայր ազգաց բազմաց: Եւ Սառա կոչեցաւ Սառա:

18/ Իսկ ընդ առաւօտուն սկսան մեկնիլ, եւ Աբրահամ՝ զհետ նոցա: Եւ ասէ ցնա հրեշտակն. «Ոչ կարեմ թաքուցանել ի քէն, զոր առնելոց եմ, զի երթամ աւերել զՍոդոմ եւ զԳոմոր, եւ մեղք նոցա հասին մինչեւ յերկինս»: Եւ ասէ Աբրահամ. «Մի՛ թէ կորիցէ արդարն ընդ ամպարշտին, թէ գտանիցի անդ Ծ. (50) արդար, աւերեցէ գնա, ոչ թէ Խ. (40), ոչ թէ Լ. (30), ոչ թէ Ի. (20), ոչ թէ Ժ. (10), ոչ:

19/ Չոգան երկուքն եւեթ եւ էին առ դրանն Ղովտայ: Կայս գնոսա Ղովտ եւ եմոյծ ի տուն իւր, եւ հրօիրեաց ընթրիս, քանզի կարծեաց, թէ մարդիկ են: Եւ աղժամայն եկին սուտ մարգարէքն, այսինքն՝ սոդոմայեցիքը, առ տունն Ղովտայ եւ ասեն. «Հա՛ն զարսն, որք[16] մտին ի տուն քո, զի գիտասցուք գնոսա»: Եւ ասէ Ղովտ. «Մի՛ առնիցէք ինձ, աղաչեմ, զայս անիրաւութիւն. են իմ երկու դստերք, առջիք գնոսա»:

---

15. The two letters րի are omitted at the end of the folio, a typical scribal error.
16. Sic!

20/ Եւ նթրա կամէին մտանել ի տունն Ղովտայ. ունէր զդուռն եւ ոչ տայր թոյլ բանալ։ Բո<ւ>ռն17 էհար հրեշտակն զՂով<տ>այ18 եւ ասէ. «Թո՛ լլ տուր մտանել»։ Եւ եբաց զդուռն եւ հարան կուրութեամբ եւ gong ինքք, որք տեսանէին, բայց ընտրութիւնս ոչ կարէին առնել։

21/ Եւ ասեն ցՂովտ. «Ե՛լ ի քաղաքէս, դու եւ մերձաւորք քո, եւ բարեկամք քո։ Չոգաւ Ղովտ եւ ասէ գնաս. «Ելէ՛ք ընդ իս, քանզի օերեցի / fol 14v / Սոդում», եւ ծաղր առնէին զևա։ Եւ ել ինքև եւ կին իւր, եւ Բ. (2) դստերք իւր։ Եւ հրամայեաց, զի մի19 ոք հայեցցի յետս։ Այլ իբրեւ լուաւ կինև նորա զդրոտումն, հայեցաւ յետս եւ եղեւ արձան աղի։

22/ Եւ ասէ Ղովտ. «Յո՞ երթիցուք։» Եւ ասեն. «Ի լեառն, ոչ այլ ի Սեգովր»։ Եւ գնացին։ Բայց ինքն զուարճացեալ ի գինոյ, ասէ յետ այնորիկ. «Ելցուք ի լեառն»։ Տեսին դստերքն զքաղաքս օերեալ՝ ասեն. «Կորեո բոլորովին ազգս ամենայն մարդկան»։ Ասէ կրսերն գերեցն. «Արբուցուք ղդա, եւ մուտ առ նա, զի զիտասցէ զքեզ, եւ ունիցիս զաւակս»։

23/ Նոյնպէս եւ ասաց երէցն, եւ եղեւ այնպէս։ Այնպէս զի ոչ իմացաւ Ղովտ։ Եւ ի միւս գիշերի եմուտ կրսերն եւ յղացաւ զՄովաբ, եւ միւսն՝ զԱմոն, ուստի ասացան մովաբացիք եւ ամուրհացիք։

24/ Ասացաք յառաջագոյն ի մէջ բաժանմանն Աբրահամու եւ Ղովտոա, թէ Աբրահամ բնակէր յերկրին Քանանու։ Եւ պատահեաց ևմա գնալ յերկիր յայլ, ուր թագաւորէր Աբամելիք։ Իբրեւ ասէր զՍառայէ, թէ քոյր իցէ իւր, առ զևա Աբամելիք ի կնութիւն, սակայն զևա ոչ զիտաց, ուստի հրեշտակն յանուրջս երեւեալ ևմա ասէ. «Մեռցիս, զի առեր ի կնութիւն զկին այլում»։20

25/ Եւ ասէ Աբամելիք. «Տէր, ողջմտութեամբ արարի», եւ ասէ հրեշտակն. «Գիտեմ, զի ողջմտութեամբ արարեր, վասն այնորիկ խնա<յե>ցի21 ի քեզ։ Իսկ նա ել ընդ առաւաոտն, պատմեաց ծառայից իւրոց եւ աղախնեաց։ Եւ ասէ ցԱբրահամ. «Ընդէ՞ր խաբեցեր զիս»։ Եւ ասէ. «Կարծեցի, թէ սպանցես զիս»։

26/ Եւ դարձոյց զևա գևա հանդերձ մեծաւ ստացուածովք, այսինքն՝ խաշամբք22 եւ արջառով եւ այլովք։ Իսկ Սառայի ետ Ռ.

---

17. Thus emending բոռն of the manuscript.
18. Thus emending զՂովայ of the manuscript.
19. The manuscript reads մի̅թ with an erasure mark over the last letter.
20. The dative case of այլում is odd.
21. Orthographic error.
22. One letter erased before շ.

(1.000) արծաթիս, զի նոքօք գնեցէ ինքեան գերեզման եւ զայլ պէտս ի թաղումն, եւ յայլ պէտս իւր: Եւ դարձո ի Քանան:

27/ Յայ{մ}ժամ²³ այց արար Տէր Աբրահամու, լցեալ զխոստումն վասն որդւոյ, զոր կոչեաց Իսահակ: Էին երկու եղբարք, այսինքն՝ Առան եւ Նաքովր: Առան մեռաւ եւ Նաքովրա եղեն որդիք ութ. ութերորդն Բաթուէլ, որոյ եղեւ դուստր Ռեբեկայ:

28/ Մեռաւ Սառայ, եւ ոչ գոյր գերեզման: Խնդրեաց զայն յորդւոցն Քետայ, յորոց միջի էր Եմովր, որ ասաց. «Առ զգերեզման իմ», եւ կամէր տալ նմա պարգեւ, եւ ետ նմա Խ. (40) արծաթիս, եւ ետ գնա զայրն կրկին եւ զազարական, յորում էր, եւ թաղեաց զնա անդ:

29/ Չկնի մահուան Սառայի կոչեաց Աբրահամ զծառայ իւր եւ ասէ գնա. «Երդուեա՛ ինձ չածել /fol 15r/ կին յորդւոյ²⁴ իմոյ, բայց եթէ յազգէ̊ իմէ»:²⁵ Եւ երդուաւ նմա եւ ասէ, «Թէ ոչ²⁶ կամեցի կինն գալ, աձի̊ գ զորդի քո յերկիր քո», եւ ասէ. «Ո՛չ»:

30/ Եւ առ ծառայն Ժ. (10) ուղտս եւ երբարձ ի բարութեանց երկրին այնորիկ: Եւ սկսաւ գնալ յերկիրն Աբրահամու, յորում բնակէր Նաքովր: Այլ նախ քան զմտանելն ի քաղաքն, սկսաւ խորհել ի սրտի իւրում եւ ասել. «Տէր, արա՛, զի աղջիկ, որ ելանիցէ ի քաղաքէս, յորմէ խնդրեցից չուր, նա եկեսցէ եւ եղիցս տեառն իմում:

31/ Եւ ահա եկն վաղվաղակի Ռեբեկա առ ջրհորն, ուր էր նա, եւ ասէ ծառայն. «Տո՛ւր ինձ ըմպել»: Եւ ետ նմա եւ ուղ<տ>ոց²⁷ իւրոց: Եւ եհարց գնա, թէ՛ ունիցի իջաւան: Եւ ասէ. «Գոյ մեր իջաւան, եւ կերակուր գրաստուց», եւ եմուտ ի քաղաքն, եւ յառաջեաց եւ պատմեաց հօրն: Եկն հայրն ընդ առաջ նորա, եւ եմոյծ զուղտն²⁸ ի տուն եւ ետ նոցա ուտել:

32/ Եւ զամենայն պէտս նոցա²⁹ կամեցաւ տալ նմա նոյնպէս, եւ ոչ առ: Այլ պատմէր զամենայն, թէ որպէս եկեալն էր, եւ ասէր ոչ ուտել, եթէ ոչ նախ գիտասցէ, թէ կամեցի երթալ ընդ իւր: Կոչեաց հայր նորա եւ հարցանէր, թէ՛ կամիցի̊ երթալ ընդ նմա: Եւ ասէ. «Երթամ,

---

23. This is an orthographic error for յայնժամ.
24. յ blurred.
25. This is an orthographic error for իմէ.
26. Unclear mark precedes.
27. Orthographic error.
28. տ above line p.m.
29. նոցա is surmounted by dots, apparently indicating an error. Indeed, նորա "his" would be a smoother reading.

զի բանս այս յԱստուծոյ էլ»: Առեալ աւրինութիւն ի հօրէն, չոզաւ ընդ նմա{ւ}:³⁰

33/ Այլ իբրեւ մերձ եղեւ յերկիր ծնընդեան իւրոյ, ետես զԻսահակ, զի զրօսնոյր ի դաշտի, եւ նա ասէ. «Ո՞ վ է այն»: Եւ ասէ. «Նա է տէրն³¹ քո»: Էշ վաղվաղակի յուղտոյն, եւ զարդարեցաւ ըստ կարի իւրում, եւ չոզաւ առ նա: Եւ առ զնա ի կին, եւ զետեղեցոյց ի տեղի մաւր իւրոյ: Իսկ Աբրահամ առ կին զՔետտուրայ, որ ըստ ումանց՝ էր Ազար, եւ ըստ այլոց՝ այլ: Եւ ծնաւ {ի նմաւ}³² ի նմանէ բազում որդիս:

34/ Եւ Ռեբեկա ամուլ էր, սակայն աղօթիք Իսահակայ յղացաւ զՅեսաւ եւ զՅակոբ, որք ընդ միմեանս մարտընչէին յորովայնի: Ուստի զարմացեալ, նա եհարց զՏէր, թէ՝ «Զի՞նչ իցէ», եւ ասացաւ նմայ, թէ՝ երկուք ազինք, յորոց ելանելոց էին երկուք ազինք. այս է՝ եդովմայեցիք եւ իսրայէլացիք, եւ աւագն կրսերոյն ծառայեցէ. այս է՝ եդովմայեցիք՝ հրէից:

35/ Ասաց Հռեբեկայ, թէ՝ «Այսպէս հանդերձեալ է լինել, լաւ էր ինձ ոչ ունել որդի»: Եւ ծնաւ Յեսաւ, եւ Յակոբ ունէր զզարշապար նորա: Եւ եղեւ Եսաւ չէկ եւ որսորդ, եւ Յակոբ՝ լերկ եւ տնասուն:

36/ Եսաւ յաւուր միում դարձո յանդէ, լքէլ եւ նքթէլ³³, եւ էր Յակոբ եփեալ սակաւուկ ոսպն. եւ խնդրեաց ի նմանէ, եւ նա ասէ.³⁴ «Ոչ տաց, եթէ ոչ տացես ինձ³⁵ զիրաւունս ան/ fol/ 15v /տրանգութեան», եւ ասէ «Քեզ լիցի, քանզի - ասէ, - լաւ է ինձ կալ,³⁶ քան մեռանել», եւ այնպէս առ ի նմանէ, եւ էլ Եսաւ:

37/ Մեռաւ Աբրահամ եւ եթող զամենայն ստացուածս Իսահակայ եւ այլ պարգեւս ետ այլոց որդւոցն: Պատմէ Մովսէս յաղագս Իսմայէլի եւ ասէ զծնունդս նորա եւ այնպէս դառնա առ Իսահակ, որ ի զաւրանալ սուրյ եմուտ առ Աբիմէլիք: Եւ ասէր վասն կնոջ իւրոյ, թէ քոյր իցէ: Եւ սակայն ոչ ոք մերձեցաւ ի նա եւ այլն: Եւ եհան հրաման, զի մի ոք ասասցէ ինչ նոցա չար: Եւ սերմանեաց զարի եւ ժողովեաց ձ.աւոր (100), ուստի արտմեցան ի վերայ նորա,³⁷ եւ հանին յերկրէն:

---

30. The final letter is a scribal error of the sort this copyist was prone to make, a number of which misspellings have been noted above.

31. An erased mark precedes this word.

32. These two words are written by error.

33. A small circle surmounts նք.

34. է above line, p.m.

35. An erased letter precedes this word.

36. Probably this should be կեալ "to live."

37. Abbreviation mark omitted.

38/ Եւ լցին զջրհորս նորա քարամ<բ>բ³⁸, եւ գնաց յայլ տեղի, եւ դարձեալ այլ լցին զջրհորս նորա, եւ դարձեալ երրորդ անգամ նոյնպէս։ Եւ յայնժամ մարտեան հովիւք նորա ընդ այլ հովիւս։

39/ Յիշեաց թագաւորն, թէ որպէս մերժեալ էր գնա։ Չոգաւ ինքն եւ Մելքող իշխան նորա ընդ նմա։ Իսկ իբրեւ ետես, ասէ. «Ընդէ՞ր եկիք,³⁹ դուք մերժեցիք զիս եւ զջրհորս իմ լցիք»։ Ասէ թագօրն. «Գիտեմ, զի Աստուած ընդ քեզ է, վասն այնորիկ կամիմք հաստատել զխաղաղութիւն։» Եւ երդուան միմեանց պահել զխաղաղութիւն։

40/ Վատեցին այքն Իսահակայ, եւ ոչ կարեր տեսանել։ Հրամայեաց Եսաւայ, զոր առաւել սիրէր. «Բե՛ր ինձ յորսոյ քումմէ, որդեա՛կ, զի աւրհնեցէ զքեզ անձն իմ, մինչ չեւ մեռեալ իցեմ»։ Եւ լուաւ Հռեբեկայ, ասէ ցՅակոբ,⁴⁰ զոր ինք առօել սիրէր. «Ա՛ռ երկուս ուլս եւ արա՛յ խորտիկ հօր քո, զի աւրհնեցէ զքեզ»։ Ասէ. «Երկնչիմ՛ զուցէ աձէ ի վերայ իմ անէծս փոխանակ աւրհնութեան»։ Եւ ասէ. «Յիմ վերայ անէծքն այն»։

41/ Եփեաց զմիսն եւ զգեցոյց զձեռս եւ զպարանոցն մորթովքն, եւ զգեցաւ զպատմուճան եղբաւրն եւ մատոյց հօրն, եւ ասէ գնա, թէ. «Այդպէս փութանակի՛ եկե՞ր, որդեա՛կ իմ»։ Եւ ասէ. «Կամք Աստուծոյ եղեւ, հա՛յր»։ Եւ ասէ. «Մատի՛ր այսր, զի մերձեցայց ի քեզ», եւ շօշափեաց եւ ասէ, «Ձեռք՝ ձեռք Եսաւայ, եւ ձայնդ՝ ձայն Յակոբայ»։

42/ Եկեր⁴¹ եւ ասէ. «Տո՛ւր ինձ համբոյր, որդեա՛կ իմ, զի աւրհնեցից զքեզ»։ Մատեաւ, համբուրեաց զնա եւ ասէ. «Ահա, հոտ որդոյ իմոյ իբրեւ զհոտ անդոյ լիոյ, զոր աւրհնեաց Տէր»։ Աւրհնեաց զնա եւ գնաց։ Մատեաւ Եսաւ եւ ասէ. «Արի՛, հա՛յր, եւ կե՛ր յորսոյ որդոյ քո», իսկ նա հիացեալ ասէ. «Եկն եղբայր քո պատրանաւք եւ մատոյց խորտիկս, եւ աւրհնեաց զնա անձն իմ»։ Եւ նա գայրացեալ ասէ. «Ճանդրանկութիւն / fol 16r / իմ նախ առ լինէն, եւ այժմ շորթեաց զաւրհնութիւն իմ։ Մի՞ թէ մի աւրհնութիւն իցէ քո հայր։

43/ Եւ ասէ. «Աւրհնեցի զնա եւ եղիցի աւրհնեալ յօրտեան։ Ի ցաւղոյ երկնից եւ ի պարարտութենէ⁴² երկրի եղիցի աւրհնութիւն քո»։ Եւ աղժամայն սկսաւ խորհել. «Եղիցին աւուրք սգոյ հաւր իմոյ,

---

38. So emend քարամք of the manuscript. Scribal error; observe մպ for մ in §8, above.

39. An erasure follows this word.

40. A superfluous sign follows the g.

41. Observe that this form is 3 pers. sing. aorist of the suppletive կերայ. It is a homograph with the 2 pers. sing. aorist of զամ seen in §60.

42. Spelled thus in the manuscript.

եւ սպանից գՅակոբ»: Վադվաղակի ազդ եղեւ մօրն եւ ասէ գՅակոբ. «Երբ առ Լաբան եղբայր իմ»:

44/ Առ էսաւ կին զդուստր Իսմայելի: Երթայր Յակոբ, իբրեւ իջաւանեցաւ ի Բեթէլ, եդ վեմ մի ընդ գլխով իւրով եւ ննջեալ եւտես սանդուխք կանգնեալ, եւ հրեշտակք ելանէին եւ իջանէին։ Յարուցեալ ի քնոյ՝ ասէ. «Արդարեւ,այս⁴³ տեղի Աստուծոյ է սա, եւ ես ոչ գիտէի»: Եւ կանգնեաց զվէմն եւ աւծ զնա ճիթով, եւ շինեաց անդ սեղան, եւ յարուցեալ գնաց ի Խառան:

45/ Այլ մինչեւ եկեալ էր ի Խառան, եզիտ հովիւս, զի պահէին զմաշինս, եւ եհարց⁴⁴ զԼաբանէ եւ ասեն. «Բարւոք է նմա: Եւ աւա դուստր նորա Հռաքել եկն», եւ սկաւ արբուցանել զմաշինս, որում աւգնելով⁴⁵ Յակոբայ յարբուցանել համբուրեաց զնա: Եւ չոգան ի միասին ի տուն:

46/ Իբրեւ ծանեաւ զնա Լաբան, ուրախ եղեւ եւ ասէ. «Կամիմ, զի եղիցիս ընդ իս»․,:Եւ ասէ. «Եղց», եւ ասէ. «Զի՞նչ վարձ կացուցից քեզ»: Եւ ասէ. «Ծառայեցից քեզ զէ. (7) ամ փոխանակ Հռաքելի»: Բայց ի կատարածի, մինչ պարտ էր տալ զՀռաքել, ի գիշերի ետ զԼիայ: Ի վաղիւն մինչ եւտես զնա եւ ասէ. «Ընդէ՞ր խաբեցեր զիս»: Յաւէր, զի գիծակն է:

47/ Եւ ասէ. «Այսպիսի սովորութիւն է առ մեզ, զի երէցն յառաջագոյն տագ ի առն, սակայն ծառայեա՛ ինձ այլ եւս է. (7) ամս, եւ տագ քեզ զՀռաքել»: Խմբեցան հարսանիք⁴⁶ Լիայի աւուր է. (7) եւ յետոյ տուաւ նմա Հռաքել. եւ խմբեցաւ նմա հարսանիքն եւս է. (7) աւուրս:

48/ Եւ բնակեաց ընդ նմա ամս չորեքտասան: Սիրէր Յակոբ <զՀռաքել>⁴⁷ առաւել քան զԼիայ: Եւ Լիայի եղեն որդիք չորք, եւ Հռաքել ամուլ էր: Եւ էր Հռաքելի աղախին. ասէ գՅակոբ. «Մո՛ւտ առ աղախին իմ Զելփա, եւ ունիցիմ որդի»: Եմուտ եւ կալաւ ի նմանէ երկուս որդիս: Ասէ Լիա. «Մո՛ւտ առ աղախին իմ Բալայ»: Մուտ եւ կալաւ երկուս որդիս՝

49/ Դարձո Ռուբէն՝ որդի Լիայ, յանդէն, եւ եբեր մանտրագորայս: Եւ ասէ Հռաքել գԼիայ. «Տո՛ւր ինձ ի մանրագորաց որդոյ քո, զի ունիցիմ որդիս»: Եւ ասէ. «Ոչ տաց քեզ, եթէ ոչ տացես ինձ յայսմ

---

43. This word is written in the marg. p.m.
44. An erased ր follow the ե.
45. ով above line p.m.
46. ն following this word is erased.
47. A word has clearly been omitted. We propose adding զՀռաքել "Rachel," or else something very similar, which must have been omitted.

/ fol 16v / գիշերի գայր քո», քանզի յայնմ գիշերի առ նա պարտ էր մտանել, եւ ասէ. «Քեզ լիցի»: Առ եւ եկեր: Ի գիշերին, իբրեւ կամեր Յակոբ մտանել առ Հռաքել, ասէ Լիա. «Ոչ մտցես, զի վարձու կալա զքեզ»: Եմուտ առ Լիա, եւ յղացաւ, եւ այնպես կալաւ ի նմանէ երկուս որդիս: Գիտաց զՀռաքել յետ այնորիկ եւ կալաւ երկուս որդիս:

50/ Ի կատարել չորեքտասանից ամից,⁴⁸ ասէ Լաբան. «Արասցուք դաշն ես եւ դու՝ ծառայեցդես ինձ, եւ տաց քեզ վարձս. ընտրեա՛ քեզ զանասուն, որք ծնանին խայտս, ցորքան ընդ իս իցես»: Առ Յակոբ գիսայտսն: Հանապազ ի ժամանակի յղութեան խաշանց երթայր յուագանսն, ուր ըմպէին ջուր, առնոյր զաւագանս եւ գերձոյր ի մի կողմանեն, եւ դներ առաջի նոցա: Եւ այնպես ծնանէին խայտախարիւս եւէք:

51/ Այսպես առներ յառաջնումն նուագի եւ ի միւսումն՝ ոչ, զի երկիցս ծնանէին ի տարւոջ: Եւ յետ այնորիկ փոխեցին զդաշն: Իսկ ի վախճանել եւթեանց ամացն ս{ս}կսաւ⁴⁹ դառնալ կանամբք եւ որդւովք, եւ ընչիւք, ոչ գիտելով աներոջն: Տարաւ ընդ իւր զՀռաքել զկուռս հօր իւրոյ: Գիտացեալ Լաբան, պնտեցաւ զհետ նոցա եւ ասէ. «Ընդէ՞ր արարեր այդպես», «Երկեա՛ գուցէ չթողուցու զիս երթալ»: Եւ ասէ. «Զկուռս ընդէ՞ր գողացար», ասէ Յակոբ. «Առ ում գտանիցես, մեռցի»:

52/ Յուզեաց եւ ոչ եգիտ, եմուտ ի խորանն Հռաքելի, եւ նորա ծրարեալ ընդ կապերտիւ, նստեր ի վերայ նորա, եւ ասէ. «Մի՛ բարկանար, տէ՛ր իմ, թէ ոչ ելանեմ քեզ, զի պատահեաց ինձ ըստ կանացի աւրինի»: Եւ գնաց ի նմանէ: Սրտմտել Յակոբայ ասէ. «Ընդէ՞ր ասիր զինէն գող», ասէ Լաբան. «Կարող եմ սպանանել զքեզ եւ զամենայն առնուլ ի քէն, բայց ի միւս գիշերի ասաց ցիս Տէր չսպանանել զքեզ: Արասցուք դաշինս, զի մի՛ անցցես զսահմանս զայս եւ ոչ ես, եւ ոչ ածցես այլ կանայս ի տուն քո ի վերայ դստերաց իմոց»: Եւ երդուան⁵⁰ ուխտիւ:

53/ Դարձաւ Լաբան ի տուն իւր, եւ Յակոբ եւ իւրքն անցին ընդ գետոն: Իսկ ինքն մնաց յետոյ եւ զատեմարտեցաւ ընդ հրեշտակի, որ այնպես ուներ զնա, զի ոչ կարեր երթալ: Եւ ասէ ցնա հրեշտակն. «Թո՛ղ զիս, քանզի մերձեցաւ առաւատ տուընջեան», եւ ասէ. «Ոչ թողից քեզ, եթէ ոչ աւրհնեցես/fol 17r /{ցես}⁵¹ զիս», եւ ասէ

---

48. Written over some other word.
49. Dittography of the first letter.
50. ու above line p.m.
51. This repetition of the last syllable of fol 16v on fol 17r is a dittography.

հրեշտակն. «Զի՞նչ անուն է քո»։ Ասէ. «Յակոբ», եւ[52] ասէ. «Ոչ կոչեցիս այսուհետեւ Յակոբ, այլ Իսրայէլ եղիցի անուն[53] քո. թէ ժուժկալեցեր ընդ Աստուծոյ, յայսմ հետէ մի երկիցես[54] յեղբաւրէ քումմէ», եւ թողեալ զնա:

54/ Բաժանեաց գործիս, եւ գօտայս, եւ զադախնայս,[55] եւ զանասունս, եւ զամենայն զոյս հօյս հօյս, եւ ասէ. «Թէ հարցէ զմին, վիրկեցցի միւսն», եւ արար առանձինն չոկա, զորս կամէր տալ Եսաւայ։ Եւ հրամայեաց նոցա, զի թէ ոք հարցանիցէ ցիս, թէ զի՞նչ իցեն, ասասցեն. «Ծառայի Եսաւայ են»։ Պատահեաց Յակոբայ Եսաւ ի Քէմոն եւ ի Սեմիր։

55/ Եհարց զնա թէ. «Ո՞ւմ իցեն այնոքիկ», եւ ասէ. «Ծառայի քո Յակոբայ, զոր Տէր ետ ինձ»:[56] Առ պայդ ամենայն, զի քո են»։ Եւ ոչ կամէր առնուլ, բայց առ զոմանս յոչխարաց։ Եւ համբուրեաց զնա եւ ելաց ի վերայ պարանոցին Յակոբայ։ Եւ ասէ. «Եկից ընդ քեզ չորեքհարիւր արամբքս այսրիպս»։ Եւ ասէ. «Ոչ, քանզի մանկունքս մատաղ են եւ անասնոց ձնունդք խառնեալ են։ Թէ ստիպեմ զսոսա, մեռանին»:

56/ Եւ ասէ. «Արձակեցից զընկերս ի ճանապարհի եւ ես եկից ընդ քեզ», եւ ասէ. «Ոչ, այլ երթ ի խաղաղութիւն։ Տեսի զե<ր>եսս[57] քո. իբրեւ զհրեշտակի»։ Մեկնեցան ի միմեանց, Յակոբ գնաց ի Սադէմ:

57/ Ասէ Դինա դուստր նորա. «Երթայց ի քաղաքն եւ տեսից զկանայս քաղաքին»։ Տեսեալ զնա Սիքէմ որդի Եմովրայ արքային{ային}[58] այնորիկ, սիրեաց եւ զիտեաց[59] զնա։ Եւ ասէ. «Կամիմ զսա ի կնութիւն», ասացաւ Յակոբայ։ Ասէ Յակոբ. «Այսպիսի սովորութիւն է առ մեզ, ո ոք կամի առնուլ կանայս ի մէնջ, թլփատի»։ Եւ հրամանաւ թագաւորին թլփատեցան ամենայն արք քաղաքին:

58/ Յերրորդումն աւուր ի զարնալ ցաւուն, Ռուբէն եւ Շմաւոն արշաւեցին ի քաղաքն եւ զամենայն մեծամեծան սատակեցին։ Բարկացեալ Յակոբայ ասէ. «Ընդէ՞ր արարէք։ Յարուցէք զքանանացիս ի վերայ իմ»։ Սակայն պաշտպանելովն Աստուծոյ ոչ ինչ չարիք հասին նոցա:

---

52. Above line, p.m.
53. An erasure follows ՟ն1°.
54. ի2° over է, p.m.
55. եւ զադախնայս is surmounted by two diacritical marks. Their purpose is unclear.
56. Erasure of a short word follows. Unclear.
57. Correcting an orthographic error, զեսսս.
58. The word is արքային and there is a dittography of the last five letters.
59. This verbal form is anomalous.

59/ Չուեաց անդի եւ եկն ի Բեթէլ, անդ կանգնեաց սեղան, մատոյց պատարագ, ուր ասացաւ նմա. «Բազմացուցից զզօակք քո»: Անդի չոգո ի Լուզա, անդ մեռաւ <Դ>եփովրայ,[60] դայեակն Հռեբեկայ, եւ անդի գնաց ի Բեթլէհէմ, որ է / fol 17v / Եփրաթայ: Անդ ծնաւ Բենիամին ի Հռաբէլայ, եւ մեռաւ Հռաբէլ: Անդ գտաց Ռոբէն[61] գիարձ հօր իւրոյ զԲալլա. այս է ոչ անգիտանալով հաւրն,անդի չոգաւն ի Մամբրէ,[62] ուր էրն Իսահակ, որ իբրեւ զոյր ամաց ՃՁ.ից (180) մեռաւ:

60/ Եսաւ ունէր Բ.ուս (2) կանայս, եւ բազում որդիս, եւ կոչեցօ Եդոմ եւ Սէիր: Ասէ Մովսէս գծնունդս նորա եւ որդւոց նորա, եւ թոռանց նորա, եւ այնպէս թողու անդէն, եւ ասէ, թէ ուր բնակեցանն: Միրէր Յակոբք գՅովսէփ,[63] քան զայլ որդիս: Եւ արար նմա պատմուճան ծաղկեա, որ պահէր գիաւտա ընդ եղբաւրս:

61/ Մի անգամ մատնեաց գեղքարան առ հայր իւր վասն յանցանաց չարաց, այսինքն՝ ի սոդոմական կամ յանասնական: Ի գիշերի միում եւեւս{եւ}[64] երազ, զի յանդի հնձէր առ եղբարս իւր, որ այս էր, զի երկիրպագին խրձունք եղբարցն իւրում խրձանն: Եւ իբրեւ ասաց, սրտմտեցան եղբարքն ի վերայ նորա եւ ասեն. «Մի՞ թէ թագօրել կամիս ի վերայ մեր, կամ հնազանդ լիցուք հրամանաց քոց»:

62/ Ի միւս գիշերի եւեւս այլ երազ եւ ասաց հօր իւրոյ. «Տեսի զարեգակն եւ զլուսին, եւ մետասան աստեղս, զի երկրպագէին[65] ինձ», սաստեաց նմա հայրն, սակա[յ]ն միտ դնէր, թէ զի՞նչ նշանակիցէ այն: Յաւուր միում յղեաց գնա հայր իւր առ եղբարան եւ ասէ. «Ե՞րբ առ եղբարա քո եւ տե՛ս, թէ բարւն ք իցէ նոցա»:

63/ Չոգաւ, եգիտ հովիւս եւ եհարց, թէ տեսի՞ն գնոսա: Եւ ասեն. «Տեսաք, զի երթային ի Դովթային»: Գնաց եւ եգիտ գնոսա, տեսին գնա եւ ասեն. «Ահա երազահանն[66] գայ. եկայք սպանցուք գնա եւ տեսցուք, թէ զինչ լինիցին նմա երազքն իւր»: Ասէ Ռոբեն.[67] «Արկցուք գնա ի ջրհորս հին եւ մի սպանցուք գնա, զի մարմին եւ արիւն մեր է»: Եւ անցանէին խմայելացիքն, եւ բարձեալ էին ստաշխին, եւ երթային

---

60. The text has, erroneously, Սեփովր 'Sebovra.'
61. Sic! compare §63 below.
62. ք below line p.m.
63. Eras. one letter precedes.
64. Dittography of the second syllable եւ in the manuscript.
65. է above line, p.m.
66. There are two diacritical marks over the middle of this word.
67. Sic!

յեգիպտոս: Եւ վաճառեցին զնա նոցա Լ. (30) արծաթոյ: Զոր տարեալ յեգիպտոս վաճառեցին զնա Փուտիփարայ՝ ներքինոյ փարաւնի:⁶⁸

64/ Զոգալ յետ այնորիկ Յուդա առ ջրհո{ւ}րն⁶⁹ եւ ոչ եգիտ, եւ ասէ. «Պատանին ոչ երեւի, եւ ես, յո՞ երթայց»:⁷⁰ Առին զպատմուճան նորա, թաթաւեցին յարիւն, եւտուն գպատանի եւ յղեցին ցհայրն: Ետես զայն հայրն, լայր եւ ասէր. «Պատմուճանն որ/ fol 18r /դլոյ իմոյ է. գազան չար եկեր զորդեակն իմ»: Կամէին մխիթարել զնա, եւ ասէ. «Ոչ մխիթարեցայց, այլ իջից ի դժոխս հանդերձ սգով որդլոյ իմոյ»:

65/ Զոգալ յայնմ ժամանակի Յուդայ առ Իրամ Ողողումացի, տեսեալ զՍուէ,⁷¹ սիրեաց զնա եւ առ ի կնութիւն, յորմէ ծնաւ երիս որդիս՝ զՄէ, զՕնան, եւ զՀէլա,⁷² ետ կին՝ էրա, անուն Թամար. որ մեռո անզաւակ, քանզի անաւրէն էր ընդդէմ Աստուծոյ: Եւ առ զնա Օնան, զի այնպիսի սովորութիւն էր առ նոսա, զի թէ մեռանէր ոք անզաւակ, յարուցանէր նմա զաւակ եղբաւրն երկրորդ, բայց նա ոչ կամէր առնել զայն, այլ հեղոյր զսերմն յերկիր, եւ վասն այնորիկ սատակեցաւ եւ նա անդրի: Ասէ Յուդայ ցԹամար. «Լինի տան քում մինչեւ աճեցէ որդին իմ Սէլայ»:

66/ Յաւուր միում երթայր Յուդայ ի կտուրս խաշանց ընդ Իրամ: Լուաւ Թամար, գերծ գհանդերձս այրութեան եւ զգեցաւ հանդերձս բոզի, եւ էր ի ճանապարհին, ընդ որ անցանելոց էր: Տեսեալ զնա կարծեաց, թէ բոզ իցէ, ասէ. «Ննջեա՝ ընդ իս», եւ ասէ. «Զի՞նչ տացես»: Եւ ասէ. «Ուլ մի յայծեաց». Եւ ասէ. «Տո՛ ւր ինձ գրաւական, զգաւազանդ եւ զգի<ն>դդ⁷³ եւ զմատանիդ», եւ ետ: Եւ դարձեալ ի տուն, յղէր նմա ուլ փոխանակ գրաւականացն, եւ նա ոչ գտեալ զնա, դարձոյց առ նա ի տուն: Եւ ասէ Յուդայ. «Ոչ կարասցէ զիս խաբել ստութեամբ»:

67/ Եւ սկսաւ այտնուլ որովայն նորա, պատմեցաւ Յուդայի եւ ասէ. «Քարկոծեցից»: Իբրեւ կամէին քարկո{ր}ծել⁷⁴ զնա, ասէ. «Ուրեմն այտրիկ նա յղացոյց զիս», «արդարագոյն, քան զիս ես, զի ոչ կամեցայ տալ քեզ զՍէլայ»:

---

68. ա1° over erasure.
69. Orthographic error of the scribe.
70. Word for word from Gen 37:30.
71. Diacritical mark over the զ-.
72. Diacritical mark over the զ-.
73. This emendation is required both by sense—զզիդդ does not exist—and by the parallel in Gen 38:18 which is զինդդ.
74. Scribal error for քարկոծել.

11. FROM ABRAHAM TO JACOB

Իսկ ի ծնընդեան իբրեւ կամէր ելանել Զարա, ձգեաց զձեռն իւր աղջիկն եւ կապեաց ի բազուկ նորա կարմիր, եւ նա քարշել յետս, ել Փարէզ:

68/ Ասացաք յաղագս Յովսեփիա, թէ վաճառեցաւ ներքինոյն: Իսկ նա եղ զնա իշխան ի վերայ տան իւրոյ: Յօուր միում մինչդեռ գոյր կին նորա ընդ նմա ի տան, կալաւ զնա զգօշակէ հանդերձին եւ ասէ. «Ննջեա՛ ընդ իս»: Իսկ նորա փախուցեալ եթող զպատմուճան[75] իւր ի ձեռի[76] նորա: Եւ նա վագվագակի ամբաստան եղեւ զնմանէ առ առն իւրում, թէ խաղ արար զնա, եւ այնու պատճառաւ եղաւ ի բանդի:

69/ Սակայն բանտապետն եղ զնա ի վերայ կալանաւորացն, որ ի բանդին: Յայնժամ եղան անդ տակառապետն արքայի եւ մատակարարն, եւ տեսին / fol 18v / նորա երազս. տակառապետն ետեւ երիս բարունակս եւ ի նոսին[77] ծաղիկս եւ խաղողս: Ճմլեր զնոսա ի բաժակն[78] փարաւոնի եւ տայր ըմպել նմա: Պատմեաց Յովսեփիա, եւ թարգմանեաց նմա. գերիս բարունակս՝ գերիս օուրս, յետոյ՝ կացուցից ի տեղի քում:

70/ Իսկ մատակարարն պատմէր զիւրն, զի ունէր երիս խանս ի գլուխ իւր, եւ վերնումն յամենայն խորտկաց, որք կարէն լինել արուեստիւ խոհարարութեան, եւ թօչունք ուտէին զնոսա: Ասէ. «Երեք խանքն երեք աւուրք են. կախեսցիս զփայտէ, եւ թօչունք կերիցեն զմարմին քո»: Եւ ասէ գտակառապետն. «Յիշեա՛ զիս, զի հանցես յայսմ բանտէ»: Իսկ նա մոռացաւ մինչեւ յերկուս ամս:

71/ Յորժամ ետեւ փարօոն երազ, զի տեսանէր է. (7) երինճս[79] պարարտս, զի ելանէին ի գետնոյն.[80] եւ է. (7) ոսինս, զի ուտէին զառաջինսն, եւ է. (7) հասկս ի փնջի միում ատոքս, եւ նօյնքան ազազունս, որք կլանէին զառաջինսն: Զամենայն զիտունս թագաւորութեան իւրոյ ժողովեալ, ոչ ոք կարաց թարքմանել: Յայնժամ յիշեաց տակառապետն զՅօվսէփի եւ պատմեաց նմա, թէ որպէս լեալ էր:

72/ Արձակեալ ի բանտէն մեկնեալ զերազն ասելով. «է. (7) երինջքն զերք՝ է. (7) ամք են առատութեան, եւ է. (7) սինքն՝ է. (7) ամք

---

75. An erasure of one letter follows.
76. This is the Medieval Armenian oblique case of this word.
77. խաղողս erased following this word. The word itself is read as a deviant spelling of նոսին.
78. ա1° above the line p.m.
79. Diacritical mark over ճ, and ջ in the margin. See Stone and Hillel, "Index" no. 86.
80. գետնոյն "ground" is clearly corrupt for գետոյն "river." See Gen 41:1.

սովոյ. նոյնպէս յաղագս հասկին»:[81] Հաճոյ թուեցաւ թագաւորին, եւ եդ մանեակ ի պարանց նորա եւ նստոյց ի կառս, եւ արար զնա իշխան ամենայն թագաւորութեան իւրոյ: Եւ Յովսէփ հրամայեաց ամենայն ցաւառացն, զի ամենայն արմտեաց դիցեն զԵ.երորդ (5) մասն ի համարս արքային յիւրաքանչիւր ամի: Ի հասանել ժամանակի սովոյն, երթային ամենեքեան առ Յովսէփ, զնել ի նմանէ:

73/ Լուեալ Յակոբ, յղեաց զորդիս իւր յԵգիպտոս զնել ցորեան: Եւ չոգան առ նա: Եհարց զնոսա. «Ուստի՞ իցէք»: Ասացին. «Որդիք եմք ամենեքեան հօր միում ծերունոյ յերկրին քանանացոց, ունիմք եղբայր մի այլ, եւ միւսն մեռաւ»: Ասէ. «Ոչ այդպէս է, այլ արբ լրտես էք դուք», եւ առաքեաց զնոսա ի բանդ: «Ո՛չ ապաքէն ասին ձեզ՝ մի սպանցուք զեղբայր մեր զՅովսէփ»: Եւ արձակեաց զնոսա անդի, եւ հրամայեաց լնուլ ի քուրձս նոցա եւ դնել զարծաթս ի բերանս քրձիցն:

74/ Եւ <աս>աց[82] զնոսա. «Թողէ՛ք առ իս զՇմաւոն եւ երբիչիք ածէք ինձ զԲենիամին»: Եւ թողեալ զնա, զնացին: Եւ ասէին / fol 19r / ցհայրն, զոր պատահեաց նոցա. եւ կամին ածել զԲենիամին առ Յովսէփ: Ասէ Յակոբ. «Յի՞մ վերայ եկն այս ամենայն. ոչ տաց ձեզ. մինն մեռաւ, եւ Շմաւոն ի կապանս. ոչ տաց ձեզ»: Սակայն ի գօրանալ սովոյն, ասէ Յուդայ. «Երդնում քեզ, զի թէ ոչ ածցուք զդայ առ քեզ, եղիցուք մեք[83] մեղապարտք առ Աստուած եւ առ մարդիկք»: Եւ անսաց նոցա:

75/ Գնացին առ[84] Յովսէփ, եւ նա հրամայեաց առժամայն պատրաստել կերակուր նոցա: Եւ նոքա կարծէին, թէ կամի յղել զնոսա ի բանդ: Եւ ասեն. «Զարծաթ քո դարձուցաք այսէն եւ այլ ունիմք»: Ասէ. «Արծաթ իմ ընդ իս է», եւ եհան զՇմաւոն արտաքս: Էին եգիպտացիքն ի մի կողմանէ, եւ նոքա ի միւսն. բաշխէր նոցա զկերակուրն: Եւ զկնի կերակրոյն արար որպէս յառաջնումն, եւ ի քրձի Բենիամենի ետ դնել զկախատակն իւր:

76/ Եւ ի զնայն նոցա յղեաց դարձուցանել զնոսա, «Զի զողացան,- ասէ, զկախատակն»: Եւ դարձան առ նա, եւ գտեալ զբաժակն քրձին Բենիամենի ասէ Յովսէփ. «Ընդէ՞ր գողացարուք զկխոտակն, յորում սովոր էի հմայել. մնացէք առ իս այն, առ որում բաժակն գտաւ»: Սկսան լալով պատմել յաղագս հօրն եւ ամենայնի, եւ եղբաւրն մեռելոյ: Եւ ասէ. «Ո՞չ է ձշմարիտ: Ես եմ Յովսէփն, զոր վաձառեցէքն յեզիպտոս: Մի՛ երկնչիք, երթայք առ հայրն մեր[85] եւ ածէք զնա առ իս:

77/ Առեալ էր Յովսէփ կին եւ ծնեալ էր զԵփրեմ եւ զՄանասէ:
Չոգան եւ ասեն զամենայն, նա, իբրու զարթուցեալ ի քնոյ, ասէ. «Շատ է ինձ տեսանել զորդին իմ»: Եկն Յակոբ, ընդ յառաջ ել Յովսէփի Սիւքեմ եւ ասէ. «Ասացէ՛ք գթացողըն, թէ տեարք հովիւք եմք»: Չոգան առ թագաւորն եւ եհարց, թէ. «Զի՞նչ իցեն», եւ ասացին, որպէս ասաց Յովսէփին: Եւ բանիլ Յովսէփայ խնդրեցին զԳեսեմ, ուր եւ բնակեցան իսկ: Եւ վաղվաղակի ետ նոցա.

78/ ի սաստկանալ սովուն յառաջնումն ամի ետուն զոսկի եւ զարծաթ, յերկրորդումն՝ զանասունս, յերրորդումն՝ զատացուածս, եւ այլպէս ոչ ինչ մնաց նոցա: Եւ ապա ստացաւ Յովսէփ զանձինս նոցա ծառայս փարաւոնի: Եւ եհան հրաման Յովսէփի, զի յամենայն ամի իւրաքանչիւր ոք զե.երորդ (5) մասն արկցէ ի համառն փարաւոնի, բայց ի քրմացն, որք առնուին ձրի ռոճիկս յարքայէն:

79/ Ապրեցաւ Յակոբ ընդ որդիսն իւր յեզիպտոս, / fol 19v / Է. եւ Ժ. (17) ամս: Եւ են ամենայն աու[ր]ք կենաց նորա ՃԽԷ. (147) ամք: Կոչեաց Յակովբ զորդի իւր զՅովսէփի եւ ասէ. «Երդուեաց ինձ, զի թաղեցես զոսկերս իմ ի Քանան», եւ երդուաւ նմա: Եւ կոչեաց զամենայն որդիս իւր եւ ասէ. «Լուարուք որդիք Յակոբայ եւ ծանուցից ձեզ, զոր ինչ լինելոց են յուրս յետինս»: Եկին իւրաքանչիւր մի ըստ միոջէ, ետ զարհնութիւն իւր:

80/ Ի մերձենալ վախձանի մահու ած Յովսէփ զերկուս որդիս իւր՝ զՄանասէ եւ զԵփրեմ, զի աւրհնեցէ զնոսա, եւ զՄանասէ յաջոյ կողմանէ, զի աւրհնեցէ զնա յառաջագոյն, եւ զԵփրեմ յահեկէ: Իսկ նա կցեալ զբազուկն եդ զձեռն ի վերայ փոքրուն: Ասէ Յովսէփի. «Մի այդպէս»: Ասէ. «Գիտեմ, որդեա կ իմ, զինչ առնեմ», եւ այնպէս աւրհնեաց զնոսա: Մեռաւ Յակոբ, եւ տարան զոսկերս նորա ի Քանան, եւ թաղեցին յայրին կրկնում:

81/ Ասացին որդիքն Յակոբայ ցՅովսէփի. «Ծառայք քո եմք. ,զի՞նչ արասցուք», քանզի երկնչէին ի նմանէ, եւ ասէ ցնոսա. «Մի՛ երկնչիք, զի ցտարիս ձեր դարձոյց Աստուած ի բարի ձեր: Արդ ասեմք, զի կկրելոց էք հալածանս յերկրիս այսմիկ, յորժամ այց արասցէ ձեզ Աստուած, տարջիք զոսկերս իմ յերկիրն խոստման»: Եւ եղեւ այնպէս:

---

85. A following ի has been erased.

Translation

1/ ... Abraham, Aram, and Nahor.[86] Aram begot Lot[87] and two daughters, Sarah and Milchah.[88] Aram died,[89] Abraham married[90] Sarah and Nahor, Milchah.

2/ At that time the Egyptians worshipped fire. And because Abraham and Nahor did not wish to worship (it), they were cast[91] into fire. Nahor died[92] and Abraham was saved. As concerns Terah, it is unknown whether he worshipped.[93]

3/ And Abraham and Lot remained. Abraham's father was told by God to go forth from the land. And he went forth[94] and he came to Haran, where Terah died. And there, it was said to him,[95] "Go forth from your land, etc."[96] Thenceforth, he had gone forth. "Go forth" means, have no wish to return.[97] And they came to the land of Canaan.[98]

---

86. Gen 11:26–27
87. Gen 11:27.
88. Gen 11:28. From Abraham to Jacob replaces Lot's daughter, Iscah, with Sarah.
89. Here an early death of Aram (thus Haran is called in many Armenian texts) is mentioned. According to the Armenian Abraham apocrypha, he burned because of his idolatry. In From Abraham to Jacob, also Nahor is assigned an early death, see §2 here.
90. Literally, "took."
91. Literally: they cast them.
92. This seems to be related to the story of Abraham who was thrown into the fire by Nimrod (Gen. Rab. 38:28). According to the Midrashic tradition, however, it was Haran (Aram), not Nahor, who was thrown into the fire. Haran saw that Abraham survived the fire and decided to ally with him, hoping that if he too would be thrown into the fire, he would also be saved. Nimrod indeed threw him into the fire, but he burned to death. In another Armenian tradition Aram (there he is called Achan) died "because he made the begetting of the mule" which miscegenation is seen as blameworthy; Stone, *Abraham*, 64. A further variant about Aram (Armenian for Haran) is that he was idolatrous and died falling into a fire in an idolatrous temple. Haran's death is explicit in Gen 11:28, which says that he died before his father Terah. The idea that Abraham overcame many trials and remained faithful is, of course, derived from Gen 22:1. This notion is already taken up in Jdt 8:26; 1 Macc 2:52; and Heb 11:17. A work enumerating the ten trials of Abraham has been published in Stone, *Abraham*, 204–5. The theme is also taken up in Step'anos Siwnec'i, *Commentary on Genesis* 2.2.46 (Stone, *The Genesis Commentary by Step'anos of Siwnik'*, 60–63).
93. This is a learned remark, like many that will be signaled.
94. Gen 11:31. The language here evokes Gen 12:1, which is also a "going forth" but in this instance directed to Abraham.
95. This is, to Abraham.
96. Gen 12:1, 4.
97. Another learned remark.
98. Gen 12:5.

11. FROM ABRAHAM TO JACOB

4/ There was a terrible famine.[99] They went to Egypt, where it was very fruitful. And while they were going, he said to his wife, "Do not say, I beg, that you are my wife, but a sister."[100] They told the king about her: he took her and kept (her).[101] But the saints[102] say that he did not draw near to her, for their religion was to keep women for one year, and then to have intercourse with them in the bath-house.[103]

5/ He was smitten with a great blow, and thus it was related to him: "She is his wife."[104] And he said, "Why did you deceive me?" And he said, "I feared lest, if I were to say that she is (my) wife, you would kill me on account of her." And he returned her with many gifts. And he[105] returned to the promised land!"[106]

6/ Lot's shepherds began to argue with his (i.e., Abraham's) shepherds.[107] Because of that he said to him, "Look to the east and take that area, and if not, to the west and I will take the other." He looked thence at the neighboring areas and took Sodom and Gomorrah. And Abraham (took) the promised land.[108]

7/ And it was said to him,[109] "I will give you and your offspring from the east and from the west," but it was not given to him, but to his offspring. He built an altar there and offered a sacrifice.[110]

8/ At that time four kings arose against the five kings who were living in Sodom and in Gomorra, in Zoar, in Semē,[111] and in Adamē.[112] Why?

---

99. Gen 12:10.
100. Gen 12:13.
101. Gen 12:15.
102. Presumably some Patristic commentators.
103. Reading as if the word were բաղանիք. This orthographic variant լ/ղ is not rare: a common example is the spelling այղ encountered in some manuscripts for այլ, and many other examples occur. I have not been able to account for the origin of this tradition about the bathhouse.
104. Gen 12:17. This is already taken up in 1QapGen ar XX.21–34.
105. That is, Abraham.
106. Gen 12:18–20.
107. Gen 13:7.
108. Gen 13:7–12.
109. That is to Abraham. This sentence is an exegetical remark.
110. Gen 13:14–15. The building of an altar is mentioned in Gen 13:18, where he built it by the oaks of Mamre, and there the sacrifice is not mentioned. On Abraham's building three altars and not offering sacrifices, see Step'anos Siwnec'i, *Commentary on Genesis* 2.1.31–33 (ed. Stone, *The Genesis Commentary by Step'anos of Siwnik'*).
111. See Gen 14:1–2. Semē corresponds to Zeboiim, there.
112. Gen 14:1–3.

Because those five kings had been giving tribute to Chedorlaomer[113] who was the senior to those four kings, for twelve years. And in the thirteenth[114] year they withheld it. And in the fourteenth, they gathered against them and they destroyed their villages and fortresses.[115] And these, having gone forth against them, were overcome.[116] And Lot, since he was dwelling with them, was taken captive with all (his) goods.[117]

9/ It was related to Abraham about his brother's son, who was in captivity.[118] He summoned his three hundred and eighteen household (warriors) and pressed after them. He freed Lot and brought back all the booty.[119]

10/ On his return, Melchizedek the priest of God Most High, went to meet him, offering the youths[120] bread and wine for food. And he[121] offered him tithes of everything which he had seized.[122] The king of Sodom heard about his victory, went forth to meet him and said, "Everything which you took, is under your control." And Abraham said, "I raise up my hand to Heaven,[123] that I have taken nothing of those things which I seized from them, except for the food of those who were with me, and that they took a portion."[124]

11/ Then it was told to him by the angel, "Fear not, for I will make you a great nation/tribe."[125] And he said, "How will this be able to take place, for I

---

113. A direct transliteration of the Armenian reads: Kʻodoł[o]gomor, which is a transliteration of LXX Χοδολλογομορ. In Gen 14:4 the text says "served," interpreted by our author to mean "paid tribute."

114. The ordinal ending -երորդ is oddly separated from the number.

115. Observe that the descriptions of fortresses must have been drawn by the writer from his contemporary realities, as were the withholding of tribute in the thirteenth year and some other details.

116. Summarized from Gen 14:8–10.

117. Gen 14:12.

118. That is, Lot.

119. Gen 14:14–16.

120. That is, the household soldiers: see Gen 14:24 where Abraham styles them "young men." Unlike various other Christian texts, the author here makes no connection here of the bread and wine with the Eucharist. This is suggestive of the idea that this work wishes just to epitomize the biblical text.

121. Apparently, Abraham.

122. Gen 14:18–20. Although Melchizedek became such a central figure in biblical retellings and this meeting was greatly embroidered, here the author does not depart from the biblical narrative.

123. That is: I swear an oath.

124. Gen 14:21–24.

125. According to Gen 15:1, God spoke to Abraham in a vision, and not "the angel" as is related in the Armenian text. Also, in Gen 15:1 God promised to Abraham protection and reward, and not to make him "a great nation": Stone, *Abraham*, 52.

am old and I do not have a son?" He said, "You will have a son." Abraham said, "Is it not that Ełeazar of Damascus, son of a house-born one, is in charge in my house. He will be my heir."[126]

12/ The angel replied, "No, but you will have a son."[127] And he said, "What will be a sign (of it)?" "Take a three years old heifer, and a three years old female goat, and a three years old male goat, and a dove, and a turtle-dove, and cut them through the middle, and not the birds." And he did thus; and birds came and he caused them to fly off.[128] Towards evening fire came from heaven and consumed (them). And he said, "This will be a sign."[129]

13/ And after that, Sarah said to him, "Go in to my maidservant, so that you may have a son." He went in to Hagar his concubine, and she conceived.[130] Then she became unruly[131] against her mistress, as a result of which she (Sarah) became angry and said to Abraham, "You are being violent to me."[132] And Abraham said, "She is in your hands (power). Do as you will."[133]

14/ And she began to beat her and to punish her with a whip.[134] From this[135] she went forth and fled on the way. An angel encountering her, said, "Where are you going, Hagar?" and she said, "I am fleeing from the presence of my mistress." And the angel said, "Return to her and be humble under her and you shall have a son from whom twelve peoples shall come forth." She returned to her to the house,[136] she bore Ishmael, from whom there were twelve princes, and from them, twelve peoples.[137]

---

126. Gen 15:1–3.
127. Gen 15:4.
128. Literally: caused them to leap up; that is, to fly off.
129. The section is based on Gen 15:9–11, 17. The prophecy to Abraham of the land is omitted. The same omission was remarked upon in Stone, *Abraham*, 15–16.
130. Gen 16:2,
131. Literally: kicked up her heels.
132. This apparently means "violent by the means of Hagar": compare Gen 16:5. That interpretation is somewhat forced and perhaps the verb should be third pers., and so: "she is being violent to me."
133. Gen 16:16:4–6.
134. Whipping is also specified in Step'anos Siwnec'i, *Commentary on Genesis* on this verse, §131, but is not in the Bible.
135. Or: as a result of this.
136. Hagar's first flight and return are narrated in Gen 16:6–9. The mention of twelve peoples here is harmonizing with Gen 25:12–15. This is, once more, a fruit of scholarly activity.
137. Gen 16:10 relates the birth and naming of Ishmael. His twelve descendants are enumerated in Gen 25:12–15

15/ At that time it was said to Abraham to circumcise his uncircumcised body, and those of his house-born.[138] "Indeed, whoever I did not circumcise, that soul shall pe[r]ish from my people."[139] That is, he will perish. And it was said to him that his family/tribe would be in Egypt for four hundred years and how they would be saved and concerning the plagues of Egypt and the splitting of the Red Sea.[140]

16/ At that time, three angels came to him, in human form. He saw three and prostrated himself to one,[141] for one of them seemed greater. And he prepared a banquet,[142] that is calf, a loaf of bread, and other things.[143] Towards evening, one said, "Where is Sarah, your wife?" And he said, "Lord, (she is) in the tent." And the angel said, "Sarah will have a son." And she, hearing (that), laughed behind the door. And he said, "Why did you laugh?" and she said, "Lord, I laughed not."[144] And he said, "Fear not, Sarah, because unknown

---

138. Gen 17:10–13. Note that the preceding verses, promising a multitude of descendants and the gift of the land are omitted. On this see p. 99 n. 129. The punishment specified in Gen 17:14 is "cutting off" and that verse is cited here, excerpted from the Armenian Bible.

139. Gen 17:14.

140. The first part of this sentence refers to the vision in Gen 15:13, while the second part is a learned comment with summary of future related events. These were considered to be alluded to in Gen 15:14. The "covenant between the pieces" (Gen 15:9–16) is one of the contexts to which later writers often attributed a more extended and detailed revelatory vision than is reported in Genesis. That is the case here. The promise of the land (Gen 15:18–21) is left aside.

141. See Gen 18:2 which has "three men," but in Gen 18:3 Abraham addresses "the angel" in the singular.

142. Literally: banquets.

143. Gen 18:6–8.

144. Gen 18:9–16.

word[145] of life, I shall return to you next year and Sarah will have a son." He spoke in human fashion.[146]

17/ Then Abraham's and Sarah's names were changed. Formerly, he was called Abram, which means, "high father,"[147] and after those things, he was called Abraham, which means "father of many nations/tribes." And Sarah was named Sarra.[148]

18/ Then in the morning they started to depart, and Abraham after them. And the angel[149] said to him, "I cannot hide from you that which I am going to do,[150] for I go to destroy Sodom and Gomorra; and their sins have reached up to the heavens."[151] And Abraham said, "Shall the righteous perish with the wicked? If there are to be found fifty righteous there, will he destroy it, nor if forty, nor if thirty, nor if twenty, nor if ten? No!"[152]

---

145. The word ուղեկցելով is not known but it may well be an orthographic variant of ուղեկից / -կցել means "to travel with, accompany." It is followed by կենաց "of life." This translates the Hebrew idiom כעת חיה, meaning "a year from now." That idiom is composed of the preposition kĕ-, the word for "time" and a derivative of the stem ḥyy "live." The LXX translate κατὰ τὸν καιρὸν τοῦτον εἰς ὥρας, the reading reflected in the Arm Bible which has in Gen 18:10 and 14 "in that time on this very day" ի ժամանակի յայսմիկ ի սոյն աւուրս. No variants are shown in Zeyt'unyan's edition: A. Zeyt'unyan, *The Book of Genesis* (Գիրք Ծննդոց), Monuments of Ancient Armenian Translations 1 (Erevan: Academy of Sciences, 1985). Our text, then, seems to derive from a reading that tried to translate the Hebrew stem ḥyy "live." In the Syriac text we read kd ḥy ḥy' which does reflect the word "to live." Also, Aquila cited in Barhebraeus has *dum tu vivis*: see John William Wevers, *Genesis: Septuaginta*, Vetus Testamentum Graece 1 (VandenHoeck & Ruprecht: Göttingen, 1974), 184.

146. This strengthen's the idea that the Lord is the central angel, which is the author's understanding of the three men.

147. The change of names is recorded in Gen 17:4-5. This etymological explanation is drawn from the *Onomastica Sacra*, such as is given in Franz Xavier Wutz, *Onomastica Sacra: Untersuchungen zum Liber Interpretationis Nominum Hebraeorum des Hl. Hieronymus*, TU 41/2 (Leipzig: Hinrichs, 1915), 850–51, 962–63. Note the confusion in the spelling of Sarah's name in this text: it appears as Սարայ, Սառայ, and Սառռայ. No etymology of Sarra is offered by the text here. See Stone, *Biblical Heroes*, 118.

148. Gen 17:5 (Abraham); Gen 17:15 (Sarah).

149. As often in this document, when the Bible has God as a speaker, the document has an angel: compare also §16.

150. Gen 18:16-17.

151. Gen 18:20. The expression "reached up to heavens" is based on Gen 18:21: compare Gen 4:10 and Rev 18:5.

152. Gen 18:23-32 retails Abraham's discussion with God.

19/ Only the two went[153] and they were by Lot's door. Lot grasped them and brought them into his house and invited them to dinner, for he thought that they were men.[154] And there came straightaway false prophets,[155] that is Sodomites, to Lot's house and said, "Bring out the men who entered your house so that we may know them."[156] And Lot said, "Do not do this unlawful thing to me, I beg. I have two daughters, take them."[157]

20/ And they wished to enter Lot's house. He held the door and did not permit to open (it).[158] The angel seized Lot and said. "Permit (them) to enter!" And he opened the door and they were smitten with blindness and with certain pains, which they saw but were unable to make choices."[159]

21/ And they said to Lot, "Go forth from this city, you and your relatives and your friends."[160] Lot went and said to them, "Go forth with me, for Sodom will be destroyed." And they made him a mockery.[161] And he himself and his wife and his two daughters went forth. And he commanded that no one should look back.[162] But, when his wife heard the thunder,[163] she looked back. And she became a pillar of salt.[164]

22/ And Lot said, "Where shall we go?" and they said, "To a mountain, to no other than Zoar (Segovr)." And they went.[165] But he was merry from wine.[166] After that, he said, "Let us go forth to a mountain." The daughters saw the cities destroyed; they said, "This whole race of all men has perished." The younger said to the elder, "Let us make him drunk and you draw near to him so he may know you and you will have offspring."

---

153. The Bible mentions two angels explicitly in Gen 19:1 and does not talk any more of the third angel after their visit to Abraham.
154. Gen 19:3 Angels were considered not to eat.
155. It is unclear why the writer would call the Sodomites, "false prophets."
156. Gen 19:5.
157. Gen 19:7–8.
158. Gen 19:9b–11.
159. The import of this last clause is unclear. The corresponding words in Gen 19:11 are "so that they were unable to find the door."
160. Gen 19:12.
161. Gen 19:13–14.
162. Gen 19:16–17.
163. Thunder is not mentioned in Genesis.
164. See Gen 19:26.
165. Gen 19:23 says that Lot came to Zoar. This bit of dialogue is an addition, and actually refers to events starting from Gen 19:30.
166. Conceivably, this phrase is misplaced and should occur later in the verse, in connection with his daughters.

23/ In the same fashion the elder one spoke and it took place in this fashion. Thus, Lot did not apprehend.[167] And the following evening, the younger one drew close (to him) and became pregnant with Moab, and the other one, with Ammon. It is said that the Moabites and the Ammonites (descend) from these.

24/ We said previously in the course of the separation of Abraham and Lot, that Abraham was living in the land of Canaan.[168] And he happened to go to another country,[169] where Abimelech[170] was king. When he was saying about Sarah that "she is my sister," Abimelech took her as wife.[171] However, he did not know her, as a result of this, for that the angel appeared to him in a dream and said, "You will die, for you took another man's wife in marriage."

25/ And Abimelech said, "Lord, I acted with rectitude." And the angel[172] said, "I know that you acted with rectitude. For that reason, I took care of you." Then he went forth in the morning, he related (this) to his manservants and maidservants, and he said to Abraham, "Why did you deceive me?" And he said, "I thought that you would kill me."[173]

26/ And he returned her to him with great possessions, that is: with sheep and cattle and other things.[174] Then, he gave Sarah one thousand silver pieces, so that with them she might buy a grave for herself and the other things needed for burial, and for all her needs.[175] And s/he returned to Canaan.

27/ At that time the Lord visited Abraham, having fulfilled the promise about a son, whom he called Isaac.[176] There were two brothers,[177] that is,

---

167. That is, that they had slept with him. These events, the latter part of §22 and §23 are related in Gen 19:31–36. In verses 37–38 of that chapter, the births of Moab and Ammon are related.

168. See above, §7. Another learned comment including a cross reference.

169. Presumably this is derived from "as an alien" (Gen 20:1).

170. The Armenian has in exact transliteration, Abamelikʻ. Abraham's settling there is related in Gen 20:1–2.

171. Gen 20:2–3.

172. Again, our text has "angel" for Genesis's "God" (20:6).

173. The incidents in this section are drawn from Gen 20:4–12.

174. Gen 20:14. In Gen 20:16 it is to Abraham that Abimlech gave a thousand pieces of silver.

175. The rest of Abimelech's speech is an expansion, presumably designed to smooth the narrative. This incident accounts for the money available to purchase the Cave of Machpelah, discussed below. Their return to Canaan is not mentioned at this point in Genesis. The expansion may well be the answer to a question: Whence did Abraham have four hundred shekels of silver to pay Ephron the Hittite? See Gen 23:16.

176. Gen 21:1–2.

177. That is, Abraham had two brothers.

Aran (Haran) and Nahor. Aran (Haran) died[178] and Nahor had eight sons. The eighth was Bathuel, who had a daughter, Rebecca.[179]

28/ Sarah died and there was no tomb. He asked that of the sons of Het (i.e., the Hittites) among whom was Hamor,[180] who said, "Take my tomb," and he wished to give this as a gift to him. And he gave him forty silver pieces, and he gave him the double cave and the field in which it was. And he buried her there.[181]

29/ After Sarah's death, Abraham summoned his servant and said to him, "Swear to me that you will not take a wife for my son, except from my family/tribe." And he swore to him and said, "If the woman will not wish to come, should I take your son to your (home)land?" And he said, "No!"[182]

30/ And the servant took ten camels and he loaded (them) with the good things of that land, and he began to go to Abraham's (home)land, in which Nahor lived.[183] But, before he entered the city, he began to think to himself and to say, "Lord, make it so that the girl who will go forth from this city, from whom I will ask water, she will come and be my lord's."[184]

31/ And behold, Rebecca came immediately to the well where he was. And the servant said, "Give me to drink!" and she gave to him and to his camels. And he asked her if she had lodgings, and she said, "There are our lodgings and fodder for the beasts."[185] And he entered the city. And she went ahead and told her father. Her father greeted him and he brought the camel into the house, and gave them food.[186]

32/ And he wished in this same way to give him all their needs, and he did not accept. But he related everything, how he had come. And he said that he would not eat if he did not first ascertain whether she was willing to come

---

178. See §1, above.

179. Gen 22:23. Here the writer skips over three incidents: the banishing of Hagar and Ishmael, the covenant between Abraham and Abimelech, and the binding of Isaac.

180. This is a confusion of Hamor of Shechem and Ephron the Hittite. Genesis 23 tells of Abraham's purchase of the Cave of Machpelah from Ephron the Hittite, while Gen 33:9 relates that Abraham bought a plot of land from Hamor, father of Shechem. The two incidents of land purchase may have catalyzed the confusion of names in our text.

181. Sarah's death, the purchase of Machpelah, and Sarah's burial are related in Gen 23:2–19. In Gen 23:16 the price is four hundred silver shekels.

182. This section is parallel to Gen 24:1–8.

183. Gen 24:10.

184. Summary of Gen 24:12–14.

185. Gen 24:15–25. Gen 24:22 and 30 relate that he gave Rebecca a gold nose ring and two gold bands. In Step'anos Siwnec'i, *Commentary on Genesis*, 2.2.59–60 the encounter is handled quite differently.

186. Gen 24:28–33.

with him.[187] Her father summoned (her) and asked if she wished to come with him. And she said, "I am going, for this matter has issued from God."[188] Receiving her father's blessing, she went with him.[189]

33/ But, when she was near the land of his birth, she saw Isaac relaxing in a field, and she said, "Who is that?" And he (the servant) said, "He is your lord." She immediately descended from the camel and ornamented herself as much as she could and went to him.[190] And he married her and established (her) in the place of his mother.[191] Then Abraham married Keturah, who, according to some is Hagar and (according) to others is someone else.[192] And he begat many sons from her.[193]

34/ And Rebecca was barren, but through Isaac's prayers she conceived Esau and Jacob, who fought with one another in the womb.[194] Amazed at this, she asked the Lord,[195] "What is it?" and it was told to her that it is two persons[196] from whom two nations, Edomites and Israelites, were to issue, and the older shall serve the younger, that is, the Edomites, the Jews.[197]

35/ Rebecca said, "If this is destined to take place, it were better for me not to have a son."[198] And she bore Esau, and Jacob was grasping his heel. And Esau was reddish and a hunter and Jacob, smooth and staying at home.[199]

36/ One day, Esau returned from the field, disheartened and famished, and Jacob was cooking <a pot>[200] of lentils. And he (Esau) asked of him, and he (Jacob) said, "I shall not give you (it) if you do not give me the right of pri-

---

187. Gen 24:33–45 is summarized in the words "related everything."
188. This statement of Rebecca's in an addition to the biblical narrative.
189. Gen 24:58–59. A number of points of the biblical story in Gen 24:49–58 are omitted, and Rachel's immediate complaisance is stressed.
190. Gen 24:63–65.
191. Gen 24:67.
192. Observe the rallying of two different views.
193. Gen 25:1–4.
194. Gen 25:22.
195. This expression often means, "consulted an oracle." Compare Gen 25:22, "she went to inquire of the Lord." In some texts she is presented as consulting Melchizedek, who serves as an intermediary to both "the Lord" and "an oracle."
196. That is, she was carrying twins.
197. Gen 25:22-23.
198. Note that in Gen 25:22 Rebecca's question, "Why do I live?" is answered by the prophecy about the struggle between two nations. In the text here, first God tells Rebecca about the two nations, and later she says: "if this is destined to take place, it were better for me not to have a son." Compare Esau's statement in §36 which is based on Gen 25:32.
199. Gen 25:25–27.
200. The text has սապատուկ ասպն, which expression is not to be found in diction-

mogeniture." And he said, "Let it be yours, because" he said, "it is better for me to live than to die."[201] And thus he took (it) from him.[202] And Esau went out.

37/ Abraham died and left all his possessions to Isaac, and he gave other gifts to his other sons.[203] Moses[204] relates concerning Ishmael and speaks of his children, and then[205] he returns to Isaac, who went into Abimelech's place when the famine grew deeper. And he said this concerning his wife, that she was a sister. And nonetheless, no one drew near to her, etc.[206] And he (Abimelech) issued an order that no one should say any evil thing to them.[207] And he (Abraham) planted barley and gathered in one hundred-fold, at which they became angry with him and expelled (him) from (their) land.[208]

38/ And they filled up his wells with stones.[209] And he went to another place, and once more they filled his wells again. And again, for a third time, in the same fashion. And at that time, his shepherds fought with other shepherds.[210]

39/ The king remembered how he had driven him away. He went, and Melk'oł[211] his prince with him. Then when he (Isaac) saw (him) he said, "Why do you come? You drove me away and you filled up my well."[212] The king said, "I know that God is with you. Therefore, we wish to establish peace." And they swore to one another to keep the peace.

---

aries. ոսպն is "lentil" and սապատուկ seems to be a diminutive of սապատ "a little." It is not listed in the dictionaries.

201. Taking the verb as a misspelling of կեալ "to live."
202. Gen 25:29–33.
203. Gen 25: 5–6. The Armenian does not mention that Isaac and Jacob buried him in the Cave of Machpelah, see Gen 25:9–10.
204. For "Moses" designating the Pentateuch, see §60 below and the discussion in introductory remarks to this document, p. 79.
205. Literally: thus.
206. Again, note the characteristic marks of scholarly writing. The preceding sentences are very compressed, mainly just tags intended for a reader already familiar with the details of events. The words եւ այլն "etc." are in the manuscript.
207. See Gen 26:1–11, which passage tells the story of Rebecca and Abimelech.
208. Gen 26:12 and 16. The biblical text does not specify barley.
209. Gen 26:15.
210. Gen 26:18–22 has both the incidents—the digging of wells and Isaac's shepherds' fight with the Philistines.
211. This name derives apparently from Phicol in Gen 26:26. Note the scribe's confusions with the labial letters, see n. 38 above. Arm Gen 26:26 has Փիքոլ P'ik'oł, which is the normal transliteration of this form.
212. This is different in detail, but has the same point as Gen 2:27. Genesis 26:26–31 deals with the covenant he made with Abimelech.

40/ Isaac's eyes degenerated and he was unable to see.[213] He commanded Esau, whom he loved more, "Bring me (meat) from your hunting, my son, so that my soul may bless you before I shall die."[214] And Rebecca heard. She said to Jacob, whom she loved more, "Take two kids and make a stew for your father, so that he will bless you." He said, "I fear lest he bring a curse upon me, instead of a blessing." And she said, "That curse (be) upon me!"[215]

41/ She cooked the meat and covered[216] (his) hands and neck with the skins, and he put on his brother's cloak[217] and he offered (it) to his father. And he[218] said to him, "Thus, you have come quickly, my son," And he said, "It was God's will, father." And he said, "Come close hither so that I may be close to you." And he felt (him) and said, "Your hands (are) Esau's hands; your voice (is) Jacob's voice."[219]

42/ He ate and he said, "Give me a kiss, my son, so that I may bless you." He drew near (and) he (Isaac) kissed him and said, "Behold, the fragrance of my son is like the fragrance of a full field, which the Lord has blessed." He blessed him and he left.[220] Esau approached and said, "Arise, father, and eat of the game of your son." Then he was amazed, saying, "Your brother came by subterfuge and offered this stew, and my soul blessed him." And he, becoming angry, said, "First he took my right of primogeniture from me and now he has purloined my blessing. Do you not have a blessing, father?"[221]

43/ And he said, "I have blessed him, and let him be blessed forever.[222] From the dew of the heavens and from the fruitfulness of the earth will be your blessing."[223] And at once he (Esau) began to consider, "There will be the days of mourning for my father, and I will murder Jacob." At once his mother was informed and said to Jacob, "Go to Laban, my brother."[224]

---

213. Gen 27:1.
214. Gen 27:3–4.
215. Gen 27:7, 9–13.
216. Literally: "dressed."
217. Gen 27:14–17.
218. That is, Isaac.
219. Gen 27:19–22.
220. Gen 27:26–30a; the last two verses 29–30a are summarized in one clause.
221. Gen 27:31, 35, 38; reflecting these selected verses which advance the storyline.
222. See Gen 27:33. Here the blessing given Esau omits the statement that he will serve Jacob (Gen 27:29 and 27:40). This might be a deliberate degrading of Jacob's blessing which might also be behind the rearrangement of events in §35. Such a speculation, however, cannot explain the assertion of the validity of Jacob's blessing in §43; cf. Gen 27:33.
223. Gen 27:37, 39.
224. Gen 27:41–43.

44/ Esau married Ishmael's daughter.[225] Jacob went (away). When he was lodging for the night at Bethel, he put a rock under his head[226] and falling asleep, he saw a ladder erected and angels were climbing and descending. Awaking from sleep, he said, "Verily this is a place of God and I knew it not." And he set up the stone and anointed it with oil, and he built an altar there.[227] And rising up, he went to Haran.

45/ And before he reached Haran, he found shepherds who were watching the sheep and he asked about Laban and they said, "It is well with him. And behold, his daughter Rachel came." And she began to water the sheep. Jacob helped her to water (them), he kissed her and they went home together.[228]

46/ When Laban recognized him, he was happy and said, "I wish you to be with me." And he said, "I will be." And he said, "What wage will I set up for you?" And he said, "I will serve you for seven years in exchange for Rachel."[229] But in the end, when he (Laban) was obliged to give Rachel, in the night he gave Leah. On the following day, when he (Jacob) saw her (Leah), he said, "Why did you deceive me?" He was pained that she was bleary-eyed.[230]

47/ And he said, "Thus is the custom among us, that first I give the older to a husband. However, serve me for another seven years and I shall give you Rachel."[231] They celebrated Leah's marriage for seven days, and afterwards Rachel was given to him and her marriage to him was celebrated for another seven days.[232]

---

225. Gen 28:9; Jacob's departure is related in v. 10. Esau's two Hittite wives (Gen 23:34–35), Rebecca's excuse for sending Jacob to Haran, are not mentioned. Perhaps this is part of the tendency to devalue Jacob, this time by omitting a blameworthy act of Esau's.

226. Gen 28:11. His dream is described in 28:12–15.

227. Gen 28:18–19. God's promise of offspring and of the land which was given in the course of the Bethel vision, is omitted. A similar omission of such promises to Abraham has been noted elsewhere: see Stone, *Abraham*, 95. See the introductory remarks to the present text.

228. Jacob's arrival in Haran; Gen 29:1–10 gives the incident of the shepherds and Jacob's assistance to Rachel, while the present text simplifies it. In comparing with Step'anos Siwnec'i, *Commentary on Genesis* 2.2.56–60, one observes that there a much more complex treatment is to be found.

229. Gen 29:15–18.

230. Gen 29:23–25 tell of the deception. Most explanations says that Leah's eyes were afflicted, but the NRSV translation gives "lovely" (29:17).

231. Gen 29:26–27.

232. Gen 29:28.

11. FROM ABRAHAM TO JACOB

48/ And he dwelt with him (Laban) for fourteen years.[233] Jacob loved <Rachel> more than Leah.[234] And Leah had four sons and Rachel was barren.[235] And Rachel had a handmaiden. She said to Jacob, "Go in to my maidservant, Zilpah[236] and I will have a son." He went in and had two sons from her. Leah said, "Go in to my maidservant, Bilhah." He went in and had two sons.

49/ Reuben, Leah's son, returned from the field and he brought mandrakes. And Rachel said to Leah, "Give me of your son's mandrakes so that I may have sons."[237] And she said, "I will not give (them) to you if you do not give me your husband this night"—for he was due to go in to her that night. And she said, "Let him be yours."[238] She took and ate (them).[239] In the night, when Jacob wished to go in to Rachel, Leah said, "You shall not go in (to her), for I have you as a reward."[240] He went in to Leah and she conceived,[241] and thus he had two sons from her.[242] He knew Rachel after that and she had two sons.[243]

50/ When fourteen years were completed, Laban said, "Let us make an agreement, I and you. You will serve me and I will give you wages. Choose for yourself the beasts that are born dappled as long as you are with me." Jacob accepted the dappled ones.[244] Always, at the time of conception of the ewes, he would go to the pools where they would drink water; he would take sticks and peel them on one side and place (them) before them, and thus they bore only dappled ones.[245]

51/ He did thus on the first time, and on the second, not. For they lambed three times in a year. And after that they changed the agreement.[246] Then,

---

233. Gen 29:30 This is reformulated.
234. Gen 29:30.
235. Gen 29:32–35, 30:1.
236. In the Bible, Gen 30:7 names Rachel's maidservant, Bilhah. Zilpah is Leah's servant, see Gen 29:24. They are reversed here.
237. Gen 30:14.
238. Gen 30:15–16.
239. The biblical text does not say what Rachel did with the mandrakes. Here it says she ate them; cf. Gen 30:25.
240. Or: a payment.
241. Gen 30:16–17.
242. Gen 30:17, 19. Her daughter, Dinah, is not mentioned.
243. This is a summary of Gen 30:22–24.
244. This sentence is a brief epitome of Gen 30:25–36.
245. Jacob's stratagem is described in much more detail in Gen 30:37–42.
246. This is an awkward transition. The changing of the agreement is referred to by Jacob in his words to his wives in Gen 31:7.

when the seven years had finished, he began to return with his wives, his children, and his goods, unbeknownst to his father-in-law. Rachel took her father's idols with her.[247] When Laban learned (this), he pursued them and said, "Why have you done thus?"[248] "I feared lest you not permit me to go." And he said, "Why did you steal the idols?" Jacob said. "With whomsoever you find (them), (that person) shall die."[249]

52/ He sought and he did not find (them). He entered Rachel's tent, and it[250] was wrapped in a cloth. She was sitting on it, and she said, "Let my lord not be angry that I do not go forth to you, for it came upon me according to the way of women." And he went from her.[251] Jacob, becoming angry, said, "Why did you say of me 'thief'?" Laban said, "I can kill you and take everything from you, but last night[252] the Lord said to me not to kill you." Let us make an agreement that you will not cross this border, nor I. And you will not bring other wives to your house, over my daughters."[253] And they swore a covenant.[254]

53/ Laban returned to his home and Jacob and his own (folk) crossed the river. Then he himself remained behind and wrestled with an angel. He held him in such a way that he could not go (walk).[255] And the angel said to him, "Let me go, because the break of day approaches." And he said, "I will not let you go, unless you bless me." And the angel said, "What is your name?" He said, "Jacob." And he said, "You shall not be called henceforth Jacob, but Israel will be your name. If you acted courageously[256] with (respect to) God,[257] henceforth, do not fear your brother."[258] And he left him.

---

247. Gen 31:19.
248. Rewriting of Genesis.
249. Gen 31:30, 32.
250. Apparently, the idols.
251. Gen 31:34–35.
252. Assuming that մյուս, which means "other of two," although it usually refers to the future with the meaning "the next day" can also be taken as "the previous day." The event is mentioned in Gen 31:24.
253. Gen 31:50.
254. Described in Gen 31:44–49.
255. This is parallel to Gen 32:24–25, 31. Although the syntax is clumsy, it appears from the next phrase that Jacob was holding the angel.
256. Or: steadfastly.
257. This is an almost literal citation from Arm Bible, Gen 32:26–28.
258. While this blessing (not to fear Esau) is not in Gen 32:29–30, Jacob's fear of Esau is featured in Gen 32:7–11 and the biblical formulation of the blessing is: "for you have striven with God and with men, and have prevailed" (RSV).

54/ He divided (his) sons and servants and maid-servants and beasts and all his goods into different groups and he said, "If he smites one, the other will be delivered."[259] And he also made into separate groups those he wished to give to Esau. And he commanded them, "If someone asks me what they might be, they shall say, 'They are Esau's servant's.'"[260] Jacob encountered Esau in Hēmon and in Sēmir.[261]

55/ He asked him, "Whose are those?" And he said, "Your servant, Jacob's, which the Lord gave me. Take all this for they are yours."[262] And he did not want to take (them), but he took a few of the sheep.[263] And he kissed him and he wept on Jacob's neck.[264] And he said, "Let me come with you with these four hundred men." And he said, "No, for the children are tender and the time of birth is upon the beasts. If I hasten them, they will die."[265]

56/ And he said, "I shall send my companions on their way and I will come with you." And he said, "No, rather go for peace. I have seen your countenance, like an angel's." They separated from one another. Jacob went to Salēm.[266]

57/ Dinah, his daughter said, "I shall go to the city and I shall see the women of the city." Shechem, son of Hamor, king of that (city) saw (her), he loved her and had intercourse with (her).[267] And he said, "I wish to marry her." It was related to Jacob. Jacob said, "Our custom is such: whoever wishes

---

259. Gen 32:8.

260. This sentence does not make sense as it stands, mainly because of the confusion of person. The verse from Genesis that inspired it reads: [17] He instructed the foremost, "When Esau my brother meets you, and asks you, 'To whom do you belong? Where are you going? And whose are these ahead of you?' [18] then you shall say, 'They belong to your servant Jacob; they are a present sent to my lord Esau" (Gen 32:17–18). Different parts of the Genesis narrative, specifically the Jabbok and Mahanaim incidents, are cobbled together here in §§53–54.

261. These names are corrupted. Sēmir is doubtless "Seir," see Gen 33:16, but Hēmon remains mysterious.

262. The last sentence corresponds to Gen 33:11.

263. This is an expansion. The Bible text has "took it."

264. Gen 33:4, but there of their meeting.

265. This incident is found in Gen 33:12–14.

266. The incidents are in a somewhat different order in Gen 33:14–17, 10. The change seems of no particular importance. Perhaps read Uhıpłu "Shechem" in accordance with Gen 33:18.

267. Gen 34:1–2. Rape is not explicit.

to take[268] women of ours is circumcised." And, at the king's command all the men of the city were circumcised.[269]

58/ On the third day, when the pain[270] grew strong, Reuben and Simeon attacked the city and slaughtered all the prominent men of the city.[271] Jacob grew angry; he said, "Why did you do (this)? You arouse the Canaanites against me."[272] However, with God's protection, no evil befell them.[273]

59/ He went from there and came to Bethel. There he set up an altar, offered a sacrifice, where it had been said to him, "I will multiply your offspring."[274] And he went from there to Luza.[275] There <D>ebora,[276] Rebecca's nurse died.[277] And from there he went to Bethlehem, which is Ephrata. There Benjamin was born of Rachel and Rachel died.[278] There Reuben had intercourse with his father's concubine Bilhah: this was not with his father's ignorance.[279] Thence he went to Mamre where Isaac was, who, when he reached one hundred and eighty years (of age), died.[280]

60/ Esau had two[281] wives and many sons, and he was called Edom and Sēir. Moses[282] recounts[283] his offspring and those of his children and of his grandchildren. And thus, he leaves this matter;[284] and he says where they dwelt. Jacob loved Joseph more than (his) other sons and he made a flowery robe for him, who herded the flocks with his brothers.[285]

---

268. That is, to marry.
269. A summary of Gen 34:3-24. Observe that the aspect of tactical deception is omitted from the circumcision demand and it is put into Jacob's mouth.
270. The pain consequent to the circumcision.
271. A brief recapitulation of Gen 34:25-29. However, in Genesis it is the brothers Simeon and Levi who slaughtered the Shechemites, not Reuben and Simeon.
272. Gen 34:30.
273. It is unclear whether this is the Israelites in general (cf. Gen 35:5), or specifically Reuben and Simeon following on Jacob's reprimand.
274. Here reference is to Gen 35:1, but the initial reference is 35:11 and that same idea is also alluded to in 48:3.
275. Here the document reads Gen 35:6 as if Luz is a separate place in the environs of Bethel.
276. Corrupt in the text to Sebora.
277. Gen 35:8.
278. Summarizing Gen 35:16-18.
279. Gen 35:22.
280. Gen 35:27-28.
281. The biblical text mentions Esau's three wives (Gen 36:2-3 and 28:8-9).
282. See §37 above for this use of "Moses."
283. Literally: says. On this technique of epitomizing, see the introductory remarks.
284. Literally: thence. Again, a scholarly note is to be observed.
285. Here, again, a conscious summary of Genesis, containing nothing notable.

61/ On one occasion he betrayed his brothers to his father because of (their) evil transgressions, that is sodomy or beastiality.[286] One night he saw a dream that[287] he was reaping in the field with his brothers. It (the dream) was this—that his brothers' sheaves bowed down to his sheaf. And when he said (this) his brothers became angry at him and said, "Indeed, do you wish to king it over us, or shall we be obedient to your orders?"[288]

62/ On the next night he saw another dream and he said to his father, "I saw the sun and the moon and eleven stars bowing down to me." His father was angry with him.[289] Nonetheless,[290] he paid attention to what that might signify. One day, his father dispatched him to his brothers and said, "Go to your brothers and see whether it is well with them."[291]

63/ He went, he found shepherds and asked whether they had seen them. They said, "We saw them going to Dotayin." He went and found them. They saw him and said, "Behold the interpreter of dreams comes. Come let us kill him and we shall see what his dreams will become for him." Reuben said, "Let us cast him into an old well and let us not kill him, for he is our own flesh and blood."[292] And the Ishmaelites were passing and they had loaded myrrh (storax) and were going to Egypt, and they (the brothers) sold him to them for thirty pieces of silver.[293] They, bringing him to Egypt, sold him to Potiphar, Pharaoh's eunuch.

64/ After that, Judah went to the well and he did not find (him) and he said, "The youth is not to be seen and I, where shall I go?" They took his cloak, wet it with blood, gave it to a youth and sent (it) to their father. Their father saw that; he wept and said, "It is my son's cloak. An evil beast has eaten my

---

286. Gen 37:2. That these specific acts were the brothers' transgressions is not stated in Genesis.

287. Or: for.

288. Genesis 37:5–8.

289. See Gen 37:9–10.

290. Reading սական as սակայն. This orthographic variant is not uncommon in manuscripts.

291. Gen 37:14.

292. Here the story, as related in Gen 37:14–22, is summarized. In Gen 37:12–36 there are many internal contradictions caused by the combining of two different narratives in the Genesis text itself. The Armenian text further harmonizes the narrative, and refers to the Ishmaelites, but not to the Midianites, whom Genesis mentions in addition to the Ishmaelites.

293. Here the next events are briefly presented; see Gen 37:25–28. Observe that the "twenty pieces of silver" of Genesis has become thirty, inspired doubtless by the price of Judas' betrayal; see Matt 26:15, 27:3, 9. Joseph, as has been remarked, is often a type of Christ, so this change should not surprise us.

son." They wished to comfort him, and he said, "I shall not be comforted, but I will go down to Hades through the mourning for my son."[294]

65/ Judah went at that time to Hirah[295] the Adullamite. He saw Shua,[296] he loved her and married her, (and) from her he begat three sons, Er,[297] Onan and Shelah.[298] He gave a wife whose name was Tamar, to Er, who (Er) died childless, for he was lawless towards God. And Onan took her, for such was the custom among them, that if someone died childless, there was raised up for him offspring of the second brother.[299] But, he did not wish to do that, but spilt (his) semen on the ground. For that reason, he too was killed childless. Judah said to Tamar, "Be in your house until my son Shelah grows up."[300]

66/ One day, Judah went to shear the sheep with Hirah. Tamar heard. She put off the widow's weeds and put on a prostitute's clothing, and she was[301] on the way along which he was going to pass. Seeing her, he thought that she was a prostitute. He said, "Sleep with me." And she said, "What will you give (me)?" and he said, "A kid of the goats." And she said, "Give me as a surety, your staff, your ring, and your seal." And he gave them. And returning home, he sent her the kid in exchange for his sureties, and he (the messenger) did not find her and he brought it[302] back home. And Judah said "She will not be able to deceive me by falsehood."[303]

67/ And her womb began to swell. It was related to Judah and he said, "Let her be stoned."[304] When they wished to stone her, she said, "Then, (see)

---

294. Close to Gen 37:31–33, 35.
295. Gen 38:1. The Armenian form of the name transliterates as Iram, coming from the LXX Ιρας.
296. According to the Hebrew text, Shua was a Canaanite man whose unnamed daughter Judah married; see Gen 38:2. In the LXX, however, Shua was the daughter of an unnamed father, a Canaanite. The Arm Bible has the sense of the LXX.
297. Armenian Sē.
298. Armenian Ēla and LXX Σηλων: see Gen 38:1–5a.
299. The text is a little confusing: the levirate marriage involved the dead childless husband's brother fathering a child upon the widow.
300. Gen 38:11.
301. That is, she waited.
302. That is, the kid.
303. See Gen 38:11–20 for this story. Judah's response here differs from that recorded in Gen 38:23 and Deut 22:22.
304. Gen 38:24. Stoning here replaces the burning of Genesis. Lev 20:10 and Deut 22:22 prohibit adultery on pain of death but do not specify the mode of execution.

these; he made me pregnant." "You are more righteous than I, for I did not want to give you to Shelah."[305]

Then, in the course of labor, when Zara (Zerah)[306] wanted to go forth, he put forth his hand. The maiden[307] tied a red thread to his hand, and he drew it back. Perez came forth.[308]

68/ We said about Joseph that he was sold to the eunuch. Then he made him ruler over his house.[309] One day, while his wife was with him (Joseph) in the house, she seized him by the edge of his garment and said, "Lie with me."[310] Then he fled, leaving his robe in her hand. And at once she made a complaint about him to her husband, that he made sport of her.[311] And for that reason, he was put in prison.

69/ However, the warden set him over the prisoners who were in the prison.[312] Then, there were placed there the king's chief cupbearer and his butler, and they saw dreams. The chief cupbearer saw three vessels and in them were flowers and grapes. He squeezed them into Pharaoh's cup and was giving (it) to him to drink. He told (it) to Joseph and he interpreted (it) for him. "The three vessels (are) three days. Afterwards, you will be appointed to your position."[313]

70/ Then the butler told his one, that he held three baskets on his head and in the uppermost, all the sorts of cakes that could possible exist through the baker's skill, and birds were eating them. He said, "The three baskets are three days. You be hung from wood[314] and birds will eat your body." And he said to the chief cupbearer, "Remember me, so that you can bring (me) out of this prison." But he forgot (him) for two years.[315]

---

305. This sentence is somewhat unclear, with an unmarked change of speaker. The passage is parallel to Gen 38:24–26.
306. Gen 38:28.
307. I.e., the midwife.
308. The story here has been so abbreviated as to be incomprehensible without the biblical text. It draws upon Gen 38:27–30.
309. Gen 39:1, 4.
310. Potiphar's wife's persistent importuning of Joseph is not mentioned (Gen 39:7–10).
311. Gen 39:11–18.
312. Gen 39:22.
313. Gen 40:1–14, much abbreviated.
314. Apparently, wooden gallows. In Esther, the gallows are called "the wood": see Esth 2:23, 5:14, etc.
315. Gen 40:16–23, much abbreviated. The last phrases are from Gen 40:14 and 40:23–41:1.

71/ When Pharaoh saw a dream, that he was seeing seven fat heifers coming forth from the ground[316] and seven lean ones that ate up the former ones; and seven fat ears (of wheat) on one stem and the same number of lean ones which swallowed the former ones.[317] He gathered all the knowledgeable men of his kingdom (and) no one could interpret (it).[318] Then the chief cupbearer remembered Joseph, and he told him (Pharaoh) what had happened.[319]

72/ He was released from the prison; he explained the dream, saying, "The seven fat heifers (are) seven years of plenty, and the seven lean ones are seven years of famine. In the same fashion, concerning the ear(s) of corn." This pleased the king[320] and he put a collar[321] on his neck and seated (him) in a chariot, and he made him ruler of all his kingdom.[322] And Joseph commanded all the regions that of every cereal they should put one fifth portion into the king's account each year.[323] When the time of famine arrived, all would go to Joseph, to buy from him.[324]

73/ Jacob heard, he sent his sons to Egypt to buy wheat. And went to him (Joseph). He asked them, "Whence do you come?" They said, "We are all sons of one old father in the land of the Canaanites. We have one other brother and other one has died." He said, "It is not thus, but you are spies."[325] And he sent them to prison. (One[326] said), "Did I not say to you, 'Let us not kill our brother Joseph.'" And he (Joseph) released them from there and he commanded to fill their sacks and to put the silver in the mouths of the sacks.[327]

74/ And he said to them, "Leave Simeon with me and go, bring Benjamin to me." And, leaving him, they went.[328] And they told (this) to their father, what had happened to them, and they wished to bring Benjamin to Joseph. Jacob said, "All this has come upon me, I will not give (him) to you. One has died, and Simeon is in chains. I shall not give (him) to you!" However, when the famine grew more severe, Judah said, "I swear to you that if we do not

---

316. Emend to "the river."
317. Gen 41:1–7.
318. Gen 41:8.
319. Gen 41:9–12.
320. This is derived from Gen 41:14–17.
321. Or: a neck chain.
322. Gen 41:38–44.
323. Gen 41:47–49. The tax of one fifth for the king is mentioned in Gen 41:34.
324. Gen 41:55–57.
325. Gen 42:1–14.
326. According to Gen 42:22 and to §63 above, it is Reuben.
327. Gen 42:25.
328. Gen 42:24.

bring him back to you, we shall be guilty to God and men." And he yielded to them.[329]

75/ They went to Joseph, and he ordered at once to prepare food for them. And they thought that he wished to send them to prison, and they said, "Your silver we have brought back from this place, and we have more."[330] He said, "My silver is with me." And he brought Simeon out.[331] The Egyptians were to one side and they were to the other. He portioned out food to them. And after the food, he did just like before, and caused his bowl to be put in Benjamin's sack.[332]

76/ And when they went, he sent to bring them back, "for they have stolen," he said, "the bowl." And they returned to him. And they found the goblet (in) Benjamin's sack. Joseph said, "Why did you steal the bowl in which it was my custom to scry?[333] Let him in whose (effects) the goblet was found remain with me."[334] They began to weep, telling concerning their father and everything and the dead brother.[335] He said, "It is not true.[336] I am Joseph whom you sold to Egypt. Fear not, go to our father[337] and bring him to me."

77/ Joseph had taken a wife and had begotten Ephraim and Manasseh.[338] They[339] went and told everything. Behold, like one awakened from sleep, he (Jacob) said, "It is enough for me to see my son."[340] Jacob came; Joseph went forth to meet him to Shechem,[341] and he said, "Say to the king that (my) lords are shepherds."[342] They went to the king, and he asked, "What might they be?" and they said as Joseph had said. And according to Joseph's word, they requested Goshen, where indeed they lived. And at once he gave (it) to them.[343]

---

329. Gen 42:36–38; 43:9–11.
330. I.e, money.
331. Gen 43:15–22; radical abbreviation.
332. Gen 43:32, 44:3.
333. It appears that here a bowl has replaced the goblet of the biblical story, though once in this section the word "goblet" slips past the author. This may reflect knowledge of lecanomantic practice among the retellers or tradents of this story.
334. Gen 44:3–10.
335. Gen 44:22. In Gen 42:18–34, the entire story is told by Judah alone.
336. That is, that he is dead.
337. Gen 45:4.
338. Cf. 41:45, 50–52.
339. That is, his brothers. They returned to Canaan.
340. Gen 45:28.
341. According to Gen 46:29 Joseph met him in Goshen, in Egypt.
342. Gen 46:29–32.
343. Gen 46:29–34; 47:1–6.

78/ When the famine grew fierce—in the first year, they[344] gave gold and silver; in the second, domestic animals; in the third, possessions. And thus, nothing remained for them. And then Joseph accepted them themselves as servants to Pharaoh.[345] And Joseph issued an order that each year everybody should contribute one fifth part to Pharaoh's account except for the priests, who were receiving freely salaries from the king.[346]

79/ Jacob lived with his sons in Egypt for seventeen years. And all the days of his life (were) one hundred and forty-seven years.[347] Jacob summoned his son Joseph and said, "Swear to me that you will bury my bones in Canaan." And he swore to him.[348] And he summoned all his sons and said, "Listen, O sons of Jacob, and I will make known to you what is to come to pass in the last days."[349] They came, each of them, one after the other, and he gave (them) his blessing.[350]

80/ When the end drew near to death, Joseph brought his two sons, Manasseh and Ephraim, so that he might bless them. And (he put) Manasseh on the right side so he might bless him first, and Ephrem on the left. Then he, joining his arms, put his hand[351] upon the younger. Joseph said, "Not thus!" He said, "I know, my son, what I am doing."[352] And thus, he blessed them.[353] Jacob died and they brought his bones to Canaan and buried them in the double cave.[354]

81/ The sons of Jacob said to Joseph. "We are your servants. What shall we do?" for they were afraid of him. And he said to them, "Do not fear, for God has turned your evil into your good.[355] Now let us say that you will undergo persecutions in this land.[356] When God will visit you, bring my bones to the promised land."[357] And thus it took place.

---

344. The people of Egypt.
345. Gen 47:13–19.
346. Gen 47:22.
347. Gen 47:28.
348. Gen 47:29.
349. Gen 49:1.
350. Gen 49:1, very close reference. The blessings to the twelve sons are given in Gen 49.
351. That is, his right hand.
352. Gen 48:1.
353. Gen 48:5–20.
354. That is, the Cave of Machpelah.
355. Gen 50:20.
356. This may be a reference to the prophecy of Gen 15:13, which was omitted by our text at that point.
357. Gen 50:24–25; Exod 13:1; and Josh 24:22; cf. Sir 49:51.

PART 4

MOSES TO DANIEL

12. Of Moses and Aaron

Introductory Remarks

This interesting text is presented in two manuscript copies. The text down to §33 is drawn from Bodleian Marsh 438 of the year 1482, fols 55r–57r.[1] Manuscript M1099B, which also preserves this text on fols 177v–182r, is of the seventeenth century and of unknown provenance.[2] The variants in §§1–33 arise from collating M1099 against Marsh 438. The text from §34 to the end is extant only in manuscript M1099. These manuscripts are both Synaxaria and so further copies of this text can doubtless can be found. At present, however, these two manuscripts suffice to convey this interesting text to the public.

The document contains the life histories of Moses and Aaron from their births to their deaths. To these narratives, M1099 appends some further traditions about Moses, including the invocation that accompanied Moses's splitting of the Red Sea, and also information concerning the origins of the Hebrew language. Note that this text does not mention the giving of the Torah, except for the Ten Commandments. There are many incidents and features that go beyond the story told in the Pentateuch on which I comment in the notes. Of them all, though, the complex of stories about Moses's Ethiopian campaign as an Egyptian general is the most intriguing. It is discussed in full in the excursus that follows.

In the apparatus, Bodleian Marsh 438 is the lemma and M1099 the variant.

There are certain consistent orthographical variations that are not recorded in the apparatus. They do not affect the meaning of the text:

- Marsh 438 nearly everywhere has ու and M1099 has օ;
- Marsh 438 nearly everywhere has խպայէլ and M1099 has խպայէղ;
- Marsh 438 nearly everywhere has Ահարոն and M1099 has Ահարովն;
- Marsh 438 has Յոցարէթ and M1099 has Յոքարէթ;

These consistent variations are not noted in the apparatus criticus.

---

1. Manuscript Bodleian Marsh 438 is discussed on pp. 8–9 above.
2. *General Catalogue* 4:307–310.

I have given English translations of those variant readings that radically affect the meaning.

Excursus: Moses in Ethiopia (§§12–13, 21–23)
by Oren Ableman

Of Moses and Aaron §§12–13 relate that Moses, having been educated in Egyptian wisdom, became a general of the Egyptian army. When the Ethiopians took captive his adoptive mother, Pharaoh's daughter Mari, Moses fought for ten years to seize Ethiopia and rescue her. He also captured T'esbi, Queen of the Ethiopians. After the death of Mari, the Egyptians, being jealous of Moses, planned to kill him. This led to Moses killing a man named K'sant'i and to his flight to Midian. Later in the text (§§21–23) there is a further reference to this tradition when the Cushite woman Moses married (Num 12:1) is identified as the same Ethiopian Queen T'esbi.[3] The text digresses at this point and relates a story about how Moses used hinds and storks in order to kill the snakes that blocked the route into Ethiopia.

The tradition of Moses in Ethiopia has its earliest known origins in two Jewish texts written in Greek. The first is by Artapanus, Fragment 3.7–18, which has survived only as a quotation in Eusebius, *Praep. ev.* 9.27.7–18.[4] Artapanus is usually dated to the second or first century BCE. The second is Josephus, *A.J.* 2.238–253, which is dated to the late first century CE.[5]

According to Artapanus, Moses's adoptive mother was named Merris and she is said to have been married to Chenephres, the king of Memphis. Once Moses became a grown man, he made many important inventions for the benefit of humankind. He also reformed the Egyptian administrative and religious system. His actions and wisdom caused him to receive divine honors and to be named Hermes. Although all of Moses's actions were done in order to strengthen the régime, Chenephres became envious of Moses's popularity and decided to find a way to get rid of him. Such an opportunity arose when the Ethiopians attacked Egypt and Moses was appointed as a general to fight

---

3. Note however that the text here seems to intentionally avoid saying explicitly that Moses married the queen of the Ethiopians. Instead he is said to have honored her and taken her out of Egypt together with the Israelites. Below I will argue that this detail is perhaps an innovation of the author of Of Moses and Aaron.

4. See translation and commentary by Erich S. Gruen, "Artapanus," in *Outside the Bible: Ancient Jewish Writings related to Scripture*, ed. Louis H. Feldman, James L. Kugel, and Lawrence H. Schiffman (Philadelphia: Jewish Publication Society, 2013), 1:675–85.

5. See translation and commentary in Louis H. Feldman, *Flavius Josephus: Judean Antiquities 1–4* (Leiden: Brill, 2000), 3:200–205.

against them. Although Moses was given untrained soldiers, he waged a successful war that lasted ten years. In order to accommodate the large army, he also founded the city of Hermopolis and he consecrated a cult of the ibis there. The Ethiopians also eventually came to love Moses and learned circumcision from him.

Once the war was over, Chenephres tried to organize a new plot against Moses and ordered a man named Chanethothes to kill him. At that time Merris died, and Moses and Chanethothes were charged with the task of burying her beyond the borders of Egypt. This was meant to create an opportunity for Chanethothes to kill Moses, but Moses was warned in advance and avoided the danger and he buried Merris in the city he then named Meroë. After this, Moses followed the advice of his brother Aaron and fled to Arabia. When Chanethothes learned of this he set an ambush for Moses. When Moses drew near him, Chanethothes attempted to draw his blade but Moses restrained his hand and then drew his own sword and killed him. Moses then reached Arabia where he found refuge with Raguel and married his daughter.

Josephus relates a similar story within his account of Moses's life, but many of the details differ from Artapanus's. In the sections of *A.J.* that paraphrase the Hebrew Bible, Josephus tends to stick close to the biblical narrative. In the story of Moses in Ethiopia he most blatantly deviates from his usual practice and adds an elaborate story not even hinted at in the Hebrew Bible.

According to Josephus, the name of Moses's adoptive mother was Thermouthis. When the Ethiopians attacked Egypt, Moses was commissioned as a general to fight against them by both the king and his daughter Thermouthis. With an army under his command, Moses led a successful counterattack against the Ethiopians by taking an unexpected route. According to Josephus, the regular route from Egypt to Ethiopia was by ship on the river. This was due to dangerous serpents that infested the land route. However, Moses devised an ingenious stratagem that allowed him to march his army safely through the dangerous land route. He prepared papyrus baskets full of ibises, a natural enemy of the serpents.[6] The ibises then attacked the serpents and allowed Moses and his army to reach Ethiopia without their approach being noticed.

---

6. Note that Artapanus also connects the worship of ibises in Egypt with Moses. This indicates that the association of Moses and this bird was part of the general tradition among Hellenistic Jews in Egypt. Both Artapanus and Josephus knew this tradition but transmitted different versions of it. Josephus also mentions deer in the context of the hunting of the serpents. The reasons for this are not entirely clear and may be the result of a mistake made either by Josephus himself or by a scribal error in the transmission of his text. Still, there are reasons to assume that there was a belief in antiquity that certain types of deer can hunt

Moses proceeded to defeat the Ethiopians quickly and they were soon pushed back to their capital city of Saba. Josephus identifies this city as the same one that centuries later was named Meroë by the Persian king Cambyses. The city was well protected by the rivers surrounding it and by massive fortifications. This led to an extended siege with no apparent end in sight. This stalemate was broken after Tharbis, the daughter of the Ethiopian king, saw Moses from the city wall and fell in love with him. She sent servants to him in order to negotiate a marriage proposal. Moses accepted the proposal on the condition that Tharbis surrender the city. Once she fulfilled her part of the agreement, Moses took the city and married her as promised. He then led his army back to Egypt. Josephus does not mention Tharbis again and it is unclear what happened to her. Shortly after this point in the narrative, Josephus relates the story of Moses's marriage to Sippora the daughter of Raguel as it appears in the Hebrew Bible. Clearly, therefore, Josephus thought that these two wives of Moses were different people.

The texts of Artapanus and Josephus contradict each other at various points, but the common themes found in both are evidence of a robust tradition among Hellenistic Jews about Moses's campaign in Ethiopia.[7] The tradition is also alluded to in Targum Pseudo-Jonathan of Num 12:1, making it clear that in some form, it was known also in rabbinic circles.[8]

The same tradition resurfaces much later in medieval Jewish sources (most notably in Yalqut Shim'oni §167 and Sefer Ha-Yashar). These sources

---

serpents (Feldman, *Judean Antiquities*, 203–4 n. 673). Regardless of the original reason deer were mentioned in Josephus's text, later texts that were dependent on his work tend to mention gazelles or hinds (as does Bodleian Marsh 438) alongside the birds used by Moses.

7. There are divergent opinions among scholars about the relationship between the accounts of Artapanus and Josephus. See Avigdor Shinan, "Moses and the Ethiopian Woman: Sources of a Story in the Chronicle of Moses," *Scripta Hierosolymitana* 27 (1978): 66–78; Tesa Rajak, "Moses in Ethiopia: Legend and Literature," in *The Jewish Dialogue with Greece and Rome: Studies in Cultural and Social Interaction* (Leiden: Brill, 2001), 257–72; Donna Runnalls, "Moses' Ethiopian Campaign," *JSJ* 14 (1983): 135–56; Robert A. Kraft, "Moses and Ethiopia: Old Scripturesque Traditions behind Josephus, *Ant.* 2.238–253," in *The Embroidered Bible: Studies in the Biblical Apocrypha and Pseudepigrapha in Honour of Michael E. Stone*, ed. Lorenzo DiTommaso, Matthias Henze, and William Adler, SVTP 26 (Leiden: Brill, 2018), 602–16. Despite some differences of opinion, there is general agreement that both Artapanus and Josephus are reworking the same earlier tradition and adapting it each to his own agenda and literary tendencies.

8. It is interesting that neither Artapanus nor Josephus connect the tradition of Moses in Ethiopia with Num 12:1. This connection seems rather obvious and it is quite likely that the entire tradition started from exegesis of that verse, as its appearance in the translation of Num 12:1 in Tg. Ps.-J. implies.

contain the kernel of the tradition found in Artapanus and Josephus and they speak of a military campaign led by Moses in Ethiopia. However, the story is set at a slightly different point of Moses's life (after his escape from Egypt but before reaching Midian) and bears very little resemblance to the tradition in Artapanus and Josephus, differing in practically every detail. These later Jewish sources represent a completely different branch of the tradition that does not stem from either Artapanus or Josephus, but may be rooted in a lost source, contemporary with or antecedent to them. The medieval Jewish sources are far more careful to integrate this story into the biblical narrative of Moses's life in a coherent way. They are also more concerned with portraying Moses as a pious Jew. This is most noticeable in their claim that although Moses married the Queen of Ethiopia, he never consummated the marriage.[9] This closer adherence to the biblical narrative and the claim that the marriage was not consummated can also be found in the Armenian text Of Moses and Aaron found in Bodleian manuscript Marsh 438 being published here.

At first glance, Moses and Aaron seems to combine elements from Josephus and Artapanus while also modifying both sources. The narrative is highly abbreviated and contains only the very basic details of the story of Moses in Ethiopia as it appears in Josephus and Artapanus. However, all the details that do appear in Moses and Aaron can be traced either to Artapanus or Josephus. Even where Moses and Aaron clearly deviates from these ancient sources, these deviations are of the type one should expect to find in the later transmission of an anterior tradition, especially of a tradition transmitted through multiple intermediary texts, as seems to be the case here.

It seems unlikely that Moses and Aaron used a third ancient source and no evidence for this has been found. Artapanus and Josephus are the only early sources of this tradition to survive in Greek and all later Christian attestations of the tradition are dependent on them. This contrasts with the medieval Jewish sources, which are dependent on a quite different version of the tradition of Moses in Ethiopia.

Interestingly, Moses and Aaron relates materials originating in different sources in different parts of the text. §§12–13 are dependent primarily on Artapanus, while §§21–23 are dependent on Josephus. This indicates that the author of Moses and Aaron or of its ancestor text(s) was perhaps using two different sources and was careful not to mix them or else he used a source that had already combined elements from Artapanus and Josephus.

---

9. Shinan, "Moses and the Ethiopian Woman," 74–76.

To understand further the relationship between Moses and Aaron and its ancient sources, let us first look at §§12–13. This section depends on Artapanus as can be demonstrated by pointing to a number of details that appear only in Artapanus or in sources dependent on him.

(1) Moses's adoptive mother is named Merris in Artapanus and Maṙi in Moses and Aaron. The Armenian here is clearly a slightly differing transliteration of the Greek name.
(2) The plot to kill Moses is connected to Merris's death.
(3) In the Armenian text, the name of the Egyptian that Moses kills is K'sant'i. This seems to be a slight corruption of the name Chanethothes that is given by Artapanus to the same character.

Moreover, in Moses and Aaron it is not completely clear why Moses needed to kill K'sant'i in order to thwart the plot against him. This is however understandable if the Armenian text assumes familiarity with the version of the story in Artapanus in which the king had despatched the assassin because he was jealous of Moses. This character was then easily identifiable as Moses's would-be assassin.

Two details in §§12–13 do not appear in Artapanus. The first is the claim that the Ethiopians captured Maṙi, Moses's adoptive mother, and he fought them in order to free her from captivity. This detail might be considered an embellishment to the story added by the author of Moses and Aaron, but, I show below that it was taken from Moses and Aaron's direct source.

The second such detail is that Moses captured the Ethiopian Queen T'esbi. This is drawn from Josephus and is placed here in Moses and Aaron. By putting this here, the author also established the premise for his digression in §§21–23 relating Josephus's version of the tradition.

Also significant is that the author of Moses and Aaron (or, of course, of an intermediary source upon which the author of Moses and Aaron drew) only used Artapanus as a source in §§12–13. This is true even at points in the narrative where additional information found in Artapanus would have made the text of Moses and Aaron clearer. The most striking example of this is the portrayal of Moses's adoptive mother. Up to §12 nothing is said about her name and she is referred to only as "Pharaoh's daughter," just as she is in Exodus. However, once the author starts relating the extrabiblical story that appears in Artapanus, the name Maṙi is introduced and she is consistently referred to as "Moses's adoptive mother." This seems to indicate that the author of Moses and Aaron (or of the intermediary document) kept the sources he used separate within his composition. As long as he was retelling the story as it appears in Exodus, he did not give this character a name. Only when he started adding details from an extrabiblical source did he start using the name that appears in that source.

In §§21–23 the story of the hinds and storks that Moses used to combat the serpents on the route to Ethiopia appears. This is a highly abbreviated summary of the narrative that is related by Josephus, with minor changes.[10] Josephus is the earliest source that includes the story of Moses's use of birds (ibises according to Josephus) during his campaign in Ethiopia and all subsequent appearances of this story are dependent on his account. Moreover, in §13 the name of the Ethiopian queen is T'esbi, clearly a corruption of the Greek name Tharbis that Josephus gives to the daughter of the Ethiopian king.

The only significant difference between Josephus and Moses and Aaron is that the Armenian text omits the story of the Ethiopian queen/princess falling in love with and marrying Moses. Instead, it simply claims that Moses captured Ethiopia and makes no mention of the negotiations for surrender found in Josephus's narrative. According to Moses and Aaron, the queen was captured by Moses and later she also joined the Israelites when they left Egypt. Moses never married the queen but he was criticized by Miriam for honoring her. This digression in the Armenian text is apologetic and is almost certainly reacting to a source that said explicitly that Moses married the Ethiopian queen. Since this particular detail is only found in Josephus, Moses and Aaron was almost certainly familiar either directly with Josephus or with a source dependent on him.

This raises a rather interesting problem when we come to identify the sources used in the composition of Moses and Aaron. This text, as we saw, is familiar with traditions attested only by Josephus and others only attested by Artapanus. One could therefore argue that it was familiar with Josephus's *A.J.* and with Artapanus through Eusebius's *Praep. ev.* This would be a surprising since there is no evidence that Josephus's *A.J.* or Eusebius's *Praep. ev.* were ever

---

10. The minor changes are: (1) The daughter of the king of Ethiopia mentioned by Josephus is portrayed as the queen of Ethiopia in Moses and Aaron. It is interesting to note that the medieval Jewish sources also identify Moses's Ethiopian wife as a queen, but in those sources, she is also portrayed as the widow of the previous king. (2) The ibises mentioned in Josephus are identified as storks in the Armenian text. A similar change in the identification of the birds can be seen in Palaea Historica §70. This is probably due to these later Christian texts not knowing what the ibis signified in ancient Egyptian culture and religion. Since neither text was composed in regions native to the Egyptian or sacred ibis, which is found throughout Africa, they probably thought that the ibis and the stork were the same. The stork is familiar in Armenia, which is on the migratory route of the white stork, and it is mentioned in Armenian songs and folktales.

translated into Armenian.[11] It is possible that the author of this text could read Greek and thus gained knowledge of these traditions, but that seems rather unlikely. Moreover, the numerous small differences between Moses and Aaron and the texts of both Artapanus and Josephus weigh against direct knowledge of those ancient sources.

These differences can be more easily understood if Moses and Aaron became familiar with the tradition of Moses in Ethiopia through intermediary sources that had already made slight changes to the tradition. One possible avenue of transmission of the tradition was through Byzantine Greek texts. However, when we compare Moses and Aaron with two Byzantine texts that contain developments of the tradition of Moses in Ethiopia, this seems unlikely.

The first is the early ninth-century Chronography of George Synkellos §139. Synkellos refers to Josephus directly when he recounts the story of how Tharbis fell in love with Moses and surrendered the city to him. Synkellos is also rather careful not to say explicitly that Moses married the Ethiopian princess. He does not mention the story about the use of birds in order to kill the serpents blocking the road to Ethiopia. Yet, since Moses and Aaron includes the story of the birds and serpents, its source is most likely not Synkellos, or any source dependent on Synkellos.

The second Byzantine text is Palaea Historica §70. The text there contains the story of the campaign along with the tradition of the use of birds to fight serpents. Moreover, in the Palaea Historica the birds are identified as storks as in Moses and Aaron. The story in Palaea Historica §70 is obviously a later development of that found in Josephus. So many details of the Palaea's story have changed that it can be considered a new story and not a version of the tradition found in Josephus. Perhaps the most obvious is that the campaign is against India, not Ethiopia. This confusion can already be found in some of the earliest Greek geographical texts, but, significantly, this is the only source reviewed here that makes this mistake. The text in the Palaea, then, belongs to an offshoot of the earlier tradition and can be clearly distinguished from

---

11. An Armenian edition of Josephus's *Jewish War* was published in 1787 on the basis of a translation from 1660. The colophons of this edition indicate that there were earlier Armenian manuscripts with translations of Josephus that had been lost. See Frederick C. Conybeare, "An Old Armenian Version of Josephus," *JTS* 9 (1908): 577–83. Conybeare also argues that there was a fifth-century Armenian translation of Josephus's *Jewish War*. All of this raises the possibility of a lost Armenian translation of Jewish Antiquities. Even if such a translation existed, there is no indication that Moses and Aaron was familiar with it and there are good reasons to assume its author had no direct knowledge of Josephus.

other versions that are closer to Josephus, among which is Moses and Aaron. In addition to this, Palaea Historica §70 does not mention the Ethiopian princess/queen at all. It therefore cannot be the source that transmitted the story found in Josephus to Moses and Aaron. Still, the fact that both texts change the ibises into storks may point to a common source somewhere in their chain of transmission.

Other variations of the Moses in Ethiopia tradition appear in various Byzantine texts (such as the Paschal Chronicle, George Cedrenus, and Pseudo-Eustathius's *Hexaemeron*), but none of these seem to be a source for Moses and Aaron.

The most probable path of transmission of the Moses in Ethiopia tradition from Artapanus and Josephus to the Armenian text of Moses and Aaron was through a series of Syriac texts. Syriac writers most likely did not have direct access to *A.J.* and Artapanus, but they probably knew the tradition of Moses in Ethiopia through quotations or adaptations of the relevant passages in Byzantine Greek chronicles. Syriac writers developed this tradition in various ways and one can speak of distinctively Syriac versions of the tradition.

Indeed, Brock makes a compelling argument for the existence of two early sources used by most later Syriac writers.[12] The first is a summary of Artapanus, while the second is a summary of Josephus that also includes some details from Artapanus. Certain texts seem to be familiar only with one of these sources and are therefore very similar to either Artapanus or Josephus. Other texts were familiar with both sources (either directly or through intermediary sources) and combined details from both Artapanus and Josephus.

An interesting inner-Syriac development of the tradition adds the name Raʿosa to the story. Some texts, dependent on the summary of Artapanus, state that Moses's adoptive mother Merris was also named Raʿosa.[13] In contrast, some texts dependent on the summary of Josephus attribute exactly the same name to Tharbis, the Ethiopian princess Moses married.[14]

---

12. Sebastian P. Brock, "Some Syriac Legends Concerning Moses," *JJS* 33 (1982): 237–55.

13. The name Raʿosa is perhaps the result of a misreading of a Greek source. See the discussion in Brock, "Some Syriac Legends," 243–44. The earliest evidence of this development can be found in two late eighth-century texts. (1) An anonymous chronicle incorrectly attributed to Dionysius of Telmaḥre. This text explicitly attributes the entire "Moses in Ethiopia" tradition to Artapanus. (2) Theodore Bar Koni's book of scholia.

14. This development first appears in an excerpt of Jacob of Edessa (d. 708), Letter 13 found in MS British Library ms Add 17193. The manuscript is dated to 874 CE and is therefore contemporary with the anonymous chronicle and Theodore Bar Koni mentioned in the previous note. It should be noted that the name Raʿosa does not appear in Jacob's

Important developments of the Moses in Ethiopia tradition first appear in the writings of Ishodad of Merv (ninth century). Ishodad is evidently the first known Syriac writer to combine the two sources and create a narrative with elements of both Artapanus and Josephus.[15] He therefore attributes the name Raʿosa both to Merris and to Tharbis, but distinguishes the two women by using a different spelling of Raʿosa for each.

Ishodad also first introduces the interesting detail that Moses studied with Jannes and Jambres. This development of the tradition spreads to all later sources that are dependent on Ishodad and is significant for tracing the transmission of the entire tradition of Moses in Ethiopia. Ishodad was used by many later Syriac writers. Therefore, texts that combine the elements of Artapanus and Josephus usually also identify Jannes and Jambres as Moses's teachers.

One of the best-known texts containing these developments of the tradition is the Chronicle of Syrian Patriarch Michael the Great (1126–1199 CE).[16] This monumental work was well known to the Armenians. Within fifty years of the completion of the original work, two Armenian versions appeared made from the original manuscript.[17] Version I was produced in 1246 through the collaborative work of Vardan Arewelcʿi—a renowned Armenian historian and

---

original text but only in the excerpt in this manuscript. Jacob does not give a name of the Ethiopian princess in Letter 13, but in his biblical commentary for Num 12:1 he gives the name Tharbis. Jacob is also the earliest Syriac writer who was familiar with the source summarizing Josephus. It is possible that all later Syriac texts that draw upon Josephus's version of the tradition are dependent on him.

15. Brock, "Some Syriac Legends," 247–48.

16. This massive work has been preserved in the original Syriac in only one manuscript. For an edition and translation see Jean-Baptiste Chabot, *Chronique de Michel le Syrien, patriarche Jacobite d'Antioche (1166–1199)* (Paris: Leroux, 1899–1910; repr. Brussels: Culture et Civilisation, 1963).

17. For the production of the two Armenian versions of Michael's Chronicle and some discussion of how they relate to each other and to the Syriac original see Felix Haase, "Die armenischen Rezensionen der syrischen Chronik Michael des Grossen," *Oriens Christianus* NS 5 (1915): 60–82, 271–84; Andrea B. Schmidt, "Die zweifache armenische Rezension der syrischen Chronik Michaels des Grossen," *Le Muséon* 109 (1996): 300–319; Schmidt, "The Armenian Versions I and II of Michael the Syrian," *Hugoye* 16 (2013): 93–128; Andy Hilkens, "'Sons of Magog' or 'Thorgmians'? The Description of the Turks (Book XIV) in Michael's Chronicle and Its Armenian Adaptations" in *Syriac Encounters: Papers from the Sixth North American Symposium, Duke University, 26–29 June 2011*, ed. Maria Doerfler, Emanuel Fiano, and Kyle Smith, Eastern Christian Studies 20 (Peeters: Leuven, 2015), 401–14. I would like to thank Andy Hilkens for bringing these papers to my attention and clarifying several points about the Armenian versions of Michael's Chronicle.

theologian [*vardapet*][18]—and a Syrian physician and priest Yeshuʻ. Vardan also made Version II[19] in 1248, but this time worked alone (Yeshuʻ had died the previous year). I refer to these texts as "versions, adaptations" and not "translations" since they cannot be described as translations even in the most generous use of the term. Not only did both versions change fundamental aspects of Michael's layout of the Chronicle, but they also modified, abbreviated, and expanded the text at numerous points.[20]

The story of Moses in Ethiopia is a good example of how these Armenian adaptations add material not found in the original Syriac of Michael's Chronicle. In the Syriac, all that is said about the Ethiopians is that Moses fought against them for ten years and captured and then married Raʻosa daughter of King Zaros, a detail taken from the inner-Syriac development of the tradition first found in Josephus.

The Syriac original of the Chronicle also mentions details that originally derived from Artapanus, including the construction of Hermopolis, the burial of Merris at Meroë, and the plot against Moses and the killing of Chanethothes. The mixing of details originating in both Artapanus and Josephus is most evident in the discussion of the name of Moses's adoptive mother. According to Michael her name was Thermouthis (as in Josephus), but she was also named Raʻosa (as found in the inner-Syriac tradition) and the "Hebrews" called her Mari (=Merris, as in Artapanus). Michael also knows the tradition first mentioned by Ishodad of Merv, that Moses received his education from Jannes and Jambres. He makes no mention of the episode of the birds and serpents.[21]

When this is compared with both Armenian versions of Michael's Chronicle several changes are immediately apparent. Version II mentions all three possible names of Moses's adoptive mother and also adds the detail that she was taken captive by the Ethiopians, who then married her off (supposedly to their king, although this is not said explicitly). Moses then wages war for ten

---

18. Tigran Sawalaneancʻ, ed., *Rev. Michael the Patriarch of the Syrians: The Chronography* (Տեառն Միխայէլի պատրիարքի Ասորւոյ Ժամանակագրութիւն) (Jerusalem: St. James, 1870).

19. Tigran Sawalaneancʻ, ed., *The Chronography of Rev. Michael, Patriarch of the Syrians* (Ժամանակագրութիւն տեառն Միխայէլի Ասորւոց պատրիարքի) (Jerusalem: St. James, 1871).

20. See Hilkens, "Sons of Magog" for in-depth analysis of only one case of significant differences between the Syriac original and the two Armenian versions.

21. It is possible that the original manuscript of the Chronicle did mention this episode briefly, but it was omitted in the one surviving Syriac manuscript.

years against "At'iupas, King of the Philistines,"²² defeats him and rescues his adoptive mother. The Ethiopian Princess is not mentioned at all. Other than this, Version II is more or less similar to the Syriac original.

Version I has even more significant changes from the Syriac: it gives only Thermouthis and Mari as the names of Moses's adoptive mother; its account of the war against the Ethiopians is much fuller; like Version II it adds the detail that Mari was taken prisoner during the Ethiopian attack and that Moses eventually rescued her; it adds that Moses used "gazelles and storks" to fight the serpents on the route to Ethiopia; and finally, Moses is also said to have captured T'esbi, the Ethiopian Queen (not the daughter of the king) but nothing is said about a marriage between them.

Thus, Version I of the Chronicle clearly uses a source that contained a summary of Josephus. This is striking since at this point Version I corrects the variant name for the Ethiopian princess/queen found in the Syriac text of Michael's Chronicle. This correction was probably done according to a Syriac text that contained a more detailed version of the tradition than does Michael's Chronicle. These details appear in Version I, but are confused in Version II, indicating that this is part of the work of Yeshu', who had extensive knowledge of a wide range of Syriac sources.

Armenian Version I of Michael's Chronicle is almost certainly the main source used by the author of Moses and Aaron for his own version of the story of Moses in Ethiopia. Certain features of the tradition appear only in these two texts. The most obvious of these is the claim that Mari was taken captive by the Ethiopians. This detail does appear in Version II, but the exact formulation of the narrative in Moses and Aaron is almost identical to that of Version I. Several other smaller details appear only in Moses and Aaron and Version I:

- The names Mari, T'esbi, and K'sant'i all appear in both texts. These are all slight corruptions of the names Merris, Tharbis, and Chanethothes that appeared in Artapanus and Josephus. Moreover, Version I corrected the original Syriac text and does not mention the name Ra'osa for either Moses's adoptive mother or the Ethiopian queen/princess. It also correctly identified the latter as Tharbis mentioned by Josephus. Most other versions of the story that could have been available to Moses and Aaron would have contained different names.
- K'sant'i, the Egyptian killed by Moses, is referred to as a "tormentor of

---

22. There is no apparent explanation for this unique name and the obvious contradiction with the previous statement about the Ethiopian attack on Egypt. One could perhaps speculate that "At'iupas" is a corruption of "Ethiopia."

Israel" only in Moses and Aaron and Version I. Even Version II does not give him this epithet.
- T'esbi (=Tharbis) is said to be the daughter of the Ethiopian king in all other texts. Only Version I and Moses and Aaron do not mention her father and give her the title of queen.
- Both Version I and Moses and Aaron say that Moses was seventy years old when God spoke to him at the burning bush. He then refused to go back to Egypt for ten years. This detail does not seem to appear in any other text. Both the Syriac original and the Armenian Version II of Michael's Chronicle give his age as seventy-eight and say nothing of him refusing to go back to Egypt for so long.

Despite all these similarities, it is interesting to note that Moses and Aaron was selective and left out some details from Version I. The most obvious of these is the tradition about Jannes and Jambres being Moses's teachers.

A significant discrepancy between the two texts is the fate of the Ethiopian queen/princess. Version I (following the Syriac original) does not mention her again, while Moses and Aaron says she joined the Israelites when they left Egypt and was "honored by Moses." Moses and Aaron also goes out of its way to frame the entire story of Num 12:1 in such a way that Moses and the Ethiopian queen were not married.

Moses and Aaron was familiar, then, with at least one other source that had the same basic story, but differed in some details. Thus, the author of Moses and Aaron used Version I as his main source, but when details there did not fit the other source(s) he would either leave them out or make some changes of his own.

In this context it seems likely that Moses and Aaron was also familiar with Jacob of Edessa's commentary on Num 12:1, which is a summary of Josephus's version of the story of Moses in Ethiopia.[23] All the basic details of the story appear there and much of the formulation of the narrative is also similar to that found in Moses and Aaron. The placement of the story of the birds and serpents in Moses and Aaron only at the point that corresponds chronologically with Num 12:1 could also be a result of this story appearing in Jacob's commentary specifically as exegesis on this verse. Above I suggested that Moses and Aaron may be polemicizing against a source that said that Moses married T'esbi/Tharbis. Jacob of Edessa does indeed relate a relatively full

---

23. See the discussion of this source in Brock, "Some Syriac Legends," 241–43. It seems likely that Version I also used Jacob of Edessa when it expanded on the original Syriac text of Michael's Chronicle.

version of the story that first appeared in Josephus, about Tharbis falling in love with Moses after seeing him from the city wall, and that they were married after the city was conquered. Jacob of Edessa also says that once Moses married Sippora he did not return to Tharbis. Even if the author of Moses and Aaron was not familiar directly with Jacob of Edessa, it is reasonable to assume that he was familiar with a similar source that probably depended on Jacob's commentary.

Moses and Aaron used its sources in the following way. First, it gives priority to the biblical narrative and recaps its main details. Next, sometimes it adds material from other sources that expand the story. In the case of the tradition of Moses in Ethiopia its source was Armenian Version I of Michael the Syrian's Chronicle. Moses and Aaron seems to be careful not to contradict anything found in Version I, but it deliberately excluded certain details, most notably that Moses was educated by Jannes and Jambres. Perhaps the author of Moses and Aaron was uncomfortable with these two notoriously evil figures being associated with Moses. Finally, Moses and Aaron makes use of some other sources (like the commentary of Jacob of Edessa) that bring slightly different versions of the traditions he is relating. These sources are used to clarify certain points and sometimes influence the way Moses and Aaron organized its narrative, but it seems that the author attributes less authority to these sources than to the text of Version I of Michael's Chronicle. When he disagreed with something in this type of source, he was willing to openly contradict what they say. In these cases, the author probably deviates from his usual tendency to maintain the vocabulary and formulation of his sources and instead offers his own exegesis of the biblical text. Thus, the detail that the Ethiopian Queen continued to wander with the Israelites in the desert and was not married to Moses, is probably an innovation of the author of Moses and Aaron.

Text

M1099/ Մարգարէից Մովսէսի եւ Ահարոն[ի]
Marsh 438/ Հոռի Թ. եւ Սեպտեմբերի ԺԲ. Տաւն է Մովսէսի եւ Ահարոնի

1/ Marsh 438 / fol 55r / Նախամարգարէն Մովսէս աստուածախաւսն, որ առաջին էր ամենայն մարգարէից եւ յԱստուծոյ աստուած փարաւոնի անուանեցաւ, եւ Ահարոն եղբայր նորին առաջին քահանայպետ ձեռնադրեալ ի Մովսիսէ: Զի Աստուած զՄովսէս ձեռնադրեաց, եւ նա՝ զԱհարոն եւ զորդիս նորա:

2/ Սոքա էին յազգէն Ղեւեա, որդիք Ամրամա, որդոյն Կահաթու, որդոյն Ղեւեա, որդոյն Յակոբա, որդոյն Իսահակա,

12. OF MOSES AND AARON

որդոյն Աբրահամու։ Եւ Յակոբ յաւրինութիւն[24] որդւոցն ետ զքահանայութիւնն Ղեւեայ եւ զթագաւորութիւնն Յուդայի։

3/ Մովսէս ծնաւ որդի Ամրամա՝ Յոզաբէդա մաւրէ, որ էր դուստր Ղեւեայ։ Եւ այսպէս եղեւ ծնունդն Մովսէսի. գէտքն Եգիպտոսի ասացին փարաւոնի, թէ. «Յայս նիշ աւուր յայս քանիս այս անուն ամսոյ փրկիչ ծնցի Իսրայէլի, եւ նա ազատէ զԻսրայէլ ի ծառայութենէ քումէ»։

4/ Զայս իբրեւ լուաւ փարաւոն, զզուշացաւ խորհրդոյն, եւ ի նոյն ամսեանն առնու զամենայն արս Իսրայէլի, եւ գնաց յորս երեցց եւ մնա ի դուրս զամիսն ողջոյն։ Իսկ նախախնամութիւն Աստուծոյ այնպէս տնաւրինեաց, որ տարաւ Ամրամ զՅոզաբէդ ընդ իւր, եւ յղացաւ ի նշանակեալ աւուրն, զոր ասացին աստղագէտքն։

5/ Եւ յորժամ ծնաւ Մովսէս, թագուցաւ ի տան ամիսս երիս։ Եւ զի էր կայտառ մանուկն, եւ թաքուցանել ոչ կարէին, վասն որոյ տապանաւ[25] ի գետն ընկեցին յահէ մանկասպանին փարաւոնի։ Չի փարաւոն յորժամ զգացաւ զծնունդ փրկչին Իսրայէլի, հրամայեաց զամենայն արու մանուկն Իսրայէլի, զորս ի ծնունդն հեղձուցանել, եւ զորս ի գետն ընկեցեն։

6/ Վասն այսորիկ զՄովսէս Գ. <ամիս>[26] թագուցին ի տան եւ այլ ոչ կարացին։ Եւ լրնկենուլն ի գետն դադարեցաւ տապանն ի պտոյտ մի գետոյն։ Եւ իջանել դստերն փարաւոնի առ ափն գետոյնէ տեսեալ նամքշտացն զտապանն, եւ առեալ ի խաղէ պտուտին, եւ տարան առաջի դստերն փարաւոնի զտապանակն հանդերձ մանկամբն։

7/ Եւ նա տեսեալ / fol 55v / խանդաղատեցաւ առ նովաւ եւ ասաց. «Ի մանկանց եբրայեցոց է դա»։ Իսկ Մարիամ քոյրն Մովսէսի, որ մի եւ նա էր ի նաժշտաց դստերն փարաւոնի, առեալ զմանուկն եւ տարեալ ետ ի մայր իւր Յոզաբէդ իբր ի դայեակ սնուցանել զտղայն վասն դստերն փարաւոնի, զոր սնոյց եւ եբեր առ նա։

8/ Եւ նա առեալ տարաւ առ հայրն իւր փարաւոն եւ ասաց. «Ի մանկանց եբրայեցոց է սա, զոր ի գետոյն առեալ՝ արարի ինձ յորդեգիր»։ Եւ էր Մովսէս մանուկ կայտառ, եւ բարետեսակ, ընդ որ հեշտացաւ փարաւոն։ Եւ առ զնա ի գիրկն իւր եւ համբուրեաց։ Եւ նոյն ժամայն բուռն եհար Մովսէս Ժ. (10) մատամբն զնուրուաց փարաւոնի։

9/ Ընդ որ բարկացեալ փարաւոն կամեցաւ սպանանել զնա։ Իսկ իմաստունքն, որ անդ կային մերձ ի նմին ժամու, ոչ թողին

---

24. This should be a locative case.
25. Arm Exod 2:3 has տապանակաւ.
26. The word ամիս "months" is missing from the text.

նենգել տղային՝ ասելով, թէ. «Ի տխմարութենէ արար զայն եւ ոչ գիտութեամբ, արքայ:

10/ «Եւ թէ կամիս, փորձեցցուք»,- ասեն: Եւ բերին առաջի մանկանն, սկտեղամբ²⁷ մի կայծ կրակ, եւ սկտեղամբ մի ոսկի կարմիր, որպէս զհուր՝ ասելով. «Եթէ զոսկին առցէ, յայտ է, որ խորամանկութեամբ էարկ զձեռն ի մորուս արքայի: Իսկ եթէ զհուրն առցէ, երեխի, թէ անմեղութեամբ արար վասն տխմարութեանն:

11/ Եւ ձգեաց Մովսէս զձեռն իւր ի հուրն, եւ կափուցեալ կայծն ի մատն տղային: Եւ նա տարաւ վաղվաղակի զմատն ի բերանն՝ լալով. կափուցեալ կայծին, եղ ի վերա լեզուին, եւ լեզուն եւս այրեցաւ: Վասն այսորիկ յառաքելն Աստուծոյ զնա առ փարաւոն ասէր նրբածայն եւ ծանրալեզու:

12/ Եւ այնպէս Մովսէս սնեալ եղեւ ի տանն փարաւոնի եւ վարժեցաւ ամենայն իմաստութեամբն եգիպտացոց, զի Մարի դուստրն փարաւոնի զնա իւր որդեգիր արար: Եւ եղեւ զայրավար եգիպտացոցն: Եւ յորժամ գերեցին երրպացիքն զՄարի զանուանեալ մայրն Մովսէսի, Ժ. (10) ամ պատերազմեալ Մովսէս՝ առ գէթոպիա եւ դարձոյց զանուանեալ մայրն իւր զՄարի:

13/ Առ գերի եւ զթագուհի նոցա զԹեսբի: Եւ յետ մահուն Մառեա անուանեալ մօրն Մովսէսի նախանձեցան եգիպտացիքն ընդ Մովսէսի եւ կամէին ըսպանանել զնա: Եւ իմացեալ Մովսէսի՝ սպան զՔսանթի գշարջարիշն Իսրայէլի, եւ փախեաւ ի Մադիամ եւ կեցեալ անդ ամս Խ. (40) ի տանն Հռաքուէլի, ուր ծնաւ Բ. (2) որդիս, զԳերսամ եւ զԵղիազար:

14/ Իբրեւ եղեւ Մովսէս Հ. (70) ամաց, երեւեցաւ նմա Աստուած հրով ի մորենին եւ ասաց նմա երթալ յԵգիպտոս եւ ազատել զազգն Իսրայէլի: Եւ նա ոչ կամէր գնալ, այլ յապաղեաց Ժ. (10) ամ՝ պատճառելով զնրբութիւն ճայինն եւ զծանրութիւն լեզուին:

15/ Եւ դարձեալ երեւեցաւ նմա Աստուած յՁ. (80) ամի կենացն Մովսէսի եւ ասաց նմա երթալ յԵգիպտոս եւ ազատել զազգն Իսրայէլի: Եւ / fol 56r / նա դեռեւս յապաղէր ի գնալ, մինչեւ ետ առնել նմա Աստուած սքանչելի նշանս: Եւ ասաց. «Ո՞ արար զխուլն եւ զհամրն, զկոյրն եւ զականին. ոչ ապաքէն ես, Տէ՛ր Աստուած»:

16/ «Եւ արդ, ե՛րթ գնա յԵգիպտոս, եւ Ահարոն եղբայր քո եղիցի քեզ բերան, եւ դու նմա պատգամաբեր յաստուածակոյս կողմանէ»: Եւ գնացեալ Մովսէս արար զնշանսն առաջի Ահարոնի եւ ամենայն

---

27. There is erasure of ե between կ and տ.

ժողովրդեանն, որք հաւատացին յԱստուած եւ ի Մովսէս ծառայ նորա:

17/ Եւ ապա զնացին Մովսէս եւ Ահարոն եւ մտին առաջի փարաւոնի, եւ արարին մեծամեծ նշանս, եւ Ժ. (10) հարուածովք պատժեալ զեգիպտոս եհան զԻսրայէլ: Եւ հերձեալ զծովն Կարմիր անցոյց զժողովուրդն ընդ ցամաք եւ ընկղմեաց զփարաւուն զաւրաւքն իւրովք[28] ի ծովն Կարմիր, եւ եհան զԻսրայէլ յանապատն:

18/ Եւ զամս Խ. (40) կերակրեաց զնոսա մանանայիւ յանապատին յերկնից եւ լորամարգիւ ի ծովէ, եւ արբոյց նոցա շուր ի վիմէ, եւ սեամպ[29] հրոյ եւ ամպոյ լուսատու եւ պահապան եղեւ նոցա ի տուէ եւ ի գիշերի:

19/ Եւ պահեաց Գ. (3) Խ. (40)[30] եւ ընկալաւ զտախտականն քարեղէնս՝ գրեալ մատամբն Աստուծոյ, զԺ.բանեա (10) օրինացն: Կազմեաց զխորանն ի նմանութիւն երկնից եւ ձեռնադրեաց զԱհարոն եւ զորդիս նորա ի քահանայութիւն Տեառն:

20/ Կարգեաց եւ զՂեւտացիսն ի կարգ պաշտաման Տեառն: Վանեաց աղաւթիւք եւ տարածմամբ ձեռացն զԱմաղէկ: Եհար զՍեհոն եւ զՈվգ արքայ եւ զամբարշտեալսն յԻսրայէլէ սատակեաց:

21/ Բորոտեաց զքոյրն իւր զՄարիամ, եւ Ահարոնի բարկացաւ Տէր սատակել զնա վասն Մովսէսի, քանզի քոյրն եւ եղբայրն բամբասեցին զծառայն Աստուծոյ զՄովսէս, որ հեզ էր քան զամենայն մարդիկ, եւ չի պատուէր մեծարանաւք զթագուհին եթովպացոց, զոր ինքն զերեալ էր անտի:

22/ Չի ի ժամանակին յայնմիկ, որ Մովսէս որդեգիր էր ‹դստերն›փարաւոնի, Ժ. (10) ամ պատերազմեցաւ ընդ Եթովպիա: Եւ սնոյց եղունս եւ ճագու արացլաց, եւ նոքաք պատերազմեցան եւ էառ զԵթովպիա: Չի աւձուտ էր ճանապարհն, որ երթայր յԵթովպիա, եւ եղունքն եւ արագիլքն զաւձան սատակեցուցին:

---

28. վ above line, p.m.
29. Phonetic variation of մբ / մպ.
30. The text here has, in Armenian numerals, "3 40" with no further specification. From the wording it is unclear whether this means "forty (days) on three occasions" or "forty-three days." However, it is made quite clear in §33 that he undertook three forty-day fasts. In the first case, it could mean the fasts of Exodus of 24:18 and 34:28. These two fasts, connected with two givings of the Torah, are repeated in Deut 9:9 and 9:18. The third forty-day fast is unidentified. See Seder Olam Rabba 6 for a Rabbinic source that also has three periods of forty days. The text does not make explicit the referent of this number. I have supplied "days," which seems evident.

23/ Եւ ապա կարաց Մովսէս ի Հապաշաստան³¹ մտանել եւ ի գերեւն զնոսա: Ջայն թագուհին, զոր գերեալ էր Մովսէս, դեռ եւս յԵգիպտոս էր յետ ԽԲ. (42) ամաց գերութեանն: Եւ ի հանել ժողովրդեանն յԵգիպտոսէ, զնա եւս եհան անտի: Իբր թէ զուր եւ ողորմութիւն առնել նմա, եւ այնպէս մեծարանաւք շրջեցուցաներ զնա յանապատին ընդ ժողովրդեանն Իսրայելի:

24/ Վասն այսորիկ բամբասեցին զՄովսէս Մարիամ եւ Ահարոն եւ պատուհասեցան: Եւ ապա վաղճանեցաւ Ահարոն, եւ թաղեաց զնա Մովսէս ի գլուխ լերինն Հովրայ: Եւ յառաջ / fol 56v / զմեռանելն Ահարոնի մերկացոյց Մովսէս զպատմուճանն ի նմանէ եւ զգեցոյց Եղիազարու որդոյ նորա, եւ քահանայացոյց զնա ընդ նորա, եւ ապա մեռաւ Ահարոն եւ թաղեցաւ ի գլուխ լերինն:

25/ Եւ լացին զԱհարոն որդիքն Իսրայելի զաւուրս Լ. (30).: Գ. (3) ամաւ յառաջ էր ծնեալ Ահարոն, քան զՄովսէս, եւ Գ. (3) ամաւ յառաջ մեռաւ, քան զնա: Եւ կացոյց Մովսէս զՅեսու որդի Նաւեա առաջնորդ Իսրայելի փոխանակ իւր: Եւ ինքն ելեալ ի գլուխ լերինն Նաբաւ եւ անդ վաղճանեցաւ Մովսէս ՃԻ. (120) ամաց:

26/ Չի յերեւմանեն Աստուծոյ լուսատրեցան երեսքն Մովսէսի զպայծառութիւն հանդերձեալ կենացն եւ զոր Ադամ ի դրախտին ունէր, մինչ զի ոչ կարէին որդիքն Իսրայելի հայել ի նա, զատ ի յԱհարոնէ եւ յԵսուա, վասն որոյ եւ է. (7) քաղ ձգէին ի վերայ երեսացն Մովսէսի, եւ ապա կարէին խաւսել ընդ նմա որդիքն Իսրայելի:

27/ Եւ մարուս ոչ ունէր Մովսէս ի պայծառ լուսափայլութենէ դիմացն: Սա ցանկացաւ տեսանել զերուսաղէմ եւ զայլ տնաւրինական տեղիսն, եւ ոչ թողացոյց Աստուած, զի բարկացոյց զՏէր ի վերայ ջուրցն բամբասանաց: Եւ պատճառն այս է, զի Մարիամ քոյրն Մովսէսի, որ էր կոյս եւ մարգարէ, մեռեալ էր, եւ Մովսէս ի սուգ մտեալ էր վասն նորա:

28/ Եւ ժողովուրդն ծարաւեալ տրտնջեաց զԱստուծոյ եւ բամբասեցին զՄովսէս, վասն որոյ զնաց Մովսէս տրտմութեամբ եւ եհար զվէմն բարկութեամբ: Վասն այսորիկ բարկացաւ Աստուած եւ ոչ ետ ջուր, զի պարտ էր խոնարհութեամբ եւ աղաւթիւք հարկանել, որպէս սովոր էր առնել, եւ ոչ բարկութեամբ:

29/ Վասն որոյ ոչ եթող նմա Աստուած տեսանել զերկիրն աւետեաց, այլ ասաց նմա ելանել ի լեառն Նաբաւ եւ անտի տեսանել զերկիրն աւետեաց, եւ մեռանել ի գլուխ լերինն Նաբաւու, մերձ ի տունն Փագովրա կոչ՝ յանդիման Երիքովի եւ Յորդանանու:

---

31. This is another name for Ethiopia.

12. OF MOSES AND AARON

30/ Եւ թաղեաց զնա Միքայէլ հրեշտակապետն, եւ ոչ ոք գիտաց զգերեզման նորա ի մարդկանէ, մինչեւ ցայսաւր, վասն Բ. (2) պատճառի: Զի աստուած անուանեալ էր Մովսէս, զադտ եւ անյայտ մեռաւ ի մարդկանէ, զի մի տեսցեն զաստուածն մեռեալ։ Եւ դարձեալ, զի մի առնուցուն մարդիկ ի պաշտել զգերեզման նորա եւ զոսկերսն:

31/ Զի ոչ եղեւ մարգարէ յԻսրայէլի իբրեւ զՄովսէս, զոր ծանեաւ Տէր յանդիման նշանօք եւ արուեստիւք, զոր արար նովաւ։ Եւ լացին զՄովսէս որդիքն Իսրայէլի յՇռաբովթ Մովարու, յանդիման Երիքովի, աւուրս Լ. (30) եւ ոչ աւելի կամ պակաս:

32/ Զի թիւ լուսնին Լ. (30) օր է, եւ անդէն նոր ծնանի, եւ ցուցանէ զմեր յարութիւնն ի հողոյ եւ զվերստին նորոգումն յանմահութիւն: Մարգարէն Մովսէս Դ. (4)[32] ծնընդեան հանդիպեցաւ. նախ՝ յՈզաբեղա, Բ. (2)՝ ի ջրոյ. Գ. (3)՝ ի հրոյ, որ մնաց առ Աստուծոյ ի գլուխ լերինն Սինեա աւուրս Խ. (40), եւ ապա ծնաւ ի / fol 57r / հրոյ, չորրորդ ծնունդն Մովսէսի՝ ի վիմէն, որ եդ զնա Աստուած ի փապ վիմին, որ ետես զետոյսն Աստուծոյ, եւ անտի ծնաւ Մովսէս որդի վիմի:

33/ Պահեաց Մովսէս Գ. (3) Խ. (40), եւ ամբ կենաց նորա էին Գ. (3) Խ. (40)՝ ՃԻ. (120) տարի օր ընդ տարոյ պահեաց։ Եւ ոչ ոք զտաւ նման նմա յամենայն մարգարէսն, զի բերան ի բերան ընդ Աստուծոյ խօսեցաւ:[33]

Text extant only in 12b (M1099):

34/ /fol 181v / Եւ էր յելիցն Ադամայ ՎՊԽԲ. (3,842) ամ, եւ ելին յաւուր հինգշաբաթու եւ անցին ընդ ծովն ի կիւրակէի։ Եւ ի ձգելն Մովսէսի զգաւազանն ի վերայ ծովուն, գայս ասաց. «Այիայ, Աստուած իմ առաջի իմ»: Եւ ի յաջակողմն ձգել զձեռն ասաց. «Շրայիայ. դու հաներ զմեզ Աստուած» եւ ի ձախն ասաց. «Ադոնիա Տէր Աստուած ընդ մեզ»: Եւ խաչանիշ նկարու դրոշմ արար նոցա ճանապարհի նոր ցամաքեալ, ոչ մի/ fol 182r /այն ցամաքեալ, այլ եւ կանաչեալ, լայնցեալ յոյժ: Մինչեւ երկոտասան ցեղքն Իսրայէլի ազխիւք իւրեանց հանդէպ միմեանց չուէին:

---

32. The letter has been damaged, but "4" agrees with the following enumeration and the surviving marks are not incompatible with Դ.

33. The text is followed directly by a colophon naming the commissioner of the manuscript and several members of his family. It is unclear whether the first four words of the colophon are a pious wish by the copyist appended to the text or the beginning of the colophon.

35/ Եւ նախ եմուտ ցեղն Բենիամենի, եւ ապա ցեղն Ղեւեայ, ապա Յուդային եւ այլոցն: Եւ աստի կոչեցան եբրայեցիք, եւ տուաւ նոցա նոր լեզու եւ բարձու Եգիպտոսին եւ նմանէ հայրենի լեզուին, զոր եւ արդ ունին, եւ այնու երգէին,.«Աւրհնեցուք զՏէր, զի փառօք է փառաւորեալ»: Եւ զկնի նոցա եմուտ փարաւոն, եւ սուզան ի ջուրն փոխանակ մանկանցն Իսրայէղի:

36/ Եւ եհան ջուրն զապանեալսն մասն բազում ի կողմն Իսրայէղի զինուքն իւրեանց, եւ իւրաքանչիւր զտեր իւր ճանաչեաց եւ թաղեաց, եւ արին զապարագինութիւնս նոցա եւ այնու կոտորեցին զԱմադէկ, որ էր հարճ որդի Եսաւայ, եւ յայնմ կալմանէ զհանեալն ի ծովէն արին եթոպացիքն, որք եկեալ էին ի Գանգէս գետոյ, եւ կատարեցաւ բան սաղմոսին «կերակրել զեթոպացիսն»:

37/ Եյյետելիցն Իսրայէղի, շարժեցաւ Եգիպտոս զէ. (7) ամիս, եւ ի³⁴ տունս ոչ բնակեցին, եւ ասեն, թէ՛ «յրնկոմին փարաւոնի» մնացեալքն յԵգիպտոս իւրաքանչիւր ոք զզորձու իւր աստուածացուցին, իբր թէ եղեն նոցա փրկութեան պատճառ:

Apparatus

Lemma is Bodleian Marsh 438 and the variant is M1099.

1/ քահանայապետ | Մովսէսէ

2/ Ամրամայ | որդոյն] որդլոյն1°, 2°, 3°, 4°, 5° | Ղեւեայ | Յակորբայ | Իսահակայ

3/ Ամրամայ | մօրէ | զետք | քումէ

4/ ամսեան | գնաց] երթայ | մնայ | նախախնամութիւն | տնօրինեաց | աստեղազետքն

5/ վասն որոյ] + պրտուեա 'of rushes' | մանկասպանն | զի] + եւ | Իսրայէղի] եբրայեցոց | հեղձուցանել | ընկենու | Գ.] + ամիս

6/ ընկենուլն | դստեր | փարաւոնի] թագաւորին

7/ խանդաղատեցաւ] խանդաղակաթեցաւ | առ նովաւ] գնվաւ | մանկանցն | մայրն | մի եւ իբր ի] իբրեւ | դայեակ] + սնուցանել զտղայն : '+ to nurture the boy' | նա] դուստրն փարաւոնի 'Pharaoh's daughter'

8/ տարաւ] + գնա | յորդէզիր | զմուրացն | առեալ] in marg. M1099 |

9/ փարաւոն (§8) --- փարաւոն (§9)] om : hpl | զայն] om

---

34. Above the line p.m.

12. OF MOSES AND AARON 141

10/ թէ] երէ | սկուտեղամբ 1° : so Marsh 438* | սկուտեղամբ 2° | երէ] զի թէ | մորուսն
11/ | իւր] om | լալով] om | | լեզուին] լեզւին | յառաքեւն] յուղարկեւն | նրբածայն] + եմ ես
12/ | զեթովպիա | երովպացիքն | պատերազմեալ Մովսէս] պատերազմեալ Մովսէսի
13/ մահուանն | սպանանել | եսպան | Հռաբւելի
14/ մորենջն | լեզւին
15/ գնալն | Աստուած 2°] om | զրսքանչելի | նշանսն | ասաց] + Աստուած
17/ արարին] արին : hplg | պատժեալ] պատեալ | եւ հերձեալ --- կարմիր եւ] om
18/ յանապատին] om | սեամբ | պահապան] հովանի 'shelter'
19/ ընկալաւ] + յԱստուծոյ | քարեղէն | բան
20/ զղեւտացիս | կարգ] սպաս | արքայ
21/ բորոտեցոյց | մարդիկք | երովպատոց
22/ <դստերն>] M1099 om | պատերազմեցաւ 2°] + ընդ երովպիա : "battled with Ethiopia" | զեթովպիա] գնա | եւ] + նորա
23/ ի 2°] om | զերել | առնելով
24/ վախճանեցաւ | նորա 1°---նորա 2°] om : hmt
25/ զահարոն] om | աւուրս | յառաջ --- զՄովսէս] յառաջ քան զՄովսէս | էր ծնեալ Ահարովն | գնա] զՄովսէս | վախճանեցաւ
26/ զատ ի] զատ | Յեսուայ | ի վերայ երեսացն] յերեսացն վերայ | Մովսէսի] om
27/ մուռուս | մտեալ] նստեալ
28/ ոչ] om | հարկանել 'have smitten'] + զվէմն 'the rock'
29/ | աւետեաց 2° 'promised'] Երուսաղէմի 'of Jerusalem' | Փագովրայ | Երեքովի
30/ պաշտել] պաշտօն |
31/ որդիքն / զմովսէս] ∞ | ըրաբովթ
32/ անդէն] անդ | յանմահութիւն] ի յանմահութիւն | Սինայ | ծնաւ] + գնա | ծնունդ / Մովսէսի] ∞
33/ ի 1°---ի 2°] om : hmt | խոսեցաւ] + ընդ Աստուծոյ

142   PART 4: MOSES TO DANIEL

Translation

Title M1099 / Of the prophets Moses and Aaron.
Marsh 438/ 9 Hoṙi and 17 September, It is the Feast of Moses and Aaron

1/ The proto-prophet Moses, the speaker with God, who was the first of all prophets, and was named by God a god for Pharaoh.[35] Aaron his brother, the first high priest, (was) ordained by Moses. For God ordained Moses and he, Aaron and his sons.[36]

2/ They were from the tribe of Levi, sons of Amram, the son of Kohath, son of Levi, the son of Jacob, the son of Isaac, the son of Abraham. And Jacob as[37] a blessing for his sons gave the priesthood to Levi and the kingship to Judah.[38]

3/ Moses was born, a son of Amram from (his) mother Jochebed, who was a daughter of Levi.[39] And the birth of Moses took place in this fashion: The savants of Egypt said to Pharaoh, "On such and such a date, on such and such a day of the month, a savior will be born for Israel and he will liberate Israel from bondage to you."[40]

---

35. Exod 7:1.
36. The Hebrew Bible does not say that Moses ordained Aaron a priest. He himself was a priest by descent, and perhaps his construction of the Tabernacle is a priestly function. Aaron was ordained by Moses, Exod 28:1; chapter 29 prescribes the ordination and associated ritual, and cf. Lev 8. The care of our author to trace the lineage of ordination is perhaps an outcome of the Christian concern with the apostolic succession of ordination.
37. The preposition ḥ comes here with the accusative, so, "as, for."
38. This is not the case in Jacob's blessing (Gen 49:5–7) but is true of the blessing of Moses in Deut 33:8–11. In ancient sources, Levi is ordained priest in ALD 4–5 and in Testament of Levi 8:1–10 he describes a vision of his investiture. The double ordination of Judah and Levi is found in Jub 31:9–20, but most likely was known to the Armenians from Testaments of the Twelve Patriarchs, where it is a common theme. No Armenian of Jubilees itself is known to have existed. On the Levi-Judah passages in Test Patr, see Harm Hollander and Marinus de Jonge, *The Testaments of the Twelve Patriarchs. A Commentary*, SVTP 8 (Leiden: Brill, 1985), 56–61. For the Armenian text of Testaments of the Twelve Patriarchs see Michael E. Stone and Vered Hillel, *An Editio Minor of the Armenian Version of the Testaments of the Twelve Patriarchs*, HUAS 11 (Peeters: Leuven, 2012).
39. See Num 26:59. Here this expression means a Levite woman.
40. The following story is familiar to several Jewish sources. In b. Soṭah 12b astrologers predict that the savior of Israel will be struck down by water, and therefore, Pharaoh decreed that all babies be thrown into the Nile. However, they erred in their application of their prediction and their vision actually referred to Moses's sin with the water from the stone. A similar story appears also in Exod. Rab. 1.18. Other sources include: Josephus, *A.J.* 2.9.2; Tg. Ps.-J.; Exod 1:15; m. Tanḥ. Vayakhel 4.9.

4/ When Pharaoh heard this, he was careful with respect to the counsel[41] and in that same month he took all the Israelite men and he went on a deer hunt and remained outside the whole month.[42] But God's providence disposed things thus, that Amram took Jochebed with him, and she conceived on the signaled day that the astrologers had said.

5/ And when Moses was born, he was hidden in a house for three months.[43] And because he was a lively child and they were unable to hide (him any more), on account of that they cast him into the river in an ark, for fear of Pharaoh's infanticide.[44] For when the birth of the savior of Israel was discerned,[45] Pharaoh also commanded with respect to all the male Israelite children, that some be suffocated on birth and others be cast into the river.[46]

6/ On account of this they hid Moses for three <months>[47] at home and were unable (to do so) any longer. And the ark that was thrown in the river was stopped at an eddy[48] in the river. And when Pharaoh's daughter went down to the river bank, and her handmaidens saw the ark, and taking it from the eddy's movement, they brought the ark with the child before the king's daughter.[49]

7/ And she saw (him and) melted with compassion for him and said, "This is one of the Hebrew children."[50] Then Miriam, Moses's sister, who was herself also one of the handmaidens of Pharaoh's daughter,[51] took the child and gave[52] it to its own (or: her) mother Jochebed[53] as a wetnurse to nurture the child on behalf of Pharaoh's daughter. She nurtured him and brought (him) to her.[54]

---

41. That is, acted according to the counsel.
42. Thus preventing the Israelite men from having intercourse, and so foiling the birth of the promised savior. The story of the deer hunt is not known to me from elsewhere.
43. Exod 2:2.
44. Exod 2:3.
45. Or: felt.
46. The suffocation of children is added by the Armenian text. According to Exod 1:22, they are cast into the river.
47. The word "months" is missing from the text. It is restored from §5.
48. Or: a bend.
49. In Exod 2:5 it is Pharaoh's daughter who spies the ark. Perhaps the writer thought it more appropriate that it be the servants.
50. The direct speech is quoted from Exod 2:6.
51. An embroidery to explain how Miriam could talk to Pharaoh's daughter.
52. Hendiadys, literally, "brought, gave."
53. The name is not in the corresponding text in Exodus. Jochebed is Amram's wife in genealogical texts in Exod 6:20 and Num 25:59.
54. Presumably, when he was weaned. The story accords with Exod 2:6-9.

8/ And she took (the child and) brought (him) to her father, Pharaoh and said, "This is one of the Hebrew children: I took him from the river and I made into my adopted son."[55] And Moses was a lively child and handsome,[56] by which Pharaoh was placated. And he took him to his bosom and kissed him. And at that very moment, Moses seized[57] Pharaoh's beard with his ten fingers.[58]

9/ At this Pharaoh was wrath (and) wanted to kill him. But the wise men who were standing there about that time, did not let (him) hurt[59] the boy. They said, "He did that from foolishness and not knowledgeably, O king!"

10/ And they said, "If you wish, we shall put him to the test." And they brought before the child in a bowl fiery coals and in a bowl red gold like fire, saying, "If he takes the gold, it will be clear that he laid hands on the king's beard out of malice. However, if he takes the fire, it makes evident that he did this in innocence because of foolishness."[60]

11/ And Moses put his hand into the fire, and the coal stuck to the boy's finger and he immediately put his finger into his mouth, crying. With the coal stuck, he put[61] it on his tongue and then (his) tongue also was scorched. On

---

55. Compare Exod 2:20. The adoption of Moses by the daughter of Pharaoh is mentioned in Exod 2:10, but his relationship to Pharaoh is made explicit by our text.

56. Some Jewish sources mention Moses's good looks just before Pharaoh tries him as a usurper; see Philo, *Moses* 1.5; Josephus, *A.J.* 2.9.6-7; Midrash Tanḥ. Exod. 8.2; Exod. Rab. 1.26.

57. Literally: smote.

58. For medieval Armenians, the pulling of someone's beard was a great insult and done by a superior to an inferior. For this reason, Pharaoh interpreted Moses's pulling his beard as a potential usurpation of the throne, demanding a death penalty. See Stone and Vardanyan, "Jacob and the Man," forthcoming.

59. խաբելւ's primary meaning is "to trick, to deceive." However, here it means "to harm," a meaning listed in NBHL, s.v.

60. This is an old story to be found in Jewish sources cited in n. 56 especially Exod. Rab. 1:26 and Josephus, *A.J.* 2.9.6-7. The form of the story in Exod. Rab. 1:26 is almost identical with that given here but adds that the angel Gabriel directed his hand towards the coals. The way the beard pulling is treated in §§4-5 makes it clear that it was regarded as a usurpation or humiliation. The incident is found in a more complex form in the Palaea Historica §69, where two traditions are found, one that Moses grabbed Pharaoh's sword and the other that he pulled his beard: MOTP 1:627-628. That form of the tradition does not have the coals and the connection to Moses's speech impediment.

61. I.e., his finger was burnt, and the coal still stuck to it. He put his finger with the coal into his mouth....

account of this, when God sent him to Pharaoh, he spoke with a delicate voice and with a heavy tongue.[62]

12/ And thus Moses was nurtured in Pharaoh's house. And he was educated in all the wisdom of the Egyptians,[63] for Mari, Pharaoh's daughter had made him her adopted son.[64] And he became a general of the Egyptians and when the Ethiopians took captive Mari Moses's adoptive mother[65] Moses battled for ten years, took Ethiopia and brought back Mari his adoptive mother.

13/ He also captured their Queen Tʻesbi. And after the death of Mari, Moses's adoptive mother, the Egyptians were jealous of Moses and wished to kill him. And Moses, learning (of this) killed Kʻsantʻi,[66] the tormentor of Israel[67] and fled to Midian.[68] And he lived there for forty years[69] in Raguel's house, where he begat two sons, Gersam[70] and Eleazar.[71]

14/ When Moses was seventy years old, God appeared to him through fire in the thorn bush and said to him to go to Egypt and free the nation of Israel.[72] And he did not wish to go but delayed for ten years,[73] giving the delicacy of his voice and the heaviness of his tongue as reason.

---

62. This of course is constructed on Exod 4:10, Moses's words to God, when he says, "but I am slow of speech and of tongue." Of the rabbinic sources, only Exod. Rab. 1:26 makes this connection.

63. The Egyptians were considered to have acquired great wisdom. Moses's education is the subject of Philo, *Moses* 1.5–7. Philo goes into great details about Moses's success as a student. He also emphasizes that he had Greek teachers (whom he quickly surpassed). Other Jewish-Hellenistic writers portray Moses as the wise man that taught various nations the particular wisdom which was in their view associated with that particular nation. This theme is perhaps connected to the present point.

64. See note 55 on §8 above.

65. Literally: "Mari called mother of Moses." She was Pharaoh's daughter.

66. On all aspects of this incident, see the excursus included in the introductory remarks to this text. There the names are also discussed.

67. In Exod 2:11 it is "an Egyptian beating a Hebrew."

68. The Armenian has "Midiam." See Exod 2:15.

69. No number is given in Exodus.

70. Exod 2:22.

71. There is some confusion here with the name of Moses's second son. Eleazar was Aaron's son, see Exod 6:22. Moses's son was named Eliezer, see Exod 18:4. Below in §24 the reverse mistake is made and Aaron's son is named Eliezer.

72. See Exod 3:2–4:17.

73. This detail is not found in the Bible. Many Rabbinic sources say that Moses was delayed for seven days at the burning bush while God tried to convince him to accept the mission. This idea is attested already in tannaitic sources, such as Seder Olam ch. 5 beginning which is on p. 16 in Milikowsky's edition: Chaim Milikowsky, *Seder Olam Rabba:*

15/ And again God appeared to him in the eightieth year of Moses's life and said to him to go to Egypt and to free the nation of Israel. And he, nevertheless, delayed going until God caused him to do wondrous signs. And he said, "Who made the deaf and the dumb, the blind and the seeing, are you not[74] the Lord God?"[75]

16/ "And now, set out (and) go to Egypt and Aaron your brother will be a mouth for you and you will be a bringer of oracles from the divine to him."[76] And Moses went (and) did signs before Aaron and all the people, who believed in God and in Moses, his servant.[77]

17/ And then Moses and Aaron went and entered in before Pharaoh.[78] And they did very great signs, and having punished Egypt with ten plagues, he[79] brought Israel forth. And splitting the Red Sea, he brought the people across on dry land. And he drowned Pharaoh with his forces in the Red Sea, and he brought Israel forth to the desert.[80]

18/ And for forty years he fed them in the desert with manna from heaven and with quail from the sea, and he gave (them) water to drink from a rock, and he guarded them with a column of fire and with a luminous cloud, both by day and by night.[81]

19/ And he fasted three forty[82] (days) and he received the stone tablets,[83] written by God's finger, the ten-utterance law. He formed the tabernacle in the

---

Critical Edition (Jerusalem: Yad Ben-Zvi, 2013), 16 [Hebrew]; Mekhilta deRabbi Shim'on b. Yoḥai on Exod 3:8 and elsewhere in later midrashic literature.

74. A 3rd pers. verb would be expected.

75. Cf. Exod 4:11.

76. Cf. Exod 4:28–31. God is the speaker of this sentence.

77. Paraphrase in Exod 4:14–16. The last phrase is taken from Exod 14:31, the narrative of the splitting of the Red Sea.

78. See Exod 5:1.

79. Observe the change from plur. to sing.; a variation often found in medieval Armenian manuscripts. See Stone and Hillel, "Index," nos. 73–77, 424–425. Here it is unclear whether Moses or God is said to bring Israel forth, but probably God.

80. This section summarizes the narrative of the Exodus from Egypt.

81. As §17 did for the exodus, so §18 neatly summarized main aspects of the wandering in the desert, reminiscent particularly of Deut 8:2–3 and 15–16.

82. See n. 30 above.

83. Exod 24:12, 31:18, 32:15–16.

12. OF MOSES AND AARON 147

likeness of the heavens[84] and consecrated[85] Aaron and his sons to priesthood of the Lord.[86]

20/ He arranged the Levites in the order of service to the Lord. Through prayer and extending his arms, he repelled Amalek;[87] he smote Sihon and King Og[88] and executed the impious of Israel.[89]

21/ He[90] made his sister Miriam leprous and the Lord became angry with Aaron, (so as) to kill him for Moses's sake, because his sister and brother calumniated Moses, God's servant, who was meeker than all men, because he honored with respect the Queen of the Ethiopians, whom he had taken captive from there.[91]

22/ For in that time when Moses was Pharaoh's <daughter's>[92] adopted son, for ten years he battled with Ethiopia. And he raised hinds and the young of storks and he battled by means of them and he took Ethiopia. For the way

---

84. That is: like that in the heavens. Observe that Bezalel b. Uri b. Hur built the Tabernacle according to a divine pattern that Moses saw; see Exod 25:9 for the pattern and 31:6 for the building of the Tabernacle in accordance with that divine pattern. This is, of course, a much older idea—namely, that the earthly dwelling of a god is built after the pattern of the god's heavenly dwelling.

85. Literally, "placed his hands upon, ordained to priesthood." Moses is not said in Exod to actually lay hands upon Aaron. See n. 36 above.

86. See Exod 28:1; 29:1,9, 20–21, 44; 40:12–16; Lev 8.

87. See Exod 17:8–13; see Joshua b. Nun Text 9, §6 in the present book.

88. Num 3:5–4:49; 8:5–26.

89. This may refer to the incident of the golden calf in Exod 32:26–28.

90. That is, God.

91. This section combines and attempts to systematize a number of different incidents: (1) Moses's marriage to a Cushite woman (Num 12:1). Observe that Moses's marriage to her is not mentioned here, and that to mitigate Moses's act, she is made into the queen of Ethiopia, whom he captured; see §7 above. In Rabbinic sources it seems that the Ethiopian wife is always understood as referring to Zipporah. (2) Miriam and Aaron's speaking against this (Num 12:1–4). (3) God's rebuke of Aaron and Miriam (Num 12:6–8). (4) God's anger and Miriam's leprosy (caused by God, not Moses, Num 12:9–10). What is not stated here is that Aaron's death, related in Num 20:23–28, is connected with this incident. Clearly the author of our text is worried about Miriam's being punished and Aaron not, for their slander of Moses.

92. This is my emendation.

by which he went to Ethiopia was swarming with snakes, and the hinds and the storks slaughtered[93] the snakes.[94]

23/ And then Moses was able to enter Ethiopia and to take them captive. That queen whom Moses had taken captive was still in Egypt after forty-two years of captivity. And when he brought the people out of Egypt, he also brought her thence, as if doing her an act of pity and mercy. And thus, respectfully, he had her wander around the desert with the people of Israel.[95]

24/ Because of this, Miriam and Aaron calumniated Moses. And then Aaron died and Moses buried him on the peak of Mount Hor. And before Aaron's death, Moses stripped him of his robe and put it upon Eleazar his son, and made him a priest in his place. And then Aaron died and was buried on the mountain's peak.[96]

25/ And the children of Israel bewailed Aaron for thirty days.[97] He was born three years before Moses and he died three years before him.[98] And Moses appointed Joshua son of Nun as leader of Israel in place of himself.[99] And he himself climbed to the peak of Mount Nebo and there Moses died at the age of one hundred and twenty years.[100]

26/ For from the revelation of God, Moses's face shone with the brilliance of the life to come and with that which Adam had in Eden,[101] so that the Chil-

---

93. This factitive of սպանակեմ translated "I slaughter" should mean "caused to slaughter." It is not listed in NBHL and, anyway, context demands that it mean "slaughtered."

94. This story is, of course, extrabiblical. See "Excursus on Moses in Ethiopia" in the introductory remarks above.

95. All this section is embroidery on the biblical story.

96. Num 20:22–28.

97. Num 20:29.

98. This contradicts Num 33:38 which explicitly places the death of Aaron in the fortieth year after the Exodus. Also, according to Rabbinic tradition, Aaron died in the same year as Moses: see Sipre Deut. 305.

99. Num 27:15–23; Deut 31:7

100. Deut 34:1, 7.

101. The luminous face of the righteous is mentioned in many sources, see the discussion in Stone, *4 Ezra*, 245, 259; for further examples, see Dan 12:3; Job 19:8; 1 En. 62.10 63.11; Odes Sol. 15:2; Mas. Geh. 7 (MOTP 1:741); 4 Ezra 7:97, 125; 10:25; 2 En. 65.11, 66.7, 69.1. Eschatological shining faces are a return to the Adamic brilliance in the garden of Eden, which reflects the idea that τὰ ἐσχάτα ὡς τὰ πρῶτα; see further concerning Adam's luminous body, Apoc. Sedr. 7:5–6; Stone, *Adamgirk'*, 169, 197, 272, 305; According to Yovhannēs T'lkuranc'i (1320–1400?), Adam's face was darkened by sin: N. Bogharian, *Yovhannēs T'lkuranc'i: Poems* (Յովհաննէս Թլկուրանցի: Տաղեր) (Jerusalem: St. James, 1958), 84–85, stanzas 95 and 102, and this idea is widely spread. Of course, the idea that Adam had luminous garments of which he was stripped when he sinned (anchored in Gen

dren of Israel could not look at him, except for Aaron and Joshua. On account of this they placed seven veils upon Moses's face and then the Children of Israel could talk with him.[102]

27/ And Moses did not have a beard due to the shining resplendence of (his) countenance.[103] He desired to see Jerusalem and the other dominical places and God did not permit (it),[104] because he angered God over the waters of calumny.[105] And this is the reason that Miriam, Moses's sister, who was a virgin and a prophet, died;[106] and Moses was in mourning on account of her.[107]

28/ And the people were thirsty (and) complained about God and calumniated Moses. On account of this Moses was sad[108] and he smote the rock in

---

3:10–11) is found in many sources: many references are given by Stone, *Traditions*, index s.v. "stripping."

102. Cf. Exod 34:29–35. That passage does not mention that Aaron and Joshua could still look at Moses. It also mentions only one veil and Moses himself puts it on.

103. Here the text appears to take account of a question, "How did Moses's face shine if he had a beard?" In Michael E. Stone, "Biblical Text and Armenian Retelling," *JSAS* 26 (2017): 82–87, this phenomenon is discussed. Further examples may be found below.

104. This verb is also, superfluously in the factitive; compare n. 93. The whole of this section is actually an embroidery and makes odd inferences from the biblical text. The statement here is actually completely anachronistic. The "dominical" places are those in which the events of Christ's life took place.

105. See Deut 32:48–52. Intriguingly Num 20:24 relates this event also to Aaron, "Aaron shall be gathered to his people; for he shall not enter the land which I have given to the people of Israel, because you rebelled against my command at the waters of Meribah." See further Deut 34:4.

106. This is an extrabiblical tradition.

107. Numbers 20:1 does not state explicitly that Miriam died because of complaints relating to water at the waters of Meribah (which name means "waters of conflict"). It is, however, a fair inference from the fact that a conflict between the people and Moses and Aaron is related in Num 20:2–8, followed by Moses's striking the rock at God's command (Num 9:13). Moses's mourning for Miriam is not mentioned in the biblical text. The tradition of Miriam's well may also be referred to here, and perhaps its cessation after Miriam's death brought about the problem of water. Alternatively or additionally, the comment may be psychological rather than aggadic, and Moses's anger might be seen as an outcome of his mourning. This seems to be implied by the first sentence of §28.

108. Literally: went sadly.

anger.[109] On account of this, God was angry and did not give water,[110] for Moses ought to have smitten (it) in humility and with prayer, as he did customarily, and not in anger.

29/ Therefore, God did not permit him to see the promised land,[111] but he said to him to climb Mount Nebo and thence to see the promised land, and to die on the top of Mount Nebo, close to the house of the idols of Peor,[112] over against Jericho and the Jordan.[113]

30/ And the archangel Michael[114] buried him and no human knew his grave until this day, for two reasons. Since Moses was called a god,[115] he died secretly and hidden from men, lest they see the god dead. And moreover, lest men take his tomb and bones for worship.

---

109. There are two stories about Moses striking the rock, one in Exod 17:1–7 and the other in Num 20:2–13. These two stories are very similar and both end with the place being named "Meribah." The main difference between them is indeed that in Exodus Moses struck the rock following an explicit commandment of God, while Numbers turns smiting the rock into a sin. Some other smaller details are also different. Another verse that may be a third version of the story is Num 21:16 (although this entire paragraph seems to be an abbreviated quotation from the lost "Book of the Wars of the Lord").

110. In Num 20:11 it says the contrary.

111. Moses was taken to a mountain top and shown the land: See Num 21:12, 27:14, and Deut 32:51, which explicitly states that Moses did not enter the land of Israel because of the incident of Meribah. But the Pentateuchal sources say that he saw the land. In Deut 32:51 God addresses Moses's death and relates it to Meribah. Elsewhere in Deuteronomy, where Moses's death is mentioned, a reason is not offered.

112. Deut 34:6 clearly places Moses's burial place near "the house of Peor," and apparently the text here reflects that.

113. Num 27:12–14; Deut 32:48–52; 34:1–5.

114. For Michael's role, see Jude 9. Rabbinic tradition offers three different explanations of Moses's burial: (1) God himself buried him—m. Soṭah 1.9; b. Soṭah 14a; b. Sanh. 39a; Gen. Rab. 8.13; Exod. Rab. 20:19; Deut. Rab. 9.5 (God with aid of the angels); Tanḥ. Beshalaḥ 2.3; and LAB 19:16; (2) Moses buried himself—Num. Rab. 10.17; Sipre Num. 32; (3) Moses never died—Sipre Deut. 357:28; b. Soṭah 13b.

115. Behind this prima facie odd statement is the verse Exod 4:16, where God tells Moses to take Aaron with him to Pharaoh, and that "He shall speak for you to the people; and he shall be a mouth for you, and you shall be to him as God." To this we may add God's words in Exod 7:1, "See, I make you as God to Pharaoh; and Aaron your brother shall be your prophet."

31/ For there was no prophet in Israel like Moses, who knew the Lord face to face,[116] through signs and miracles[117] which He did through him.[118] And the Children of Israel bewailed Moses in Araboth Moab, over against Jericho, for thirty days, not more and not less.[119]

32/ Because the number of the moon[120] is thirty days and immediately it is born anew, it demonstrates our resurrection from dust and (our) renewal again to immortality. The prophet Moses encountered four births: first, from Jochebed; the second, from the water;[121] the third, from fire, for he remained with God on the top of Mt. Sinai for forty days and then was born of fire; Moses's fourth birth, from the rock—that God placed him in a crevice of the rock so that he saw God's back.[122] And thence Moses was born as a son of the rock.[123]

33/ Moses fasted 3 x 40 days and the years of his life were 3 x 40, (that is) one hundred and twenty years, he fasted a day for each year.[124] And none among all the prophets was found (to be) similar to him. He spoke face to face[125] with God.[126]

Text extant only in M1099

---

116. Thus I translate յանդիման, which usually means "against, in the presence of." Here it is used as an adverb.
117. See Exod 7:3, Deut 4:34, 6:22, etc. This common phrase is the same in the Armenian Bible.
118. Cf. Deut 34:10-11.
119. Cf. Deut 34:8. The phrase "not more and not less" does not appear in the verse. It is perhaps an interpretation of the end of the verse which says that after thirty days the mourning ceased.
120. That is, of the lunar month and the lunar cycle.
121. When Pharaoh's daughter took him out of the river. See §7 above.
122. Compare Exod 33:20-24:"But," he said, "you cannot see my face; for man shall not see me and live." 21 And the Lord said, "Behold, there is a place by me where you shall stand upon the rock; 22 and while my glory passes by I will put you in a cleft of the rock, and I will cover you with my hand until I have passed by; 23 then I will take away my hand, and you shall see my back; but my face shall not be seen." The expression is found in Vardan Arewelc'i (M1267) fol 5r i: եւ ապա ի վիմն եդեալ արար զնա ծնունդ վիմի "and then, having placed him in the rock He made him a birth (one born) of rock."
123. This expression, "son of the rock" is not found elsewhere of Moses. With his four births, compare Jonah 2 §§2, 29. The reason for this idea is unclear.
124. We observe the Christian piety in the stress on fasting; see p. 243 n. 29. Here the age of one hundred and twenty years given in Deut 34:7 is viewed as corresponding to Moses's three forty-day fasts. Those fasts are discussed on p. 139 n. 30.
125. Literally: mouth to mouth. In §31 above the text uses the word յանդիման.
126. The last two sentences are a paraphrase of Deut 34:9-10.

34/ And it was the three thousand, eight hundred and forty second year from Adam's going forth.[127] And they went forth on Thursday and crossed the sea on Sunday.[128] And when Moses extended his staff over the sea, he said this, "Ayiay, my God is before me." And when he extended his hand to the right, he said, "Srayiay, you brought us out, God," and to the left he said, "Adonia, the Lord God is with us."[129] And with a cruciform image he made a seal.[130] A new path dried up, (indeed) not only dried up but also greened, and it widened greatly, until the twelve tribe of Israel with their baggage advanced against one another.[131]

35/ And first the tribe of Benjamin and then of Levi and then of Judah and of the others. And from this point they were called Hebrews, and a new tongue/language was given to them and the Egyptian one was removed, and from it (comes) the ancestral language which now they have. And in it they were singing, "Let us bless the Lord for he is glorified through glory."[132] And Pharaoh entered (the sea) after them and they were immersed in the water in recompense for the Israelite children.[133]

36/ And the water brought forth the dead,[134] the major part in the Israelite direction, with their weapons. And each recognized his master and buried (him). And they each took their armaments and with that they cut down Amalek, who was Esau's concubine's son,[135] And through this seizing of those brought forth from the sea they took the Ethiopians that had come

---

127. The text uses the word ելից which means "going forth, Exodus" perhaps deliberately. The common verb for Adam's expulsion from the Garden is հանել "bring forth." Does ելք here deliberately evoke the Exodus from Egypt, for which is is the fixed term? The numbers here are in the range yielded by the chronological text published in *Angels and Heroes*, part 2, but not identical.

128. This pattern is taken from the Easter chronology.

129. This invocation of three magical divine names occurs quite often in Armenian retellings of the Exodus: see, Stone, *Angels and Heroes*, 248 and n. 1099. The same appears in Stone, *Angels and Heroes*, text no. 4.10 §6 and so both the idea and the specific names are quite widely distributed.

130. The sign of the cross: this signals the Christian character of this text.

131. This is an elaboration of Exod 14:15–22.

132. Exod 15:1. On the sacred tongue, see Question concerning Adam's Language, p. 63 above.

133. Cf. Exod 14:23–28. The biblical text does not say explicitly that Pharaoh also drowned in the sea.

134. Exod 14:30.

135. For Amalek's ancestry see Gen 36:12. According to that verse, Amalek was not Esau's son, but rather his grandson.

from the River Ganges, and the saying of the Psalm was carried out, "To feed the Ethiopians."[136]

37/ And after the Exodus of Israel, Egypt was quaking for seven months, and they did not dwell in houses and they said, "In the drowning of Pharaoh." Those who remained in Egypt, each made his own work into a god, as if they were the cause of their salvation.

Scribe's Colophon

---

136. The reference is unclear. The confusion of India and Ethiopia is quite common; see the excursus above, and cf. Jonah, text no. 17 below.

13. Question concerning Moses's Countenance

Introductory Remarks

This short document appears in manuscript miscellany, Matenadaran M1134 (1695), 152r–152v, with its own rubricated title and it is followed by a different work.[1] The document is included in a section of the manuscript comprising Question and Answer texts. This independent question with its answer are embedded among them. The same manuscript also contains a retelling of Daniel, two parts of which have appeared in the present series: see Story of Daniel in Stone, *Biblical Heroes* and text no. 19, which is published in the present volume. These Daniel works are in a quite different handwriting to the Question and Answer texts that include Moses's Countenance. The writing is notrgir, and very clear. There are very few scribe's corrections to be observed.

The document deals with Moses's shining countenance, which was manifested after the second giving of the Ten Commandments related in Exodus 34. The relevant biblical passage reads:

> Exod 34:29–35 29 ¶ When Moses came down from Mount Sinai, with the two tables of the testimony in his hand as he came down from the mountain, Moses did not know that the skin of his face shone because he had been talking with God. 30 And when Aaron and all the people of Israel saw Moses, behold, the skin of his face shone, and they were afraid to come near him. 31 But Moses called to them; and Aaron and all the leaders of the congregation returned to him, and Moses talked with them. 32 And afterward all the people of Israel came near, and he gave them in commandment all that the LORD had spoken with him in Mount Sinai. 33 And when Moses had finished speaking with them, he put a veil on his face; 34 but whenever Moses went in before the LORD to speak with him, he took the veil off, until he came out; and when he came out, and told the people of Israel what he was commanded, 35 the people of Israel saw the face of Moses, that the skin of

---

1. See *General Catalogue* 4:395–398.

13. QUESTION CONCERNING MOSES'S COUNTENANCE

Moses' face shone; and Moses would put the veil upon his face again, until he went in to speak with him. (RSV)

Shining countenances occur quite frequently in late antique texts and Armenian documents as well, and we have remarked on them before.[2] A notable instance concerning Moses may be observed in the text preceding this one, in §27. Shining faces are a sign of divine grace and perhaps a sign of superhuman nature.[3] To Armenian authors, the shining countenance often recalled Adam's Edenic luminosity, that of the eschatological righteous and, as here, Christ's luminosity on Mount Tabor, that is, in the Transfiguration.

Text

M1134 / fol 152r / Լուսաւորիլ երեսացն:
Հարց: Վա՞սն էր լուսաւորեցաւ երեսքն Մովսիսի:
Պատասխանի: Վասն բազում պատճառի մեծահրաշ սքանչելիքս, որ եղեւ առ Մովսէս:

- Նախ՝ զկերպն Ադամա, որ ի դրախտին
  երեւեցոյց ինքեան, զոր[4] էտես մահ եւ ընկեց զքազն իւր:
  Ըստ այնմ թագաւորեաց մահ յԱդամա մինչեւ զՄովսէս, զի
  ի Մովսէս օրինակաւ եւ ի Քրիստոս[5] ճշմարտութեամբ
  կործանեցաւ մահ, եւ ի յարութեան[6] մեր առհասարակ:
- Երկրորդ՝ զի դէմ յանդիման էտես զՏէր, եւ
  նշան լուսոյ նմանեաց ի տեսութիւն:
- Երրորդ, զի փարք տախտակաց[7] մեծացի ի լոյս
  երեսացն:
- Չորրորդ, զի զարհուրին ժողովուրդն եւ
  հնազանդին Մովսիսի:

---

2. For similar examples, see the discussion in Stone, *4 Ezra*, 244–45; see further, e.g., Robert W. Thomson, *The Armenian Adaption of the Ecclesiastical History of Socrates Scholasticus: Commonly Known as "the Shorter Socrates,"* HUAS 3 (Leuven: Peeters, 2001); see also 1QH 11:3–4; 1 En. 38.4; 2 En. A 65.11; 66.7; 4 Ezra 7:97, 125; 10:25; LAB 12; Syr. Men. 2:309; Ques. Ezra A20; Death Adam14; Ques. Greg 42: and compare 2 En. 69.1. In Armenian, see, e.g., *Adamgirkʽ* 3.5.2. (Stone, *Adamgirkʽ*, 59); 2.1.5 (p. 272).
3. See preceding notes.
4. This should be որ, nominative.
5. A genitive would be expected; the construction of ի + instr. is strange.
6. Three erased letters follow this word.
7. An illegible sign follows.

- Հինգերորդ՝ խնայեաց⁸ ի նա Տէր ոչ ցուցանել
  գերեաս իւր։ Այն, որ կոչեաց զնա Տէր, եւ արար քաշս նորա
  Տէր եւ պատժող։
- Վեցերորդ, զի իմանալի ունի լոյս, ցուցանէ
  զզալի լոյսն, զի ի զիշերի եղեալ ի խորանէն՝ հալածէր
  զիւարն եւ լուսաւորէր անապատն։
- Եւթներորդ՝ զի որ աշակերտի Մովս/ fol 152v /
  իսի, զլոյսն ընդունի. եւ որ ոչ աշակերտի, ի խաւար մնասցէ,
  որպէս քանանացիքն։
- Ութերորդ՝ զի տեսիլ աչացն առաւել պարզեցց
  զլեզու նորա, փոխանակ ճարտարութեան լեզուի։
- Իններորդ՝ ի յորինակ արդարոցն լուսոյ, որ ոչ
  կարօտանայ արտաքին լու<ս>ոյն, նոյնպէս եւ Մովսէս
  ոչ կարօտէր, զի ոչ բնական էր լոյսն, զի այժ բնական
  տեսութիւն ունի, այլ ոչ թէ լոյս։
- Տասներորդ, զի որ զայնպիսի լոյսն յինքն
  ընկալաւ, զմուք առ կենացն Ադամայ ոչ ստացաւ։
- Մետասաներորդ՝ յորինակ Տեառն, որ
  պայծառացաւ ի Թափօր։
  Եւ սոյնպէս զանազանին.
    – Նախ՝ զի Տէրն բոլոր մարմնով լուսաւորեցաւ, եւ նա
      մատամբ։⁹
    – Եւ դարձեալ՝ Տէրն բնութեամբ ունէր զլոյսն, եւ նա
      արտաքուստ ստացաւ։
    – Դարձեալ՝ Տէրն այլոց տա զլոյսն, եւ Մովսէս ոչ կարէ։
- Երկոտասաներորդ՝ լուսաւորեցաւ, զի քող
  արկցէ երեսացն, որ օրինակ է զչին Կտակարանս, որ քող
  է արկեալ, եւ առ<ագ>աստ¹⁰ մտաց նոցա, մինչեւ դարձցին
  առ Տէր հոգին, որպէս զՄովսէս, եւ ապա վերասցի քողն, եւ
  յայտնեցցի լոյ<ս>¹¹ գիտութեան նոցա։

---

8. A following ի erased in text; a diacritical marks the marginal correction ի նա p.m.:
9. Dr. A. Arakelyan has suggested emending մատամբ "with his finger" to մասամբ "partly." I am uncertain, because the phrasing is suggestive of Exod 31:18, "And he gave to Moses, when he had made an end of speaking with him upon Mount Sinai, the two tables of the testimony, tables of stone, written with the finger of God." Both this event and the transfiguration happen on mountains.
10. The text has առաս, which is not a word and is apparently corrupt for առագաստ "veil, cover" (A. Arakelyan).
11. Correcting an error of the copyist.

13. QUESTION CONCERNING MOSES'S COUNTENANCE

Translation

Question: Why did Moses's face shine?
Answer: Because of many reasons, most wonderous miracles that happened to Moses.

- First, the form of Adam,[12] which He caused to appear to him in the Garden, who saw death and whose crown fell.[13] According to this, death ruled from Adam up to Moses; for by Moses's example and by Christ<'s> truth death was destroyed, also in our general resurrection.
- Second, because he saw the Lord face to face, he resembled a sign of light in the seeing.[14]
- Third, that the glory of the Tablets was made greater by the light of his face.[15]
- Fourth, that the people are afraid and obey Moses.
- Fifth, The Lord cared for him, so as not to show His face.[16] That he called him Lord, and the Lord made his eyes punishing.[17]
- Sixth, because he has intelligible light, he exhibits the perceptible light. For, if he went out of his tent at night, he chased darkness away and illuminated the desert.
- Seventh, because the one who is Moses's disciple receives the light, and the one who (is) not his disciple will remain in darkness, like the Canaanites.
- Eighth, because the sight of his eyes would further clarify his tongue,[18] instead of dexterity of the tongue.
- Ninth, after the pattern of the light of the righteous, which does not need external light, thus also Moses did not need (external light), for

---

12. That is, he took on Adam's Edenic luminous form.
13. The crowned Adam is notably present in Armenian iconography of Eden; see, e.g., J1667, of 1529, fol. 58v.
14. Or: the vision.
15. See above p. 146.
16. This refers to Exod 33:22–23, where God shelters Moses so he should not see His face. This statement apparently contradicts Exod 33:11 "The Lord used to speak to Moses face to face." Compare Num 12:8; Deut 34:10. The statement in this text does not resolve that crux interpretationis.
17. The sense of this sentence is not clear.
18. That is, his speech.

the light was not natural. For the eyes have natural vision, but not light.[19]

- Tenth, for the one who took that sort of light into himself, does not receive the gloom of the life of Adam.[20]
- Eleventh, after the pattern of the Lord, who shone on Tabor.[21]
  And thus they are differentiated.
    - First, because the Lord was made luminous with his whole body and Moses with his finger.
    - And again, the Lord had the light by nature, and he (Moses) received it from outside.
    - Moreover, the Lord gives the light to others and Moses cannot.
- Twelfth, he was luminous so that he might put a veil over his face, which symbolizes the Old Testament, which puts on a veil and a cover to their mind, until their spirit turns to the Lord, like Moses. And then the veil will be removed and the light of their knowledge will be revealed.

---

19. The theory behind vision here is that "ordinary" or "natural" light is not needed to create or perceive the special light of the righteous or of Moses.

20. That is, his luminosity is not affected by Adam's loss of it: this is a restatement of the view that the righteous will shine with Adam's Edenic luminosity, which Adam lost on his expulsion from the garden.

21. Referring to the transfiguration.

14. Joshua B. Nun: Text 9

Introductory Remarks

This brief biography of Joshua occurs in Bodleian ms Marsh 438/1 fol 32v. The manuscript is written in clear regular bolorgir script, and shows careful, highly professional presentation and exact grammar. It is composed in standard Ancient Armenian. This manuscript Menologium was copied in 1482 and it contains the recension of the Armenian Menologium edited by Grigor Xlatʻecʻi Cerencʻ in the early fifteenth century, so it was copied quite close to the date of Grigor Xlatencʻiʼs editorial labors.[1] The text of this entry, dedicated to Joshua b. Nun, has many connections with the various Armenian apocryphal Joshua works, of which a number exist. Previously, I listed seven such works, and counting the present text, together with Joshua b. Nun 1, also published in the present volume, the number now stands at nine.[2]

Text

Marsh 438 / fol 32v / Title/ Նաւասարդի ԻԲ. (22) եւ Սեպտեմբերի Ա. (1). Սոն է Յեսուայ որդոյ Նաւեայ

1/ Յեսու որդին Նաւեայ աշակերտեր Մովսեսի նախամարգարէին մեծի: Եւ ի պահելն Մովսեսի Խ. (40) տիւ եւ Խ. (40) գիշեր, պահեաց եւ Յեսու ընդ նմա ի լեառն: Եւ լուաւ զպատգամն Տեառն, զոր խօսեցաւ Տէր ընդ Մովսեսի:

2/ Եւ էր Յեսու կուսան եւ սուրբ պատկեր ճշմարտին Յիսուսի, եւ կայր հանապազ առ դրան խորանին վկայութեան, եւ անդադար աղաւթեր առ Աստուած:

3/ Եւ յառաջ քան զվախճանելն իւր, Մովսես եդ զձեռն ի վերայ Յեսուա եւ աւրհնեաց զնա, որոյ հնազանդեցան ամենայն ժողովուրդն

---

1. See Bodleian Catalogue, no. 30, cols. 32–69. On the recensions of the Armenian Menologium, known as the Yaysmawurkʻ, see Jean Mécérïan, "Introduction à l'étude des Synaxaires arméniens," in *Bulletin Arménologique*, Mélanges de l'Université de St. Joseph 40 (Beirut: Imprimerie Catholique, 1953), 99–238.
2. These are listed in Stone, *Biblical Heroes*, text no. 6.2.

Իսրայէլի, որպէս ծառային Աստուծոյ Մովսէսի։ Եւ յետ Մովսէսի, զնա ետ Աստուած առաջնորդ Իսրայէլի եւ ասաց նմա, թէ «Որպէս էի ընդ Մովսէսի, նոյնպէս եւ եղէց ընդ քեզ»։

4/ Որով բաժանեաց զՅորդանան գետ եւ անց Իսրայէլ ընդ ցամաք, որպէս եւ յաւուրն Մովսէսի ընդ ծովն Կարմիր։ Նա ինքն Յեսու հրաման ետ արեգականն եւ լուսնին եւ դադարեալ կացոյց զնոսա ի գնացից իւրեանց։

5/ Սա եւեթ զՏէր ի նմանութիւն զինուորի՛ եկեալ յաւգնականութիւն նմա, որով կոտորեաց զԼԲ. (32) թագաւորսն քանանացոց զօրօքն իւրեանց եւ զերկիր նոցա բաժանեաց վիճակաւ որդոցն Իսրայէլի։

6/ Սա յառաջին յաղթութեանն իւրում եհար վանեաց զԱմաղէկ եւ սաստիկ կոտորեաց զնա համբարձմամբ ձեռացն Մովսէսի։ Եւ եհար զնոսա բարեա կարկտիւ։

7/ Զի Մովսէս տարածեալ զձեռսն աղաւթէր, եւ Յեսու պատերազմէր, եւ որքան բարձրանայր բազուկն Մովսէսի, յաղթէր Յեսու Ամա/ fol 33r /ղեկայ։ Եւ յորժամ խոնարհեալ ցածնոյր ձեռքն Մովսէսի, տկարանայր Յեսու եւ ի պարտութիւն դառնայր։ Վասն որոյ Ահարոն եւ Ովր կացին ի ներքո բազկացն Մովսէսի եւ ի վեր ունէին զբազուկն նորայ, որով ի պարտութիւն մատներ Ամաղեկ։

8/ Սա եւ զէ. (7) տակ պարիսպն Երիքովի զանդամանդեայն հալեաց աղաւթիւք եւ ձայնիւ կործանեաց։[3] Եւ հասեալ ի բարուր ծերութեան մեռաւ պակասեալ ամսի Ճ. եւ Ժ. (110) ամաց։ Եւ յաւելաւ առ ժողովուրդ իւր

ի փառս Քրիստոսի Աստուծոյ մերոյ։

Translation

Title/ Nawasard 22, September 1. It is the feast of Joshua son of Nun.

1/ Joshua son of Nun was the disciple of the great proto-prophet[4] Moses. And when Moses fasted for forty days and forty nights, Joshua fasted with

---

3. This is a strange aorist form.

4. This title, while appropriate for Moses, is notable. Intriguingly, in text 19 §9, Moses and "the proto-martyr human" are mentioned side by side. That "human," of course, is Stephen, often called "proto-martyr" (Acts 7:58–60). Moses is called "proto-prophet" in Of Moses and Aaron §1.

him on the mountain.[5] And he heard the Lord's oracle, which the Lord spoke with Moses.[6]

2/ And Joshua was a virgin[7] and a holy image of the true Jesus.[8] And he remained always by the entry of the tent of witness and prayed to God.[9]

3/ And before his death, Moses laid his hand upon Joshua[10] and blessed him. All the people of Israel obeyed him (Joshua), as (they had) Moses, servant of God.[11] And God gave him to Israel as a leader after Moses and said to him, "As I was with Moses, so also I will be with you."[12]

---

5. See Exod 24:13, 34:28, and Deut 9:9, 18. The tradition of Joshua's ascent and fasting with Moses is not to be found in Exodus. Indeed, Exod 34:3 reads, "No man shall come up with you, and let no man be seen throughout all the mountain; let no flocks or herds feed before that mountain." However, in the text being presented here, Joshua is said to have fasted or conceivably guarded or waited (with պահել all three translations are possible) with Moses for forty days and nights. The biblical story line is broken in these chapters. Joshua's participation could be asserted from reading Exod 24:13 together with 32:1. The ninth-century m. Lekaḥ Ṭob Exod. 32:19 does exactly this. In the Brief History of Joshua §3 in Stone, *Biblical Heroes*, 86–87 he stands for forty days outside the cloud (see Exod 19:9) and holds Moses's shoes. This last detail is presumably inferred from the incident of the burning bush where God commands Moses to remove his shoes for the place is holy (Exod 3:5). The bush is said to be on the mountain of God, Horeb (Exod 3:1). Horeb was another name of Sinai, "the mountain of God" (Exod 3:1, Deut 1:2, and elsewhere). See G. Ernest Wright, "Art: Sinai," *IDB* 4:376 on the usage and distribution of these names. See also Sir 48:7.

6. This is not asserted in other Joshua texts nor in the Bible, though here is probably an interpretation of Exod 33:11.

7. The word կուսան means "virgin" and see b. ʿErub. 63a–b, which interprets 1 Chr 7:27 to mean that Joshua's line ends abruptly with him, not recording any descendants of Joshua. Of course, interpreting childlessness as implying virginity is a strategy reflecting Christian ascetic values. Nothing is said in the Pentateuch about Joshua's descendants.

8. Joshua as type of Christ is commonly derived from the identity of names, so the expression "true Jesus" is to be understood. See Brief History of Joshua §5, which reads, "And that one letter of his name is missing is because he was human and the savior Jesus was incarnated God and because his salvation was bodily and imperfect, and Christ's (was) a perfect and an eternal spiritual salvation." The missing letter is perhaps the final "s" of "Jesus." The name Joshua adds a single letter at the beginning of Hosea in the Hebrew forms of these names. See further the introductory remarks to Brief History of Joshua.

9. See Exod. 33:11.

10. That is, consecrated him. See Num 27:18–23 where the election and consecration of Joshua is described. Cf. Deut 1:38, 3:28, 31:7, etc.

11. Thus Josh 1:13: "Moses the servant of the Lord," and other places. This title is common in the historical books of the Bible.

12. Deut 34:9: "And Joshua the son of Nun was full of the spirit of wisdom, for Moses had laid his hands upon him; so the people of Israel obeyed him, and did as the Lord had

4/ Through whom[13] He divided the River Jordan, and Israel crossed on dry land, even as (they crossed) the Red Sea in Moses's day.[14] Behold, Joshua himself commanded the sun and the moon and he stood them still in their courses.[15]

5/ He saw the Lord in the likeness of a warrior, who came to help him.[16] With him he cut down thirty-two Canaanite kings with their forces.[17] And he divided up their land by lot to the Children of Israel.[18]

6/ He in his first victory smote (and) repelled Amalek and cut them down fearsomely, through Moses's raising up of his hand.[19] And he smote them with stony hail.[20]

7/ Moses, extending his hands wide, prayed and Joshua battled. And as long as Moses's arm was held high, Joshua defeated Amalek. And when having been lowered, Moses's hands were lowered, Joshua weakened and began to be defeated.[21] On this account, Aaron and Or (Hur) stood beneath Moses's arms and held his arms up, by which Amalek was delivered to defeat.[22]

---

commanded Moses." Note also Josh 3:7: "as I was with Moses, so I shall be with you," which is cited here.

13. That is, Joshua.

14. Josh 3:16–17 and compare Exod 14:21–22; see also Ps 66(65):6; Brief History of Joshua §§11, 13, 24, 27–28, 41, etc. The crossing of the Red Sea is related in Exod 14–15 and the two miracles, the crossing of the Red Sea and the crossing of the Jordan, are explicitly equated in Josh 4:23.

15. Josh 10:12–14.

16. Josh 5:13–14. Strangely, our text identifies this warrior epiphany as God, while in Josh 5:14 the warrior identifies himself as "commander of the Lord's army," the heavenly archistrategos.

17. In Josh 5 the vision of the angel is connected with the conquest of Jericho, while in the present text it is mentioned in connection with the battle against the thirty-two kings. Joshua 12:24 in the MT reads "thirty-one," LXX εἴκοσι ἐννέα "twenty-nine," and Arm Josh also has "twenty-nine." These readings seem to be based on the list of kings in Josh 12:9–24 as given by these witnesses.

18. The latter part of the book of Joshua is devoted to the allotment of the land to the Israelite tribes (Josh 13:7–19:51)

19. In Josh 8:18, 26, Joshua's raising up of his own hands was viewed as being done after the pattern of Moses's actions in the battle against the Amalekites (Exod 17:8–13). Indeed, this similarity is expanded upon in Brief History of Joshua §58. The association in the present context draws the narrative back to the incident in the desert, as is clear in the following section.

20. See Josh 10:11. This event is not related to Joshua's battle with Amalek, but rather to his much later battle against the alliance of the five Amorite kings.

21. Exod 17:10–13.

22. Exod 17:12 describes this.

8/ He also melted the seven-based adamantine wall of Jericho[23] by prayers, and destroyed it by noise. And, having reached a good old age he died, leaving here[24] at hundred and ten years.[25] And he was gathered to his people.[26]

For the glory of Christ, our God.

---

23. The wording here is difficult. The Brief History of Joshua b. Nun published in Stone, *Biblical Heroes*, in §48 says of Jericho's walls: "And Jericho had seven foundation walls of magnetic stone, unworkable by iron, invincible and impregnable." This obviates the difficulty. The noise is the shouting and blowing of trumpets related in Josh 6:5.

24. That is, this world.

25. Josh 24:29 and also Judg 2:8.

26. The book of Joshua does not use this expression in chap. 24, which relates Joshua's death. It is a standard biblical phrase, however, and may be observed in Gen 25:8; 25:17; 35:29; 49:33; Deut 32:50 of Abraham, Ishmael, Isaac, Jacob, and Aaron respectively. Its use in the case of Joshua here may be deliberate, putting him into the series of the leaders of Israel. After the death of Joshua in Judg 2:8, it is said that "and also all that generation were gathered unto their fathers" (Judg 2:10).

15. Eli the Priest

Introductory Remarks

This text is the entry for Eli the priest as it occurs in the Yaysmawurkʻ (Synaxarium) in Bodleian Marsh 438, fol 450r.[1] This narrative, like certain of the other entries relating to other Old Testament saints, is drawn from Vitae Prophetarum. In that work, it is extant in Recensio Anonyma.[2] There are two text forms of that recension, both with confusions in their opening sentences, and they identify Eli with Ahaiah and Selōm. No such identifications is given here. An Armenian text of this Vita from manuscript M1500 of the thirteenth century (before 1281) and a retroversion of its Greek original were published in Stone, *Patriarchs and Prophets*, 150–51.

Text

1/ Marsh 438 / fol 450r / Յայսմ աւուր յիշատակ է եւ Հեղեայ քահանայի

2/ Սա ծնաւ ի Սելով քաղաքի, անդ ուր էրն յառաջ խորանն Տեառն: Եւ ի սկզբան քահանայութեանն իւրոյ մարգարէացաւ Հեղի վասն Սողոմոնի, թէ՛ անցանէ զաւրինօքն Աստուծոյ վասն կանանց, քանզի խոտորեցուսցեն զնա կանայք իւր եւ դարձուցանեն զնա յիրաւանցն Աստուծոյ:

3/ Եւ վասն Ռոբովամու, որ ասաց էթէ՛ նենգութեամբ զնաց ընդ Տեառն եւ ընդ Իսրայէլի:

4/ Եւ եսետ Հեղի զոյցս եգանց իգաց որ կոխէին զժողովուրդն, եւ յարձակէին ի քահանայիցն վերայ: Զայս նախասաց Հեղի յառաջ քան զքահանայանալն որդոց իւրոց:

---

1. Concerning the manuscript, see the introductory remarks to text no. 9 above on pp. 8–9.

2. Theodor Schermann, *Prophetarum Vitae Fabulosae Indices Apostolorum Discipulorumque Domini Dorotheo Epiphanio Hippolyto Aliisque Vindicata* (Leipzig: Teubner, 1907), 91–92. A shortened form of this Vita occurs in the Dorothean Recension (54).

15. ELI THE PRIEST

5/ Եւ մեռաւ նա ի ծանր ծերութեանն եւ ոչ բարւոք. այլ ի լինել գրաւք զերութեան տապանակին. անկաւ յետուստ եւ բեկաւ ողն նորա:[3]

Translation

1/ On this day is also the memorial of Eli the priest.

2/ He was born in the city of Shiloh[4] where formerly the tabernacle of the Lord was.[5] And in the beginning of his priesthood, Eli prophesied concerning Solomon, that he would transgress the laws of God on account of women, because his wives/women caused him to turn aside and they would make him turn from God's laws.[6]

3/ Also concerning Rehoboam, (of) whom he said that he went by deception against the Lord and against Israel.[7]

4/ And Eli saw a pair of heifers[8] who were trampling the people[9] and they were attacking the priests. Eli foretold this before his sons became priests.[10]

5/ And he died at a great old age[11] and not well, but when the heard ill tidings of the captivity of the ark, he fell backward and split his brain.[12]

---

3. The text is followed by a scribe's colophon.
4. Shiloh is mentioned as the place where Eli served as priest, see 1 Sam 1:9, etc.
5. The Tabernacle was set up in Shiloh according to Josh 18:1.
6. In this paragraph a prophecy concerning Solomon is attributed to Eli. This prophecy, like those in the next two sections, is apocryphal. The Solomon texts are listed in Stone, *Biblical Heroes*, 159–61, and see further references there.
7. This and the next section present prophecies of Eli's which have no biblical basis.
8. Literally: female oxen.
9. Perhaps the image is drawn from Rehoboam's response to the people, which refers to a weight of a yoke he would put on them (1 Kgs 12:14). Another possibility is that this draws upon the pair of golden calves built by Jeroboam and placed in Dan and Bethel (1 Kgs 12:28).
10. The prophecy refers, of course, to Eli's sons. Their consecration as priests is not mentioned in the biblical text.
11. According to 1 Sam 4:15 he was ninety-eight years old when this event took place.
12. 1 Sam 4:18. This incident is also related in Story of the Ark of the Covenant §§16–19; see Stone, *Biblical Heroes*, 109–22.

16. Elisha

Introductory Remarks

This document occurs in the Menologium Bod Marsh 438, fol 510v–513r.[1] The text devoted to Elisha is hagiographical in character and opens with a version of the Vita of Elisha (§§1–2) that differs from the published text in a number of respects.[2] Following §3, this Menologium entry presents several pages of further narrative. All this additional narrative is drawn from the Armenian Bible, utilizing the narrative sections about Elisha. This technique was sometimes used in Armenian pseudepigrapha to compose writings devoted to the doings of various biblical saints. To illustrate this editorial method, I have given a sample here, the first part of the compiled text (§§3–9). In order to highlight its relation to the biblical text, I have italicized all words that are quoted directly, or almost directly from that text. The manuscript's text related to Job, occurring on fols 454v–456v of the same manuscript, is a similar combination of narrative verses from the book of Job. Another technique, used, for instance, in the entries on Eli, Zephaniah, and Habakkuk, is simply to adopt the text of the Vita of the prophet from the Vitae Prophetarum, without adding any narrative drawn from the Bible. This may be seen in Bod Marsh 438, fols 450r and 174r–174v, and these texts contain a number of variants when compared with the Vitae of these prophets in Armenian Vitae Prophetarum.[3]

---

1. On this manuscript, see the introductory remarks on p. 159 above.
2. See Stone, *Patriarchs and Prophets*, 144–45, with a Greek retroversion.
3. See Yovsēpʻeancʻ, 213–15. Naturally, a new edition of Armenian Vitae Prophetarum is very desirable, and it is to be hoped that it will include, in addition to those Vitae often found in manuscript Bibles, also texts also preserved in Čaṙĕndir and Synaxaria, as well as from other, nonbiblical manuscripts. Inter alia, it would be interesting to know which textual and recensional traditions of Vitae Prophetarum were used by the Armenians. A Čaṙĕndir, is a collection of various sorts of lections, including biblical, apocryphal, and hagiographic texts, arranged by dates on the ecclesiastical calendar.

16. ELISHA

Text

Marsh 438 / fol 510v / Մարգացի ԺԱ. (11) եւ Յունիսի ԺԷ. (17). Tοն է Եղիսէի մարգարէին

1/ Մարգարէն Եղիսէ էր յԱ{գ}բէղմաուլայ, յազգէն Ռուբենի: Եւ յորժամ ծնաւ ի մօրէն, Բ. (2) երինջքն ոսկի, որ կային ի Դան եւ ի Բեթէլ, այնպէս գոչեցին մեծաձայն, որ լսելի եղեն յերուսաղէմ:

2/ Եւ քահանայապետն, որ կայր ի տաճարին, ասէ. «Մարգարէ մեծ ծնաւ այսաւր, որ բառնայ զկռապաշտութիւն յԻսրայէլէ»:

3/ Եւ եղեւ մեծանալ Եղիսէի եւ վարէր երկոտասան եզամբք, եւ եկն եհաս առ նա Եղիա մարգարէն բանիւ Տեառն եւ ընկեց զմաշկեակն իւր ի վերայ նորա, եւ ինքն անց գնաց:

4/ Եւ եթող Եղիսէ զեզինսն եւ ընթացաւ զհետ Եղիայի, եւ ասէ. «Համբուրեցից զհայր իմ եւ զմայր իմ եւ եկից զհետ քո»: Ասէ ցնա Եղիա. «Ե՛րթ, դարձի՛ր անդրէն, եւ արա՛ այնպէս, եւս, զոր ինչ առնելոց էր, արարի քեզ»:

5/ Եւ դարձաւ ի նմանէ Եղիսէ առ զոյգս եզանցն եզին,[4] եւ գործովք եզանցն հատոյց զնոսա, եւ ետ ժողովրդեանն եւ կերան: Եւ ինքն Եղիսէ գնաց զհետ Եղիայի եւ պաշտէր զնա:[5] Եւ յետ վերանալոյն Եղիայի յերկինս առ Եղիսէ զմաշկեակն, զոր ընկեց ի վերայ նորա[6] Եղիա, ծալեաց եւ եհար զջուրն:

6/ Եւ Յորդանան բաժանեցաւ յայս կոյս եւ յայն կոյս, եւ անց Եղիսէ ցամաք ոտիւք, ընդ որ ուրախացեալ որդիք մարգարէիցն Երիքովի, որ[7] կային հա<ն>դէպ[8] եւ հայէին, զի հանգեաւ հոգին Եղիայի ի վերայ Եղիսէի:

7/ Եւ մտեալ Եղիսէ յԵրիքով եւ բժշկեաց զջուրն Երիքովի հոգովն Եղիայի, եւ ել Եղիսէ անտի ի Բեթէլ, եւ մինչդեռ ելանէր ընդ ճանապարհի, մանր մանկտին ելին ի քաղաքէն, աղաղակէին առ մարգարէն եւ ասէին. «Ե՛լ կնդակ, ե՛լ կնդակ»:

---

4. The reading եզին most likely an orthographic variant of եզէն "he slaughtered," which occurs in Arm 1 Kgs (3 Kgdms) 19:21.

5. From this point and for the next two phrases the author departs from the text of 1 Kgs (3 Kgdms) 19.

6. The word is abbreviated, but the abbreviation mark is omitted.

7. This is most probably corrupt for ուր "where" and so I translate it. See Stone and Hillel, "Index," 434.

8. Letter omitted by the copyist.

8/ Դարձաւ մարգարէն եւ անէծ զնոսա յանուն Տեառն, ասելով. «Որդիք յանցանաց եւ դատարկութեան»։ Յայնժամ ելին Բ. (2) արջք յանդառէն եւ պատառեցին ի նոցանէ ԽԲ. (42) մանկունս։

9/ Եւ կին մի ի Սամարիա ադադակէր առ Եղիսէ մարգարէ եւ ասէր. «Այրդ Աստուծոյ, ծառա քո այր իմ, մեռաւ, եւ դու ինքնին գիտես, տէ՛ր իմ, զի / fol 511r / ծառայ քո երկիւղած էր ի Տեառնէ, զի յորդոց մարգարէիցն էր, եւ փոխատուն եկն առնուլ զԲ. (2) որդիսն իմ իւր ի ծառայութիւն։

Translation

11 Maragac' 11 and 17 June. It is the feast of Elisha the prophet.

1/ The prophet Elisha was from A{z}bełmauoul,[9] of the tribe of Reuben. And when he was born from his mother, the two golden calves that were standing in Dan and in Bethel, cried out so loudly that it was heard in Jerusalem.

2/ And the high priest who was in the temple said, "A great prophet has been born today, who will remove idolatry from Israel."

3/ And when Elisha had grown up and he was ploughing with twelve oxen. Elijah[10] came (and) reached[11] him at the Lord's word, and cast his leather cloak over him, and he himself passed by and went.

4/ And Elisha left the oxen and ran after Elijah and said, "I will kiss my father and my mother and I will come after you." Elijah said to him, "Go, return again, and do so. That which He was going to do,[12] I have done to you."

5/ And Elisha went back from him to the yokes of oxen, he slaughtered (them) and with the oxen's tools, he cooked them and he gave (them) to the people, and they ate. And Elisha himself went after Elijah and served him.

---

9. The -q- is a corruption. There were early confusions with this place name "Abel Maoul," which is Abel Meholah, and which was erroneously thought to be located in the north of Israel, when it was actually in the centre of the country. See for a fuller discussion of these variations: Jonas C. Greenfield, Michael E. Stone, and Esther Eshel, *The Aramaic Levi Document: Edition, Translation, Commentary*, SVTP 19 (Leiden: Brill, 2004), 135–37. The name is found also in T. Levi 2.3.

10. Literally: and Elijah

11. An instance of hendiadys, a frequent stylistic feature.

12. The whole section is drawn from 1 Kgs 19:20. This phrase seems to mean: "that which the Lord intended to be done to you."

And after Elijah went up to heaven, Elisha took the leather cloak that Elijah had thrown over him, he folded it up and smote the waters.[13]

6/ And the Jordan was divided into this side and that side, and Elisha passed over with dry feet.[14] At this the sons of the prophets in Jericho rejoiced, where they were standing opposite and looking,[15] for Elijah's spirit rested upon Elisha.[16]

7/ And Elisha entered Jericho,[17] and he healed the water of Jericho through the spirit of Elijah.[18] And Elisha went up from there to Bethel; and while he was going up on the road,[19] small boys went forth from the city. They were calling to the prophet, and saying, "Climb, bald one! Climb, bald one."[20]

8/ The prophet turned around and cursed them in the name of the Lord, saying, "Sons of transgressions and emptiness." Then two bears came forth from the forest and rent forty-two youths from among them.[21]

9/ And a woman of Samaria beseeched Elisha the prophet[22] and said, "Man of God, your servant my husband died. You yourself know, my lord, that your servant feared the Lord for he was of the sons of the prophets and the creditor came to take my two sons into slavery."

---

13. This incident is described twice in 2 Kgs 2:8 and 2:14. In 2:8 it precedes Elijah's ascent to heaven and in 2:14, which is the direct source being used here, it follows that event.
14. 2 Kgs 2:14, cf. 2:8. This is, of course, based on the crossing of the Red Sea (Exod 14:21–22) and Joshua's crossing of the Jordan (Josh 3:16–17). Dry feet, mentioned here, are not present in the 2 Kgs passage, but are drawn from Josh 3:15.
15. This is based on 2 Kgs 2:16. The rejoicing is not explicit there.
16. 2 Kgs 2:15.
17. The incident is related in 2 Kgs 2:19–22.
18. "Spirit of Elijah," an addition in line with 2 Kgs 2:15.
19. 2 Kgs 2:23.
20. So 2 Kgs 2:23. The boys were teasing Elisha who was bald.
21. 2 Kgs 2:24.
22. In 2 Kgs 4:1 the woman is identified not as of Samaria but, "the wife of one of the sons of the prophets." This is only specified in the next section.

17. Jonah

17.1. Jonah 1

Introductory Remarks

This document, which I designate Jonah 1, is preserved among many other biblical stories, in M1099 on fols 202r–207v.[1] This manuscript Miscellany was copied in the fifteenth century. The document opens, as does the text that I titled Jonah 2, which is found in the manuscript Menologium, Bodleian Marsh 438 (1482), fols 61r–v, with text extracted from the Vita of Jonah, in §§1–2 and another extract occurs also in §25.

The known Jonah texts to date are:

1. Jonah 1, the composition from M1099 being published here.

2. Jonah 2 is preserved in Bodleian Marsh 438, fols 61r–v and it also published in the present volume.

3. The Armenian translation of the Vita of Jonah, published in 1896.[2]

4. The Story of Nineveh, already published.[3]

5. The Ninevehites, already published.[4]

6. The Sermon of the Prophet Jonah in Nineveh.[5] This text was published in 1896 and a new English translation of it is presented below.

7. The Pseudo-Philonic *de Jona*, a work to be found in the Armenian corpus of Jonah writings.[6]

---

1. The introductory remarks to Daniel and the Three Young Men presents information about this manuscript; see pp. 220–21.
2. Here cited from Yovsēpʻeancʻ, 211–12.
3. To be found in Stone, *Angels and Heroes*, 266–76.
4. To be found in Stone, *Biblical Heroes*, 200–206.
5. Published by Yovsēpʻeancʻ, 343–48.
6. Hans Lewy, *The Pseudo-Philonic De Jona*, part 1, *The Armenian Text with a Critical Introduction*, Studies and Documents 7 (London: Christophers, 1936). An English translation was prepared by Gohar Muradyan and Aram Topchyan, "Pseudo-Philo, On Samson and On Jonah," in *Outside the Bible: Ancient Jewish Writings Related to Scripture* (Philadelphia: Jewish Publication Society, 2013), 1:750–803.

In the present edition of Jonah 1, references to parallel material in the text and annotation of Jonah 2 are given in footnotes. The same procedure is also followed for the parallel material in Vita Ionae, The Story of Nineveh, The Sermon of Jonah and, of course, for the biblical book of Jonah. Other material in the present text is not paralleled in the above sources. Its origin is unknown, for the present. The wide range of sources used perhaps indicates that its editor/author wished to produce an "omnibus" text and to this end he combined a number of Jonah texts into one document, together with his own ideas.[7]

This story shares, as far as the Jonah story proper is concerned, much text with The Story of Nineveh. It is not yet possible to determine which document is dependent on the other. At some points one, and elsewhere the other, is more detailed. If there is not a direct relationship of dependency between them, it seems likely that they share a source. The story in Jonah 1 continues after the withering of the gourd, with Jonah's return to his land, and then with elements drawn from the Vita Ionae, with §26 serving as a narrative bridge.

Orthographic peculiarities of this manuscript are:

բ -- փ   §5
զ -- ք   §13
դ -- թ   §§32, 33. etc.

Text

Յովնանու մարգարէի

M1099 / fol 202r / 1/Յովնան էր ի Կարիաթարիմայ, որ է մերձ յԱզովտոս ի ծովեզերին, ի քաղաքն այլազգեաց:

2/ Սորա Դ. (4) մայր երեւի. նախ՝ ի յիւր մօրէն, Բ. (2)՝ ի նաւէն ի ծովն, եւ Գ. (3), որ ծովն ետ ի ձուկն, եւ Դ. (4), որ ձուկն եթուք ի ցամաք:

3/ Յորժամ Նինուէացիքն բազում չարիս գործեցին եւ մեղօք ապականեցան, կամէր Տէր սատակել զնոսա, բայց վասն մարդասիրութեան Աստուծոյ հրամայեաց Հոգին Սուրբ Յովնանու եւ ասէ. «Ե՛րթ ի Նինուէի, քարոզեա՛ եւ ասա՛, թէ հասեալ է բարկութիւն Աստուծոյ ի վերայ ձեր. կամի Տէրն սատակել զձեզ, զի ահայ, Գ. (3) օր այլ ոչ եւս իցեն ի Նինուէի»:

4/ Ասէ Յովնան. «Տէ՛ր, զի գիտեմ դու քաղցր եւ ողորմած ես, զի քարոզելն իմ նոքա զղջան, եւ դու ողորմած ես, յետս եւ ողորմիս, եւ լինիմ սուտ մարգարէ»:/ fol 202v /

---

7. Perhaps a similar purpose may be discerned in the Daniel text in M1099, Daniel and the Three Young Men.

5/ Դարձեալ կրկին հրամայեաց Տէր երթալ ի Նինուէ եւ քարոզել, իսկ Յովնան աճապարեաց[8] փախչել ի Թարսիս։ Եւ գնացեալ եմուտ ի նաւ, զի փախչից ի Թարսիս։ Իսկոյն հողմ սաստիկ եղեւ եւ ալեկոծումն, ամենեքեան ի լաց հարան, եւ աղաղակէին ամէն մարդ յաստուածս իւրոց։

6/ Իսկ Յովնան գմաշկեակն ընկալեալ էր ի գլուխն. ննջէր եւ խորդայր։ Իսկ մի ոմն ասէ. «Օ՛վ ես դու, որ անհոգ ննջես. ահա, կորընչիմք։ Արի՛, կարդա՛ առ Տէր Աստուած քո, միթէ ողորմած լիցի մեզ եւ քեզ»։

7/ Իսկ Յովնան ասէ. «Այս բարկութիւնս վասն իմ է։ Եթէ կամիք ապրել, առէ՛ք զիս եւ ի ծովն ընկեցէ՛ք»։[9] Ասեն. «Չի՞նչ արարեալ է քո»։ Ասէ Յովնան. «Տէրն, որ ստեղծիչն[10] է երկրի եւ երկնի, հրամայեաց ինձ գնալ ի Նինուէ եւ քարոզել, եւ ես կամիմ փախչել ի Թարսիս. վասն այն բարկացաւ Տէր ի վերայ իմ, կամի կորուսանել զիս։ Թէ ոչ արկանէք զիս ի ծովն, կորընչիք եւ դուք ընդ իս»։

8/ Իբրեւ լուան, որ ասաց թէ. «Տէրն իմ ստեղծողն է երկնի եւ յերկրի»,[11] եւ եւս աւելի երկեան արկանել ի ծով։ Արկին վիճակ, թէ վասն ում իցէ. ելաներ վիճակն ի Յովնան։ Մինչեւ Գ. (3) անգամ վիճակ արկին, անկաներ վիճակն առ Յովնան։ Առին գնայ եւ ընկեցին ի ծով, եւ առժամայն հանդարտեաց ծովն։

9/ Հրամայ/ fol 203r /եաց Տէր ձկան մեծի, եւ կալեալ զնա եւ պահեաց գնայ ի փոր կետին կենդանի։ Եւ յետ Գ. (3) աւուրց թքեաց զՅովնան կենդանի ի յեզր ծովուն առ կողմն Նինուէի։ Դարձեալ հրամայեաց Հոգին Սուրբ Յովնանու երթալ ի Նինուէ եւ քարոզել։

10/ Իսկ Յովնան մտեալ ի մէջ Նինուէի եւ համարձակ բարձրաձայն քարոզէր ի մէջ Նինուէի եւ ասէր. «Ահա Գ. (3) օր՝ այլ ոչ եւս իցէ Նինուէի»։ Մինչեւ բանն եհաս առ թագաւորն, առաքեաց եւ եբեր Յովնան, եւ մեծարեաց զմարգարէն, աղաչէր եւ ասէր. «Ուսո՛ մեզ եւ խրատեա՛, թէ որպէ՞ս աղաչեսցուք զԱստուած, զի փրկեսցէ զմեզ»։

11/ Ասէ մարգարէն. «Բարկացեալ է Տէր ի վերայ ձեր. ոչ աղօթիւք եւ ոչ ողորմութեամբ, եւ ոչ այլ բարեգործութեամբ ոչ կարէք ապրել։ Ահա եւս Գ. (3) օր, ոչ դուք մնաք եւ ոչ քաղաքս. ամենեքեան կորձանիք»։

---

8. Orthographic variant of աճապարել "to flee."
9. Medieval Armenian form.
10. ն above line p.m. presumably an erroneous hypercorrection.
11. Initial յ- is superfluous: see Stone and Hillel, "Index," s.v. "addition/omission."

17. JONAH

12/ Ասէ թագաւորն. «Յորժամ բարկանայր Աստուած իսրայէլացոցն, առաջնորդ նոցա Մովսէս ադաչեր վասն ժողովրդեանն, հաշտեցուցանէր զԱստուած ընդ նոսա եւ փրկեր զժողովուրդն ի պատուհասէն: Նոյնպէս եւ դու մարգարէ եւ առաջնորդ լեր մեզ, զի թէ բարկացեալ է Տէր ի վերայ մեր, մեզ ոչ լսէ վասն մեր մեղաց.

Բայց դու արդար ես եւ մարգարէ, աղաչեմ զքեզ, միջնո´րդ լեր մեզ եւ հաշտեցո´ զԱստուած ընդ մեզ, եւ անցո´ զբարկութիւն նորա, զի ապրես/ fol 203v /ցուք ի պատուհասէ»:

13/ Ասէ Յունան. «Ես բազում անգամ աղաչեցի զՏէր վասն ձեր, եւ ոչ լուաւ: Փախեա եւ ի նաւ մտայ, ի ծով անկայ եւ ձկան կլանեցայ, եւ մահն իմ կամէի, եւ ձեզ զուժ մահոյ ոչ կամէի տալ: Եւ զիս կենդանի հանեալ ի փորոյ ձկան եւ առաքեաց զուժ մահու տալ ձեզ. ըստոյքն¹² ասեմ ձեզ, զի ահա Գ. (3) օր´ ոչ եւս իցէ Նինուէ. այսպէս ասէ Աստուած»: Զայս ասաց Յունան եւ ել ի քաղաքէն:

14/ Հրամայեաց թագաւորն եւ կոչեաց զիշխանս եւ մեծ եւ փոքր, եւ առհասարակ քաղաքն ամենայն: Ելաց թագաւորն եւ ասէ. «Այրս այս ըստոզգ մարգարէ, զոր ինչ խոսի, ի բերանոյ Աստուծոյ խոսի: Թէ զիստէի այլն այն սուտ էր, կարող էի սպանանել, բայց զոր ինչ խոսի, ի բերանոյ Աստուծոյ խոսի»:

Մինչ թագաւորն զայս ասէր, եւ ահայ, շարժումն մեծ եղեւ, մինչեւ ամենեքեան անկան ի վերայ երեսաց, անկաւ եւ թագաւորն ի աթոռոյն: Ահա տեսանէին, զի սեւ ամպ հրախառն պատեաց զշուրջ քաղաքին, որպէս պարիսպ հրեղեն:

15/ Իբրեւ եռես թագաւորն, արտասուէր եւ ասէր. «Ահա´ յայտնի եղեւ բան մարգարէին, ո´վ իշխանք մեծ եւ փոքր, զի ահա ամենեքեան ունկն դրէ´ք, զի շատ աղաչեցի զմարգարէն եւ ոչ լուաւ, քանզի մարգարէն այն մարդ է իբրեւ զմեզ, պահելով զպատուիրանն Աստուծոյ´ քաղցրա/ fol 204r /ցաւ Աստուծոյ: Իսկ մեք, ոչ պահելով զպատուիրանն Աստուծոյ, հեռացաք ի նմանէ, եւ կամի կորուսանել զմեզ վասն մեր մեղաց:

16/ Բայց զիտեմ, յորժամ բարկանայ հայր ի վերայ զաւակաց, հարկանէ քարիւ եւ փայտիւ. յորժամ որդին արտասունք հանէ¹³ եւ լայ, ողորմի հայրն եւ ոչ հարկանէ: Քանզի Աստուած հայր է ամենայն կենդանեաց, որոշեցէք հայր ի որդոյ եւ դուստր ի մորէ, զնորածին եւ

---

12. Variant orthography of ստոյգ, see below.

13. This appears to be the reading, but it is not completely visible, a fault on the page having largely obscured the writing.

կաթնակեր տղայքն, որոշեցէք զգառն ի ոչխարէն, գործն ի կովէն, զբուրակն ի ձիէն, գձուտն ի հաւէն:

17/ Մարդ եւ անասունք, սղղունք եւ թռչունք, ամէնն անսուա՛ղ պահեցէք, ամենեքեան Աստուծոյ ստեղծուածն են, ամենայն ստեղծուածքն անօթի հառաչեն եւ բառանչեն, լան եւ կոծեն, միթէ քաղցրասցի Աստուած վասն մեր, կամ վասն անմեղ մանկանց, վասն գրաստից, կամ վասն անասնոց, վասն գազանաց, կամ վասն հաւուց ողորմեսցի եւ ազատեսցէ զստեղծուածս իւր եւ անցուսցէ զբարկութիւն իւր: Իսկ թէ ոչ ողորմեսցի, կորուսանէ զմեզ, զի թէ աստ կորնչիմք, անդ ոչ կորնչին ապաշխարանքն մեր»:

18/ Զայս ասաց թագաւորն եւ առեալ զթագն իւր եւ զարկ ի գետին, պատառեաց զհանդերձն իւր եւ զգեցաւ զթուրծ, արկ մոխիր ի գլխովն, ձՈիւեր զմորուսն, ծեծէր զգլուխն, բախէր զկո/ fol 204v /րծն, ճանկէր զերեսն, ձայներ ողբալով եւ ասէր. «Վա՜յ թագաւորութեանս իմոյ եւ Ռ. (1,000) վա՜յ մեծութեանս իմոյ: Երանի՛ էր, թէ մուրացկան եւ աղքատ էի եւ չէի թագաւոր աշխարհիս, ամենայն վասն իմ մեղացս անցանի երկիրս, վասն իմ կործանի քաղաքս, վասն իմ քակի մարդ, եւ անասուն վասն իմ պատուհասի», եւ այլ բազում բանս պաղատանաց խօսէր. վա՜յ եւ եղո՜ւկ կարդայր, արտասունք թափեր եւ մոխիր թաւալէր:

19/ Իսկ թագաւորն, որ թագն ի գետինն ձգէ եւ հանդերձ մազեղէն հագնի: Իսկ ո՞վ է, որ զարդարի եւ պձնի: Թագաւորն, որ մոխրով թաւալի եւ ազայ: Իսկ ո՞վ է, որ խնդայ: Թագաւորն որ մոխիր տայ: Այլ ո՞վ է, որ զինքն լուանայ: Թագաւորն, որ անսուաղ կայ: Այլ ո՞վ է՛ ուտէ եւ ըմպէ: Ջոկեցին կաթնակեր տղայքն ի մօրէն, յորդն ի կովէն, զառն ի ոչխարէն, քուռակն ի գրաստէն, ճուտն ի հաւէն, մարդ եւ անասուն, սղղուն եւ թռչուն, շուն եւ կատուն ամէնեքեան անսուաղ ձայն արձակեալ, տղայքն լային, եւ ծնողքն ողբային, կանայքն սուգ առնէին, եւ մարդիք կոծէին, ձին խառնջար, անասունքն հառաչէին եւ զրաստք[14] բառանչէին, շունք կնձային, եւ կատունքն մղային, բարկութիւն սաստկացաւ, եւ լոյս խաւարեցաւ, երկիր շարժէին եւ քաղաք / fol 205r / դղղային, վէմք պատառէին եւ շինուածք քակտէին, երկինք գոռային եւ երկիր որոտային, շուրջ զբաղաքան կրակ եւ կայծակ բորբոքէին, եւ քաղաքն որպէս նաւ ի վերայ ծովու տապալէին, ոսկի եւ արծաթ, բեհեզ եւ ծիրանի իբրեւ զաղբ կոխէին:

20/ Ո՞վ էր, որ հայէր ի նոսա, ամենեքեան, որ տեսանէին զբարկութիւնն, անյոյս լինէին, զի այլ ոչ ուսանային, թէ փրկիմք

---

14. ք above line, p.m.

17. JONAH

ի պատուհասէ: Հարցանէին մանկունքն զծնողս իւրեանց, թէ. «Մէկ օրն անցաւ, Բ. (2) օր այլ ոչ լինիմք կենդանի», իսկ Բ. (2) օրն հարցանէին, թէ. «Հա՛յր, մա՛,յր Բ. (2) օր անցաւ, մի օր այլ ոչ լինիմք կենդանի. այսօր կենդանի, եւ վաղն մեռանիմք ամենեքեան, այլ ոչ տեսանեմք զմիմեանս»: Անկանէին ծնողքն ի վերայ զաւակաց

եւ սուտ յուսով խաբելով ասէին. «Որդի՛ք, քանի դուք ծուտ գործէիք, մեք փայտիւ ծեծէինք եւ խրատէինք, երբ լայիք, ողորմէինք եւ համբուրէինք զձեզ. նոյնպես եւ Աստուած խրատէ զմեզ, եւ յորժամ աղաչեմք, ողորմի եւ փրկէ»:

21/ Ի վճարել Գ. (3) աւուրն տեսանէին, զի որոտմունքն օր ըստ օրէ բորբոքէին, եւ թնդմունքն դողային. ամենեքեան անյոյս լինէին: Անկանէին հայրքն ի վերայ որդոց եւ որդի ի վերայ հարց, մայր ի վերայ դստեր, եւ դուստր ի վերայ մոր, քոյր ի վերայ եղբարց, եւ եղբարք ի վերայ քորց, փեսայ ի վերայ հարսին / fol 205v / եւ հարսն ի վերայ փեսին, սիրելիք եւ բարեկամ<ք>[1] ի վերայ իրերաց լային եւ ողբային, կոծէին եւ ասէին, թէ. «Մինչ այս ժամս դեռեւս յոյս ունէինք. Գ. (3) օրն վճարեցաւ, եւ բարկութիւնն սաստկացաւ, եւ յոյս մեր բարձաւ. այս է յետին ժամն, այլ ոչ տեսանեմք առաւտ կամ արեգակն: Մինչ այսպէս լային եւ ողբային, ո՞վ կարէ պատմել զարտասունքն եւ զլաց նոցա, թէ որպես աղաղակէին կամ ինչպես գոչէին.:

Մինչ նոքա այսպէս ողբային, քաղցրացաւ Տէր եւ ողորմեցաւ նոցա: Ծագեաց արեգակն, վերացաւ մութն, եղեւ խաղաղութիւն եւ խնդութիւն, ուրախութիւն եւ գնծութիւն: Գնացին ատ թագաւորն մեծամեծք եւ փոքունք, թագն ի գլուխ թագաւորին եդին, փառօք զարդարեցին եւ ի կառս իւր նստեցուցին: Ո՞վ կարէ պատմել, թէ որպէս բաժանէին զտուրս եւ ողորմութիւն առնէին, գձատյան ազատէին, զզերիքն փրկէին, զիւրեանց բաշխէին եւ այլ ոչ առնէին, աւրհնէին զԱստուած, գովէին եւ փառաւորէին. ո՞վ կարէ պատմել[2] զտուրք եւ ողորմութիւն կամ ասել զխնդութիւն եւ ուրախութիւն նոցա:

22/ Իսկ Յունան էր եզր քաղաքին: Իբրեւ ետես, թէ ողորմեցաւ նոցա Տէր, տրտմեցաւ եւ ասէ. «Տէ՛ր, զիտէի զի ողորմած ես, վասն այն փախչէի ի Թար/ fol 206v /սիս»:[3] Իսկ տրտմեալ Յունան եւ զաւզականն ցցեալ, կրկնոցն ի վերայ հովանի արար եւ նստեաց, եւ զարթուցեալ ետես դղղմենի մի կանաչեալ եւ ելեալ ի վերայ զաւզականին, եւ հովանի լինէր նմա: Ուրախ եղեւ եւ ասաց. «Փառք քեզ, Տէ՛ր, զի մխիթարեցեր զիս եւ հաներ ի տրտմութենէս»:

---

1. The plur. ending has apparently fallen.
2. մ above word p.m.
3. See Jonah 4:1–2.

23/ Դարձեալ ևս ևս և զարդուցեալ ետես դրդմենին չորացեալ, տրտմեցաւ ևս ասէ. «Ո՛ Տէր, հան զհոգի իմ յինէն, քանի՞ տրտմեցուցանես զիս», ասէ Հոգին. «‹Յ›ունան, դու ոչ սերմանեցեր. ի միում ժամու բուսաւ դրդմենիդ ևս հովանի արար քեզ, ևս ի միում ժամու չորացաւ։ Ոչ ունէիր աշխատանք ի վերայ դորա, ևս վնաս ինչ ոչ արար քեզ. դու վասն դրդմենոյդ տրտմեցար, ընդէ՞ր դժարանաս վասն փրկութեան Նինուէի, որ ՃԻՌ. (120,000) կաթնակեր մանկունք կայ ի մէջն, որս աջ ևս ‹ձ›ախ⁴ ոչ ճանաչեն։

24/ Եւ ապա ելեալ թագաւորն մեծամեծ ևս փոքունք միաբան գնացին առ ոտսն Յունանու, ևս Յունան ամօթոյ ոչ կարէր հայել երես նոցա։ Իսկ թագաւորն ևս ամենայն մեծամեծքն անկան առ ոտսն մարգարէին, աղաչէին. «Մի՛ տրտմիր ‹Յ›ունա՛ն,⁵ ի քոյին քարոզից ծանեաք զԱստուած, վասն քո բանիդ՝ ապաշխարանք մտաք, լացաք ևս արտասուեցաք, հառաչացաք ևս պաղատեցաք, ևս զԱստուած յուսացաք, ևս ի ստակմանէ ապրեցաք, մեղաց մաքրէ/ fol 206v / ցաք, բանիդ քո արդարացաք։ Սո՛ւրբ մարգարէ, ընդէ՞ր տրտմիս ևս նեղանաս. ի քենէ ծանեաք զԱստուած, ևս դու ես պատճառ փրկութեան մերոյ»,- ևս այլ բազում բանս պաղատանաց խօսէին ընդ մարգարէին ևս զուտս համբուրէին, ևս մեծաւ պատուով տարան ի քաղաքն։ Եւ ուսանէին զիրատ ի նմանէ ևս առին զալիհնութիւն նորա։

25/ Եւ յետ սակաւ աւուրց ելեալ Յունան երթայր յաշխարհն իւր. ուռք նորա ինչ տեղ որ կոխեր, զհողն առնէին վասն ալիհնութեան։ Եւ բազում մարդիկ, հրաժարեալ ի տանէ, երթային ընդ մարգարէին։

Իսկ Յունան խաբեր գնոսա՛ ասելով, թէ. «Մեր թագաւորն հրամայեալ է ոչ թողուլ օտար մարդ իւր աշխարհին, զի մի ժողովուրդքն իւր ուսցեն ի օտարաց անօրէնութիւն գործել։ Դուք կացէք ի յաշխարհի⁶ ձեր, մինչ պատմեցից թագաւորին վասն դարձին ձերոյ, ապա ծանուցից ձեզ. յայնժամ գայցէք յաշխարհն»։ Այսպէս ասելն պատճառն այն էր, զի բազում անօրէնութիւն գործէին երկրայեցիքն, իսկ ինքն Յունան գովեալ էր զերկրայեցիքն, թէ սուրբ են. վասն այն ոչ թողոյր զնոսա ընդ ինքն երթալ, զի մի յայտնի լիցին երկրացոցն զուտ ասելն իւր։ Տես որ Յունան ոչ քարոզէր Նինուէի թէ ոչ ստեաց ինքն։ Իսկ տես, թէ քանի սուտ ասաց։

26/ Եւ ի դառնալն Յովնա/ fol 207r /նու ի Նինուէէ, ոչ մնաց յերկրի իւրում, այլ առեալ զմայրն իւր ևս չոգաւ պանդխտեցաւ ի Սուրի զաւարին այլազգեաց, ընդ հեթանոս։ Քանզի ասէր, թէ. «Այսպէս

---
4. Correcting the scribe's orthographic error: ծախ.
5. Initial Յ omitted, a fairly common orthographic error.
6. Sic!

բարձից զնափատինս իմ, զի ստեցի ի մարգարէանալն իմում վասն Նինուի քաղաքին մեծի»:

27/ Յայնժամ Եղիայ յանդիմանէր զԱքայաբ եւ զկին նորա զեզաբէլ, վասն որոյ կոչեաց սով ի վերայ երկրի, եւ ինքն Եղիա գնաց փախստական ի Սարեփթայ եւ անդ եզիտ զայ<ր>ին[7] հանդերձ որդւովն: Այս է զՅունան եւ զմայրն իւր, եւ մնաց առ նոսա, քանզի ոչ կամէր լինել ընդ անթլփատոսն: Եւ աղիւեաց զնոսա վասն օտարընկալութեանն, եւ զի յառաջագոյն ձանաչէր զնոսա ի վաղուց հետէ:

28/ Չորրոյ զորդին յարոյց Աստուած աղօթիւք Եղիայի, որ էր նա ինքն Յունան մարգարէն: Եւ այսու երեւի Ե. (5) ծնունդ Յունանու: Եւ յարուցեալ Յունան յետ սովոյն, եկն երկիրն Յուդա, եւ մեռաւ մայր նորա ի ձանապարհին, եւ թաղեաց զնա մօտ ի կաղնին Դեբովրայ:

29/ Եւ բնակեցաւ <Յունան>[8] յերկրին Սարարայ, որ մեռաւ անդ, եւ թաղեցաւ յայրին Կենեզայ դատաւորին եղելոյ ի ցեղէ միոջէ յաւուրս անիշխանութեանն: Եւ յետ Յունան նշան յերուսաղէմ, զի յորժամ տեսցեն զքար, զի աղաղակելով գոչեսցէ զորդ/ fol 207v / վալիր եւ զբութտ, զի ի փայտէ աղաղակեսցէ մերձ լինել զվիրկութիւն:

30/ Յայնժամ տեսցեն զերուսաղէմ տապալեալ ի հիմանց, եւ մտցեն ի նա ամենայն հեթանոսք յերկրպագութիւն Տեառն: Եւ առեալ զքարինս նորա դիցեն ի կողմ արեւելից դէպ յարեւմուտս. եւ անդ լիցի երկրպագութիւն օծելոյն:

Մեռաւ խաղաղութեամբ եւ թաղեցաւ յայրին:

Translation

Of Jonah the Prophet

1/ Jonah[9] was from Kiriath Jearim, which is close to Azotus[10] on the coast, in a city of gentiles.[11]

---

7. Correction of orthographic error.
8. The ms reads Յուդայ "Judah," a contamination from the end of the preceding section. We have emended to <Յունան>,
9. Jonah 2 §1
10. See Jonah 2, n. 94.
11. See Jonah 2, n. 95.

2/ Four mothers (i.e., births) are seen for him. First, from his own mother; second, from ship to the sea; third, that the sea gave him to the fish; fourth, that the fish vomited him up on dry land.[12]

3/ When[13] the Ninevehites did many evil deeds and were corrupted by sins, the Lord wished to cut them down.[14] However, on account of God's love of humans, the Holy Spirit commanded Jonah and said, "Go to Nineveh, preach and say, 'God's wrath has come upon you. The Lord wants to cut you down. For, behold, in three more days,[15] those in Nineveh shall no longer be.'"

4/ Jonah said, "Lord, since I know (that) you are kind[16] and merciful, for, at my preaching they will repent, and you are merciful. (So) you will hearken (to them) and be merciful,[17] and I shall become a false prophet."[18]

5/ Again, for a second time, the Lord commanded (him) to go to Nineveh and preach, but Jonah hastened to flee to Tarshish. And going, he boarded a

---

12. See Jonah 2 §3 and the introductory remarks, there. This distinctive tradition shows the relationship of these Jonah works. Compare Moses's four births in Of Moses and Aaron §32. In Step'anos Siwnec'i #17 in Stone, *Traditions*, 329, four births of Christ are mentioned. In the instance in On Moses and Aaron the births seem related to the four elements. A full understanding this idea of multiple births still remains undiscovered.

13. The parallel to Jonah 2 stops here. That text moves to events following his return from Nineveh. The text of Jonah 1 §3 follows the biblical storyline.

14. See Jonah 1:2 with different wording.

15. So also Story of Nineveh §1; in Jonah 3:4 it is forty days. Three days is the period Jonah spent in the fish's belly (Jonah 1:17) and it is also the time it took to walk across Nineveh (Jonah 3:3).

16. Literally: sweet.

17. This section is parallel to Jonah 4:2. In Story of Nineveh §3 the same theme is found. Moreover, there Jonah 3 adds: "Because he was a prophet he knew that the Lord would not destroy Nineveh, and his heart did not bear witness."

18. This passage is an addition to the biblical text. The idea that Jonah was angered by the Lord's mercy that gave the lie to his prophecy is much developed in this text. It is inferred directly from Jonah 4:3–4 and, in fact, it is implied by the central message of the biblical book. As is clear from §5, all the preceding narrative, though drawing on Jonah's arrival in Nineveh, is attributed to an apocryphal first divine command given in the Holy Land. A second command, also given before Jonah attempted to flee, is related in §5 and similarly in The Story of Nineveh §3, though there it follows the discussion of Jonah's reluctance to be known as a false prophet. Following this second command, the tale of his flight, etc. ensues, in accordance with Jonah 1:3. This section here is connected with Story of Nineveh 2, but is shorter.

ship so that he might flee to Tarshish.[19] However, there was a mighty and stormy wind.[20] All began to cry and they besought each his own gods.[21]

6/ Then Jonah wrapped the leather cloak around his head; he fell asleep and snored.[22] Then someone said, "Who are you that you sleep uncaring? Behold, we shall die! Arise, call on the Lord your God, perchance he will be merciful to us and you."[23]

7/ Then Jonah said, "This wrath is on my account. If you wish to live, take (me) and cast me into the sea." They said, "What have you done?" Jonah said, "The Lord who is Creator of earth and heaven commanded me to go to Nineveh and to preach. And I wish to flee to Tarshish. Because of that, the Lord is angry with me; he wishes to destroy me. If you do not cast me into the sea, you too will perish with me."[24]

8/ When they heard that which he said, that "My Lord is the Creator of heaven and earth," they were even more afraid to throw (him) into the sea.[25] They drew lots, (to discover) on whose account it was. The lot fell upon Jonah. They drew lots three times; the lot fell upon Jonah.[26] They took him and cast him into the sea and at once the sea calmed.[27]

---

19. Jonah 1:3. As observed in n. 18 above, here the author returns to be biblical story. Our text is much shorter than the Bible at a number of points.

20. The tale as told in The Story of Nineveh is much longer than here.

21. This is based on Jonah 1:4.

22. Two elements go beyond the biblical text in Jonah 1:5c. That he sheltered beneath of a leathern cloak is not to be found there. The association of a leathern cloak with the prophetic role is to be found in the Armenian of 3–4 Kgdms (2 Sam 19:19 and 1 Kgs 2:8, 13, 14) where Elijah's and Elisha's אדרת "mantle" appears in the Armenian Bible as մաշկեակն "leather cloak." This developed from the corresponding LXX reading at that point, μηλωτής "sheep skin." The second point is Jonah's snoring which is an embroidery here.

23. Jonah 1:6.

24. The text of his speech is added to the biblical text, where only its existence is mentioned: Jonah 1:10. This expands the text quite considerably. These events are related in Jonah 1:12, but here the story is rearranged, putting Jonah's confession before the casting of lots.

25. This is inferred from Jonah 1:13–14.

26. Here the lots serve to confirm Jonah's confession and the throwing him into the sea. In biblical Jonah, the lots occur earlier in the narrative and served to indicate the culprit responsible for the storm (1:7). Only a single casting is recorded in that verse.

27. Jonah 1:15. These events are related in Jonah 1:12, but in the text being published here the story is rearranged, putting Jonah's confession before the casting of lots.

9/ The Lord commanded a great fish and it seized him and He[28] preserved him alive in the great fish's belly.[29] And after three days, it vomited Jonah up alive on the sea coast in the region of Nineveh.[30] Again the Holy Spirit commanded Jonah to go to Nineveh and to preach.[31]

10/ Then Jonah entered into the midst of Nineveh and he preached fearlessly in a loud voice in the midst of Nineveh, and said, "Behold! Nineveh will exist not more than three days,"[32] until this matter reached the king. He sent and brought Jonah and he honored the prophet, he besought (of him) and said, "Teach and instruct us how we may beseech God to save us."[33]

11/ The prophet said, "God has become angry with you. You cannot be saved by prayers, nor by mercy, nor by any other good deeds. Behold! In three days neither you nor this city will remain. You will all perish."[34]

12/ The king said, "When God was angry with the Israelites, their leader Moses besought on behalf of the people. He reconciled God with them and saved the people from the punishment.[35] In the same way, you too, be a prophet and leader for us. For if God has become angry with us, he will not listen to us because of our sins, but you are righteous and a prophet. I beseech you, be a mediator for us and reconcile God with us, and make his anger pass away so that we may be saved from punishment."[36]

13/ Jonah said, "I have besought the Lord many times on your behalf and he did not hearken. I fled and boarded a ship, I was cast into the sea. And I was

---

28. That is, God.

29. This sentence is based on Jonah 1:17. Jonah's hymn to God, which constitutes chap. 2 of the biblical book, is not included in the present document.

30. This is expanded beyond the biblical verse 2:10 which has simply: "Then the Lord spoke to the fish, and it spewed Jonah out upon the dry land." Compare also Story of Nineveh §11 (Stone, *Angels and Heroes*, 273). The similar text there in §11 is somewhat longer than Jonah 1 here.

31. Again, giving instructions is attributed to the Holy Spirit, rather than to God. In the Book of Jonah, the text upon which this passage is based may be found in 3:1–2.

32. Here again, the Bible has forty days.

33. The words from "when --- king" are based on Jonah 3:6a, but the following, including Jonah's summons to before the king, his reception, and the king's speech, are not to be found in the biblical book.

34. This speech of Jonah's is not in the biblical book. Jonah's brief words to the king in The Story of Nineveh §16 are not related to this discourse.

35. Compare 4 Ezra 7:106.

36. This sentence is based on Jonah 1:17. Jonah's hymn to God, which constitutes chap. 2 of the biblical book, is not included in the present document.

swallowed by a fish and wished for my own death.³⁷ And I did not wish to give you the sad news of death. And having brought me forth alive from the belly of the fish, he sent me to give you the sad news of death. I speak accurately to you that in three days Nineveh will be no more. Thus says the Lord."³⁸ Jonah said this and went out of the city.

14/ The king commanded and summoned the princes, both great and small, and all the city together. The king wept and said, "This man is a true prophet. Whatever he says, he says from God's mouth. If I knew (that) that man was false, I would have killed (him). But, whatever he says, he says from God's mouth."³⁹

While the king was saying this, behold! a great earthquake took place, so strong that everybody fell on (their) faces. The king, too, fell from the throne.⁴⁰ Behold! they were seeing that a black cloud mixed with fire surrounded the city's environs, like a fiery wall.⁴¹

15/ When the king saw (this), he wept and said, "Behold! The prophet's discourse has been revealed, O princes great and small, for behold! all pay attention, for I greatly besought the prophet, and he hearkened not. For that prophet is a human like us, through (his) observing the commandment of God, He relented.⁴² But we, not keeping God's commandment, have grown distant from Him, and he wishes to destroy us on account of our sins.

16/ "But I know that when a father is angry with (his) children, he hits them with a stone and wood. When the child weeps and cries, the father has mercy and does not hit (him). Because God is a father of all living beings, (you) separate father from (his) son and daughter from (her) mother, separate

---

37. Jonah in this section attributes all his own actions which were taken to escape having to reproach Nineveh, as being intercessory on behalf of the citizens of Nineveh. Of course, the whole section is authorial embroidery.

38. This discourse is closed with the prophetic seal, "thus says the Lord," common in the biblical prophetic books. On three days, not forty, see nn. 15 and 32 above. This section and the following are quite different from the corresponding sections of Story of Nineveh.

39. No explanation of the king's certainty about Jonah's prophetic role is given. Nor is this explained in the Book of Jonah, but the king is affected by Jonah's prophecy and he issues the commandment to repent (Jonah 3:7–9). Note the repetitiveness of the style here.

40. This is a dramatization of Jonah 3:6.

41. The whole section has no basis in the biblical source. A similar cloud is mentioned in The Preaching of the Prophet Jonah in Nineveh, text no. 17.3 below.

42. That is, Jonah was saved from the whale's belly, because he was God-fearing. One might remark that this comment runs up against Jonah's attempt to disobey the divine command to go and prophesy in Nineveh.

new born and suckling males—the lamb from the sheep, the calf from the cow, the foal from the filly, the chick from the hen![43]

17/ Human and beasts, reptiles and birds, keep them all fasting, all of them are created by God. From hunger, all creatures sigh and bellow, weep and lament. Perhaps God will relent for our sake, or He will have pity for the sake of the sinless infants, for the sake of the beasts of burden, or for the sake of the domestic animals, for the sake of the wild beasts or for the sake of the birds and He will liberate his creatures and make his anger pass away. But, if he does not have pity upon us, he (will) destroy us. For (even) if we perish here, there[44] our penitential deeds will not perish."[45]

18/ The king said this. And he took his crown and cast it to the ground, he rent his garment and put on sack-cloth, he threw ashes on his head, he <pulled out>[46] his beard, he hit his head, he beat his breast, he scratched his face.[47] He cried, lamenting, and said, "Woe to my kingdom, and a thousand woes to my greatness. It would be better if I were a beggar and a poor man, and I were not king of this land. This earth undergoes all (this) because of my sins. On my account this city is perishing, on my account it is destroyed: humans and animals are punished because of me." And he spoke many other words of entreaty. He was calling out, "Woe and alas," he was weeping and he was rolling in ashes.[48]

19/ Then the king cast his[49] crown to the ground and put on haircloth garments:[50] yea, who is there that is embellished and ornamented? The king rolled in ashes and mourned: yea, who is there who rejoices? The king put ashes on his head: who else is there who washes himself? The king who remains hungry: again, who else is there that eats and drinks? The suckling

---

43. Apparently separating the young from the parents was to make them sad as part of a program of affliction to assuage divine anger.

44. That is, in the world to come.

45. This is the retelling of Jonah 3:7–9. The point of the last sentence is that even if the acts of penance do not succeed in averting destruction, nevertheless in the world to come the penances will survive and be worthwhile.

46. The word անխեղ is difficult. If it were derived from անխ "opulent, wealthy" the sense would be difficult. The context requires "pulled out" or "shaved off" (see, e.g., Isa 15:2; 50:6). I cannot imagine what the original reading might have been. On the plucking out or cutting the beard, see Stone and Vardanyan, "Jacob and the Man."

47. Compare the simpler description of the king's mourning in Jonah 3:6.

48. Story of Nineveh is much shorter in its description of the penitence of Nineveh and of the natural disturbances that our text describes as accompanying it.

49. Literally: who cast.

50. This is penitential or ascetic clothing.

child was separated from its mother, the calf from the cow, the lamb from the ewe, the foal from the beasts of burden, the chick from the bird. Human and beast, reptiles and birds, dogs and cats, all fasting raised (their) voices. The children wept, and the parents lamented, the women mourned, and the men wore mourning, the horse whinnied,[51] the beasts sighed, the beasts of burden lowed, dogs barked and cats mewed.[52] Wrath decimated and light was darkened, the earth was quaking,[53] the city was trembling,[54] rocks were split and buildings were destroyed, the heavens were making a great noise, the earth was rumbling, around the city fire and lightning flamed up, and the city suffered like a ship at sea. Gold and silver, byssus and purple were trodden underfoot like dung.

20/ Who was it that looked at them? All who saw the anger lost hope, for they were no longer learning that "we are (to be) saved from this punishment." Children were asking their parents, "If one day has passed, for two more days will we not be alive?" Then, on the second day they were asking, "Father, mother, two days have passed, will we live for one more day? Today (we are) alive and tomorrow shall we all die? Shall we not see one another any more?" The parents were falling upon[55] the offspring and deceiving them with false hope, they were saying, "Children, as far as you were acting crookedly, we struck and rebuked, (but) when you cried, we had mercy and kissed you. Thus, too, God rebukes us and when we beseech (him), he has mercy and saves (us)."[56]

21/ When three days were ended, they saw that the thunders flamed up day by day, and noises shook, all lost hope. The fathers fell upon (embraced) the sons and a son upon (his) father, mother upon daughter and daughter upon mother, sister upon brothers and brothers upon sisters, groom upon bride and bride upon groom, beloved and friends upon one another.[57] They wept and mourned, wailed and said, "Up till this hour we still had hope. The third day is ended and anger has menaced and our hope has been taken away. This is the last hour, we shall no more see morning or the sun." While

---

51. Translated as if it were խարբնշար.
52. The meanings of the two verbs used in the Armenian text are obscure and here the translation is a surmise.
53. The verb is actually 3 pers. plur.
54. The verb is plural.
55. That is, embracing.
56. A similar but much shorter description of the children's questions occurs in Story of Nineveh §18.
57. Such lists of familial relations are ancient: see the discussion in Stone, *4 Ezra*, 111–13, 247–48, 392, 398, 402; other ancient sources exist.

they wept and mourned thus, who can tell their tears and weeping, how they begged and in what way they called out?

While they were lamenting thus, the Lord relented and had mercy on them. The sun shone, the darkness lifted, there was peace and rejoicing, joy and gladness and happiness. The great and small ones went to the king; they put his crown (back) on the king's head; they ornamented (him) with glory, and sat him in his carriage. Who can tell how they distributed gifts and acted mercifully? They freed slaves, they redeemed captives, they distributed their own (goods) and they did nothing else (but) bless God; they praised and glorified (him).

Who can tell the gifts and mercies, or tell their joy and happiness?[58]

22/ Then Jonah was at the edge of the city. When he saw that God had been merciful to them,[59] he became gloomy and said, "O Lord, I knew that you are merciful. For that reason, I fled to Tarshish." Then Jonah, being gloomy, planted his staff, made a shelter from his outer garment and fell asleep.[60] And, awaking, he saw a gourd vine that had greened and climbed upon the staff and was a shelter for him. He was happy and said, "Glory to you, Lord, that you consoled me and brought (me) forth from my gloom."[61]

23/ He slept again, and awakening, he saw that the gourd vine had dried up. He became gloomy and said, "O Lord, bring forth my soul from me: How gloomy have you made me!" The Spirit said, "<J>onah,[62] you did not plant (it). In one hour, this gourd sprouted and made a shelter for you, and in one hour it dried up. You did not labor over it and it did you no harm. You were gloomy on account of this gourd, why are you vexed because of the delivery

---

58. The first part of this section has no parallel in biblical Jonah. The second paragraph corresponds to Jonah 3:10, talking of God's mercy upon them. The text of Jonah 2, is much expanded and embellished. Jonah 4:3 is omitted here.

59. In Story of Nineveh §19, Jonah gives a prophecy of comfort, which is not to be found here.

60. This incident uses the same terminology as is found in the apocryphal story of Mamre, part of the Armenian Abraham saga: see Stone, *Abraham*, 45, 117, 118, 152. The planting of the stick in the present text corresponds to Jonah 4:5 where he "made a booth." His sleep at this point is additional. The planting of the stick is not mentioned in Story of Nineveh §21.

61. Jonah 4:6.

62. This corresponds to Jonah 4:9–10. Notable is the interpretation of "persons who do not know their right hand from their left" in Jonah 4:11, as infants. This point is the end of the book of Jonah.

17. JONAH

of Nineveh,[63] in which are one hundred and twenty thousand infants, who do not know right from left?"[64]

24/ And then the king (and) the great and small (nobles) went forth (and) together they went to Jonah's feet. And Jonah, for shame, could not look at their faces. Then the king and all the grandees[65] fell at the prophet's feet, they begged (him), "Do not be gloomy, Jonah. Through your preaching we have recognized God. On account of your discourse we repented,[66] we cried and wept, we sighed and implored and put our hope in God, and we were delivered from extermination. We cleansed our sins; through your discourse we became righteous. Holy prophet, why are you gloomy and afflicted? Through you we recognized God and you are the cause of our deliverance." And they spoke many other imploring words with the prophet and they kissed his feet and they brought (him) to the city with great honor. And they learned instruction[67] from him and received his blessing.

25/ And after a few days, going forth, Jonah went to his land. His feet made earth on every place on which he trod,[68] for the sake of blessing. And many people renounced (their) homes (and) went with the prophet.

Then Jonah deceived them, saying, "Our king has commanded not to permit foreign people in his land, lest his people learn from the foreigners to act unlawfully. You, remain in your land until I tell the king about your repentance, and then I will inform you.[69] Then, you will come to (our) land." The reason that he spoke thus is the following,[70] that the Hebrews were doing many unlawful things, but Jonah himself had praised the Hebrews, (saying,) that they are holy. Therefore, he did not permit them[71] to go with him, lest his having spoken a lie be revealed to the Hebrews. See how Jonah did not preach to Nineveh, or did not lie himself.[72] But see how great a lie he spoke!

---

63. The east wind, which aggravated Jonah's suffering after the withering of the vine, according to Jonah 4:8, is absent as is the worm that killed the vine (4:7).
64. At this point in the narrative, Story of Nineveh ends.
65. Or: great ones.
66. Literally: we entered penitences. The noun ապաշխարանը should not be in the nominative case and this is another instance of an odd medieval usage of the nom. plur. ending -ը.
67. Or: reproof.
68. This sentence seems to mean, "They went in his footsteps."
69. That is, of his decision.
70. Literally: that.
71. That is the Ninevehites.
72. This passage is not quite clear.

26/ And Jonah, having returned from Nineveh, did not remain in his own land, but taking his mother,[73] he went and sojourned with the heathens in Tyre, a region of the gentiles. Because he said, "Thus I will remove my shame, that I lied in my prophecy concerning Nineveh the great city."[74]

27/ At that time, Elijah was rebuking Ahab and his wife Jezebel. On this account he summoned a famine upon the land, and Elijah himself fled to Zarephath and there he found the widow with her son. They were Jonah and his mother. And he[75] stayed with them because he did not wish to be with the uncircumcised. And he blessed them for their hospitality to foreigners and because he knew them formerly from of old.[76]

28/ God resurrected her son, who was Jonah himself, through the prayers of Elijah and through this, the fifth birth of Jonah was revealed.[77] And Jonah rose up after the famine (and) came to the land of Judah. And his mother died on the way and he buried her close to the oak of Deborah.[78]

29/ And <Jonah> dwelt in the land of Sarara. He died there and was buried in the cave of the judge Kenaz, who had been from a certain tribe in the days of anarchy.[79] And Jonah gave a sign in Jerusalem, that when they will see a rock that, crying out, will beseech tenderly and that the worm that will beseech from wood, salvation is near.[80]

30/ Then they will see Jerusalem overthrown from (its) foundation and all the heathen shall enter it to do obeisance to the Lord, and taking its stones, they will place (them) from the eastern part to the west, and there there will be obeisance (to) the Anointed One.

Jonah died peacefully and was buried in the cave.

---

73. Jonah 1 §6, like the Armenian version of Vitae Prophetarum, mentions the prophet's mother. Here this section serves as a bridge, leading from the story of Nineveh to the events following Jonah's return from Nineveh, which are drawn from the Vita Ionae.

74. Here the text transitions to the rest of the Vita Ionae, which is discussed in the context of Jonah 2 in the present volume. Jonah 1 §§4–5 correspond to the present text.

75. That is, Elijah.

76. This is very close to the text of Vitae Ionae (Yovsēpʻeancʻ, 211).

77. On the other four births, see §2 above.

78. Again, the passage is very close to Vita Ionae.

79. That is, before there were kings.

80. The text of Vitae Ionae continues. The passage is annotated in Jonah 2 §§9–10, which may be consulted.

17. JONAH

17.2. JONAH 2

INTRODUCTORY REMARKS

This text is found in the Synaxarium ms Bodleian Marsh 438, fol 61r–v and it is followed by a colophon.[81] Jonah 2 is mainly drawn from the Vita or Life of Jonah in the Vitae Prophetarum,[82] using a form of the Vita based on the same textual type as that published by Sargis Yovsēpʻeancʻ.[83] In the notes, we will remark on significant variant readings of Yovsēpʻeancʻ's text.

The narrative in this text does not deal with the incident of Jonah and Nineveh, but with what happened to him after he returned home. It takes up the incident of Elijah and the widow of Zarephath, whose son Elijah revived from the dead (1 Kgs 17:8–24, esp. v. 9). The text connects this incident with Jonah who is identified as the revived son. This form of the story is found in both the Greek and Armenian texts of the Vita Ionae and its origin is unclear, but it is quite old.[84] The same tradition occurs in several forms in midrashic sources[85] and in the prologue to his commentary on Jonah, Jerome mentions it and attributes it to Jewish exegetes.

The text, as do many of the Lives in Vitae Prophetarum, then gives some signs by which the people should recognize that salvation is near. In the present instance, the signs hint at Christ and the conversion of the gentiles. Another point of interest is that the author goes out of his way to connect Jonah with preceding prophets and heroes. He is buried in "the cave of the judge Kenaz" for one thing (§9), and for another, he buried his mother, the widow of Zarephath, near the oak of Deborah (§8). According to Gen 35:8, Deborah, Rebecca's nurse was buried by an oak. An oak tree is also related

---

81. See Bodleian Catalogue, 32-69. See p. 159 (Joshua Text 14) above for details of this manuscript.

82. The standard edition of the Greek text is Schermann, *Prophetarum Vitae Fabulosae*. The Armenian text is printed in Yovsēpʻeancʻ, 211–12.

83. Yovsēpʻeancʻ, 211–12.

84. See the preceding text, which also knows the incident. The story is also known to Names, Works, and Deaths of the Holy Prophets §17: see Stone, *Patriarchs and Prophets*, 172–73. It is also known in some midrashic works, not notably ancient: See Ginzberg, *Legends of the Jews*, 6:351.

85. See, e.g., Gen. Rab. 99.13, y. Sukkah 5.1. These two sources do not say explicitly that Jonah was the revived son, but they imply it. The midrash discusses which tribe Jonah belonged to. The command to Elijah to go to Zarephath is then quoted as part of a proof that Jonah was from the tribe of Asher. Later rabbinic sources, as we have noted, make explicit that Jonah was the son of the widow of Zarephath: see Pirkei deRabbi Eliezer ch. 33; m. Tehillim 22.

to a prophet in 4 Ezra 14:1.[86] The "judge Kenaz" is puzzling, since in the Bible, Kenaz appears as the father of the first judge, Othniel. The name may be a familial or tribal indicator, for according to Gen 36:11, 15, etc. Kenaz is a grandson of Esau. It is notable that in the retelling of the biblical book of Judges found in Liber Antiquitatum Biblicarum, chaps. 25–29 the judge Kenaz plays a major role, unparalleled in the book of Judges. Do these two occurrences of this otherwise secondary character hint at the existence of a substantial extrabiblical tradition about Kenaz that has not survived? Perhaps more evidence will turn up.[87]

An interesting theme, not of inherently Christian character, is that the text attributes multiple "births" to Jonah, in addition to his natural birth.[88] Of course, Jonah's sojourn in the fish's belly was talked of as a sort of death in biblical book of Jonah,[89] and so his escape from there was a rebirth. Similarly, once Jonah became identified as the widow's son, his revival by Elijah joined his birth from the fish's belly as a another sort of birth.[90] The precise function of this theme in the narrative is unclear, but one wonders how it might connect in its Armenian context with the Christian idea of baptism as a sort of new birth. A few expansions or changes to the text of Vita Ionae have been observed, and these are signalled in the notes. They do not cohere into a single *Tendenz* of the editor who adopted and adapted the Vita Ionae for the Armenian Synaxarium, resulting in the present text.

---

86. A survey of the occurrences of the oak tree in the Bible shows that on occasion this tree tends to have some special significance.

87. Elsewhere, I have pointed out similar hints at a developed Naphtali tradition that, though it perished, left traces in surviving texts: Michael E. Stone, "Warum Naphtali? Eine Diskussion im Internet," *Judaica: Beiträge zum Verständnis des Judentums* 54 (1998): 188–91; trans. "'Why Naphtali? An Internet Discussion," in Stone, *Apocrypha, Pseudepigrapha and Armenian Studies*, 1:261–64.

88. Jonah 2:6: "I went down to the land whose bars closed upon me forever; yet thou didst bring up my life from the Pit, O Lord my God." See §§2, 28 and notes on Jonah's multiple births.

89. Certain elements in the Jonah story, such as the phrase "in Sheol" (Jonah 2:2) already imply a certain "transcendence of death." In the fish's belly, Jonah is in Sheol and, following his appeal for deliverance (Jonah 2:9) the fish spews him up onto the dry land. This theme was then interpreted slightly differently by Jews and Christians. It is still interesting to note that also in Jewish tradition Jonah is seen as a "proto-Messiah" (remark by O. Ableman).

90. 1 Kgs 17:19–22.

17. JONAH

Text

1/ Marsh 438 / fol 61r / Յայսմ աւուր տաւն է Յունանու մարգարէին

2/ Սա էր ի Կարիաթարիմա, որ է մերձ յԱզովտոս ի ծովեզերին, ի քաղաքն այլազգեաց:

3/ Սմա Դ. (4) մայր երեւի. նախ՝ յիւր մալրէն, Բ. (2)՝ ի նաւէն ի ծովն, եւ Գ. (3), որ ծովն եռ ի ձուկն, եւ Դ. (4), որ էթուք ի ցամաք:

4/ Եւ ապա գնաց ի Նինուէ հրամանաւն Աստուծոյ[91] եւ ի դառնալն անտի ոչ մնաց յերկրի իւրում, եւ չոգաւ, պանդխտեցաւ ի Սուր գաւառին այլազգեաց ընդ հեթանոս:

5/ Քանզի ասէր, թէ. «Այսպէս բարձից զնախատինս իմ, զի ստեցի մարգարէանալն իմում վասն Նինուէի քաղաքին մեծի»:

6/ Յայնժամ Եղիա յանդիմանէր զԱքայաբ եւ զկին նորա զեզաբէլ, վասն որոյ կոչեաց / fol 61v / սով ի վերայ երկրի, եւ ինքն Եղիա գնաց փախստական ի Սարեփայ: Եւ անդ էջիտ զայրին հանդերձ որդովն: Այս է գՅունան եւ զմայր իւր, եւ մնաց առ նոսա, քանզի ոչ կամէր լինել ընդ անթլփատսն:

7/ Եւ ալրնեաց զնոսա վասն աւտարընկալութեանն, եւ զի յառաջագոյն ճանաչէր զնոսա ի վաղուց հետէ, զորոյ զորդին յարոյց Աստուած ի մեռելոց աղաւթիւքն Եղիայի, որ էր նա ինքն Յունան մարգարէն:

8/ Եւ այսու երեւի Ե. (5) ծնունդ Յունանու: Եւ յարուցեալ Յունան յետ սովոյն՝ եկն յերկիրն Յուդայ, եւ մեռաւ մայր նորա ի ճանապարհին, եւ թաղեաց զնա մերձ ի կաղնին Դերովրա:

9/ Եւ բնակեցաւ Յունան յերկրին Սարարայ, որ[92] մեռաւ անդ եւ թաղեցաւ յայրին Կենեզայ դատաւորին, եղելոյ ի ցեղէ միոջէ յալուրա անիշխանութեանն:

10/ Եւ յետ Յունան նշան յերուսաղէմ, զի յորժամ տեսցեն զքար, զի աղաղակելով գոչեսցեն[93] գորովալիր եւ զբռտոտ, զի ի փայտէ աղաղակեցգ մերձ լինել փրկութիւն:

11/ Յայնժամ տեսցեն զերուսաղէմ տապալեալ ի հիմանց եւ մոցեն ի նա ամենայն հեթանոսք յերկրպագութիւն Տեառն: Եւ առեալ

---

91. Here, Vita Ionae in both Greek and Armenian has various readings, none identical with our text.

92. Very likely որ should emended to ուր. It is not preserved by Yovsēpʻeancʻ.

93. Presumably this is a mistake for գոչեսցէ-ն, for the subject, քար "stone" is singular. We so translate it and in this we follow the Greek text.

զքարինս նորա՝ դիցեն ի կողմանէ արեւելից դէպ յարեւմուտս, եւ անդ լիցի երկրպագութիւն աձելոյն:

12/ Մեռաւ Յունան խաղաղութեամբ եւ թաղեցաւ յայրին:

Translation

1/ On this day is the feast of the Prophet Jonah.

2/ He was from Kiryath Jearim, which is close to Azotus[94] on the sea coast, (in) the city of gentiles.[95]

3/ Four mothers are evident for him:[96] First, from his own mother; second, from the ship into the sea; third, that the sea gave him to the fish; and fourth, that it vomited (him) up on dry land.[97]

4/ And then he went to Nineveh at God's command, and when he returned thence, he did not remain in his land, and went and sojourned in the region of Tyre of the gentiles, with heathens.[98]

---

94. Strikingly, these two locations are prominent in the story of the captivity of the ark at the hands of the Philistines; see 1 Sam 5–7:2. See the Armenian traditions in Michael E. Stone, "Two Stories about the Ark of the Covenant," in *Sion, mère des églises: Mélanges liturgiques offerts au Père Charles Athanase Renoux*, ed. M. D. Findikyan, Daniel Galadza, and André Lossky (Münster: Aschendorff, 2016), 253–66 and also Stone, *Biblical Heroes*, text no. 7.

95. This sentence is from the Vita Ionae in Vitae Prophetarum. Azotus is Ashdod, one of the cities of the Philistines on the coast of the Mediterranean. Kiryath Jearim, however, is in the Judean Hills, about twelve kilometers west of Jerusalem. There is clearly a geographical confusion here. The confusion is, however, the name Kiryath Jearim (or: Kiriath Ye'arim; Arm Կարիթարիմ). This name is already found in Greek variants, where it replaces the name found in the text of Greek Vita Ionae, which varies in the different recensions: Rec. Anonyma gives καριαθμους and the other recensions have differing forms, all with a μ: see Schermann, *Prophetarum Vitae Fabulosae*, 82 line 15 and parallels. The Armenian translation of that Greek name is found in the text of the Vita Ionae, as printed in Yovsēpʻianc‛, 211. This name does not appear in the Bible and no suggestion has been made to date as to its possible location or identification in terms of historical geography. Anna Maria Schwemer (*Studien zu den frühjüdischen Prophetenlegenden Vitae Prophetarum: Einleitung, Übersetzung und Kommentar*, Texte und Studien zum Antiken Judentum 49, 50 [Tübingen: Mohr Siebeck, 1995], 2.53–60) presents a long discussion of the place names but this point is not resolved.

96. This is the literal meaning; the phrase means, "four births." See further §8 below, which isolates a fifth birth for this prophet.

97. This section does not appear in the Vita Ionae and the only other source with which it is connected is found in Jonah 1 §2. It reflects, of course, the story told in the book of Jonah.

98. This section is also found in the Vita of Jonah in Yovsēpʻeanc‛.

17. JONAH

5/ Because he said, "Thus I cast off my shame, that I spoke falsely in my prophesying about Nineveh the great city."[99]

6/ At that time, Elijah was rebuking Ahab and his wife Jezebel, on account of whom he summoned a famine on the land, and Elijah himself fled to Zarephath.[100] And there he found the widow with her son, that is Jonah and his mother, and he stayed with them because he did not wish to be with the uncircumcised.[101]

7/ And he blessed them on account of their hospitality to strangers and since previously he knew them from before, (for they were those) whose son God raised up from the dead at Elijah's prayer, who was indeed[102] the very prophet Jonah.[103]

8/ And through this the fifth birth of Jonah is evident.[104] And Jonah rose up after the famine and he came to the land of Judah. And his mother died on the way and he buried her near the oak of Deborah.[105]

---

99. This section is nearly completely identical with the Vita of Jonah. Jonah's fear of being proven a false prophet, derived from the book of Jonah 4:2, is evident elsewhere, e.g., Pirqei deRabbi Eliezer, ch. 10.1; m. Tanḥuma 8. See also The Story of Nineveh and Jonah, in Stone, *Angels and Heroes*, §§ 2–4, 20, 270–71, 275 and The Sermon of Jonah in Yovsēpʻeancʻ, 186 and here, p. 181 n. 41.

100. 1 Kgs 17:9.

101. Again, the text follows the Vita Ionae here; it is rather close to Armenian recension printed in Yovsēpʻeancʻ.

102. That is, the son.

103. The explicit identification of the widow's son with Jonah is not found in other known Armenian Jonah tales. In Vitae Prophetarum it is found most recensions, such as Recensio Anonyma (Schermann, *Prophetarum Vitae Fabulosae*, 83), in Recensio Epiphanii Prior (Schermann 19), and in Recensio Dorothei (Schermann 31). The sentence is rather clumsy.

104. See p. 188 above.

105. See Gen 35:6; this place near Bethel, was north of Jerusalem. This statement is modified from the Vita Ionae.

9/ And Jonah lived in the land of Sarara, where he died. And he was buried in the cave of the judge Kenaz,[106] who had been from a certain tribe in the days of anarchy.[107]

10/ And Jonah gave a sign in Jerusalem, that when they see a rock crying out[108] and beseeching tenderly,[109] and a worm that will beseech from the wood,[110] salvation is near.[111]

11/ Then they will see Jerusalem overthrown from (its) foundation[112] and all the heathen shall enter it to do obeisance to the Lord, and taking its stones they will place (them) from the eastern part to the west, and there will be obeisance (to) the Anointed One.[113]

12/ Jonah died peacefully and was buried in the cave.[114]

---

106. See Montague R. James, *The Biblical Antiquities of Philo* (London: Society for Promoting Christian Knowledge, 1917; repr. with prolegomenon by L. Feldman, New York: Ktav, 1971), 146–47 for a discussion of the judge Kenaz. The chief text about him is in LAB chaps. 25–28. His death, related in LAB at the end of chap. 28 is not connected with a cave. In the Bible, Kenaz is most prominent as the father of the first judge, Othniel. In LAB he has replaced Othniel and his story is expanded enormously. His deeds include dedication of the Temple, victories and more. The tradition that is surfacing here is unknown beyond these Jonah texts. See p. 188 above.

107. In Gen 36:11 makes him a son of Esau. "Anarchy" presumably means before the institution of the monarchy.

108. See 4 Ezra 5:5, perhaps deriving from Hab 2:11 (LXX). See Stone, *4 Ezra*, 111.

109. This is not known elsewhere.

110. The phrase about the wood is to be found in the Vita Ionae as found in Yovsēpʻeancʻ and in one Greek recension (Recensio Scholiis: Schermann, p. 101.2-3). Do these signs hint at Christ's Cross? The significance of the worm does not seem to be symbolic and perhaps, like the crying out of the rock and the text implies that a small and negligible creature like a wood-worm cries out.

111. On such omens in Vitae Prophetarum, see David Satran, *Biblical Prophets in Byzantine Palestine: Reassessing the Lives of the Prophets*, SVTP (Leiden: Brill, 1995), 63–68.

112. The message of redemption from this point on is present only in the Recensio Scholiis of the Life of Jonah and in Yovsēpʻeancʻ, and there it is more extensive than in the text presented here.

113. This word is nom/acc here, where an oblique case is demanded, as in Yovsēpʻeancʻ.

114. It is not clear which cave. Again, an unknown tradition.

17.3. The Preaching of the Prophet Jonah in Nineveh

Introductory Remarks

This text was published by Yovsēpʻeancʻ (343–348) from manuscript V1541, of the year 1627[115] and an unsatisfactory English translation was prepared and published by J. Issaverdens.[116] The work needs a new edition, which will take the quite plentiful manuscript witnesses into account.[117] Since a number of Jonah texts have been published in the present volume as well as in two preceding volumes of this series, I decided for the readers' convenience, to include a new translation of Yovsēpʻeancʻs edition here with the present group of Jonah texts. The translation has been supplied with page and line numbers from Yovsēpʻeancʻs edition.

No attempt has been made to annotate the text, with the exception of references to the Bible. Discussion of this text itself should await a new edition.

Translation

[p. 343] Preaching (Sermon) of the prophet Jonah in the City of Nineveh.

For Nineveh was a great city and (of) Assyria, which king Ninos built and it was called after his own name, Nineveh. And this king Ninos had a wife named Shamiram (Semiramis). And Ninos feared / 5 / his wife because of her insatiable promiscuity. He left the kingdom and fled to the Hellad.[118] And Shamiram ruled for fifteen years and afterwards, she was killed by her sons.

And in seven days, a man went from Babylon to Nineveh / 10 / to the South East.[119] And the place was rich and full of good things like the land of Sodom. They ate and drank and perfumed their bodies, food for the unsleeping worms.[120] They abandoned sanctity and righteous marriage, and they pursued promiscuity. They went forth from God's / 15 / eyes and enraged God, he who, though he is angry with the sinner, has pity, and does not wish

---

115. See Yovsēpʻeancʻ 343–48.
116. Jacques Issaverdens, *The Uncanonical Writings of the Old Testament Found in the Armenian MSS. of the Library of St. Lazarus*, 2nd ed. (Venice: Mechitarist, 1934), 185–91.
117. I have noted over the years that the text occurs in J669, 383r–398r; J6312, 334r–349v; J0694, 135r–154v; J0811, 408–438; J1012, 123–142; J1047, 155v–177r; J1136, 134–146; M2939, 217r–221r; M6340, 47r–50r; M0059, 9r–11a, and more copies doubtless exist.
118. Issaverdens: Greece.
119. I.e., Nineveh was seven days' travel from Babylon.
120. Cf. Isa 66:24.

to punish him, but remains (waiting) for repentance and penitence, as he says, "I do not desire the death of the sinner, but his turning back and (continued) life" (Ezek 18:23, 33:11). On account of that, he pitied Nineveh, and desired first to send a herald (or: a prophet, a preacher) and, if they do not repent, then to punish (them).

[p. 344] And the Lord said to <J>onah the prophet, "Go to Nineveh, a great city, and preach penitence there, for their cry has come up before me,"

And Jonah did not wish to go, for two reasons: / 5 / the first, he did not wish to preach to pagans and to be with uncircumcised, (for he said), "(If) I preach,[121] I leave my tree thirsting and I water that of others. Of what benefit is it to me?" And the second reason, "I know," he said, "that You are merciful, long-suffering and You will be sorry for humans. / 10 / (If) I go," he said, "(and) I preach that this city will perish, they will be sorry and repent and you will not destroy (them). My prophecy (will) remain unfulfilled and my name (reputation) becomes of a false prophet. It is better for me to die than for my name to become that of a false prophet."[122]

/ 15 / Because of these two reasons he did not wish to go, but went down to Jaffa and boarded a ship with the merchants and wanted to flee to Tarsus. And when he boarded the ship, the Lord God cast turmoil and a storm onto the sea, and they began each to beseech / 20 / his god and the sea did not stop, but moved even more in turmoil. And Jonah, descending into a compartment of the ship, fell asleep and snored. And they woke him up and said, "Why are you sleeping? Arise, call upon the Lord your God, so that perhaps he will save us and / 25 / we shall not perish."[123] And the sea did not cease its turbulence and they cast the food into the sea and then the cargo to make the ship lighter, and there was no quietude.[124]

And they said, "Let us cast lots and let us see on account of whose sins this evil has come upon us."[125] And they cast lots, and / 30 / the lot fell upon Jonah. And they said to him, "What sort of man are you, from which nation

---

121. I.e., if I preach to them.

122. The theme of Jonah not wanting his prophecy to fail, even because of divine mercy, is found prominently in the apocryphal Jonah writings. It is based on Jonah 4:2–3.

123. Based on Jonah 1:8.

124. The sea was not quiet, peaceful. This is based on Jonah 1:5, but the order of events here differs.

125. Jonah 1:8, almost literally.

or from which people?"[126] And Jonah said, "I am a servant of God, and I serve the Lord of heaven, who made the earth."[127]

/ 35 / And they were greatly afraid for they learned that he had fled from the face of God, because he had told them, and they said to him, "Why did you do this?" and

[p. 345] they wished to turn the ship back and to bring it to dry land,[128] and they could not, and they said, "Far be it, Lord. Do not bring innocent blood upon us, for you did that which you wished."[129]

/ 5 / And Jonah said, "Cast me into the sea and this storm will cease from you."[130]

And they seized Jonah and cast (him) into the sea, and then the sea became peaceful. And at that very time the Lord commanded a whale, a great dragon of the fish, and it swallowed Jonah.[131] And the men went forth onto dry land, sacrificed offerings to the Lord and sought / 10 / the forgiveness of (their) sins.[132] And the dragon took Jonah, it descended to the depths of the earth, and bringing (him) to the sea, it went around the land of the Ethiopians, and by the river of the Indians it brought him to the sea of the Persians and from the sea of the Persians it brought him forth to the River Sarankas in the blinking of an eye, (which) was fifteen / 15 / days on foot.

And Jonah was in the belly of the whale for three days and three nights,[133] standing with his arms outstretched he prayed, alive by the power of God.[134] And after three days the dragon brought Jonah to before the city of Nineveh, it spewed (him) out onto the dry land,[135] / 20 / three days travel distant from the city. And it returned to its place. And Jonah was not familiar with the place, so that Jonah might realize that humans cannot flee from God, and his omnipotent hand reaches every place. / 25 /

And the word of the Lord came a second time to Jonah and said, "Arise, go to Nineveh, the great city, and preach penitence there." When Jonah had

---

126. The three questions occur in Jonah 1:6b.
127. Cf. Jonah 1:9b.
128. Based on Jonah 1:10–11, 13.
129. Cf. Jonah 1:14.
130. Jonah 1:12a.
131. Jonah 1:15, 17.
132. Expanded from Jonah 1:16.
133. Jonah 1:17.
134. Jonah's prayer is in Jonah 2:1–9.
135. Jonah 2:10.

gone a three-days' journey, he reached the city.[136] He began / 30 / to preach and to say, "Behold in three days and Nineveh will be destroyed." And the dwellers in the city saw Jonah's face more resplendent than the sun, and fiery flames went forth from his mouth, and running, they told the king and said, "A foreign man and frighteningly clothed, has come and he is preaching thus." And the king said, "His discourse is true."[137]

/ 35 / And when he said this, the city began

[p. 346] to shake, and at first, he wished to flee. And a fiery cloud descended; it surrounded the city like a wall, and no one was able to flee. The king said, "Fear not. That God who sent the prophet, if he / 5 / wanted our destruction, indeed he would destroy (us), and he would not send us a herald (preacher) and prophet. But he sent (him) for the following reason, that he might rebuke us by means of the prophet's preaching, so that we should be sorry for (our) sins and repent. / 10 / We turn away from sins (and) God from his anger."

And it was proclaimed in Nineveh by the king and his grandees, "Every human, man and woman, greybeard and child—let them not eat for three days; and let them not give sustenance to the beasts and let the mothers not / 15 / give the breast to children." And all put on sackcloth, the king and the grandees, and all the whole city."[138]

The dark cloud produced thunder and lightning. And they began to encourage one another and were saying, "God is caring, a <lover>[139] of humans. He does not annihilate the work of (his) hands." / 20 / Children were asking their mothers, "When will that last day come on which our city will perish?" The mothers answered, saying to their children, (as) they held out hope, "God is caring, merciful, he does not annihilate his servant." The parents were saying to their offspring, "You / 25 / beseech God. It may be that through your mercy[140] we too shall escape." And everybody turned wholeheartedly to God and were sorry for their evils and were saying, "Who knows? (Perhaps) God will repent and turn away from his anger." And thus,

---

136. In Jonah 3:3 three days' walk is the distance across the city of Nineveh. In this text, and certain other apocryphal texts, Jonah's preaching is said to be that in three days Nineveh will be destroyed, not in the biblical forty days (Jonah 3:4, etc.).

137. The text greatly expands the following incidents of the repentance and adds many details of supernatural and meteorological events that are not in the book of Jonah.

138. Sic!

139. Speculation of Yovsēpʻeancʻ.

140. That is: through His mercy on you.

/ 30 / beating their breasts, they were weeping and lamenting in the midst of the darkness.

And Jonah went forth from the city to the midst of the fiery cloud and he was not harmed. And he sat over against the city to see the fulfillment/completion and he wished that the city would perish and his prophecy be fulfilled.

/ 35 / Then the inhabitants of the city for three days, by day and by [p. 347] night did not discern one another, but fasting, human and beast, by repentance, by sorrow, and by tears they turned back the punishment of the divine wrath. And after three days the cloud lifted and the quaking ceased, and the sun shone on them and the fear of death and gloom / 5 / dissipated. And they began to bless God and to praise him.

And Jonah was gloomy and heat was cast around his head,[141] and he was kept in suspense. And God said to Jonah, "Do you grieve / 10 / greatly?" And Jonah said, "Is not this (situation) those words that I was saying while in my land? For I knew that you are merciful and caring and you repent over the evils of humans?"[142]

The Lord wished to rebuke his pitiless / 15 / conduct by example, and on the following morning, a gourd sprouted, climbed up and made a shelter for Jonah's head.[143] And he sat under its shelter and he was somewhat comforted. And when that day had passed and on the following day, at God's behest, the earthworm smote the gourd and / 20 / it dried up and heat was cast around his head, (he was excited) and he was kept in suspense.

And Jonah said, "It were better for me to die than (to live) this sort of life."

And the Lord said to Jonah, "Are you very gloomy on account of the gourd."[144]

And Jonah said, "I am very gloomy, for it was my comfort."

And the Lord said, "You cared about the gourd which came into being without even one hour of work in it, but came forth in a night and perished / 30 / on the next night.[145] The perishing of one gourd upset you and was reckoned a pain," said the beneficent One, "how shall I not care about Nineveh, the great city, in which there live more than one hundred and twenty thousand people, who do not know their right hand and left, and very many

---

141. That is: he became (over-)excited.
142. Jonah 4:2, to which is prefaced a phrase from Jonah 4:4.
143. Jonah 4:5–6 is rewritten here.
144. Jonah 4:9.
145. Jonah 4:10.

beasts?[146] If I punish the / 35 / sinners," he said, "how shall I not care for the children without sin. You were bitter

[p. 348] for one gourd," He said, "how much more does the destruction of my creations pain me?"

And then Jonah was conciliated. Then the inhabitants of Nineveh, who caused the punishment to pass away through penitence, / 5 / stood before the holy prophet and served and honored him in a god-like way. And the prophet remained among them for six months and wished to go away and the inhabitants said to the prophet, "You are our illuminator, burning lamp and sun, do not go and do not / 10 / draw distant from us, lest the darkness of sin and faithlessness surround us. And if you do not wish to live with us, take us with you." And he did not want to remain with them or to take them (with him), giving as a reason the {annual}[147] of the land. "The bread of our land is {annual}," he says, "if a person / 15 /eats it, he gets stomach pain, and cannot overcome (it)."

And they went weeping after the prophet, and with love set him on the way; they blessed the nation of Israel and his people. And the prophet did not wish to bring them, lest their[148] shame, the / 20 / faithlessness and dissension of the Israelite nation become known (to) the Syrians.[149] And the prophet did not go to his land but, taking his mother, and he went and he sojourned in the land of Ishmael, "so that thus," he said, "I shall remove my shame, that I lied in my prophecy concerning the city of Nineveh." And his mother died on the way and he buried her by the oak of Řakʻel.[150]

---

146. Jonah 4:11.
147. Corrupt. Issaverdens emends "hurtfulness."
148. The Israelites' shame.
149. Perhaps intending "Assyrians." Odd!
150. This last sentence comes from Vita Ionae.

18. Job the Righteous

Introductory Remarks

This text, found in Marsh 438 fols 454v–456r under the rubric for the date 29th Ahekan and 6th May is to be read on the day on which the biblical Job was celebrated.[1] The author composed the text using the verses from the book of Job that constitute the narrative elements of the story. He has modified the wording of those verses has introduced some further minor apocryphal traditions. In making this determination, I have consulted the text of the Armenian Bible, specifically Zohrab's edition of 1805, and I have compared this apocryphal tale with it.[2]

This text, therefore, like the text on Elisha above,[3] is an example of an apocryphon in which there is very minor departure from the biblical narrative, with few exegetical embroideries, or other additional materials. It is one end of a spectrum, at the other end of which are texts whose relationship to the Bible may be characterized as radical reworking, re-interpretation and invention.

Text

Marsh 438 / fol 454v / Title / Ահկի ի ԻԹ. (29) եւ Մայիսի Զ. (6). Տաւն է Յոբայ Արդարոյ:

1/ Երանելին Յոբ՝ հայրն համբերութեան,[4] էր թոռանցն Եսաւայ՝ այր արդար եւ ճշմարիտ, մեկնեալ եւ զատեալ յամենայն իրաց չարեաց:

---

1. Concerning the manuscript, see the introductory remarks on p. 159 above.
2. J. Zohrabean, ed., *The Scriptures of the Old and New Testaments* (Venice: Mekhitarist, 1805). See also Claude Cox, *Armenian Job: Reconstructed Greek Text, Critical Edition of the Armenian with English Translation*, HUAS 8 (Leuven: Peeters, 2006).
3. From Text 16 Elisha §3 on.
4. The virtue of patience is particularly celebrated in connection with Joseph, see The Third Story of Joseph 25, 93 (Stone, *Biblical Heroes*, 176–228).

2/ Եւ էր թագաւոր որդոցն Եսաւայ, անարատ եւ աստուածապաշտ, եւ առաջին անուն նորա Յոբաբ էր։ Եւ էր հուրընկալ եւ աստուածասէր, ողորմած եւ գթած ըստ նմանութեան նախնոյն իւրոյ հաւրն հաւատոյ Աբրահամու։

3/ Եղեն որդիք նորա է. (7) եւ դստերք Գ. (3), ունէր եւ խաշինս բազումս, ոչխարք ԵՌ. (5,000), ուղտ ԳՌ. (3,000), լուծք եզանց ԵՃ. (500) եւ այլ սպասք բազում յոյժ։

4/ Եւ միաբանեալ՝ որդիք նորա գային առ միմեանս եւ առնէին ուրախութիւն, ունելով ընդ ընթեանս գերեքին քորսն իւրեանց, ուտել եւ ըմպել ընդ նոսա։

5/ Եւ ի կատարման ուրախութեանն առաքէր Յոբ եւ սրբէր զնոսա, եւ մատուցանէր զոհս ըստ թուոց նոցա, եւ զուարակ մի վասն մեղաց ըստ ոգւոց նոցա, քանզի ասէր Յոբ, թէ․ «Գուցէ որդիքն իմ ի միտս իւրեանց իմացան չարութիւն ինչ զԱստուծոյ»։

6/ Եւ այսպէս առնէր Յոբ զամենայն աւուրս նոցա,[5] եւ այլ մեծամեծ գործք բարութեան էին Յոբայ ի վերայ երկրի, զոր տեսեալ սատանա մախայր եւ խնդրեաց յԱստուծոյ փորձել զնա։ Եւ ետ զնա Աստուած ի ձեռս նորա, եւ թէ որպէս ետ, ասացից։

7/ Յաւուր միում կային հրեշտակք ի սպասու իրը ի հանդիսի, եկն ընդ նոսա եւ սատանա։ Ասէ Տէր ցսատանա. «Դու ուստի՞ գաս», պատասխանի ետ սատանա Տեառն Աստուծոյ եւ ասէ. «Շրջեալ ընդ ամենայն երկիր եւ յածեալ ի ներքոյ երկնից եկեալ կամ»։

8/ Ասէ Տէր ցսատանա. «Նայեցար մտաւք ընդ ծառայն իմ Յոբ, զի ոչ գոյ իբրեւ զնա այր անարատ, արդար եւ ճշմարիտ աստուածապաշտ ի վերայ երկրի»։ Ասէ սատանա. «Մի՞ թէ ձրի պաշտէ Յոբ զՏէր, ոչ ապաքէն դու ամրացուցեր զարտաքին եւ զներքինս տան նորա, զգործս ձեռաց նորա աւրհնեցեր եւ զանասունս նորա բազմացուցեր ի վերայ երկրի։ Բայց աղէ առաքեա զձեռն քո եւ արկ յամենայն ինչս նորա, եւ տես, թէ աւրհնեցէ՞ զքեզ արդարութեամբ»։

9/ Եւ ասէ Տէր ցսատանա. «Ահա զամենայն ինչս նորա տաց ի ձեռս քո, բայց ի նա մի մերձենայցես»։ Եւ ել սատանա յերեսաց Աստուծոյ։ Եւ որդիքն Յոբայ եւ դստերք նորա ուտէին եւ ըմպէին ի տան աւագ եղբաւրն իւրեանց։ Եւ ահա ծառայ մի յեզնավարացն եկն առ Յոբ եւ գոյժ ի բերանն ասէլ[ով].[6] «Լուծք եզանցն վարէին, եւ էշք, / fol 455r / մատակք արածէին առ նոքօք, յանկարծակի հասին առ

---

5. The singular, նորա, would be expected.
6. The ending of this word is illegible. Probably it was ասելով "saying."

նոքայք ասպատակաւորք եւ զերեցին զամենեսեան, եւ զմանկտին կոտորեցին սրով։ Ես միայն ապրեցայ եւ եկի պատմել քեզ։

10/ Եւ մինչդեռ նա զայն խաւսէր, այլ բաւթա{ա}ւ⁷ եկն եւ ասէ ցնոր. «Ասպատակաւորք ասպատակեցին զմեզ երիս առաջս եւ պատեցան զուղտաւքն եւ զերեցին զնոսա եւ զմանկտին կոտորեցին սրով. ես միայն ապրեցա եւ եկի պատմել քեզ»։

11/ Իսկ Յոբ ամենայն զուժկա{կա}նիք⁸ զայս պատասխանէր. «Տէր ետ եւ Տէր էառ. եղիցի անուն Տեառն աւրհնեալ»։

12/ Եւ մինչդեռ զոհութիւնն Յոբա ի բերանն էր, այլ զուժկան եկն եւ ասէ ցնոր. «Մինչդեռ ուտէին եւ ըմպէին որդիքն քո եւ դստերքն, ատ էրէց եղբայրն իւրեանց, յանկարծակի կործանեցաւ տունն ի վերայ նոցա ի չորից կողմանց, եւ եսպան զամենեսեան. ես միայն մնացի ապրեալ եւ եկի պատմել քեզ»։

13/ Յայնժամ յարուցեալ Յոբ, ելաց եւ պատառեաց զհանդերձս իւր եւ կտրեաց զհերս վարսից իւրոց, եւ անկեալ երկիրպագանէր Տեառն Աստուծոյ եւ ասէր. «Մերկ իսկ եկի յորովայնէ մաւր իմոյ եւ մերկանդամ դարձայց անդրէն։ Տէր ետ եւ Տէր էառ, որպէս համաճոյ թուեցաւ, այնպէս կատարեցաւ. եղիցի անուն Տեառն աւրհնեալ»։

14/ Եւ յայսմ ամենայնի, որ անցին ընդ նա, ոչ մեղաւ Յոբ առաջի Տեառն, այլ ընդ ամենայնի զոհութիւն տայր Աստուծոյ։ Եւ դարձեալ արար Տէր հանդէս հրեշտակաց իւրոց կալ առաջի Տեառն Աստուծոյ։ Եկն եւ սատանա ընդ նոսա կալ առաջի Տեառն Աստուծոյ ի մէջ նոցա։

15/ Եւ ասէ Տէր ցսատանա. «Դու ուստի՞ գաս, ո՛վ պեղծ»։ Ասէ սատանա. «Սահեալ ի ներքո երկնից եւ շրջեալ ընդ ամենայն երկիր, իբր թէ զամենայն ինձ բաժին արարի, ահաւասիկ եկեալ կամ»։

16/ Ասէ Տէր ցսատանա. «Ապաքէն հաճեցար ընդ ծառայն իմ Յոբ, զի ոչ գոյ իբրեւ զնա մարդ ի վերայ երկրի, այր ճշմարիտ, արդար, աստուածապաշտ, զատեալ եւ մեկնեալ յամենայն չարեաց եւ տակաւին կա յանմեղութեան։ Եւ դու տարապարտ խաւսեցար կորուսանել զինչս նորա։

17/ Ասէ սատանա. «Ջինչ պակասեաց ի նմանէ եւ ոչինչ, ոչ ապաքէն մորթ ընդ մորթո, եւ որ ինչ իցէ ընդ նորա, իցէ մարդոյ. լոյս աչացն եւ լոյր ականջացն, հոտոտումն ոռնկացն, եւ ճաշակ բերանոյն, բարբառ լեզուին եւ շաւշափումն ձեռացն, գնացք ոտիցն եւ առողջութիւն մարմնոյն, ընդ անձին մարմնոյ նորա է, / fol 455v / եւ լիապէս ունի զամենայն։

---

7. The second ա is a dittography.
8. The second կա is a dittography.

18/ Ապա թէ ոչ, առաբեա զձեռն քո եւ արկ զոսկերաւք եւ զմարմնով նորա, եթէ ոչ յերեսս աւրհնեսցէ զքեզ»։ Ասէ Տէր ցսատանայ. «Ահա մատնեմ զնա քեզ, բայց միայն զոգին պահեսցես եւ ոչ մեղանչիցես ոգոյ նորա»։

19/ Եւ ել սատանա յերեսաց Տեառն, եւ եհար զՅոբ չարաչար կեղտով, յոտից մինչեւ ցգլուխ, եւ անպատիւ արարին զնա հացաբոյծ եւ արծաթագին ծառայքն իւր։ Եւ հանեալ ընկեցին արտաքոյ տանց եւ ապարանից իւրոց, այլ եւ ի քաղաքէն իսկ արտաքսեցին, որ անկեալ դներ յաղբիսն։

20/ Եւ առեալ կոշտ եւ խեցի եւ քերեր նոքաւք զթարախ վիրացն. եւ այնպէս եկաց զամս Է. (7): Եւ ապա ասէ ցնա կին իւր. «Մինչեւ յե՞րբ ժուժկալեալ ասիցես, թէ համբերեցից տակաւին, ահաւասիկ ապականեալ է յիշատակ քո ի վերայ երկրի. ուստերքն քո եւ դստերքն իմոյ որովայնի երկունքն, յորս տարապարտուց վաստակեցի տառապանաւք.9

21/ Դու որբա՞ւ ն ի զազրութիւն որդանց նստիս, անձրեւքաց եւ արեւակէզ, ճիւնաթաթախ եւ ցրտասառոյց, եւ ես մոլորեալ տանէ ի տուն, եւ դրանէ ի դուռն, շրջիմ սպասելով, թէ երբ մտանիցէ արեգակնն, զի սակաւ մի հանգիստ առից ի տառապանաց եւ ի ցաւոց, որ այժմ պատեալ են զինեւ։ Ադէ՛ ասա բան ինչ ի Տէր եւ վախճանեաց»։

22/ Եւ Յոբ սաստեալ նմա ասաց. «Իբրեւ զմի ի կանանց անզգամաց խաւսեցար. եթէ զբարիսն ընկալաք ի Տեառնէ, չարեացս ո՞ւչ համբերեմք»։ Եւ յայսմ ամենայնի, որ ինչ անցք անցին ընդ նա, ոչ մեղաւ Յոբ Աստուծոյ, այլ միայն աւրհներ զԱստուած եւ ասէր. «Տէր ետ եւ Տէր էառ. եղիցի անուն Տեառն աւրհնեալ»։

23/ Եւ լուեալ երից բարեկամացն Յոբայ զամենայն չարիսն, որ հասին ի վերայ նորա, եւ եկին առ նա յիւրաքանչիւր քաղաքաց եւ յաշխարհաց մխիթարել զնա. Եղիփազ արքայ Թեմնացոց, Բաղդատ բռնաւոր Սաւքեցոց, եւ Սոփար խան Մինեցոց։

24/10 Եւ տեսեալ զնա ի բացուստ ոչ ծանեան եւ բարբառ արձակեալ լացին մեծաձայն, պատառեցին զպատմուճանսն, եւ արկին հող ի վերայ գլխոց նոցա։ Եւ նստան շուրջ զնովաւ զզգենի զէ. (7) աւր եւ զէ. (7) գիշեր ընդ երկինս հայելով հառաչէի[ն] լռութեամբ, եւ ոչ ոք ի նոցանէ խաւսեցաւ ընդ նմա բան մի, քանզի տեսանէին զանհնարին հարուածսն եւ հիացեալ ապուշ մնացին։

---

9. LXX and Arm Job 2:9. Those texts have a long expansion here.
10. The whole section follows Arm Job 2:12-13 with some variants.

25/ Եւ ապա երաց Յոբ զբերան իւր եւ ասաց. «Կորիցէ օրն, յորում ես ծնայ, եւ գիշերն {յո}[11] / fol 456r / յորում ասացին, թէ ահա առու. անիծեալ այր ծննդեան իմոյ, եւ մի եղիցի նա յաւուրս տարոյ եւ մի թուեցցի նա յաւուրս ամաց:

26/ Յայնժամ երեւեալ Տէր ամպով ի վերայ Յոբայ եւ ասէ սաստիկ որոտմամբ եւ ահագին հրնչմամբ. «Ո՞ վ է դա, որ թագուցանէ յինէն զբանս»: Եւ ասաց զամենայն ինչ ի ստեղծմանէ արարածոց եւ յայտնեցաւ Յոբա զամենայն: Եւ ապա առողջացոյց զնա զեղեցկագոյն, քան զառաջինն, որ էր նախ քան զտառապանսն փորձանացն:

27/ Եւ եկին եղբարքն եւ քորքն Յոբայ, կերան եւ արբին ընդ նմա, եւ ետուն նմա իւրաքանչիւր ոք մէն մի որոչ եւ ստեր մի ոսկի: Եւ եղեն նորա որդիք Է. (7) եւ դստերք Գ. (3): Եւ կոչեաց զմինն Տիւ, եւ զմիւսն Կասիա, եւ զմիւսն Ամաթեղջիւր. եւ աւրինեաց Տէր Աստուած զՅոբա վերջինն, քան զառաջինն:

28/ Եւ եղեն նորա ոչխարք ԺՌ. (10,000), լուծք եզանց Ռ. (1,000): Եւ յետ փորձանացն եկաց Յոբ ՃՀ. (170): Որպէս զամենայն ինչ կրկին ետ Տէր Յոբայ, նոյնպէս եւ զկեանս ժամանակաց: Զի առաջին ժամանակ թագաւորութեանն Հ. (70) ամ էր, եւ Է. (7) ամ ի վիշտն եկաց, եւ յետ վշտացն հարիւր եւ Հ. (170) ամ թագաւորեաց, որ գայ ամենայն ժա<մա>նակ[12] կենաց նորա ԲԽԷ. (247) ամ:

29/ Եւ ետես Յոբ զորդիս որդոց իւրոց մինչեւ ի չորրորդ ազգու եւ վախճանեցաւ Յոբ ի քառասուն ծերութեան: Էր նա յՕսիտ աշխարհէ, որ այժմ ասի Թլկուրան, եւ է անդ յայտնի գերեզման նորա: Եւ է Յոբ Զ. (6) ծնունդ յԱբրահամէ, որպէս եւ ազգահամարն ցուցանէ. Աբրահամ, Իսահակ, Յակոբ, Դեւի, Կահաթ, Ամրամ, Մովսէս:

30/ Եւ դարձեալ յԻսահակայ՝ Եսաւ, Ռակուէլ, Զարեհ, Յոբ, որ գայ Յոբ յաւուրս Ամրամայ հարն Մովսիսի եւ յերկարեալ յետ Մովսէսի ամս բազում: Եւ գիտելի է, զի Յոբ պատկեր էր Ադամայ. կրիւք անձինն եւ թագաւորութեամբն, եւ տառապանաւքն փորձանացն, եւ վերստին նորոգութեամբն, եւ թագաւորութեամբն:

31/ Եւ թէ ո՞ վ գրեաց զբանք սորա եւ զպատմութիւն. ասեն, թէ Մովսէս գրեաց մարգարէաբար, որպէս զպատմութիւն, եւ յետոյ Սողոմոն ստքսեաց,[13] այսինքն՝ տնատեաց եւ քաղցրացոյց, որպէս զիւր բանս Առակացն.

ի փառս Քրիստոսի:
Colophon

---

11. Dittography at the end of a folio.
12. Haplography at head of a column.
13. Spelling variant of ստիքսեմ "put into poetry."

Translation

Title/ 29th Ahekan and 6th May: It is the feast of Job the righteous.

1/ The blessed Job, father of patience, was one of Esau's grandsons,[14] a righteous man and true, departing and separated from all evil things.

2/ And he was king of the sons of Esau, without blemish and pious, and his former name was Yobab.[15] And he was hospitable and god-loving, merciful and caring according to the likeness of his forefather, the father of faith, Abraham.

3/ His sons were seven and his daughters three. He had many flocks, five thousand sheep and three thousand camels and five hundred[16] yokes of oxen and very many other possessions.[17]

4/ And his sons agreeing, they used to come to one another and make a feast, having their three sisters with them, to eat and drink with them.[18]

5/ And at the end of the feast Job would send and purify them and offer sacrifices according to their number, and one heifer[19] on account of sins according to their souls,[20] because Job said, "Perhaps my sons have apprehended some evil concerning God."[21]

6/ And Job did this all their days, and Job had other very great deeds of goodness upon the earth. Satan seeing this, was envious and he asked God

---

14. Cf. T. Job 1:6. I am indebted to Oren Ableman who helped in the preparation of the annotations to this text and has made several important suggestions about its exegesis.

15. Cf. T. Job 1:1. Job is identified as Jobab son of Zerah who was the second king of Edom according to Gen 36:33. This would make Job Esau's great-grandson. Incidentally, this would mean that he was also a descendant of Abraham through Esau's wife Basemath, daughter of Ishmael.

16. The figure in MT, LXX, and Armenian Bible is five hundred. Note that T. Job 9–10 mentions all of this property (including she-donkeys) and much more. The numbers there are inflated, but this seems to be deliberate and systematic, since there Job mentions the numbers of each animal which he allocated to charity. The figure given to charity is always identical to the total figure given in the biblical Book of Job (including the number five hundred for the oxen).

17. Cf. Job 1:2–3.

18. Job 1:4.

19. MT does not mention the heifer but it occurs in LXX.

20. That is, one heifer for each of them.

21. Job 1:5.

18. JOB THE RIGHTEOUS

to test him.[22] And God gave him into his power and I shall say how he gave (him).[23]

7/ One day the angels stood in service as in a ceremony. Satan also came with them. God said to Satan, "Whence do you come?" Satan answered the Lord God and said, "I come and stand (here), (after) having gone around all the earth and having walked around beneath the heavens."[24]

8/ The Lord said to Satan, "Consider[25] my servant Job, for there is none like him upon the earth, a man without blemish, just, and truly pious." Satan said, "Does Job serve the Lord gratuitously? And did you not strengthen the outside and inside of his house? You blessed the labor of his hands and you multiplied his beasts[26] upon the earth. But, come! Put forth your hand and cast (it) against all his possessions and see whether he will bless you righteously."[27]

9/ And the Lord said to Satan, "Behold, I have given all his possession(s) into your power, but do not draw near to him." And Satan went forth from God's presence.[28] And Job's sons and daughters were eating and drinking in the house of their eldest brother. And behold, a slave of the ox-herders came to Job with lamentation[29] in his mouth, sayin[g], "They were herding yokes of oxen and she-donkeys were pasturing with them. Suddenly marauders came to them[30] and captured them all and cut down the youths with the sword. I alone survived and I have come to tell you (this)."[31]

---

22. That is, Job. It is also unclear why this sentence is located here. Section 7 commences the narration of Satan's interaction with God and gives a rather complete retelling of the biblical narrative. Thus, perhaps it was a summary of the story, or a heading (O. Ableman).

23. Both the reading of the abbreviation as a nomen sacrum and the meaning, particularly of the last phrase, are unclear. This section is not paralleled in biblical Job.

24. Job 1:6–7. The biblical text has been expanded.

25. Literally: Regard with the mind. This is the expression in Arm Job 1:8.

26. Thus the Armenian Bible reads, as well.

27. Job 1:8–11. Note the softening of the biblical text in this last phrase: Job 1:11 has, "that he will curse you to your face."

28. Direct quotation of Arm Job 1:12. The next sentence is adapted from Arm Job 1:13.

29. Or: sad news.

30. Literally: by, with them. The "marauders" of our document are derived from գերեվարք "captors, exilers," in Arm Job (1:15) and "Sabeans" in Hebrew Bible. Indeed, שבא "Sabeans" of the Hebrew Bible is taken by the LXX to derive from the root šb"y "to exile."

31. Job 1:12–15. Job 1:16 is not represented in the paraphrase.

10/ And while he was speaking this, another one came with sad news and said to Job, "Marauders[32] attacked us on three fronts[33] and the camels were surrounded and they captured them and cut down the young men with swords. And I alone survived and I have come to tell you (this)."[34]

11/ Then Job answered each giver of ill news, "The Lord giveth and the Lord has taken away. Blessed be the name of the Lord!"[35]

12/ And while that praise was in Job's mouth, another bringer of ill news came and said to Job, "While your sons and daughters were eating and drinking at their eldest brother's place, suddenly the house was destroyed upon them from the four sides, and it killed them all.[36] I alone remained alive and I came to tell you."[37]

13/ Then Job arose and wept and rent his garments and cut off his hair[38] and prostrate, he worshipped the Lord God and said, "Naked I came forth then from my mother's womb and with naked limbs I shall return thither. The Lord gives and the Lord takes away. As seemed pleasing,[39] thus He did.[40] Blessed be the name of the Lord."[41]

14/ And in all this which befell him, Job did not sin before the Lord, but though all of it, he gave praise to God.[42] And again the Lord made a second gathering of his angels, to stand before the Lord God. Satan also came with them to stand before the Lord God in their midst.[43]

15/ And the Lord said to Satan, "Whence do you come, O abominable one?" Satan said, "Having wandered beneath the heavens and having gone about through the whole earth, I made a division as if all was mine.[44] Behold, having come, I stand (here)."[45]

---

32. Here the Hebrew Bible Job 1:17 reads "Chaldeans."
33. Or: thrice.
34. Job 1:17.
35. Job 1:21. This quotation is drawn from 1:21, but in this apocryphal retelling it occurs both at that point, and here, following the text corresponding to Job 1:17.
36. According to Job 1:19 a wind destroyed the house.
37. Job 1:18–19.
38. Literally, "the hair of his waves."
39. Implying "to the Lord," which is explicit in the Arm Bible Job 1:22.
40. Reformulating the biblical որպէս եւ եղեւ.
41. Job 1:20–21 quoted from the Armenian Bible.
42. Based on, but not identical with Job 1:22.
43. Job 1:22–2:1.
44. Unclear phrase.
45. Compare Job 2:2. The last part of this section has no biblical parallel. The text here describes Satan explicitly as an evil character. This attribute of his does not appear in the biblical account, but is perhaps implied there.

16/ The Lord said to Satan, "Then, were you pleased with my servant Job? For there is no human like him upon the earth, a man true, righteous, God-serving, separated and departing from all evil, and still he remains in sinlessness. And you unjustly said to destroy his possessions."[46]

17/ And Satan said, "Why did he lack nothing? Is it not skin in exchange for skin? And what he will have, (every) human has: light of the eyes and hearing of the ears, smelling of the nostrils, and taste of the mouth, speech of the tongue, and touch of the hands, walking of the feet and health of the body. These are with his own body and he has all fully.[47]

18/ If not, put forth your hand and take hold of his bones and body (and see) if he will not bless you to your face." The Lord said to Satan, "Behold I deliver him to you, but only preserve his spirit, and do not sin against his spirit."[48]

19/ And Satan went forth from the presence of the Lord and he smote Job with a very evil blemish, from (his) feet up to (his) head.[49] And his slaves dishonored him, those who ate his bread and were bought with his silver. Also, bringing (him) out, they expelled (him) from his own houses and his palace. Moreover, they even put him out of the city, him who, having fallen, was placed on/in the dung.[50]

20/ And he took a lump of earth and a potsherd and was scraping the pus of (his) sores with them.[51] And thus he remained for seven years.[52] And then his wife said to him, "How long will you restrain yourself and say, 'I shall still be patient.' Behold your memory[53] is spoiled upon the earth, your sons

---

46. Job 2:3. It is interesting that in the Bible God acknowledges that he himself was responsible for Job's calamities, implying that Satan is just his messenger. In the present text there seems to be some ambiguity about this point (O. Ableman).

47. Cf. Job 2:4. The text expands and explains Satan's somewhat ambiguous statement in the biblical account.

48. Job 2:5-6. This means, "save his life."

49. Job 2:7.

50. This material, from "(his) head" to the end of the section is an expansion of Job 2:7. Note that LXX and Arm Job 2:8 have, at the end of the verse, "outside the city," which is probably the point of departure for this embroidery.

51. Cf. Job 2:8.

52. This is not in Hebrew Job or in LXX or Arm. Indeed, from this point the text is taken from the expansion in the Armenian version of Job in Zohrabean's Bible, with some variants.

53. Or: reputation.

and daughters, fruit of my womb, whom I labored (to bear) with undeserved pains."[54]

21/[55] How long will you sit in filth of worms, soaked by rain and burned by the sun, snow-covered and icy cold, and I, wandering from house to house and from door to door, I go about waiting for[56] the sun to set so that I may take a little rest from the tribulation and pains that now encircle me. Now, say a word against God and die."[57]

22/ And Job reprimanding her, said, "You have spoken like one of the foolish women. If we accepted good things from the Lord, will we not be long-suffering at bad things?" And whatever events came upon him in all of this, Job did not sin against God,[58] but only praised God and said, "The Lord gives and the Lord takes away, blessed be the name of the Lord."[59]

23/ And Job's three friends, having heard all the bad things that had come upon him, came to him from their several cities and lands to comfort him: Eliphaz king of Teman, Bałdat (Bildad) ruler of Sawk'ites, and Sophar, monarch of the Mineans.[60]

24/ And seeing him from afar, they did not recognize (him) and delivering a speech, they wept loudly. They tore their robes and cast dust upon their heads and sat around him on the ground for seven days and seven nights; looking up to heaven, they sighed quietly. And not one of them spoke a word with him, for they saw (his) insupportable afflictions, and being astounded they were flabbergasted.[61]

---

54. The latter part of this section draws verbatim on Arm Job 2:9. §10 here continues with the rest of the text of 2:9. Thus the apocryphon, as is its habit sometimes, rearranges the biblical story line slightly.

55. The text drawn from Arm Job 2:9 resumes down to "sit." The following words of his wife's speech are not in Arm Job 2:9, but it resumes with "and I wander ... die." The citation from Arm Job 2:10 continues in §20,

56. Literally: when will.

57. See Job 2:9.

58. At this point the citation from Arm Job 2:10 ceases. The "sin against God" throughout means to speak ill of him or curse him. That sin, Job does not commit.

59. The apocryphon's author clearly feels uncomfortable with the idea of cursing God and softens it whenever it occurs. At the end of Job 2:10 the apocryphon adds "before God" with LXX and Arm, and then Arm Job adds "and did not malign God." It is this text that raises the author's hackles and he replaces it with Job 1:21b.

60. The names of the three kingdoms follow the Armenian Bible, as transliterated from Greek. This whole section is from Arm Job 2:11, with some variants.

61. This follows Job 2:12–13, while the last phrase is an addition.

25/ And then Job opened his mouth and said: "Perish the day on which I was born and the night in which they said, 'Behold, a male (child)!'[62] Cursed be the day of my birth and let it be not in the days of the year and let it not be counted in the days of the years."[63]

26/[64] Then the Lord appeared in a cloud above Job and he said with terrible thunder and fearful cries, "Who is that one who hides his words from me?"[65] And he said everything from the creation of the created things, and revealed them all to Job.[66] And then he healed him (so that he was) more beautiful than previously,[67] which he was before the sufferings of his trials.

27/ And Job's brothers and sisters came (and) ate and drank with him. And they each gave him, a lamb and a stater of gold.[68] And he had seven sons and three daughters, and he called one Day, and another Kassia, and the other Amat-horn.[69] And the Lord God blessed Job in the latter more than the former.

28/ And he had ten thousand[70] sheep, one thousand yokes of oxen.[71] And after his trials, Job lived for one hundred and seventy years.[72] Just as the Lord gave Job everything twofold, thus (he doubled) the time of his life. For the time of his first reign was seventy years and he was in sufferings for seven years, and after the sufferings, he ruled for one hundred and seventy years, which makes the whole time of his life two hundred and forty-seven years.[73]

---

62. This follows Arm Job 3:2–3 down to արու "male!"

63. This sentence is based on Job 3:6b. The rest of Job's speech is omitted.

64. Here the apocryphon skips all the speeches that form the main part of the biblical book and it resumes with Job 38.

65. Cf. Job 38:1–2.

66. This is an interpretation of God's appearance from the whirlwind in Job 38–41. The apocryphon understood the biblical text as God's revelation of all secrets to Job (and this is perhaps inferred from Job's response in Job 42:1–6 (O. Ableman).

67. According to Job 42:10 the healing took place only after Job asked for repentance for his three friends.

68. Cf. Job 42:11. The lamb and the gold coin are in accordance with the LXX and Arm Bible.

69. See Job 42:13–14 for these names. Here they are in accordance with the LXX and Arm Bible.

70. The biblical sources in Job 42:12 all have fourteen thousand.

71. Cf. Job 42:12.

72. Job 42:16. According to MT it was one hundred and forty years.

73. The MT does not give a total. In the LXX the total given is two hundred and forty-seven like in the text here.

29/ And Job saw his children's children up to the fourth generation. And Job died in good old age.[74] He was from the land of Ōsit, which now is called T'lkuran, and his renowned tomb is there. And Job is the sixth generation from Abraham as the number of the generations shows: Abraham, Isaac, Jacob, Levi, Kohath, Amram, Moses.

30/ And again from Isaac: Esau, Raguel, Zareh, Job. So, Job comes in the days Amram, Moses's father and lived long after Moses for many years. And it is to be known[75] that Job was an image of Adam in the suffering of himself and in kingship and in afflictions of trials and again in renewal of kingship.

31/ And who wrote his words[76] and his tale? They say that Moses wrote it in a prophetic fashion as history,[77] and later Solomon <put it into poetry>, that is, versified and sweetened (it) just like his own discourses of Proverbs.

For the glory of Christ.
Colophon

---

74. Job 42:16–17. The Arm Bible, like our text, then draws upon the addition found in the LXX of Job. This additional passage says that it was taken from a Syriac book, and it places Job in biblical genealogy. The addition to LXX correctly puts Job in the fifth generation. The information in the next paragraph is also correct about Job's lineage. It is, therefore, puzzling why he is said to be of the sixth generation. (Perhaps it is in order to make him a contemporary of Moses: O. Ableman.)

75. This formula introduces a preexistent piece of information or tradition.

76. That is, the discourse about him.

77. This tradition appears also in Rabbinic literature. See b. B. Bat. 15a; y. Soṭah 5.6.

19. Daniel Epitome, Part 2

Introductory Remarks

In this section we publish Part 2 of the Epitome of the Daniel stories that is preserved on folios 84r–86v of ms M1134, which was copied in 1695. Part 1 of this work, recounting the story of Susanna, was published in Stone, *Biblical Heroes*, 207 where the manuscript is discussed in detail.[1] In addition, before giving the text of the Daniel Epitome that is parallel to Daniel chap. 1, I take the opportunity to present a coda to Part 1 of this composition, since it was omitted from the previous edition.

19.1. Coda to Daniel Epitome, Part 1

Text

M1134 /fol 84r / Յովակիմս առաջին ի գիրս Դանիէլի եւ[2] Յովակիմս առաջին ի տնօրէնութիւն Տեառն մայրն սուրբ կուսին Մարիամ‹այ›. փառք Աստուծոյ Հօրն

Translation

The first Joakim (is) in the Book of Daniel. The first[3] Joakim[4] is for the disposition of the Mother of the Lord, the holy Virgin Mary.

Glory to God the Father.

---

1. See Stone, *Biblical Heroes*, 207 who gives the details of this manuscript.
2. This first phrase was written vertically in the margin. It was omitted by haplography.
3. This is odd: Should it be "the second"? Note that the first phrase of this sentence was omitted in the manuscript and written by the original scribe in the right-hand margin.
4. That is "Jacob the father of Joseph the husband of Mary, of whom Jesus was born," Matt 1:16, here called Joakim.

19.2. Daniel Epitome, Part 2

Text

Title/ Տեսիլ ասէն ի Դ. (4) բաժանի:

1/ Առաջին՝ պատմութիւն, Բ. (2)՝ Հոգոյն Աստուծոյ յայտնութիւնն տեսիլ ասի, Գ.դ (3)՝ երազ թագաւորին, Դ. (4) տեսիլ՝ ասի գերութիւն:

2/ Երկրորդ ճառն. Աբգար թագաւորն. որդին Նաբուբալսարայ գնաց յԵրուսաղեմ

յԲ. (2) ամի թագաւորութեան իւրոյ եւ գերեաց զիսրայէլացիքն:[5]

3/ Եւ Գ. (3) որդի թագաւորին Յովակիմայ. / fol 84v / զԱնանիա,[6] որ ասի շնորհք, Ազարիա՝ համարձակութիւն, Միսայէլ՝ շօշափումն, եւ զԴանիէլ, հօր[7]եղբօր որդիք նոցա՝ Սեդրակ, Միսրակ, Աբեդնագով: Դանիէլի, որ կոչի դատաստան, եդ անուն Բաղդասար, զանուն աստուծոյ իւրոյ:

4/ Եւ ետուն Յասփանեա ներքինապետ, զի սնուցանէ զնոսա, եւ վարժին քաղդէական գրովն եւ ուսուցին զամենայն լէզուս, եւ այլ բազում գերիսն յորդոցն գերութեան: Եւ վերակացու նոցա եդին զայր ումն Ամելասադ անուն,

5/ Գ. (3) ամ սնուցանել զնոսա եւ վարժել ուսմամբն քաղդէացոց: Եւ ապա առաջի թագաւորին կացուցանել, իսկ Դանիէլ եդ[8] ի մտի ոչ ճաշակել[9] ի պիղծ զոհից եւ ի սեղանոյ թագաւորին:

6/ Եւ ոչ մանկանցն ետ թոյլ ճաշակել ոչ ի հացէ, ոչ ի մսոյ, ոչ / fol 85r / ի զինոյ, եւ ոչ յայլ կերակրոց: Այլ միայն ընդով{ով}ն[10] շատացան, որ է՝ սիսեռն, ոսպն, ոլոռն, բակլա եւ հատիկն գործենոյ:

7/ Եւ զսահմանեալ[11] կերակուր թագաւորին վերակ<ա>ցութն[12] ուտէին: Իսկ յորժամ Գ. (3) ամն լցաւ, Հոգոյն Աստուծոյ իմաստութեամբն լցան բանական գիտութեամբ, եւ շահական, եւ

---

5. Observe the use of -ք, a nom. plur. ending, where a -u (accusative) would be expected. This is a common error in medieval Armenian. See further p. 185 n. 66; p. 266 n. 49.

6. The prefixed q- occurs on two of these names and is absent from the other two.

7. This word is in the marg. p.m.

8. There is a letter blotted out in this word.

9. ճաշ՝կել is overwritten by ճաշել.

10. The dittographic second occurrence of -ով is surmounted by delete marks.

11. q below line p.m.

12. The text has վերակցուքն, an abbreviation for վերակացուք, with the abbreviation mark omitted.

ստացական, եւ փառաւորեալ վերին աստուածային իմաստութեան եւ գիտութեան:

8/ Եւ դէմք կերպարանաց նոցա եղեն իբրեւ զերեսս հրեշտակի, իբրեւ զգՄովսիսին եւ զնախավկային, մինչ զի ամենայն քաղաքացիքն զարհուրեալ դողային:

9/ Եւ բազում[13] բանս իմաստութենէ հարցին, եւ ամենայնի պատասխանի ետուն: Եւ կացոյց զնոսա թագաւորն ի վերայ տան թագաւորութեան եւ ամենայն աշխարհին,

10/ զի Աստուած զփառաւորիչս իւր փառաւորէ, զի ասէ մարգարէիւն. «Որ զիսն սիրեն, սիրեմ զնոսա», եւ զկամս երկիւղածաց եւ աղօթից նոցա լսէ եւ կեցուցանէ: Եւ Աստուած փառաւորեալ է ի խորհուրդս / fol 85v / նոցա:

11/ Չի զեղան թագաւորին անարգեցին եւ զգարշելի կերակուր նոցին, վասն որոյ Աստուած պատոյց զնոսա աստ մարմնաւոր մեծութեամբ: Եւ ի հանդերձն պատուին յԱստուծոյ հոգեւոր մեծութեամբ:

12/ Եւ սեղան երկնաւոր թագաւորին բազմին եւ զաստուածային կերակուրն ճաշակեն, որ է նորա վարդապետելն եւ մեզ ուսանելն: Եւ դարձեալ Աստուծոյ օրինութիւն, որ ասէ. «Եկայք օրհնեալք հօր իմոյ»: Եւ Դաւիթ ասէ. «Տացես[14] նմա ալրինութիւն յալիտեանս յալիտենից ուրախ <ա>ր<ասցես....»:[15] Եւ աստ նշխարք նոցա պատուեցաւ ի անիւատից:

13/ Չի յորժամ Կիւրոս թագաւորն կամ Ատտիկոս նահատակեաց զնոսա, ընկալան երեք եղբարքն զզլուխս ինքեանց ի գիրկս իւրեանց: Եւ Դանիէլ զերիսն յինքն ընկալալ: Եւ եդ զզլուխս նոցա առ մարմինս իւրեանց: Եւ հրամանաւ Արարչին կացեալ մի/ fol 86r /ւորեցան ընդ իրար:

14/ Եւ տեսեալ բաբելացն կրկին, եւ երեք կին օրհնեցին զԱստուած: Իսկ Դանիէլ այրն ցանկալի Աստուծոյ,[16] հրեշտակաց եւ մարդկան իւր մահուամբ վախճանեցաւ:

---

13. There is a blot on the page following բազում.

14. ս above line, p.m.

15. This is a citation of Ps 21:6 (20:7), including the word ուրախ "happy." The final ր added onto ուրախ remains without obvious explanation. In the Psalm, the next word is արասցես 'you will make' and the ր may be from that word, which is how we have reconstructed.

16. Daniel is addressed by this title in Dan 10:11, 19. The phrase found here is exactly the same as is present in the Armenian Bible from which it was doubtless taken.

15/ Եւ եղաւ ոսկի տապանօք ի զանձատուն թագաւորին: Իսկ Մօրիկ թագաւորն Յունաց խնդրեաց զն2խարք¹⁷ Դանիէլի ի Խոսրովու արքայէն Պարսից, որ էր որդեգիր նմայ:

16/ Եւ նորա եղեալ ի չորոց¹⁸ եւ բացում զանձ ընդ նմայ, եւ աժամայն Բ. (2) գետրն Եփրատ եւ Տիգրիս գամաքեցան եւ ամենայն աղբերք աշխարհին ընդ նմա: Եւ Շիրին թագուհի ազգաւ ասորի ժողովեաց զամենայն բազմութիւն հաւատացելոցն յեկեղեցին:

17/ Եւ ուժգին գոչմամբ եւ արտասուօք պաղատին առ Աստուած եւ առ սուրբն Դանիէլ: Եւ աժամայն դարձան չորիքն ի քաղաքն, եւ չուր գետոցն եւ աղբերացն վաղվաղակի բղխեցին

18/ /fol 86v / ի յաղօթից եւ ջերմեռանդ հաւատոցն Շիրին թագուհոյն, եւ ամենայն քաղաքացիքն հաւատացեալք եւ անհաւատք, եւ Աստուծոյ աղբիւնութիւն ի բարձունս առաքեցին անճառելի եւ անպատմելի խնդութեամբ, եւ Քրիստոսի փառք յաւիտեանս:

TRANSLATION

Title/ The meaning of "vision" is divided into four (parts):

1/ First (it means) story; second, the revelation of the God the Spirit is called "vision;" third, the king's dream (is called "a vision"); fourth, captivity is called "a vision."[19]

2/ Second discourse: King Abgar, son of Nabubalsar went to Jerusalem in the second year of his rule and captured the Israelites.[20]

3/ And the three sons of King Jehoiakim (were) Ananiah which means "grace," Azariah, (which means) "daring," Mishael (which means)

---

17. An accusative plur. ending would be expected; see n. 5 above.

18. This is, apparently, a scribal misspelling of չորոց < չորի "mule." The classical Armenian gen. plur. of չորի would be չորեաց.

19. This is clarified below.

20. The two exiles, the Assyrian in 720 BCE and the Babylonian in 586 CE are related in 2 Kgs 17:5–6; 24:13–15; 25:11, 2 Chr 36:20, 1 Bar. 1:1–2 respectively. Neither of these events took place in the second year of Abgar, or of his father Nabopolassar (Nabubalsar), whoever that was. Indeed, the name Nabopolassar is not included in the book of Kings nor, indeed, is Abgar mentioned there. The Bible relates that the Babylonian Exile was executed by the captain of Nebuchadnezzar's guard, Nebuzradan; see 2 Kgs 25:11; Jer 39:9, etc. King Nabupolassar (625–605 BCE) was Nebuchadnezzar's father. This name introduced here, therefore, is an extrabiblical item. King Abgar V of Edessa, known as the first Christian king, lived at the time of Christ and features in texts extant in Armenian, including Movsēs Xorenacʻi 2.26–33. He does not fit the dates implied in this text which refer to the sixth century BCE. He was a member of the "Abgar" dynasty of Edessa which ruled between the first century BCE and the third century CE.

"tenderness,"[21] and Daniel (was) their uncle; their children,[22] Sedrach, Meshach, Abednego.[23] He gave Daniel, which means judgment,[24] the name Baltasar,[25] the name of his god

4/ And they caused Yesp'anēs the chief eunuch[26] to nurture them. And they were instructed in the Chaldean writing.[27] And they were taught all

---

21. Two of these meanings are drawn from the onomastic lists of biblical names called Onomastica Sacra. The meanings and even the word choice are in accordance with these lists. Thus Ananiah in Ona IV 22 (Stone, *Signs of the Judgement*, 110) is said to mean: շնորհքն Աստուծոյ "grace of God," Azariah is explained as համամակութիւն կամ այգնութիւն "daring or help" (Wutz, *Onomastica Sacra*, 958), and Mishayel as ով խնդրուածք "who enquiries" in (Wutz, *Onomastica Sacra*, 964) or ով խնդրեալ "who, having enquired" in Ona V (Wutz, *Onomastica Sacra*, 964). The text's explanation of Misayel is not found in the Armenian onomastic lists. Its origin remains obscure.

22. This is unclear. If the text read որդի in the singular, then one could translate: Daniel, son of their uncle, which would make sense. The specific relationships of the three companions to Daniel and to King Jehoakim (Jehoiakim), as well as Daniel's relationship to them are quite fanciful. No source in the Bible says that they were sons of King Jehoiakim of Judah. All that Dan 1:3 says about them is that they are "of the royal house and of the nobles"; on this see Michael E. Stone, "A Note on Daniel 1:3," *ABR* 7 (1959): 67–71.

23. These are the Babylonian names given to Daniel's three companions according to Dan 1:7. The Armenian, however, does not state that, but appears to say that three persons with Babylonian names were the children of Daniel's three companions. This is unparalleled.

24. In the onomastica, Daniel is said to mean judgement; see, e.g., Ona V 153 Դանիել. դատաստան Աստուծոյ "Daniel, God's judgement." dw"n is the Semitic root meaning "judge." It might be suggested, by the way, that the story of Susanna, which is included in the Greek and Armenian recensions of Daniel, is in fact a name midrash on "Daniel."

25. In the Hebrew of Dan 1:7 it is traditionally transliterated Belteshazzar. Armenian here has Baltasar, and says it was the name of the king's god. "Bel" was a god's name, but Balthasar is not known as the name of a divinity, though it is theophoric, Bal- or Bēl- deriving from Baal and known as a divine name in later Mesopotamia. Note also the story of Bel and the Dragon, included in Greek and Armenian recension of Daniel. That might be the reference here.

26. Dan 1:3. The biblical text does not state explicitly that the youths were castrated. Some later traditions asserted that the four youths did indeed become eunuchs, while others contend that they remained uncastrated (primarily on the basis of the statement later in the verse that they were "without blemish"). For a summary on various later traditions see John J. Collins, *Daniel: A Commentary on the Book of Daniel*, Hermeneia (Minneapolis: Fortress, 1993), 134–35.

27. Dan 1:4: "to teach them Chaldean writing and language."

languages, and[28] many other captives of the children of the Exile. And they appointed a certain man, Amēlasad[29] by name as their overseer,

5/ to feed (them) and to instruct (them) for three years in the learning of the Chaldeans, and then to present them before the king.[30] But Daniel decided not to eat of the abominable sacrifices, nor of the king's table.[31]

6/ And he did not permit the children to eat, not of bread, not of meat, not of wine, and not of other foods, but only legumes they did (eat) often, which are chickpeas, lentils, peas, broad beans, and grains of wheat.[32]

7/ And the overseers ate the food allotted by the king.[33] But when three years were completed,[34] they[35] were filled with wisdom of the spirit of God,[36] and rational knowledge, both profitable and acquisitive,[37] and they praised the celestial, divine wisdom and knowledge.

8/ And the countenances of their form became like the face of an angel, like Moses and the Protomartyr human,[38] so that all the inhabitants of the city being astounded were quaking.[39]

---

28. That is: as were.

29. So Arm Dan 1:11, translating LXX Αβιεσδρι. Hebrew is ham-melṣar. Greek might be derived from a graphic confusion of ר/ד and a doublet retaining both readings.

30. Dan 1:5.

31. Dan 1:8.

32. Dan 1:12.

33. See Dan 1:16. The incident of the ten days' trial and so forth, found in Dan 1:11–15 and taken up in The Three Hebrews, a work published as text no. 20 in this volume, is omitted by the present composition.

34. In Dan 1:5, the king orders that they be nurtured and educated for three years.

35. That is, the three young men.

36. The expression "filled with the spirit of God" is used referring to Bezalel's skilled craftsmanship in Exod 31:3; 35:31.

37. Dan 1:17.

38. This is predicated of Stephen the Protomartyr in Acts 6:15. The brightness of Moses's countenance after his second descent from Sinai is famous; see Exod 34:29–30, 33–35. This is taken up in the work Question concerning Moses's Countenance, text no. 13 in the present book. The shining faces of celestial beings and of the righteous are commonly mentioned from Second Temple times on. The text here is perhaps interpreting Dan 1:15, where the four youths are said to look healthier than any of the other pupils under the chief eunuch's care. A similar assertion is made about Joseph, who also ate only permitted food, in T. Joseph 3:4. Compare with Dan 12:3: "And those who are wise shall shine like the brightness of the firmament; and those who turn many to righteousness, like the stars for ever and ever."

39. This section is an expansion and does not correspond to anything in Daniel chap. 1. Compare, however, the transformation of Moses's countenance described in Of Moses

9/ And they were asked[40] about many matters through wisdom,[41] and they answered all.[42] And the king appointed them over the royal palace and all the land.[43]

10/ For God glorifies those who glorify him, for he said through the prophet, "Those who love me, I love them."[44] And he hearkens to the wishes of those who fear him and listens to their prayers and keeps them alive; and God is glorified in their councils.[45]

11/ Because they scorned the king's table and their[46] abominable victuals, on account of which God surrounded them here[47] with bodily greatness[48] and in the future (world) they are honored by God, with spiritual greatness.[49]

12/ And they sit at the table of the heavenly king and eat divine food, which is his teaching and our learning.[50] And again, (they receive) God's blessing which says, "Come blessed of my Father;"[51] and David says, "You will give him blessing forever and ever, you will make (him) happy."[52] And here[53] their remains[54] are honored by the unfaithful.[55]

---

and Aaron §26 and in Question concerning Moses's Countenance, both published in this volume.

40. Literally: "they asked," which we take as an impersonal.

41. The exact force of the ablative case here is unclear. It might be a partitive, so meaning: "many matters appertaining to order."

42. A paraphrase of Dan 1:19-20.

43. The specifics of their appointment are an embroidery on the biblical story. Next there follows a homiletic discourse on the preceding narrative.

44. The quotation is from Prov 8:17. This is, of course, attributed to Solomon, not usually called a prophet. This indicates that the word "prophet" is being used in a broad sense, as it is often in Christian literature, to designate any individual to whom a biblical book is attributed, and even other biblical worthies.

45. Or: counsels.

46. That is, the Babylonians'.

47. That is: in this world.

48. See Dan 1:19.

49. The last phrase is an embroidery as, in fact, is the rest of this document.

50. The table and food are metaphorical here, of course. The image of the heavenly banquet is widespread.

51. Matt 25:34.

52. Ps 21:6 (20:7).

53. That is: in this world.

54. Or: relics. This seems to be a reference to the Inventio of their relics, published by G. Garitte and in other forms by Stone. See the works cited in notes 56 and 57 below.

55. Or: the unbelievers. The last phrase is an embroidery, as is the rest of this document.

13/ For when King Cyrus or Atticus[56] martyred them, the three brothers accepted their heads in their bosoms and Daniel[57] received the three to himself and he put their heads by their bodies. And, at the Creator's command, having waited, they were united with one another.

14/ And when the Babylonians saw this they praised God doubly and triply. Then, Daniel, the man beloved of God,[58] of angels, and of men came to an end through his death.[59]

15/ And he was placed with a golden coffin into the king's treasury.[60] Then Maurice, King of the Greeks[61] sought the relics of Daniel from Xosrov the king of the Persians,[62] who was his adopted child.

---

56. The author is apparently familiar with two recensions of this story, one featuring Cyrus (M1500) and the other, Atticus (Synaxaria, Greek and Armenian recensions 1, 2, 3). These texts are given in Michael E. Stone, "An Armenian Tradition Relating to the Death of the Three Companions of Daniel," *Le Muséon* 86 (1973): 111–23; repr. Stone, *Selected Studies in Pseudepigrapha and Apocrypha*, 90–102.

57. This martyrdom is reported with some variants in M1500, fol 362r (Stone, "Three Companions," 90–91; Stone, *Patriarchs and Prophets*, 154–55). The story is also to be found in Kirakos Arawelc'i's recension of the Armenian Synaxarium (Stone, "Three Companions," 113–14) in a form close in detail to the present text. G. Garitte published a similar Georgian tale (see Stone, "Three Companions," 115): G. Garitte, "L'Invention géorgienne des Trois Enfants de Babylone," *Le Muséon* 72 (1959): 69–72. See further Garitte, "Le Texte arménien de l'invention des Trois Enfants de Babylone," *Le Muséon* 74 (1961): 91–108. It is also included in various other Armenian hagiographical works (Stone, "Three Companions," 91–108).

58. This is a particular title of Daniel, see Dan 10:11–19.

59. The Book of Daniel relates his death in 12:13, "But go your way till the end; and you shall rest, and shall stand in your allotted place at the end of the days" (NRSV). The text here is more specific.

60. The origin of this detail is unknown.

61. That is, of the Byzantines.

62. Xosrow Parviz was one of the last Sasanian emperors. He fled to Syria when, on his father's death, a usurper seized the throne. There he was under the protection of Byzantine emperor Maurice. His wife, Shirin, was a Christian. After Xosrow succeeded in taking the throne, Shirin did much to encourage and aid the Christians in the Sasanian realm. Xosrow ruled from 590 to 628. The story told in our text is related to the events narrated by Sebēos, *The Armenian History*, chap. 13. See Robert W. Thomson, James Howard-Johnston, and Tim Greenwood, *The Armenian History Attributed to Sebeos*, Translated Texts for Historians 31 (Liverpool: Liverpool University Press, 1999), 29. Maurice was emperor of Byzantium 582–602 CE. These historical references suggest a date post quem for the present work of 602 CE. Of course, that comes as no surprise.

16/ And he,[63] having placed (it)[64] on a mule, and much treasure with him, instantly the two rivers, the Euphrates and the Tigris, were dried up[65] and all the springs of the land with it.[66] And Queen Shirin, a Syrian by race, assembled all the multitude of the faithful in the church.

17/ And they besought God with mighty cries and tears and also (besought) the holy Daniel. And the mules at once turned to the city.[67] And the water of the rivers and springs started flowing at once.

18/ From the prayers and ardent faith of Queen Širin and all the citizens, believers and unbelievers, they sent the blessing of God upwards with ineffable and indescribable joy. To Christ eternal glory.

---

63. That is, his relics.

64. That is, the body or the coffin.

65. The drying up of waters so that special persons or objects can pass most likely takes its origin from the incidents of the Red Sea (Exod 14:21) and of the splitting of the Jordan (Josh 3:15-17). Similar events are found in the Vita of Ezekiel 7 and elsewhere. The drying up of the Euphrates before the returning exiles at the eschaton is related in 4 Ezra 13:43-44.

66. A plur. would be expected.

67. This phrase is not quite clear. դարձան could also be translated "turned back."

20. Daniel the Prophet and the Three Young Men

Introductory Remarks

M1099 is a miscellany.[1] It is composed of two different parts. That which interests us is of the seventeenth century and it contains a series of texts about biblical figures, arranged in chronological order. Thus, it forms a sort of "Embroidered Bible," a narrative retelling of substantial sections of Old and New Testament by biblical paraphrase and expansion.[2] The text published here is one of these unpublished apocryphal texts dealing with a favorite topic, Daniel and his three companions, Ananiah (Ḥananiah), Mishael, and Azariah.

The main Old Testament apocryphal narratives in M1099 are the following (*General Catalogue* 4:308):

1. 157r–171r is drawn from the Armenian translation of *The Chronography of Michael the Syrian*, as in the edition of the Armenian translation, Jerusalem: St. James, 1870.[3]

---

1. *General Catalogue* 4:303–10.
2. This phenomenon of an embroidered sequence of biblical events achieved by the placement of biblical and apocryphal passages in one manuscript was observed for Armenian manuscripts in Michael E. Stone, "Two Armenian Manuscripts and the Historia Sacra," in *Apocryphes arméniens: Transmission, traduction, création, iconographie; Actes du colloque international sur la littérature apocryphe en langue arménienne, Genève, 18–20 septembre, 1997*, ed. V. Calzolari Bouvier (Lausanne: Zèbre, 1999), 21–36; repr. in Michael E. Stone, ed., *Apocrypha, Pseudepigrapha and Armenian Studies*, 2 vols. (Leuven: Peeters, 2006), 1:399–414. The same phenomenon is studied in detail in Bulgarian manuscripts by Anissava Miltenova in her work *South Slavonic Apocryphal Collections* (Sofia: Iztok-Zapad, 2018).
3. Michael the Syrian, *The Chronography of Rev. Michael the Syrian Patriarch* (Jerusalem: St. James,1870) and T. Sawalaneacʻ edited a different copy of this document in 1871: *Chronography of Rev. Michael, Patriarch of the Syrians* (Jerusalem: St. James, 1871). On the two Armenian recensions of this Chronography, see nn. 18–19 on p. 131.

20. DANIEL THE PROPHET AND THE THREE YOUNG MEN   221

2. 171r–174v, Of the Patriarchs, Abraham, Isaac, and Jacob.[4]
3. 174v–177r, Of Melchizedek, the High Priest of God—to be published in the next volume of this series.
4. 174r–177v, Memorial of Job the Righteous.
5. 177v–182r, Of the Prophets Moses and Aaron—published in this volume.
6. 182r–183v, Of Daniel the Prophet—a text summarizing parts of the book of Daniel. This is not simply a version of the Vita of Daniel that was published in two recensions by Yovsēpʻianc', 218–22. Nor is it identical with the Epitome of Daniel from M1134, of which two sections have been published.
7. 183v–188r, Daniel the Prophet and the Three Young Men, Anania, Mishael, and Azariah—the text being published in this section.
8. 188r–193r, Of Elisha the Prophet.
9. 193r–197r, Of Jeremiah the Prophet and His Disciples.
10. 197r–199r, Of Ezekiel the Prophet and of Ezra.
11. 199r–200r, Of Isaiah the Prophet
12. 200r–201r, Of Asasias (a graphic corruption for Asaph) the Prophet and of Nathan—these texts are copies of the same documents published in Stone, *Angels and Heroes*, text nos. 4.11 and 4.12 with some variants. The text about Nathan has an additional sentence at the end.
13. 201r–202r, Of the Prophets Zephaniah and Habakkuk.
14. 202r–207v, Of Jonah the Prophet—published in this volume as Jonah 1, text no. 17.1.

Following the texts relating to the Hebrew Bible and its prophets come twenty-seven texts dealing with New Testament figures.

This document combines stories drawn from the book of Daniel (chaps. 1, 3, 6, Susanna, Bel, and the Dragon), from hagiographic literature (the Inventio of the relics of the Three Companions of Daniel), and it also refers to relevant information from other sources, such as 3 Maccabees and Susanna. The author also knows the Prayer of Azariah and the Three Young Men and the story of Habakkuk feeding Daniel in the lions' den, found in the Greek versions of Daniel and consequently in Armenian Daniel.[5]

---

4. Not having images of this document at hand, I cannot determine whether it is a copy of one of the documents published in Stone, *Abraham*.

5. For the text of Armenian Daniel, see S. Peter Cowe, *The Armenian Version of Daniel*, UPATS 9 (Atlanta: Scholars Press, 1992) and S. Peter Cowe, "The Reception of the Book of Daniel in Late Antique and Medieval Armenian Society," in *The Armenian Apoca-*

From §§20–28 the text follows the text of the fourth recension of the Armenian Synaxarium, which is close to that of the Greek Synaxarium Constantinopolitanum.[6] It was compared with the text of that entry and variants recorded. They follow the text below, and precede that translation.[7] Below, we discuss the relationship of this story to the Inventio in Georgian and Armenian published by G. Garitte.

Following the conclusion of this narrative, in §30 the author/editor provides a bridge back to the main narrative, which is drawn again from the book of Daniel. The question posed about the identification of the capital city, Babylon or Isfahan (Šoš) might indicate the time of the combination of the various elements into one document. Editorial, too, is the reference to Daniel chap. 7 in this section, which although its detail is not given, serves to take account of it. The rest of the document is an abbreviated form of Daniel chap. 6, the story of Daniel in the lions' den. This is interpolated with the story of Habakkuk's feeding him miraculously, which occurs in the recension of Daniel known in Greek and Armenian. Into the end of this section are introduced both passages relating to the stories of Bel and the Dragon, and a burial tradition known in Vitae Prophetarum, of his burial in Babylon.

In fact, as Garitte already noted, the ancient Greek sources are silent about the Inventio of the relics of the Three Young Men, which story he found in two Georgian manuscripts. He observes that the text lacks certain of the genre markers of an Inventio, while on the other hand, it strives for historical verisimilitude.[8] Garitte showed that the text was translated into Georgian from Armenian, and some years later he published the Armenian text.[9] This Armenian text, he claimed, was in turn translated from Syriac.[10] He knew the Armenian text from manuscript V303 of the year 1220 CE[11] and from V225 of the nineteenth century. He also observed that the text is found in J1 (1419)

---

lyptic Tradition: A Comparative Perspective, ed. Kevork Bardakjian and Sergio La Porta (Leiden: Brill, 2014), 81–125.

6. Allied Armenian traditions are published in Stone, "An Armenian Tradition," 111–23. There, the text of the Synaxarium Constantinopolitanum in Greek is published as well. Similar traditions are to be found in Georgian and were published by Garitte, "L'Invention géorgienne," 69–100. Garitte also published a paper on the Armenian forms of this tradition; Garitte, "Le texte arménien," 91–108.

7. The text is published in Stone, "An Armenian Tradition," 112–13. Obvious typological errors in that text are not recorded.

8. Garitte, "L'Invention géorgienne," 72–73.

9. Garitte, "Le texte arménien," 91–108.

10. Garitte, "L'Invention géorgienne," 82–84.

11. Basile Sarghissian, Grand Catalogue des manuscrits arméniens de la bibliothèque

and that copy remains unstudied. Doubtless, further copies exist. I compared the text of §§20–28 published below with Garitte's Armenian text; it is clearly the same writing, but in another, longer rather different form and cannot be simply included in the Apparatus criticus. Nor is the direction of the genetic relationship of the texts firmly established at the present stage of research. In the edition below, we have used M1099 as the text and noted the variants of the fourth recension of the Synaxarium.[12] Garitte's editions and notes must be consulted for the Venice manuscript, as for the Georgian version.

Text

M1099 / fol 183v / Title Դանիելի մարգարէին եւ երից մանկանցն՝ Անանիայի, Ազարիայի եւ Միսայելի

1/ Սոքա որդիք էին թագաւորին Յովակիմայ, որ յԵրուսաղէմ, յազգէն Յուդայ, յորդղցն Դաւթի, թոռունք բարեպաշտին Եզեկիա եւ Յովսեայ։

2/ Եւ Դանիէլ մարգարէն հօրեղբօր որդի էր սուրբ Անանիանցն, որդի էր Յոհանու եղբօրն Յովակիմայ արքային։

3/ Սոքա յաւուրս աւերմանն Երուսաղէմի գերեցան ի Բաբելոն, զոր տեսեալ Նորգոդոնոսոր արքայ գնաստ ուշիմ եւ իմաստուն, զեղեցիկ երեսօք եւ վայելուչ տեսլեամբ

4/ եւ ասաց Ասփանեհայ՝ ներքինապետին իւրոյ, տալ գնոստ ի դպրոց յիմաստունն քաղդեացոց, զի ուսանիցին գիր եւ լեզու քաղդարէն, կալ առաջի արքային ի պաղատն[13] արքունի։

5/ Եւ ասաց տալ նոցա կերա/ fol 184r /կուրս յարքունուստ օր ըստ աւուրց, ուստի ուտէր եւ ըմպէր ինքն, սնուցանել գնոստ ամս Գ. (3) եւ ապա կացուցանել առաջի թագաւորին։

Եւ եղին նոցա անուանս քաղդէարէնս. Դանիէլի՝ Բաղդասար, եւ Անանիայի՝ Սեդրաք Ազարիայի՝ Միսաք, եւ Միսայելի՝ Աբեդնագով։

Եւ զոր ինչ տային նոցա կերակուր յարքունուստ, ոչ ուտէին, այլ միայն ընդովք շատանային։

---

des PP. Mekhitaristes de Saint-Lazare (Venice: Mekhitarist, 1914–1924), vol. 1/2:1129–38 (Armenian).

12. In Stone, "Three Companions" a form of the story known from M1500 (before 1282 CE) was published and compared with the entry for the Three Young Men in the editions of the Armenian Synaxarium. The story in a form closer to M1099 than to V303 is incorporated into the fourth recension of the Synaxarium.

13. This is an alternative spelling of պալատ which means "palatial building, palace." The alternation of ղ / լ is a common orthographic phenomenon.

6/ Ասաց Ասփանեի ներքինապետն ցԴանիէլ, զի նա էր աւագագոյն եւ էր ամաց ԲԺ.-անից (12), որ եւ ի նոյն աւուրսն մարգարէացաւ եւ ազատեաց զՇուշան յանիրաւ ծերոցն, զՇուշան ապրեցոյց եւ զծերսն մահու մատնեաց:
Յնա ասաց Ասփանեի. «Վահեմ ես ի թագաւորէն, զի մի զուցէ տեսանիցէ զերեսս ձեր տրտում եւ զձեզ նիհար եւ սպանանէ զիս»:
7/ Ասաց Դանիէլ. «Դու փորձեա՛ զմեզ աւուրս Ժ. (10) եւ տո՛ւր մեզ ունդս, զի կերիցուք. ոսպն, սիսեռն եւ բակլայ, զի կերիցուք եւ չուր, զի արբցուք։ Եւ երեւեսցին առաջի քո գոյնք մեր եւ գոյնք մանկանցն, որ ուտեն ի սեղանոյ թագաւորին։ Եւ յայնժամ արա՛ ընդ մեզ, որպէս եւ հաճոյ թուի քեզ:
8/ Եւ նա արար ըստ կամացն Դանիէլի եւ փորձեաց զնոսա Ժ. (10) օր։ Եւ յետ Ժ. (10) աւուրցն ետես Ասփանեի զերեսն Դանիէլի եւ զերից մանկանցն առաւել պայծառ, զեր / fol 184v / եւ զեղեցիկ, քան զայլ մանկանցն, որ ուտէին ի սեղանոյ թագաւորին:
9/ Եւ ետ Աստուած Դանիէլի հանճար եւ իմաստութիւն, որ այլ ոչ էր լեալ բնաւ այնպիսի խելամտութիւն մանկանցն քաղդէացոց, եւ ոչ գտաւ բնաւ նման Դանիէլի եւ երից մանկանցն։ Եւ այնպէս կային առաջի թագաւորին:
10/ Եւ արար Նաբուգոդոնոսոր արքայ պատկեր ոսկի՝ զԲելայ նմանութիւն։ Կ. (60) կանգուն երկայն եւ Զ. (6) լայն, եւ կանգնեաց զնա ի դաշտին Տարայու[14] եւ հրամայեաց ամենայն ումեք երկիր պագանել նմա:
11/ Իսկ Դանիէլ եւ Գ. (3) մանկունքն արհամարհեցին զիրամանս թագաւորին եւ պատկերին ոսկոյ ոչ երկրպագեցին։ Վասն որոյ բարկացեալ թագաւորն եւ ետ արկանել զնոսա ի հնոցի հուրն:
12/ Ուր եւ էջ հրեշտակ Տեառն ի մէջ հրոյն, նոյն ինքն Բանն Աստուած Որդին միածին էջ առ նոսին եւ զբոց հրոյն տարածեաց որպէս կամար ի վերայ նոցա։ Եւ ի բըցոյ հրոյն գոյ էր նոցա որպէս զցօղ անձրեւաց մեղմագոյն:
13/ Իսկ Անանիանքն զուարճացեալ ի մէջ հնոցին՝ զբանս աւրհնութեան երգէին ընդ հրեշտակին։ Եւ զայն տեսեալ անօրէն արքային, զի ոչ այրէին մանկունքն ի հնոցին եւ զկերպարան չորրորդին առաւել պայծառ եւ ահագին՝

---

14. This name is Dūra' in Hebrew and *dwr*' in the Peshitta; in Theodition Greek deïra and this gave rise to the forms Դեհերա, Դահերա, and Դեերա in the Armenian Daniel: see Cowe, *Armenian Version of Daniel*, 163. The origin of the form here is unclear.

զահի հարեալ ասէր. «Ո՞չ երիս արս արկաք ի հնոցին, եւ արդ՝ Դ. (4) տեսանեմ:/ fol 185r / Իսկ միւսոյն կերպարանն զարհուրեցուցանէ զիս, զի նման է Որդոյն Աստուծոյ»:

14/ Յայնժամ ձայնեաց թագաւորն ի հնոցն՝ ասելով. «Եկայք արտաքս ծառայքդ Աստուծոյ, զի եւ ես ընդ ձեզ աւրհնեմ զՏէր Աստուածն Դանիէլի»:

Եւ հանեալ զնոսա արտաքս ի հնոցէն՝ կարգեաց յեւս գերագոյն փառս եւ ի պատիւ:

15/ Եւ տուան յԱստուծոյ շնորհք Դանիէլի, որ մեկնեաց զահագին երազն արքային, որ եւտես յանիւն դաշտի մի. մարդոյ պատկեր մի, որ էր գլուխն ոսկի, լանջքն եւ թիկունքն արծաթի, միջովն ի վայր եւ կշտերովն մինչեւ բարձքն պղնձի եւ բարձքն երկաթի, եւ սրունքն կէսն երկաթի եւ կէսն խեցի, եւ թաթ ոտիցն ամենեւին խեցի կաւեղէն, եւ վէմ մի հատեալ ի լեռնէ միոջէ առանց ուրուք ձեռին:

16/ Եւ եկեալ ի վերայ պատկերին եւ ջարդեալ խորտակեաց զնա մանր, եւ արար զոսկին եւ զարծաթն, զպղինձն եւ զերկաթն ընդ խեցոյն որպէս փոշի: Եւ այն վէմն լայնացեալ, բարձրացեալ, լեռնացեալ ելից զյարձակութիւն դաշտին եւ արձանացաւ անդէն:

17/ Զոր տեսեալ զայն թագաւորն՝ զարհուրեցաւ եւ հատաւ քունն ի յայցաց նորա: Կոչեաց զիմաստունսն եւ զգէտսն քաղդէացոց եւ հարցանէր ի նոցանէ զմեկնութիւն երազին: Եւ նոքա ասեն, թէ. «Ասասցէ արքայ զերազն, եւ ապա մեք / fol 185v / ասեմք զմեկնութիւն նորա:

Ասաց թագաւորն, թէ. «Ի զարհուրանացն թռեաւ ի մտաց, եւ ոչ գիտեմ»:

18/ Ասեն զետքն. «Այդ գործ դիցն է՝ գիտել զխորհուրդս արքայի եւ յայտնել զմոռացեալ երազն»:

Յայնժամ բարկութեամբ հրամայեաց¹⁵ թագաւորն սպանանել զգէտսն: Եւ մինչ տանէին ի սպանումն, ասաց Դանիէլ դահճապետին. «Մի՛ սպանաներ զնոսա, այլ տար պահեա, զի մի գիտասցէ արքայ»: Եւ ինքն խոստացաւ Դանիէլ յետ երից աւուրց ասել զերազն եւ տալ զմեկնութիւնն: Եւ ի խնամոցն Աստուծոյ արար դահճապետն զասացեալն ի Դանիէլէ:

19/ Եւ զաւուրս Գ. (3) կացեալ Դանիէլ ի պահս եւ յաղօթս Գ. (3) մանկամբքն: Եւ խնդրեցին յԱստուծոյ տալ նմա գիտութիւն գիտել զերազն արքայի, եւ յայտնեաց նմա Աստուած: Եւ մտեալ Դանիէլ

---

15. այ above line, p.m.

առաջի արքայի՝ ասաց զերազն եւ զմեկնութիւն նորա: Եւ մեծարեցաւ Դանիէլ յարքայէ, եւ ազատեաց զզետոսն ի սպանմանէ:

20/ Եւ յոյժ մեծարեաց արքայն Նաբուգոդոնոսոր զԴանիէլ եւ զերիս մանկունսն, որքան եկաց նա կենդանի, եւ յետ նորա՝ որդին Բաղտասար, եւ յետ նորա՝ Դարեհ, եւ յետ նորա՝ Կիւրոս, եւ յետ Կիւրոսի՝ Արտաշէս, եւ յետ նորա՝ Ատտիկոս: Զոր բազում անգամ յանդիմանէին զնա Դանիէլ եւ Գ. (3) մանկունքն վասն ամ/ fol 186r /բարբշտութեանն իւրոյ, եւ նա բարկացեալ ետ սպանանել զնոսա:

21/ Եւ ի հատանել զգլուխն Միսայէլի՝ տարածեաց Ազարիայ զքղամիթն իւր եւ առ ընկալաւ զգլուխ նորա: Նոյնպէս եւ Անանիայ էառ զգլուխն Ազարիայի ի գոգն իւր, էառ եւ Դանիէլ զգլուխն Անանիայի եւ զայլ Բ. (2) եղբարցն ի պատմուճանն իւր:

22/ Եւ ժողովեալ հրէիցն բարձին զմարմինս նոցա եւ եդին յարձաթի տապանս, եւ անդէն միացան հատեալ գլուխքն ի մարմինս նոցա, եւ տարեալ ամբուփեցին[16] ի ծածուկ տեղոջ, զի մի առեալ թագաւորն այրեցցէ զմարմինս նոցա:

23/ Եւ եղեւ յետ բազում ժամանակաց յաւուրս քրիստոնէութեան, յամս Վռամայ Պարսից արքային, յայտնեցան նշխարք սուրբ երից մանկանցն Անանիանցն եւ յայտնեցան այսպէս.

այր ումն հրէայ ի Բաբելոն նստէր առանձին ի տան իւրում, եւ զային առ նա բազումք ի հիւանդաց եւ առողջանային ի ցաւոց իւրեանց: Եւ այր ումն քրիստոնեայ՝ անուն Մալխութայ յազատ ազգէ, կարգեալ իշխան յարքայէն Պարսից կողմանց Բաբելացոց:

24/ Լուաւ զքահանչելիսն, զոր առնէր հրէայն, եւ բան եղ միում ի ծառայից իւրոց՝ իշխանն Մալխութայ՝ ձեւանալ ի կերպ հրէի եւ երթալ առ այրն հրէայ, եւ տեսանել, թէ ո/ fol 186v /րո՛վ զօրութեամբ առնէ զքահանչելիսն զայն:

25/ Եւ առեալ հաց եւ միս, եւ գինի եւ գնաց առ հրէայն: Եւ նստաւ առ նմա օր մի եւ եւտես, զի բազում ցաւագարք զային առ նա, եւ նա առնոյր լի ամանով ջուր եւ դնէր ի մէջ տանն յերեկորեայ մինչեւ ցառաւօտ: Եւ ի վաղիւն առեալ զջուրն՝ լնոյր ի վերայ հիւանդացն, եւ ողջանային:

26/ Եւ քրիստոնեայն, զոր տարաւ ընդ իւր, եղ առաջի հրէին, եւ նստեալ կերան եւ արբին ի միասին: Եւ ուրախացոյց զհրէայն եւ ապա սկսաւ հարցանել զնա, եւ ասաց.

---

16. Unusual orthography of ամփոփեցին.

27/ «Տէ՛ր իմ, ի՞ւ առնես գրժշկութիւնդ զայդ։ Չի արժան է ինձ ասել, որ հրէայ եմ իբրեւ զքեզդ։ Եւ արդ, տեսանեմ, զի բան ինչ ոչ ասես եւ տաս ամենայն ցաւոց առողջութիւն մարդկան»։

Եւ իբրեւ կարի ստիպեաց զնա, ասաց հրէայն. թէ. «Յայնմ տեղոջ, յորում դնեմ զամանն շրով, են նշխարք սրբոց երից մանկանցն՝ Անանիանցն, ի մէջ տան։ Չի անդ շինեալ են շիրիմք նոցա, եւ ի նոցանէ լինին բժշկութիւնքդ, զոր տեսանես ի փառս Աստուծոյ եւ սրբոց նորա։

28/ Եւ այնպէս տեղեկացեալ այրն եւ գիտացեալ գծշմարիտն, դարձաւ առ իշխանն Մալխութայ եւ ասաց նմա։ Եւ իշխանն ասաց իւրոյ վանաց երիցուն Անտոնի, եւ նորա զգուշացան, եւ սպասեցին շաբաթ / fol/ 187r/ գիշերոյն, յորում երթայր հրէայն ի ժողովարանն հրէից։ Քանզի յուրբաթու երեկոյին՝ ի մուտս շաբաթուն, վառեր զկանթեղն եւ աձեր խունկ ի տանն եւ ինքն երթայր ի ժողովարանն։

29/ Իսկ վանաց հայրն Անտոն,[17] առեալ ընդ իւր արս ժիրս եւ ճարտարս, եւ գնացեալ եհան գնշխարս սրբոց Անանիանցն, եւ տարան զաղտաբար ի վանս իւրեանց

եւ ժամանակս ինչ անյայտ պահեցին վասն հրէից, զի մի գիտասցեն, եւ լինիցի խռովութիւն։ Եւ ապա յայտնի արարին, եւ եղեւ ուրախութիւն մեծ ամենայն քրիստոնէից վասն սքանչելեացն, որ լինէին ի սուրբ նշխարացն Անանիանցն։

30/ Իսկ Դանիէլ մարգարէն էր ի պաղատն արքայութեանն Պարսից Դարեհի եւ Արտաշիսի եւ յօրն Գ. (3) անգամ ի մէջ կռապաշտիցն աղօթեր ի դարպասն ի վերայ Երուսաղէմի, ուր եւ լինէր պալատն թագաւորաց՝ թէ ի Բաբելոն, եւ թէ՛ ի յԱսպահան, որ է Շօշ քաղաք։

Ուր եւտես Դանիէլ գտեսիլն ահագին գազանացն եւ գոսկալի դատաստանն Քրիստոսի, ուր հին աւուրցն Աստուած նստաւ, եւ Որդին մարմնով գայր ընդ ամպս երկնից։

31/ Անդ՝ յԱսպահան, աղօթեր Դանիէլ ի վերայ Երուսաղեմի, ընդ որս շարեալ մոգուցն՝ մախային եւ խափանել զԴանիէլ յաղօթիցն ոչ կարէին։ Ապա խորհուրդ արարին եւ ուխտ եդին ի մէջ / fol 187v / իւրոց մոգքն եւ գէտքն պարսից, թէ մի ոք իշխեսցէ տալ զանունն աստուծոյ ամսօրեա մի ժամանակ, բայց միայն լիշեսցեն գԴարեհ արքայ։ Զայս խորհուրդ կնքեցին ի գրի մատանեաւ թագաւորին։ Իսկ սուրբն Դանիէլ ոչ կասէր յաղօթից իւրոց, այլ համարձակ լիշեր հանապազ գահեղ անունն Աստուծոյ։

---

17. n above line, p.m.

32/ Վասն որոյ մատեան գէտքն առ արքայ եւ ասեն. «Արքա՛յ, յաւիտեան կեաց, ո՞չ դու ետուր հրաման՝ մի յիշել զանուն այլ աստուծոց ամիս մի, բաց արքայէ»:
Եւ նա ասաց. «Այո՛, այնպէս գրեցաւ», յորմէ համարձակեցան գէտքն եւ առեալ զԴանիէլ՝ ընկեցին ի գուբն առիւծոց՝ կերակուր լինել գազանացն: Եւ թողին զգազանսն անօթի զաւուրս է. (7), զի կերիցեն զԴանիէլ:
33/ Եւ գազանքն քաղցեալ՝ ի մարգարէն ոչ մերձեցան, այլ զհող ուտիցն լեզուին:
Եւ մարգարէն Ամբակում յԵրուսաղէմ հոգայր զինձոս արտին իւրոյ: Եւ առեալ հաց եւ թան տանել հնձողացն: Եւ յորժամ եդ զմի ոտն արտաքոյ սեմոց տանն եւ միւս ոտն դեռեւս ի տանն էր, ազդեաց ի նա Հոգին Սուրբ, եւ մարգարէացաւ: Ասաց ընտանեացն, թէ. «Ես երթամ յերկիր հեռաստան», եւ առեալ հրեշտակն զԱմբակում եդ ի հորն Դանիէլի:
34/ Զոր առեալ Դանիէլ / fol 188r / զճաշ հրնձուորացն Ամբակումայ՝ եկեր ինքն եւ ետ առիւծոցն: Եւ Ամբակում փակեալ դրօք եմուտ ի գուբն եւ ել: Եւ գնացեալ ի տունն իւր՝ ամսոյ միոյ ճանապարհի, եւ տարաւ ճաշ հնձողացն՝ ոչ յամեալ ինչ զտվորական ժամն:
35/ Եւ յետ է. (7) աւուր թափեալ Դարեհ արքայ յիմարութենէն՝ խնդրեաց զԴանիէլ: Եւ ազդեցաւ նմա, թէ ի գուբն առիւծոց է: Եւ եկեալ արքայ իւրովի ինքն ի բերան զբին կոչեաց զԴանիէլ եւ ելան ի գբոյն, եւ ետ ընկենուլ զչարախօսսն Դանիէլի ի գուբն, եւ նոյն ժամայն պատառեցին զնոսա առիւծքն[18] եւ կերան:
36/ Եւ դարձեալ յայլում ժամանակի արկաւ Դանիէլ ի գուբն Բ. (2) մարդակեր առիւծոց եւ յետ երից աւուրց ել անվնաս:
37/ Եւ սպան զվիշապն, որում զոհէին քաղդէացիքն, եւ խայտառակեալ յանդիմանեաց զիսքերութիւն մոգուցն: Եւ այլ բազում նշան արար Դանիէլ ի Բաբելոն յամս Ե. (5) թագաւորացն Նաբուգոդոնոսրայ եւ որոց զհետ նորա:
38/ Եւ մեռաւ Դանիէլ խաղաղութեամբ, եւ թաղեցաւ ի գերեզմանս բաբելացոց: Էր Դանիէլ աչօքն գեղեցիկ նման Քրիստոսի, եւ մօրուացն քարզ,[19] եւ տեսլեամբն ցամաք լի շնորհօքն Աստուծոյ:

---

18. Diacritical sign above ք.
19. We read this word as an orthographic variant of քարձ "thin (of beard)."

20. DANIEL THE PROPHET AND THE THREE YOUNG MEN

Apparatus

| M1099 | text |
| Synaxarium 4 | variant |

20/ յոյժ] + սիրեաց եւ | եւ ... Բաղդասար] om | Դարէի | Ատտիկ | ամբարշտութեան | իւրոյ] նորա

21/ հատանելն | Ազարիա | գքդամիդն | Անանիա

22/ հատեալ] կցեալ | ամփոփեցին | տեղւոջ | նոցա3°] սրբոցն

23/ Անանիանցն եւ յայտնեցան 'and they were revealed'] om | առանձին] follows իւրում առանձինն | Մալխութա | կողմանցն բաբելացւոց

24/ մհում ի] om | ի2խանն Մալխութայ] om

25/ յերեկօրեայ | ողջանային] առողջանային վաղվաղակի

26/ տարաւ] տարեալ էր | զնա] + անոյ2

27/ զքեզ | ոչ ասես] որ ասես | ամենայն ցաւց / առողջութիւն ∞ | տեղւոջ | զամանա | ջրոյ | լինի | բժշկութիւնդ | զոր տեսանես] om

28/ գձշմարիտն] գձշմարտութիւն իրացն | Մալխութա | եւ սպասեցին] om | հրէից | ուրբաթ աւուրն | յերեկոյին + ժամուն | ի մուտս շաբաթուն] om

29/ ճարտարս] իմաստունս | եհան] հանին | Անանիանցն] մարտիրոսացն | յայտնի արարին] յայտնեցին | քրիստոնէիցն] քրիստոնէից | լինէին] լինէր | սուրբ ն2խարացն] ն2խարաց սրբոցն ի փառս միոյն Աստուծոյ | Անանիանցն] om : doxology follows

Translation

Title/ Of the Prophet Daniel and the Three Young Men, Anania, Azariah and Mishael.

1/ They were children of King Jehoiakim[20] who was in Jerusalem, from the tribe of Judah, of the sons of David, and grandchildren of pious Hezekiah and Josiah.[21]

---

20. In Dan 1:1 Jehoiakim is mentioned, but as part of a dating formula, not as a father of Daniel.

21. The text has Յովսեայ, where Յովսիա might be expected. However, the identification is clear.

2/ And Daniel the prophet was the cousin of the holy Ananianes'[22] uncle, he was son of Johan,[23] brother of King Jehoiakim.[24]

3/ They were exiled to Babylon in the days of the destruction of Jerusalem. King Nebuchadnezzar saw them (to be) intelligent and wise, with handsome countenances and pleasing appearance.[25]

4/ And he told Asp'aneh, his chief eunuch, to give them to school, to the wise men of the Chaldeans, so that they might learn Chaldean writing and language, so as to stand before the king[26] in the royal palace.

5/ And he said to give them food daily from the royal supply, from which he himself ate and drank, to nurture them for three years and then to have them stand before the king.[27] And they gave them Chaldean names, to Daniel—Baldasar, and to Anania—Sedrak, to Azariah—Misak', and to Mishael—Abed-Nago.[28] And they did not eat whatever they gave them from the royal supply, but they were content only with legumes.[29]

6/ Asp'aneh the chief eunuch said to Daniel, for he was the oldest and was twelve years old—what is more, in those same days he prophesied and freed Susanna. And he saved Susanna from the lawless old men and delivered the old men to death.[30]

Asp'anēh said to him, "I fear[31] the king, lest he see your countenances gloomy and you become thin and he kill me."[32]

---

22. So the three companions are sometimes called in the Armenian tradition.

23. 1 Chr 3:15: Johanan (Johan) is not mentioned in Daniel or in 3–4 Kgdms (1–2 Kgs). His relationship to Daniel is apocryphal.

24. §§2–3, on the ancestry of Daniel and his companions, is doubtlessly based on Dan 1:3, where Ashpenaz is commanded "to bring some Israelites of the royal family." See Stone: "A Note on Daniel 1.3," 67–71.

25. See Dan 1:4 where both their intelligence and their good looks are mentioned.

26. That is, to enter the royal service.

27. §§4–5 are dependent on Dan 1:5.

28. Dan 1:6.

29. This is based on Dan 1:6, but expanded in line with Dan 1:12.

30. Here a reference to the story of Susanna is introduced. In the Greek translation of Daniel, it precedes Dan 1.

31. There is a confusion of խ and հ in two words in this sentence—վահել < վախել and նիխար < նիհար. This shift also occurs in mediaeval inscriptions and in certain modern dialects. See Josef Karst, *Historische Grammatik des Kilikisch-Armenischen* (Strassburg: Trübner, 1901), 90. For other instances of this phoenetic variation, see Stone and Hillel, "Index," no. 345, p. 441.

32. Dan 1:10.

20. DANIEL THE PROPHET AND THE THREE YOUNG MEN

7/ Daniel said, "You test us for ten days and give us legumes to eat: lentils, chick-peas and broad beans to eat and water to drink, and let our colors[33] be seen before you, and the colors of the young men who eat of the king's table, and then do with us as seems pleasing to you."[34]

8/ And he did according to Daniel's wish and tested them for ten days. And after the ten days, Aspaneh saw the countenances of Daniel and the three young men, more brilliant and plumper and more handsome that those of the other young men, who were eating from the king's table.[35]

9/ And God gave Daniel talent and wisdom, such intelligence that no other young man of the Chaldeans was found like Daniel and the three young men. And thus, they were standing before the king.[36]

10/ And King Nebuchadnezzar made an image of gold, the likeness of Bel. (It was) sixty cubits long and six cubits wide. And he set it up in a field of Dara[37] and commanded everybody to worship it.[38]

11/ But Daniel and the three young men disdained the king's order and did not bow down to the gold statue. On account of this the king was wrath and caused them to be cast into the fiery furnace.[39]

12/ There the angel of the Lord descended into the midst of the fire, the very Word, God the Son, the only-begotten, descended to them. And he spread the flame of the fire like an arch over them.[40] And from the fire's flame, dew descended for them just like the dew of rain, very gently.[41]

---

33. That is, the colors of our countenances.
34. Dan 1:12-14.
35. Dan 1:15.
36. In Dan 1:17 the knowledge is attributed to all four men, but dreams and visions only to Daniel. Here, the special skill of Daniel is not mentioned.
37. See Dan 3:1 which has the statue erected in the field of Dura: on the name see p. 222 n. 14 above.
38. Dan 3:1-6.
39. Dan 3:12-19 are briefly summarized here. Daniel is not included among the young men according to the book of Daniel.
40. The origin of the image is unclear.
41. This explicit explanation of how they were saved and of the descent of the angel who is also a Person of the Trinity, is an apocryphal embroidery. It is based, however, on 3 Macc 6:6, which says: "The three companions in Babylon who had voluntarily surrendered their lives to the flames so as not to serve vain things, you rescued unharmed, even to a hair, moistening the fiery furnace with dew and turning the flame against all their enemies." The miracle is described differently in Azariah 26, which says that the angel drove the fire and the heat out. The idea of angelic descent brought the author to identify it with Christ's descent, thus interpreting Dan 3:25.

13/ Then the Ananiaians rejoiced in the midst of the furnace; they were singing the words of the blessing with the angel.[42]

And when the lawless king saw that, that the young men were not burned up in the furnace and that the form of fourth one was more brilliant and fearsome, smitten by fear, he said, "Did we not throw three men into the fire and now I see four? but the form of the fourth one frightens me, for he is like the Son of God."[43]

14/ Then the king called out to the furnace, saying, "Servants of God, come forth, for I too with you bless the Lord God of Daniel."[44]

And he brought them forth outside the furnace, he prescribed (for them) even greater glory and honor.[45]

15/[46] They gave thanks to the God of Daniel,[47] who explained the king's fearful dream. He saw in an immense field an image of a man which had a head of gold, breast and shoulders of silver, from the middle down and the belly down to the thighs of bronze, the thighs of iron and the shanks, half iron and pottery, and the feet completely of clay pottery, and a rock was cut out of the midst of a mountain, without any hand.[48]

16/ And it (the rock) came upon the image and destroyed it, breaking it up into little parts. And it reduced the gold and silver, the bronze and the iron together with the pottery, to a dust.[49] And that rock was widened, elevated, becoming a mountain filled the attack[50] of the field. And it became fixed there.

17/ When the king saw that, he was affrighted and sleep was banished from his eyes. He summoned the wise men and the magicians of the Chaldeans, and asked of them the interpretation of the dream. And they said, "Let

---

42. See Azariah 1. This refers to the Songs of Azariah and of the Three Children, occurring in the Greek versions of Daniel and so in the Apocrypha. They also occur among the Odes that are associated with the Psalter in Eastern Church usage.

43. A Christian reading of Dan 3:25 which has "a son of God."

44. Dan 3:26. In this text, the king expresses his desire to join the praise of God. That sentiment is not in the verse in Daniel, though his praise is found there, in Dan 3:28.

45. The rest of Daniel chap. 3 is not represented here.

46. Here the narrative transitions to the story of Nebuchadnezzar's dream in chap. 2 of Daniel. The order of events is adapted to the story line here. No text corresponds to Dan 2:2–19.

47. See Dan 2:47 where Nebuchadnezzar praises God. Daniel blesses God in 2:20, 28.

48. This is an epitome of Dan 2:31–34.

49. Dan 2:34–35.

50. The word յարձակութիւն "attack, pouncing on," etc. is odd in this context.

the king say the dream and we will say its interpretation." The king said, "In the affright it flew from my mind, and I know it not."[51]

18/ The magicians said, "That is the work of the gods, to know the king's thought and to make the forgotten dream known."[52] Then, in anger, the king ordered (them) to execute the magicians.[53] And while they were being taken to execution, Daniel said to the chief executioner, "Do not execute them, but keep them distant so that the king shall not know."[54] Daniel himself promised to tell the dream after three days, and to give its interpretation.[55] And by God's care, the chief executioner did that which Daniel said.

19/ And Daniel with the three young men fasted and prayed for three days, and they asked God to give him knowledge to know the king's dream.[56] And God revealed it to him. And Daniel, entering the presence of the king, related the dream and its interpretation.[57] And Daniel was honored by the king, and freed the magicians from execution.[58]

20/ And King Nebuchadnezzar honored Daniel and the three young men greatly as long as he stayed alive. And after him, his son Balthasar, and after him, Darius, and after him, Cyrus, and after Cyrus, Artashes, and after him, Atticus.[59] Daniel and the three young men often rebuked him on account of his impiety, and he, growing angry, caused them to be executed.

21/ And when Mishael's head was cut off, Azariah spread out his cloak and took (and) received[60] his head. Thus, also Anania took the head of Aza-

---

51. This section corresponds to Dan 2:1–4.
52. Dan 2:10–11.
53. Dan 2:12.
54. Dan 2:13. This theme of the wise man who intervenes to save courtiers and their eventual vindication, is also found in Story of Aḥiqar the Wise, and is old. Compare the analogous story of St. Gregory in *Agat'angełos*.
55. Dan 2:16. The length of the delay is not mentioned in the book of Daniel. Here it is a standard number of three days.
56. The fasting is an embroidery.
57. This summarizes the preceding. The interpretation of the dream is not given, for the focus of the text is on Daniel and his companions and not on God's message to the king.
58. See Dan 2:48 on Daniel's honors. The last phrase is the author's. From this point, the story is that of the martyrdom of the three Young Men, which is not in the Book of Daniel.
59. This king, with his odd genealogy, is mentioned by Garitte, who refers to an unedited Greek text, BHG 3.484z–484*: See Garitte, "L'Invention géorgienne," 71. With this transitional sentence, the material drawn from the biblical book of Daniel comes to an end and the material related to the hagiographical traditions of the Three Young Men start.
60. An instance of hendiadys, a favored construction in Ancient Armenian.

riah into his bosom. Daniel also took the head of Anania and the other two brothers into his garment.

22/ And, the Jews having assembled, the took their bodies and placed them in a silver coffin. And at once the cut-off heads united with their bodies, and taking them, they confined them in a secret place, lest the king, having taken their bodies, burn (them).

23/ And it came to pass after many times, in the days of Christianity, in the years of Vṙam, king of the Persians, the remains (relics) of the holy three Ananian Young Men were revealed, and thus they were revealed. A certain man, a Jew, in Babylon[61] was living[62] alone in his house. Many of the sick were coming to him and were being cured of their pains. And a certain Christian man, by the name of Malxut'a[63] of a noble family, was appointed prince of the region of Babylon by the king of the Persians.

24/ He heard of the miracles (wonders) that the Jew was doing, and the prince Malxut'a spoke to one of his servants. The prince Malxut'a disguised him as a Jew and he went to the Jewish man to see by what power he was doing those miracles.

25/ He took bread and meat and wine and went to the Jew, and he sat down with him, and he saw that many people suffering pains were coming to him. And he would take a vessel full of water, and would put it in the house from evening to morning. And on the following day he would take the water and he would spread it over the sick and they would recover.

26/ And the Christian set what he had brought with him before the Jew and they sat and ate and drank together. And he made the Jew happy and then he began to ask him and said,

27/ "My Lord, by what means do you do this healing of yours? For, it is fitting that you say to me, who am a Jew like you. And now I see that you say nothing and you give healing to people from all pains."

When he urged him strongly, the Jew said, "In this place on which I put the vessel with the water there are the remains of the holy three Ananian young men, inside my house. For there their tombs are built and through them these healings come which you see, for the glory of God and his saints."

---

61. Babylon was the traditional site of the cult of the relics of the Three Young Men; see Garitte, "L'Invention géorgienne," 71.

62. Literally: seated.

63. In the version of this story in the manuscript miscellany of Mxit'ar Ayrivanec'i (1271–1288), fol 362r the name of the prince was Mazlut'a, clearly a variant of the same Syriac name: See Stone, "An Armenian Tradition," 111.

28/ And the man, having been thus informed and having apprehended the truth, he returned to Prince Malxut'a and said (it) to him. And the prince said (it) to the presbyter of his convent, Anton. And they were careful and waited for the night of the Sabbath, when the Jew would go to Jewish synagogue. Because on Friday eve, at the coming in of the Sabbath, he would light the lamp and bring incense to the house and he, himself, would go to the synagogue.

29/ Then Anton, the abbot of the monastery, taking lively and clever men with him, went (and) bought forth the relics of the holy Ananiaites, and brought (them) secretly to their monastery. And for some time, they kept (this) unknown on account of the Jews, lest they learn (of it) and disturbances take place. And then, they made (it) public and there was great rejoicing for the Christians, on account of the miracles that were taking place through the holy relics of the Ananiaites.

30/ Then Daniel the prophet was in the palace of the kingdom of the Persians, of Darius and of Artashes, and thrice daily, amidst the idolaters, he prayed over Jerusalem in the palace.[64] Where was the kings' palace? in Babylon or in Isfahan, which is the city of Šōš?[65]

There, Daniel saw the fearsome vision of the beasts and Christ's dread judgment, where the God, the Ancient of Days sat, and the Son came in the body with the clouds of heaven.[66]

31/ Now, in Isfahan Daniel was praying over Jerusalem. The magi, being at odds with this, were envious and they were unable to prevent Daniel from his prayers. Then the magi and the magicians of the Persians took counsel and made a covenant among themselves, that no one could mention the names of gods for the period of one month, but they would only mention King Darius.[67] They sealed this plan in writing with the king's ring.[68] Then the holy Daniel

---

64. See Dan 6:10 for Daniel's prayer facing towards Jerusalem. All of §30 is bridging text serving to resume the story after the narrative of the Inventio of the relics. Moreover, the vision of the four beasts is referred to here thus accounting for its absence from the present document, This, as well as the question discussed in the next section, indicate the editorial character of this section.

65. Some later traditions are referenced here, and in the seventeenth and eighteenth centuries Isfahan was the capital of Safavid Persia. This question, to which no answer is given, seems to be a gloss added to an earlier document.

66. The reference is to the vision of the four beasts, Dan 7.

67. The magicians' idea of a conspiracy, as well as the actual plot, are related in Dan 6:4–6.

68. The signing is mentioned in Dan 6:9, but a sealing with the royal signet is not

did not hold back from his prayers and openly mentioned God's fearful name continually.[69]

32/ On account of which the magicians approached the king and said, "O King, live forever! Did you not give a commandment not to mention the name of any other of the gods for one month, except for the king?" And he said, "Yes, thus it is written."[70] By this the magicians were emboldened and seizing Daniel, they cast him into the lions' den, to be food for the beasts.[71] And they had left the beasts hungry for seven days, so that they would eat Daniel.

33/[72] And the beasts, (though) hungry, did not approach the prophet, but were licking the dust of (his) feet. And the prophet Habakkuk in Jerusalem was tending to the reapers of his field. And he took bread and tʻan[73] to bring to the reapers. And when he put one foot outside the threshold of the house and the other foot was still in the house, the Holy Spirit informed him and he prophesied. He said to his household, "I am going to a far land." And the angel, taking Habakkuk, put him into Daniel's pit (cistern).

34/ Daniel received the reapers' meal from Habakkuk, he ate himself and gave (some) to the lions. And Habakkuk, closed in by the door, entered the den and left (it). And he went to his house, a month's journey, and brought a meal to the reapers, not having delayed the customary time at all.[74]

---

found there. Sealing is found in a different context in the continuation of this story, where the king closed Daniel into the lions' den and sealed the entrance: Dan 6:17.

69. Dan 6:10. The expression "fearful name" recalls Pr. Man. 3 where sealing by the name is mentioned. The magical power of the divine name was also known in Armenian Christian sources. Perhaps also the words of power used by Moses to invoke the splitting of the Red Sea are related to this idea: see Stone, *Angels and Heroes*, text no. 4.8 §33 and text no. 12 Moses and Aaron §34.

70. Dan 6:12. In Dan 6:14 tells that the king wished to save Daniel, but was outsmarted by the accusers.

71. Dan 6:16. The starving of the lions for a week is not related in Dan 6:16. This feature is to be observed in other Daniel texts; see Bel and the Dragon 14:31.

72. In this section the legend is introduced that Habakkuk was brought wondrously from Judea to Babylon with food for Daniel. This story is found in the Greek Daniel (Bel and the Dragon) 14:33–39: see Satran, *Biblical Prophets in Byzantine Palestine*, 101. The story is repeated in many sources including the Vitae Prophetarum, the Greek Palaea, §168 (MOTP 1:670). On the Vita of Habakkuk, see Satran, *Biblical Prophets in Byzantine Palestine*, 60–61. The story is known, of course, to the Armenian Vitae Prophetarum, as well as to Names, Works, and Deaths of the Holy Prophets §12.

73. A soup or a drink of buttermilk or yoghurt.

74. Thus, it is once more evident that the document we are studying evinces knowledge of the longer recension of Daniel, which is included in the Septuagint and the Armenian Bible.

20. DANIEL THE PROPHET AND THE THREE YOUNG MEN

35/ And after seven days[75] had passed, King Darius foolishly sought Daniel. And he was informed that he is in the lions' den. And the king came by himself to the mouth of the den. He called Daniel and brought him out of the den[76] and caused Daniel's slanderers to be cast into the den, and straight away the lions tore them to pieces and ate (them).[77]

36/ And again at another time Daniel was cast into the den of two man-eating lions, and he came forth after three days unharmed.[78]

37/ And he killed the dragon to which the Chaldeans were sacrificing; having put them to shame he reproached the deceit of the magi.[79] And Daniel did many more signs in the years of the five kings, Nebuchadnezzar and his successors.

38/ And Daniel died peacefully and was buried in the tombs of the Babylonians.[80] Daniel was handsome to the eye, like Christ and thin-bearded and in appearance dry, full of the grace of God.[81]

---

75. According to the book of Daniel 6:19–30 Daniel spent only one night with the lions.
76. Dan 6:20.
77. Dan 6:24.
78. It is not certain that this is a reference to Daniel's stay in a lions' den as related in Bel and the Dragon (Dan 14:31–32). That text speaks of seven lions, while here there are two lions; the number of days differs too, being three here, and six days in Dan 14:31. Yet, the next section draws upon Bel and the Dragon.
79. This is clearly a reference to the story of Bel, and the priests' deception also related in the apocryphon.
80. His burial in Babylon is also to be found explicitly in the Vita of Daniel, *Epiphanii Recensio Prior*.
81. No ancient descriptions of Daniel are known.

21. The History of the Three Young Men

Introductory Remarks

This text is found in Oxford Bodleian manuscript arm f11. That manuscript, no. 55 in the Bodleian Catalogue, is titled "Apocrypha of O. and N.T. and Legends" and it was copied in 1651–1655. The volume contains a number of apocryphal texts such as History of Melchizedek on fols 93r–94r (incomplete), History of Joseph on fols 94v–104v, History of the Captivity of Israel on fols 104v–116v; and History of the Ark of the Covenant on fols 116v–122r. In addition, there are in it a number of extracts from the Synaxarium, among which is the document published here.[1]

The text is a narrative of The Three Young Men (or: Hebrews) in the furnace, explaining the context in which the prayers of Azariah and the three young men were pronounced. These prayers are preserved in the Greek versions of Daniel, and so in Armenian, but not in the Hebrew-Aramaic form of the book that is to be found in the Hebrew Bible.[2] The narrative elements of the story here are based on various sources within the book of Daniel. Rightly, this should be compared with the LXX form of Daniel and not the MT.

In addition to the narrative text published here, which is intended to provide a context for the prayers embedded in the LXX and Armenian versions of Dan 3, there are other texts in both Armenian and Georgian that deal with the discovery of the relics of The Three Hebrews. A number of these inventio stories have been published, both in Armenian and Georgian.[3]

---

1. Bodleian Catalogue, 115–17.
2. See George W. E. Nickelsburg, "The Bible Rewritten and Expanded," in *Jewish Writings of the Second Temple Period*, Compendia rerum judaicum ad Novem Testamentum 2.2 (Philadelphia: Fortress; Assen: van Gorcum, 1984), 149–52.
3. Stone, "An Armenian Tradition"; Garitte, "L'Invention géorgienne"; Garitte, "Le texte arménien." In Stone, *Biblical Heroes*, 28 mention is made of an unpublished text, Sermon concerning the Three Young Men surviving in M2242 (seventeenth century).

21. THE HISTORY OF THE THREE YOUNG MEN

Text

Title/ / fol 179v / Այս է պատմութիւն սրբոց երից մանկանց՝ Անանիայի, Ազարիայի եւ Միսայէլի

1/ Ի ժամանակին, որում գնաց Նաբուգոդոնոսոր արքայն ի յԵրուսաղէմ եւ գե/fol 180r/րեաց զնա, ընտրեաց զայս Գ. (3) մանկունս եւ ետ յուսումն, եւ ասաց վարպետի նոցա լաւ պահել կերակրով եւ զգեստով:

2/ Իսկ այս Գ. (3) մանուկս խորհեցան եւ ասացին. «Այս ի՞նչ էր, զի եկն ի վերայ մեր, զի մեծ հարքն մեր Աբրահամ, Սահակ, եւ Յակոբ, եւ Յովսէփի աստուածախօսք էին եւ Աստուծոյ սիրական, ընդէ՞ր գերի ետ զմեզ ի ձեռն այլազգեաց։ Մի՞ թէ հարքն մեր չար գործեցին, Աստուած բարկացաւ ի վերայ հարցն մերոց եւ գերի ետ զմեզ ի ձեռն այլազգեաց։

3/ Իսկ այժմ մեք յուսացեալ եմք ի յԱստուած հարցն մերոց, Աստուած Աբրահամու, Աստուած Սահակայ, Աստուած Յակոբայ։ Մի՞ թէ փրկեսցէ զմեզ ի ձեռաց նեղչաց մերոց»։ Յուսացան յԱստուած, պահէին ծոմ եւ պաս,[4] եւ առնէին յաղօթս:

4/ Իսկ վարպետ նոցա ոչ թոյլ ետայր[5] նոցա պահել զպաս եւ զծոմ, թէ. «Վախեմ, թէ զոյն երեսաց ձեր փոխի,[6] բարկանայ ինձ թագաւորն»։[7] Ասեն Գ. (3) մանկունքն, զի. «Ազգն մեր քանի սակաւ ունեն եւ զմ/ fol 180v /պեն, այլ զեղեցկագուն լինին։ Թէ ոչ հաւատաս, շաբաթ մի պահեմք, փորձեա՛ եւ տե՛ս, թէ մաշուիմք կամ դեղնուիմք, այլ մի՛ թողուլ պահել, եւ թէ ոչ մաշուիմք, թո՛ղ զմեզ ի կամս մեր կացցուք»:

5/ Եւ հաձոյ թուեցաւ զբանս[8] նոցա վարպետին իւրոց։ Իբրեւ փորձեաց զմանկունս եւ տեսաւ, զի ոչ մաշեցան եւ ոչ փոխեցան զոյն յերեսաց նոցա, դեռ եւս այլ պայծառանային դէմք նոցա:

See above, text no. 20 Daniel the Prophet and the Three Young Men and the introductory remarks to that text.

4. Note the orthographic variant for պահս, also found in other manuscripts of this vintage.

5. Strange imperfect of տամ, with an augment.

6. Note this late passive form. The asyndeton is bridged by the addition of "and" in the translation.

7. See Dan 1:10.

8. Observe the anomalous grammar of թուեցաւ զբանս. If զբանս is the subject it should be in the nominative, so the verb must have been used as an impersonal. That is how we have translated it. The prefix q- is superfluous, as often happens in medieval texts. In Ancient Armenian, q- is either a preposition or the nota accusativi.

6/ Իբրեւ զարգացան եւ ուսան զամենայն⁹ զիրս իմաստասիրական, տարեալ թագաւորն, ետես զնոսա, <Անանիայ>¹⁰ հաւանեցաւ եւ մեծացոյց զնոսա. Անանիայ վերակացու քաղաքին, Ազարիայ՝ գանձապետ իւր, եւ զՄիսայէլ՝ դպրապետ իւր.¹¹

7/ Եւ ի ժամանակին այնմիկ Նաբուզողդոնոսոր արքայն շինեաց պատկեր մի ոսկեղէն Կ. (60) կանգուն բարձրութիւն նորա եւ Զ. (6) կանգուն լայնութիւն նորա, եւ ԺԲ. (12) երգարան եդ ի մէջ նոցա,¹² եւ անուանեաց անուն նորա Բէլ: / fol 181r / Չի յորժամ հնչէին զերգարանս սրընկի, թմբկի, քնարի եւ տօղի, ամենայնք¹³ անկանէին, յերկիր պագանէին:

8/ Եւ արար տեղ հնգի եւ փորեաց ԽԹ. (49) կանգուն, եւ վառին ի նմա հուր եւ ձայն տուեալ՝ ասէին, թէ. «Որք ոչ երկիրպագանէին պատկերին Բէլայ, անկանին ի հուրն եւ այրին»:

9/ Եւ յայնմ ժամուն ումանք կացին առաջի արքային եւ ասացին. «Արքայ յաւիտեան կաց, զի դու մեծացուցիր Անանիայ, Ազարիայ, եւ զՄիսայէլ, քան զամենայն մեծամեծս, զի ամենայն հեծեալք եւ ժողովուրդք քեզ հնազանդին եւ երկիրպագեն Բէլայ պատկերին, քո ծառայքն Անանիայ, Ազարիայ եւ Միսայէլ, եւ նորա ոչ հաւանեցան հրամանաց քոց եւ ոչ երկիրպագանեն պատկերին Բէլայ»:

10/ Եւ հրամայեաց թագաւորն եւ կոչեաց զնոսա, եւ բերին առաջի թագաւորին: Ասէ թագաւորն Նաբուքողդոնոսոր.¹⁴ «Եկա՛յք ընտրեալ ծառայք իմ՝ Անանիայ, Ազարիայ եւ Միսայէլ, / fol 181v / զի տեսանեմ զձեզ, թէ ինչպէս երկիրպագանէք նորաշէն աստուծոյն իմոյ Բէլայ»: Ասէ Անանիայ. «Ո՛չ լեր, թագաւո՛ր. մեծ ամօթ է շինուածոց աստուած ասել: Աստուած այն է, որ յերկնից¹⁵ եւ երկրի ստեղծօղ է, զի մեր մահն եւ կեանքն ի ձեռին, արեգակն եւ լուսինն ամենայն նորա են ստեղծուած: Թէ դու ծանիցես զնա, մեծ փառքի¹⁶ հասանես»:

11/ Ասէ թագաւորն. «Դուք ուստի՞ ճանաչէք զնա»: Ասէ Անանիայ. «Ձայրցն մերոց խօսեցաւ¹⁷ Աստուած, զի օրէնս եւ գիրք ի նոցանէ

---

9. գ° over կ* or ե*.
10. This word is the result of dittography and contamination by the next phrase.
11. There is no reason for two names, Անանիայ and Ազարիայ not to have the nota accusativi, while the third name, Միսայէլ exhibits it.
12. °նցա is written over *նորա.
13. ք is a correction p.m., beneath the line.
14. Note this spelling variant with -ք-.
15. The prefixed յ- is superfluous.
16. Observe the late form փառքի, which would be փառաց in Ancient Armenian.
17. An erasure of one letter precedes.

ունիմք եւ նովաւ[18] ճանաչեմք զԱստուած, զի նա է փրկիչ եւ կեցուցիչ մեր: Ասէ թագաւորն. «Երբ այդպէս[19] պահող Աստուած ունիք, ընդէ՞ր ոչ կարաց փրկել զձեզ ի ձեռաց իմոց»:

12/ Ասեն մանկունքն, զի. «Ժամանակ առաջին հարցն մերոց, քան զքեզ այլ մեծ թագաւորք յարեան ի վերայ ազգին մեր եւ ոչ ինչ կարէին առնել, այլ ոտնակոխ լինէին, իսկ վասն ծնօղացն մեր, որ բազում մեղք / fol 182r / եւ չարիք գործեցին, վասն այն բարկացաւ Աստուած ի վերայ մեր եւ զմեզ գերի ետ ի ձեռս քո»:

13/ Ասէ թագաւորն, զի. «Արկանեմ զքեզ ի մէջ հրոյն բորբոքելոյ, երբ տեսանեմ զԱստուած ձեր փրկէ զձեզ ի հրոյս, եւ ես պաշտեմ զԱստուած ձեր»: Ասեն մանկունքն. «Ի մահ պատրաստ եմք, տանջանք[20] եւ ի հուր վասն անուան Աստուծոյ մերոյ, զի զոր ինչ գիտես, այնպէս արա »:

14/ Եւ հրամայեաց թագաւորն կապել զերեքն[21] ի վերայ մի տախտակի, եւ Ձ. (6) մարդով առեալ զմանկունս, արկին ի մէջ հնոցին: Եւ առժամայն ամպ մի հովանի եղեւ ի վերայ նոցա եւ ցօղեր զցօղ ի մէջ հնոցին, եւ ցուրտ քամի ելաներ ի նմանէ, եւ զբոց հրոյն փախուցաներ ի նոցանէ, եւ զքշնամիսն այրեր, որ շուրջ զնովաւն էին:

15/ Եւ թագաւորն բարկացայր, եւ տարածեալ ի վերայ նոցա նիւթ եւ ձէթ, երկայն ձողով եւ փայտիւ տայր բորբոքել զբոցն, եւ այրեցին շուրջ զնովաւ, զոր եւ գտանէին:

16/ Իսկ թագաւորն հայէր եւ տեսանէր, զի արձակեալ ման / fol 182v /կունքն ի մէջ հնոցին աղօթէին, աւրհնէին եւ գովէին զԱստուած եւ ասէին. «Օրհնեա՛լ ես, Տէ՛ր Աստուած հարցն մերոց. աւրհնեալ, փառաւորեալ անուն քո յաւիտեան»: Եւ ասացին զհարց սաղմոսն ի մէջ հրոյն մինչեւ այն տեղն, որ ասեն. «Աւրհնեցուք Անանիայ, Ազարիայ եւ Միսայէլ, զՏէր աւրհնեցէ՛ք»:

17/ Եւ տեսանէր թագաւորն Դ. (4) հոգի երեւէր ի մէջ հրոյն, զարմանայր եւ ասէր. «Գ. (3) հոգի արկի ի մէջ հրոյն եւ, ահա, Դ. (4) երեւին, եւ ի միւսին տեսիլն ահեղ է եւ զարհուրելի»: Եւ ձայնեալ թագաւորն եւ ասէր. «Եկա՛յք արտաքս ծառայք Աստուծոյ, զի եւ ես ընդ ձեզ բարեբանեմ զթագաւորն ամմահ»:

18/ Իսկ այնչափ աղօթեցին երեք մանկունքն ի մէջ հնոցին, որ շիջաւ հուրն, եւ ապա ելին ի հնոցէն եւ յայտնապէս քարոզէին

---

18. A plur. would be expected after "laws and books," but the pronoun is in the singular.
19. ս below line p.m.
20. The case of this word is strange and perhaps the text is defective here.
21. An accusative would be expected.

qԱստուած։ Իսկ թագաւորն ազատ արար զամենայն Իսրայէլ, ազատ
եւ առանց հարկի նստէին ի Բաբելոն։

Եւ յետ Նաբուքոդոնոսրի թագաւորեաց որդի նորա։

Translation

Title/ This is the Story of the Three Holy Youths, Anania, Azariah, and Mishael.[22]

1/ At the time when King Nebuchadnezzar went to Jerusalem and took it captive,[23] he chose these three young men and gave (them) for instruction. And he said to their tutor/teacher to keep them well, with food and raiment.[24]

2/ Then these three young men considered and said, "What is this that happened to us?[25] For our great ancestors, Abraham, Isaac, and Jacob and Joseph[26] were speakers with God and beloved of God. Why did He give us as

---

22. The order of the names in Dan 1:5 Ananiah, Mishael, and Azariah. This variant order is maintained consistently in this document.

23. These events are related in 2 Kgs 25:1–8.

24. Cf. Dan 1:1–6. In the Book of Daniel, it is Daniel who is the hero. In this text, Daniel is omitted and only his three companions are mentioned. This is undoubtedly because the work was written as praise of the three young men, and by omitting Daniel it highlights them the more.

25. Literally: came upon.

26. Here Joseph is added to the standard list of three Patriarchs. The substantial role Joseph plays in the Armenian apocryphal literature should be observed and his popularity may be in part due to his being viewed as a paradigm or type of Christ. Note that in the similar invocation of the prayer in §3 of the present text, Joseph is not mentioned. Among the Armenian apocrypha, in addition to the Joseph stories in Testaments of the Twelve Patriarchs, the following compositions also exist: Third Story of Joseph (Stone, *Angels and Heroes*, 176–229); unpublished forms of Yusuf and Zuleika, a widespread Moslem Joseph story that survives titled Joseph the Beautiful in M2126, 204–220, M2234 208r–221r, and other copies; Pseudo-Ephrem, *Seven Vahangs of Joseph*, apparently the so-called "Life of Joseph" (A. H. Serjuni, "St. Ephraem's 'On the Seven Vahangs[?] of Joseph,'" *Sion* 47 [1973], 26–37, 137 [Armenian]); Joseph and Asenath (Christoph Burchard, *A Minor Edition of the Armenian Version of Joseph and Asenath*, HUAS 10 (Leuven: Peeters, 2010]); The Story of Joseph in Biblical Paraphrases (Stone, *Patriarchs and Prophets*, 104–8), and other compositions as well. It is uncertain which work the "History of Joseph" in ms Bodleian arm f11 94r–104v may be.

captives into the hand of gentiles?[27] Perhaps our fathers did evil (and) God was angry with our fathers and gave us as captives into the hand of gentiles.[28]

3/ "But now we have hoped in the God of our fathers, God of Abraham, God of Isaac, God of Jacob. Perhaps he will save us from the hands of our oppressors." They hoped in God, observed a fast and abstinence, and prayed.[29]

4/ Then their tutor did not permit them to observe the abstinence and the fast, saying,[30] "I fear (lest) the color of your faces changes (and) the king will be angry with me." The three young men said, "The less our people eat and drink, the more handsome they become. If you do not believe (this), we shall fast for one week.[31] You (then) check and see: If we are worn out and sallow, permit us to fast no longer, and if we are not worn out, permit us (and) we shall remain as we want."[32]

5/ And their discourse seemed pleasing to their tutor. When he checked the young men, then he saw that they were not worn out and that they had not changed with respect to the color of their faces,[33] (but) their countenances were even more resplendent.[34]

6/ When they grew up and had studied all the philosophical books, the king having brought (them), he saw them. He was pleased and made them great: Ananiah, overseer of the city; Azariah, his treasurer; Mishael, his chief scribe.[35]

---

27. See a similar question in a quite different context and with quite different conceptual underpinnings in 4 Ezra 3:28–36.

28. The language is somewhat repetitive here. It should be noted that the author is, apparently, drawing a distinction between "our great fathers" the three Patriarchs and "our fathers" who sinned, who must be more recent ancestors of the three young men.

29. These actions are typical of the Christian ascetic life in the Armenian and other traditions: see, e.g., Ques. Greg. 32–34. In Dan 1, they eat very limited types of food because of issues of purity; see Dan 1:8–13 and the interpretation of this abstinence as fasting is a typical strategy employed in various Christian texts.

30. Thus I translate pt here.

31. In Dan 1:12 the trial is for ten days, and here for a week.

32. Cf. Dan 1:10–13. Cf. T. Jos. 3:4. In other texts they eat only legumes for ten days.

33. This clumsy translation takes the subject of the phrase as the plural, "young men," as is demanded by the verb form. However, if the verb is falsely plural, and should be singular, then we should translate, "the color of their countenances had not changed."

34. Cf. Dan 1:14–16.

35. Cf. Dan 1:17–20. The biblical text does not mention the exact offices of the young men, which are given here but have no known textual basis.

7/ And at that time, King Nebuchadnezzar built a golden statue, sixty cubits in height (and) six cubits wide.[36] Twelve[37] musical instruments he put in its midst, and he called its name "Bēl."[38] When the musical instruments were sounding: a flute, a drum and tōł,[39] all fell down (and) worshipped.

8/ And he made a place for a furnace, and he dug forty-nine cubits[40] and he lit a fire in it and they announced, saying, "Those who do not worship the statue of Bēl will be cast into the fire and burned."[41]

9/ And at that hour certain men stood before the king and said, "O King, live forever. You made Ananiah, Azariah, and Mishael greater than all the grandees. For all the cavalry[42] and the people are obedient to you and bow down to the statue of Bēl. As for your servants, Ananiah, Azariah, and Mishael, they did not obey your commandments and did not worship the statue of Bēl."[43]

10/ And the king commanded and summoned them, and they were brought before the king. King Nebuchadnezzar said, "Come my chosen servants, Ananiah, Azariah, and Mishael, so I may see how you worship my newly constructed god, Bēl."[44] Ananiah said, "May the king be well. It is a great shame to say that constructed things are god. God is that one who is the creator of heavens and earth, for our death and life (are) in (his) hand.[45] The

---

36. These are the dimensions of the statue in Dan 3:1.

37. Dan 3:5, 10, and 15 all list six instruments but also mention "all kinds of music." Apparently, the Armenian text doubled the number of listed instruments.

38. The idol's name "Bēl" is not mentioned in Dan 3, but occurs in LXX chap. 14, which is also referred to as Bel and the Dragon in verses 2, 6, etc. Bel was well known to the Armenian tradition as a wicked Babylonian king, who expelled Hayk, the eponymous ancestor of the Armenians, from Mesopotamia, after which they settled in the Armenian highlands: See Movsēs Xorenacʻi 1.10–11.

39. This word is unknown.

40. Cf. Prayer of Azariah 24. The figure of forty-nine is perhaps derived from Dan 3:19 where Nebuchadnezzar orders the fire to be heated seven times more than usual. Otherwise, no source known to me has this figure.

41. Cf. Dan 3:6.

42. Perhaps meaning "the minor nobility."

43. Cf. Dan 3:8–12.

44. Cf. Dan 3:13–14. The king's attitude is portrayed as less hostile than in Dan 3:13 where he falls into "a furious rage."

45. Cf. Deut 30:19.

sun and the moon all[46] are created by Him. If you recognize Him, you will achieve great glory."[47]

11/ The king said, "Whence do you know him?" Anania said, "God spoke concerning our fathers, for we have laws and books from/by them, and by that we know God, that he is our Savior and Vivifier."[48] The king said, "When you have a God (who is) such a protector, why was he not able to save you from my hands?"[49]

12/ The young men said that, "In the former time of our fathers, kings even greater than you arose against our people and they were unable to do anything, but were trampled underfoot. Then, on account of our parents who did many sins and evils, because of that God was angry against us, and gave us as captives into your hands."[50]

13/ The king said that, "I will cast you into the midst of the flaming fire. When I see (that)[51] your God saves you from this fire, I too will worship your God." The young men said, "We are ready unto death, tortures and for fire for the sake of the name of our God, so do that which you know."[52]

---

46. Perhaps "all" is a relic of another phrase, somewhat like, "and all the stars," or "and all the host of heaven." This second phrase is quite common in the Hebrew Bible.

47. The dialogue which is reported in §§10–11 is more complex than in Daniel. There, moreover, all three young men speak in concert. Here the spokesman is Azariah in §10 and Ananiah in §11. Only their final answer, reported in 3:12, is given jointly. The argument from creation is common and is very prominent in the Abraham traditions: see Stone, *Abraham*, 42, 51–53, etc.

48. This argument is uncommon and hard to parallel from the Bible or the apocryphal literature. That is natural, of course. The existence of ancient books becomes a stronger argument as the idea of inspired scripture develops. The appeal to ancient writings as probative is to be found in a wide range of Jewish, Christian, and pagan literature. It is discussed in a broad perspective by Wolfgang Speyer, *Die literarische Fälschung im heidnischen und christlichen Altertum: Ein versuchlicher Deutung* (Munich: Beck, 1971).

49. The text here is constructed on Dan 3:15 where there is a similar question, though there it is rhetorical and not a real enquiry.

50. The idea that exile is due to sins is commonplace, see Azariah 4–9. Moreover, that it was due to the sins of the exiles' ancestors is to be found in Dan 9:8, 16; Ezra 9:7; Neh 9:2, 26–30 and other sources.

51. Perhaps the common corruption of qḥ into q-. Thus we translate.

52. Compare Dan 3:17. The biblical text regards the furnace as a means of execution (Dan 3:19–22). In the text here, the event is formulated as an ordeal, a trial of God's power, like in Bel and the Dragon 8–9. If the young men survive, the king will accept God. The acceptance of God by the king is related in Daniel in v. 26 of this chapter and elsewhere in the book. Bringing about the king's explicit acknowledgement of the might of God is one of the main points of the court tales of Daniel. See Dan 3:28–29; 4:37; 6:26–27. On the intention of these court tales in Daniel see John J. Collins, *Daniel, with an Introduction to*

14/ And the king commanded to tie the three onto one plank. And six men seized the young men and cast (them) into the midst of the furnace.[53] And directly, a cloud became a shelter over them[54] and dropped dew in the midst of the furnace. And from it a cold wind went forth and put the fire's flame to flight from them and it burnt the enemies who were around it.[55]

15/ And the king was wrath and having spread <naphtha>[56] and oil over them[57] with a long beam and wood[58] he caused the flame to flame up. And it burnt whoever was there[59] around them.

+1016/ Then the king looked and saw that the freed young men in the midst of the furnace were praying, blessing, and praising God.[60] And they were saying: "You are blessed, Lord God of our fathers. Your name be blessed (and)

Apocalyptic Literature, FOTL 20 (Grand Rapids: Eerdmans, 1984), 58–59, 65, 73. The element of God's intervention is absent from most other examples of the court tale genre and is rather unique to the Book of Daniel. Cf. Lawrence M. Wills, *The Jew in the Court of the Foreign King: Ancient Jewish Court Legends* (Minneapolis: Fortress, 1990), 22–23.

53. Cf. Dan 3:21–22. Daniel 3:21 says, "Then these men were bound in their mantles, their tunics, their hats, and their other garments, and they were cast into the burning fiery furnace." The garments are not mentioned by our text, while the plank is not in Daniel. The binding, however, is found in both Azariah and Daniel. It is an essential part of the narrative, required so that their release from their bonds may form part of the miracle: See Dan 3:25.

54. A cloud becomes a shelter for the hidden ark of the covenant according to Story of the Ark of the Covenant §32 in Stone, *Biblical Heroes*, 121; Concerning the Ark of God in Stone, *Biblical Heroes*, 127

55. Cf. Prayer of Azariah 26–27. There, and in Dan 3:25, 28, an angel is mentioned, who is not present here. Paradisiacal dew is mentioned in LAB 26:8 and in Hours of the Day and Night Nviii (Stone, *Adam and Eve*, 171—a unique reading of the Armenian there). This description here is apparently a development of Azariah 27 which relates that the angel "made the midst of the furnace like a moist whistling wind, so that the fire did not touch them at all or hurt or trouble them."

56. Reading նաւթ "naphtha," as in the text of Azariah 23, for նիւթ "material" of the manuscript, from which it differs by one letter.

57. These details are drawn from Azariah 23.

58. The origin of this detail is unclear but it involves stoking the fire with additional fuel.

59. Literally: whatever (people, things) were found. A second attempt to burn the three is not mentioned by Daniel or Song of Azariah. However, it arose as a result of reading Daniel and the Song as part of one continuous text, which is how they appear in the Armenian Bible, as well as in the LXX. It is likely then, that Song of Azariah 23–27 was interpreted as a second attempt to burn the three. This is confirmed by the detail of the flammable materials that the king's servants fed to the fire.

60. In the biblical text the king does not see them pray, but only walking unhurt with a fourth figure. Once again, the angel is missing from this text.

glorified forever."[61] And they said the psalm "Fathers"[62] in the midst of the furnace up to that point at which they say, "Bless Anania, Azaria, and Mishael, praise the Lord."[63]

17/ And the king looked; four persons appeared in the midst of the fire and he was amazed and said, "I cast three persons into the midst of the fire and, behold, four are visible, and the appearance of the other[64] is fearsome and terrifying."[65] And the king called out (and) said, "Come out you servants of God, for I will praise the undying King with you."[66]

18/ Then the three young men prayed so much in the midst of the furnace that the fire was extinguished.[67] And then they went out of the furnace and openly preached God.[68] Then the king freed all Israel; free and without impost they dwelt in Babylon.[69]

And after Nebuchadnezzar, his son ruled.

---

61. This is adapted from the first line of the Songs of Azariah and The Three Hebrews, found in Greek Dan 3:26–86. This paean of praise is included among the Odes in the Armenian Psalter, but its text there is not identical with the text preserved in Daniel.
62. The reference is to the Songs of Azariah and The Three Hebrews Dan 3:26.
63. This refers to Dan 3:88. The prayer is not mentioned in MT Daniel.
64. That is, the additional.
65. Cf. Dan 3:24–25.
66. Cf. Dan 3:26.
67. This is not in accordance with the biblical text, see Dan 3:26.
68. Again, a nonbiblical detail. The king's praise of God, undertaken in §3 above, is not recorded.
69. Another nonbiblical element.

PART 5

THE SIBYL AND KING SOLOMON

22. Concerning the Sibyl, a Woman Philosopher

Introductory Remarks

The text is found in Matenadaran M101 on fol 104v. Manuscript M101 is a miscellany copied in 1740.[1] In the catalogue description of this manuscript, item 1 covering fols 1c–210r is *The Writings of John Damascenus*.[2] From that entry it may be inferred that this paragraph on the Sibyl originated in some learned work, perhaps of compilatory character. Fol 104v also contains, in addition to the text given here below paragraphs on Aristotle, Vergil and the heading for a section on Plato. Thus, it makes the impression of being a doxographic collection,[3] parallel to those surviving in Greek and other oriental languages. In addition, the manuscript includes an adaptation of The Short Story of Elijah, which has been published.[4]

The ancient and medieval Sibylline literature is extensive and it is discussed by various scholars, such as Herbert W. Parke and others.[5] Much information may also be found in two works by John J. Collins, which focus primarily on the older corpus of Sibylline oracles that includes Jewish and Christian elements.[6] Collins also produced a translation and commentary on

---

1. *General Catalogue* 1:419–432. The existence of this short work in the manuscript is not noted by the *General Catalogue*.
2. The work by John Damascenus is listed in that catalogue on p. 419 as no. 1.
3. See Jaap Mansfeld, "Doxography of Ancient Philosophy," Stanford Encyclopedia of Philosophy, online, 2004.
4. Stone, *Biblical Heroes*, text no. 14, 175–79.
5. Herbert W. Parke, *Sibyls and Sibylline Prophecy in Classical Antiquity* (London: Routledge, 1988).
6. John J. Collins, *The Sibylline Oracles of Egyptian Judaism*, SBLDS 13 (Missoula, MT, Scholars Press: 1974) and Collins, *Seers, Sibyls and Sages in Hellenistic-Roman Judaism*, JSJSup 54 (Leiden: Brill, 1997).

these traditional collections with a solid introduction.[7] The texts by and about the various Sibyls did not cease with the emergence of the corpus of the well-known Jewish and Christian Sibylline Oracles and it is clear that the fragment published here is part of a developed later tradition.[8]

In general, the Armenians knew medieval traditions the origins of which lay in classical antiquity.[9] In the last section of Names, Works, and Deaths of the Holy Prophets we find a reference to a pagan prophet, to a Cyclops, and to Polyphemus apparently drawn from a Latin source[10] and other instances exist.[11]

Lorenzo DiTommaso graciously added the following remarks on the medieval Sibylline tradition, a subject of his current research.

Regarding the Armenian Text, "Concerning the Sibyl, A Woman Philosopher" (Matenadaran M101, fol 104v)
Lorenzo DiTommaso

This short Armenian Sibylline piece does not appear to exist in other languages or versions. Indeed, it does not mention a Sibyl except in its title, and even here she is called only "the Sibyl." Yet the text's connection with the Sibylline tradition is evident in its setting in the temple of Apollo and in the prophecy of Christ's birth.

Many of the Sibyls of classical Greece and Rome were associated with temples and sites connected to Apollo, including the Cumaean Sibyl of Vergil's *Aeneid*, who pronounced her oracles in her role as the priestess of the Apollonian temple at Cumae near Naples. Although most Sibylline prophecies that were uttered in response to supplicants in situ went unrecorded, written oracles and books of oracles associated with various Sibyls were common-

---

7. In James H. Charlesworth, ed. *The Old Testament Pseudepigrapha* (Garden City, NY: Doubleday, 1983), 1:317–472.

8. A good example of this is Paul Julius Alexander, *The Oracle of Baalbek : The Tiburtine Sibyl in Greek Dress* (Washington: Dumbarton Oaks, 1967).

9. Gohar Muradyan, *Echoes of Ancient Greek Myths in Medieval Armenian Literature* (Հին հունական առասպելների արձագանքները հայ միջնադարյան մատենագրության մեջ) (Erevan: Nairi, 2014) deals in detail with the knowledge of Greek mythology among the Armenians. This useful work is soon to appear in a new edition in English. The present text is an excellent example of what could migrate into Hellenistic and various Christian cultures and thence into Armenian.

10. Stone, *Patriarchs and Prophets*, 172–173.

11. On the subject of medieval Armenians' knowledge of ancient Greek traditions, see the abundant sources adduced in Muradyan, *Echoes of Ancient Greek Myths*.

place. The most famous collection was the Libri Sibyllini of Rome. Disposed in Greek epic hexameters, the Libri were kept in the temple of Jupiter Capitolinus and officially consulted in times of national emergency. Reconstituted after a fire in 83 BCE, they survived until the early fifth century CE. Unlike the Libri Sibyllini and much of the religious universe of classical antiquity, the Sibyls survived the Roman Empire's conversion to Christianity, mainly for two reasons. First, the early Christians accepted the Sibylline Oracles of early Judaism, and eventually composed new oracles, rounding out the collection to the twelve "books" now known to scholars. Like their classical antecedents, these Sibylline Oracles are set out in Greek hexameters, but are apocalyptic in their outlook and eschatological in their focus.[12]

Second, the church fathers regarded the Sibylline Oracles and Sibyls in general as vehicles for a special dispensation in which Christian "truths" such as monotheism and the Trinity were revealed by God to the pagans. This understanding stood behind the composition of short prophecies about the life of Christ that were attributed to the classical Sibyls, either singly or as part of a group of ten or twelve, and to which an iconography was later added wherein each Sibyl was associated with a special symbol.

This, I suspect, is the context of the Sibylline piece of manuscript M101. Most of the Sibylline prophecies concern Christ's birth, as we find in the text here, and a few also refer to the cross of the crucifixion, which is the "wood" mentioned in line 1. The Sibyls have an old connection with the cross. In Sib. Or. 6.26–28 (second century CE), the Sibyl prophesizes, "O wood, o most blessed, on which God was stretched out; / earth will not contain you, but you will see heaven as home / when your fiery eye, o God, flashes like lightning" (transl. John J. Collins, cf. also Sib. Or. 5.257). By the eighth century CE, a Babylonian or Egyptian Sibyl ("Sabba") had become fused with the biblical queen of Sheba, and in this form was later inserted into the "Legend of the Wood of the Cross" as a prophetic figure with foreknowledge of the Passion. That said, I am unaware of a Christian Sibylline prophecy that parallels this text's reference to Christ's form as "fire and man" or its reference to an offering of "bread and wine."

---

12. The best edition remains that of Johannes Geffcken, *Die Oracula Sibyllina* (Leipzig: Hinrichs, 1902).

Text

Սիբիլայ կնոջ իմաստասիրի

M101 Ո՛վ երանեալ փայտ, քանզի օծեալ Միածինն տարածէ ի վերայ քո զանարատ բազուկս իւր:

Ուն գետնակոչ ի տաճարին Ապողոնի հարցին եւ ասեն. «Մարգարէաց մեզ, ո՛վ սուրբդ եւ գէտ, պարգեւող գիտնական, զի՞նչ լինի տաճարիս այսմիկ»։ Եւ նա ասէ. «Երրորդութիւնն մի է՛ միայն Աստուած բարձրեալ, եւ Բան նորա անպակասն գայ եւ ի կուսէ երիտասարդուհւոյ ծնանի, եւ ի կերպ հրոյ եւ մարդոյ յաշխարհի շրջի, զամենայն ըմբռնէ, եւ հաց եւ գինի իւր պատարագ մատուցանէ, նմա լինէ տունս այս, զի Տէր է անուն նորա»:

Translation

Of the Sibyl, a Woman Philosopher.

O, Wood, blessed because the anointed Only-begotten spread out his immaculate arms upon you.

They asked a certain geomancer in the temple of Apollo and said, "Prophesy to us, O holy one and knower,[13] learned giver of gifts, "What will happen in this temple?" And he said, "The Trinity is only one: God Most High and his Word comes lacking nothing. He is born from a young virgin, and in the form of fire and man he goes around in the world. He comprehends all and offers bread and wine as his offering. His will be this house (i.e., the Temple of Apollo) for Lord is his name."[14]

---

13. Or: magician.

14. This is, perhaps, a reminiscence of the Christian Byzantine Empire's conversion of pagan temples into churches. Gohar Muradyan drew my attention to a passage in which Grigor Magistros (tenth century) refers to the stripping of stones from temples of Apollo and their reuse in churches; see MH (Matenagirkʻ Hayocʻ), vol. 16, letter 17 [ԺԷ], p. 254.

23. Questions and Answers from Holy Books

Introductory Remarks

Lists and Questions and Answers

It is worth noting that the many Armenian apocryphal traditions are embedded in different instances and varieties of lists.[1] Such list literature is rather ancient, and it seems most likely that in the Armenian cultural realm, it was cultivated in a scholastic tradition and context. Examples of varied lists that have been published include:[2] Lists of Prophets' Names;[3] The Seventy-Two Languages;[4] Names of the Patriarchs;[5] Names of the Wives of the Forefathers and Patriarchs;[6] Names of the Four Matriarchs;[7] The Ten Trials of Abraham;[8] Concerning the Twelve Hours of the Night;[9] Concerning the Names of the Twenty-Four Hours of the Day and Night;[10] The Twelve Gifts Lost by Adam;[11]

---

1. The importance of these lists from an apocryphal perspective was already noted in Michael E. Stone, "The Armenian Apocryphal Literature: Translation and Creation," in *Il Caucaso: Cerniera fra culture dal mediterraneo alla Persia (secoli IV–XI), 20–26 aprile 1995*, Settimane di studio dal centro italiano de studi sull'alto medioevo 43 (Spoleto: Presso la Sede del Centro, 1996), 638.
2. Chronological lists are not included in the enumeration below. A number of such are published in Stone, *Angels and Heroes*, 25–64.
3. Stone, *Adam and Eve*, 174–75, four lists.
4. Stone, *Adam and Eve*, 161; the oldest form of this material is to be found in the Chronography of Philo of Tikor, MH, 906 §57 and see p. 66 n. 80 above.
5. Stone, *Adam and Eve*, 164. Lowndes W. Lipscomb. "A Tradition From the Book of Jubilees in Armenian," *JJS* 29 (1978): 149–63.
6. Philo of Tikor, MH, §165.
7. Stone, *Adam and Eve*, 167.
8. Stone, *Abraham*, 204–5.
9. Stone, *Angels and Heroes*, 1.
10. *Angels and Heroes*, 1–4.
11. Stone, *Angels and Heros*, 12–16, two lists.

and Signs and Wonders of the Temple.[12] This literary genre and its function in the Armenian tradition are worthy of monographic study.[13]

Within the general category of lists, and of very considerable antiquity, is a subcategory constituted of lists of Questions and Answers focused on a specific text, predominantly biblical texts. The oldest documents of this type surviving in Armenian are most likely the two treatises, Questions on Genesis and on Exodus originally composed by Philo of Alexandria at the turn of the era and early translated into Armenian. These Jewish texts are related, in turn, to the exegetical school developed in Alexandria at the focus of which stood the Homeric epics.[14] So this genre's origins lie in the Hellenistic exegetical tradition and it was adopted in late antiquity as an exegetical and polemical tool. Lists of Questions and Answers subsequently became, in Christian hands, a favored tool both of exegesis and of polemic.[15]

Thus, there exist in Armenian, as in many other Christian languages, documents composed of texts of questions and answers about the Bible, usually elucidating details of the biblical narratives. This genre of texts is widespread.[16] In addition to such lists of questions, there are instances in parabiblical narratives where it is transparent that a particular turn of the tale is taken

---

12. Stone, *Further Armenian Apocrypha*, forthcoming.

13. I first wrote about these lists in 1996; see Stone, "The Armenian Apocryphal Literature: Translation and Creation."

14. On the connection between Alexandrian Homeric scholarship and Rabbinic learning, see Yakir Paz, "From Scribes to Scholars Rabbinic Biblical Exegesis in Light of the Homeric Commentaries," PhD diss., Hebrew University of Jerusalem, 2014.

15. However, there were also forms of Second Temple Jewish literature that cultivate series of questions set in the mouth of a biblical hero or of a saint or other significant figure together with answers given by angels or God. Thus, as well as texts in which the questions are posed by an anonymous interlocutor, there are dialogic compositions in which the questions are asked by a named hero. Such erotapokritic dialogues are to be found in many apocalyptic revelatory texts, an early example being the Book of the Watchers. Not dissimilar series of questions occur in heavenly ascent visions such as 3 Baruch; and in the Dialogic Dispute form, so beloved of 4 Ezra. For examples of such texts in Armenian, see the published writings Questions of Ezra and Questions of St. Gregory, as well as the sapiental erotapocritic work, translated into Armenian from Syriac, Questions of the Queen and Answers of King Solomon. Moreover, this literature is even more complicated than this and must await discussion at a future time. See the preliminary discussion in Stone, *Biblical Heroes*, 9–11.

16. In addition to the works mentioned in the discussion above, there are also some lists that contain only answers in the form of a staccato series of assertions that frequently betray the questions that generated them.

or a specific detail is stressed that implicitly responds to a question, though the question itself is suppressed as not appropriate for use in a narrative text.

There are very substantial medieval Armenian assemblages of questions and answers concerning narratives and other subjects from the Bible. The most famous are, perhaps, parts of both the *Book of Questions* of Vanakan vardapet Taušecʻi (1181–1251) and the *Book of Questions* of Grigor Tatʻewacʻi (1346–1409), but a number of other texts exist, some attributed and some anonymous.[17] The texts published here are a sample of a very extensive literature. Certain of the texts in this and preceding volumes of Armenian pseudepigrapha may be reckoned with this genre. Such include, in addition to the text immediately following, Abel and Other Pieces (Stone, *Adam and Eve*, 141–157); History of the Forefathers, Adam, Sons and Grandsons §15 (Stone, *Adam and Eve*, 187–200); Abraham in an Elenchic Text (Stone, *Abraham*, 125–26); Questions on Melchizedek, (*Abraham*, 239–40); Questions on Archangels (Stone, *Angels*, 72–75); Praises of Angels (Stone, *Angels*, 77–81); Questions concerning Angels (Stone, *Angels*, 83–92); History of the Discourse (Stone, *Angels*, 101–6); Concerning Tower 2 (Stone, *Angels*, 114–15); Concerning Jannes and Mambres, Angels (Stone, *Angels*, 257–61). A number of such texts are included in the present volume.

Questions and Answers from Holy Books

The text of part of this work was published in Stone, *Angels and Heroes*, 92–101 from a miscellany, M1654 (1336), fols 189v–197v.[18] The photographs then available to me of the text in M1654 were incomplete, and so I edited the amount of text then available. Since that time, two developments have taken place. The first is that I have received the photographs of the rest of Questions and Answers from Holy Books contained in M1654. Intriguingly, one folio (two pages) in the middle of the work was blank, but from the photographs, it appears its paper is the same as that bearing the adjoining document. So, I concluded that these blank pages represent a lacuna in the manuscript's

---

17. See Roberta R. Ervine, "Antecedents and Parallels to Some Questions and Answers on Genesis in Vanakan Vardapet's Book of Questions," *Le Muséon* 113 (2000): 417–28; Tatʻewacʻi, *Book of Questions*. It is my hope to conduct a further study of such features of these bible-related texts with the aim of gaining insight into at least one nexus of the genesis of Armenian parabiblical creativity, that it, the scholastic tradition. Other features relevant to such an enquiry are the calendary, astronomical, and astrological knowledge exhibited by some documents.

18. *General Catalogue* 5:767.

exemplar. This was borne out when the text preserved in M1254 became available to me.

In addition to M1654, I now have at my disposal two further, later copies of this work, one taken from M1254, a seventeenth-century miscellany, fols 156v–159v[19] and the other from M1405, an eighteenth-century miscellany, fols 146r–148v.[20] Certain of the questions and answers that occur in M1254 are not found in the older ms M1654. These additional questions and answers are introduced into our diplomatic text of M1654 at the appropriate points, as is the text corresponding to the two blank pages of M1645. Thus, the text presented here is that of M1654 with complements from M1245. Such complementary text, introduced from M1254, is set off both by notices embedded in the text and by use of a different type face. Newly available text in M1654, following the end of that published in *Angels and Heroes*, is assigned section numbers sequential to those of the previous edition.[21] Where additional text occurs in M1254 between sections already numbered, it is noted as 00A/, 00B/, etc. The question and answer form has been discussed above, and these works undoubtedly originated in learned tradition.[22]

The critical apparatus contains readings in which M1254 differs from the text of M1654 printed here. Of course, there is no apparatus for those sections in which M1654 does not exist. Intriguingly, there are no blocks of text found in M1654 that are omitted from M1254. The apparatus and the text are followed by an annotated translation.

In addition to the text witnessed by the two manuscripts just mentioned, a much-shortened version of the document is preserved in M1405. This manuscript has one question unparalleled in the earlier copies (published as §65) and it abbreviates the questions and answers at many places, occasionally to detriment of clarity. Where its text is substantially like that of the longer recension, comments made in the context of the long recension are not repeated. Except for §1, the text in M1405 omits the tags հարց "question" and պատասխանի "answer."

---

19. *General Catalogue* 4:751.
20. *General Catalogue* 4:1188.
21. In *Angels and Heroes*, 92–93 an excursus on the Lamech traditions found in this document was published, authored by Asya Bereznyak. Since it is available in that work it is not reprinted here.
22. See also Michael E. Stone, "Biblical Text and Armenian Retelling," *JSAS* 26 (2017): 82–87.

23. QUESTIONS AND ANSWERS FROM HOLY BOOKS

The Present Edition

The present edition is organized as follows: First, I present a diplomatic edition of the text of M1654, into which I have introduced segments of text preserved in M1254 that do not appear in M1654. After that, I give the apparatus criticus of variant readings of M1254 collated against the diplomatic text of M1654. The lemma is M1654 and the variant is M1254.

The following variants are of purely orthographic character and occur regularly and are not included in the Apparatus Criticus.

-այ and -ոյ / -ա and -ն
-այա- / -աա-
այն / այնյ
դարձեալ / դարձել
-եաց / -եց in verb 3 pers sing. aor.
եթէ / եթէ and other instances of է- / ե-
Կաեն / Կայեն

I do not note instances of variation between Armenian numeral notations and the fully written-out numbers.

The previous translation has been revised throughout and translations of the newly published text added. The existing notes have also been reviewed and supplemented, and new notes added as required.

23.1. The Long Recension

Text

Title// M1654 / fol 189v / Հարցմունք եւ պատասխանիք ի Գրոց Սրբոց [Հարց: Մ]ինչ ոչ էին ստեղծեալ հրեշտակք եւ մարդիք, զաստուածութիւնն ո՞վ փառաւորէր։
Պատասխանի: Հայր յՈրդոյ փառաւորի, եւ Որդի ի Հաւրէ, եւ Սուրբ Հոգին ի նոցունց. փառաւորէին զմիմեանս։

2/ Հարց: Զի՞նչ յանցեւ սատանա:
Պատասխանի: Զի նման բարձրելոյն խորհեցաւ լինել։

3/ Հարց: Հրեշտակք կա՞ն ի նոյն երկեղի, եթէ՞ գուցէ անկան։
Պատասխանի: Այո՛, կան ի նոյն երկեղին հանապազ, վասն այնորիկ կան անդադար ի փառաբանութիւն։[23]

4/ Հարց: Մարդն Աստուծոյ պատկեր ի՞ւ կոչեցաւ, յորժամ ոչ էր նման պատկերի նորա։

---

[23]. A locative case would be expected.

Պատասխանի: Մարդն պատկեր Աստուծոյ վասն անձնիշխանութեանն կոչեցաւ:

5/ Հարց: Ս*ա*/ fol 190r /տանա գիտէ՞ր, եթէ քանի ծառ հրամաեց Աստուած ուտել Ադամա:

Պատասխանի: Գիտէր, վասն այնր, զի լուաւ ի Տէառնէ զասացելն առ Ադամ, վասն այնմիկ[24] եդ բանս ընդ կնոջն:[25]

6/ Հարց: Ադամ եւ կինն ի դրա՞խտն ստեղծան, եթէ՞ արտաքո դրախտին:

Պատասխանի: Արտաքո ստեղծան, վասն զի գրեալ է, թէ՝ «եդ անդ զմարդն, զոր ստեղծ»:

7/ Հարց: Քանի՞ ժամանակ եկաց Ադամ ի դրախտին, զի զինք՝ բազում ասեն, եւ այլք՝ ոչ աւր մի:

Պատասխանի: Վասն զի ի դրախտին ոչ տիւ կայր եւ ոչ գիշեր, այլ հանապազ լոյս էր, վասն այնր ոչ ոք գիտաց զսահմանս կենացն Ադամա:

8/ Հարց: Աւձն մարդկայի՞ն բարբառով խաւսեցաւ ընդ [կն]ոջն,[26] եթէ՞ իւր բարբառովն:[27] Պատասխանի: Ցանկայր աւձն մարդկային բարբա/fol 190v/ռոյս, վասն այնորիկ էմուտ ի նա սատանա եւ խաւսել ետ մարդկային բարբառովն:

9/ Հարց: Սատանա ունէ՞ր իշխանութիւն մտանել յաւձն, եթէ՞ ոչ: Պատասխանի: Ունէր, վասն զի թոյլ ետ Աստուած մտանել յաղագս փորձելոյ զմարդն:

From manuscript M1254:

9A// fol 157r / Հարց: Զի՞նչ է մաշկեղէն հանդերձն Ադամայ: Պատասխանի: Մաշկեղէնն յաղագս թանձրամած եւ ընդդիմամարտ[28] մարմնոյ է, որ մեք ստեղծաք:

M1654 resumes:

10/ Հարց: Բոցեղէն սուրն դեռ եւս պահէ՞ զդրախտն, եթէ՞ ոչ: Պատասխանի: Ի ձեռն խաչին բարձաւ սուրն ի միջո եւ բացաւ մեզ ճանապարհի ծառոյն կենաց:

---

24. This should, by standard grammar, be այնորիկ, a genitive and not a dative.
25. Observe the orthography for կնոջն.
26. Apparently, the text's ոջն is a remnant of <կնոջն> "woman" (GM).
27. վ over ւ p.m. in M1254.
28. M1405 has ընդդէմ մարդ մարմնոյ "against human body."

23. QUESTIONS AND ANSWERS FROM HOLY BOOKS 261

11/ Հարց: Եթէ Ադամ չէր յանցել, ի դրախտին կա՞յր հանապազ, թէ՞ ոչ:
Պատասխանի: Այո՛, փոխելոց էր որպէս թագաւոր յապարանից յապարանս:

12/ Հարց: Ապաշխարէ՞ց Կաեն, թէ՞ ոչ:
Պատասխանի: Ապաշխարեց ստոյգ, զի վասն նորա եկն ջրհեղեղն, եւ ապրեցաւ ի ջրհեղեղէն:²⁹

13/ Հարց: Կաեն յի՞նչ պատճառի եսպան զԱբէլ:/ fol 191r/
Պատասխանի: Զի իւր գործքն չար էին եւ եղբաւրն՝ բարիք:

14/ Հարց: Եւ Ղամեք յի՞նչ պատճառի եսպան զԿաեն:
Պատասխանի: Վասն նախատանաց ազգին իւր:

15/ Հարց: Մաթուսադա է՞ր ապրեցաւ շատ, քան զայլ մարդիկ:
Պատասխանի: Վասն առաքինութեանէ³⁰ հաւրն իւր Էնովքա:

16/ Հարց: Եւ զի՞նչ էր առաքինութիւնն Էնովքա:
Պատասխանի: Զի ի պոռ աշխարհիս ոչ ճաշակեցաւ:

17/ Հարց: Քանի՞ ամ կուսութեամբ եկաց Նո:
Պատասխանի: Շ. (500) ամ:

18/ Հարց: Եւ զի՞նչ պատճառի եկաց զայնչափ ժամանակս:
Պատասխանի: Վասն զի երկեւ ի չար ծննդոց ժամա<նա>կին,³¹ զի իւր ծնունդն էլ³² չար չլինէր:

19/ Հարց: Յորժա՞մ առ զկինն:
Պատասխանի: Յորժամ առ հրաման զտապանն շինելո:

20/ Հարց: Եւ քանի՞ ամ շինեց զտապանն Նո:
Պատասխանի: ՈՃ. (600) ամ:

21/ Հարց: Եւ քանի՞ աւր եկն ջրհեղ<եղ>ն:³³
/ fol 191v / Պատասխանի: Խ. (40) աւր:

22/ Հարց: Եւ ո՞ւր եղին զտապանն:
<Պատասխանի>: Ի լերինն Սարարադա յազատ Մազիս:

23/ Հարց: Եւ Նո վասն է՞ր անիծեց զորդին որդո իւրո, եւ ոչ զիւր որդին, որ յանցեւ:

---

29. The words եւ ապրեցաւ ի ջրհեղեղին are in the marg. s.m.: the omission was by haplography.
30. The use of the ablative is bizarre. Observe the odd case usage following վասն, which takes a genitive.
31. The text has ժամակին, which is corrupt.
32. Postclassical form of այլ. Indeed, this text has a lot of postclassical forms, such as երկեւ, անիծեց, and others.
33. The manuscript has ջրհեղն, which is corrupt by haplography.

Պատասխանի: Վասն զի Աստուած աւրհնել էր գանդրանիկն, վասն այնորիկ ոչ կարաց զաւրհնութիւն Աստուծոյ ընդ անիծաւք արկանել:

24/ Հարց: Ջաշտարակն յերկինս ելանելո պատճառա՞ւ շինեցին, թէ՞ յայլ պէտոս:

<Պատասխանի:>: Բ. (2) պատճարի[^34] շինեցին. մինն՝ յաղագս այնր, եթէ դարձե[ա]լ ջրհեղեղն լինելոց է, եւ միուսն[^35] այլ պատճառի, վասն զի կարի անհոգացել էին:

25/ Հարց: Մի՞ս յԱդամա՞յ եղեւ սկիսքն ուտելը:
Պատասխանի: Ոչ յԱդամա, այլ ի Նոէ հրամաեցաւ ուտել, նոյնպէս եւ զինին:

26/ Հարց: Ջի՞՞նչ խորհուրդ էր, զի զՄովսէս թաքուցին ձնդքն:
Պատասխանի: Վասն զի ի ձեռն նորա էր լինելոց փրկ/ fol 192r/ ութիւն Իսրայէլի:

27/ Հարց: Մովսէսի զի՞ր ետ Աստուած, եթէ՞ պատուիրան:
Պատասխանի: Ջերկունն՝ զիր եւ պատուիրան:

28/ Հարց: Ջի՞՞նչ պատճառաւ հրամեց Աստուած ժողովրդեանն խաբէութեամբ կողոպտել զեգիպտացիսն զզանձս իւրոց, մինչեւ ինքն հրամաեաց ամենեցուն Տէրն զարդար վաստակս վաստակել:

Պատասխանի: Ոչ եթէ կողոպտէր, այլ չորէք Ճ. (100) ամին դառն եւ խիստ ծառութեանն, զոր ծառեցին էգիպտացիոցն, զայն վարձ հրամաեց առնուլ

29/ Հարց: Մովսէսի ընդէ՞ր ոչ հրամաեց առնուլ:
Պատասխանի: Վասն զի ոչ էր աշխատել ի կան եւ յաղիսարկութիւնն:

30/[^36] Հարց: Ջքառասուն ամ ընդէ՞ր կացոյց զժողովուրդն յանապատին:

Պատասխանի: Վասն զի էգիպտական մոլորութեամբն թալալեալ էր /fol 192v / ժողովուրդն, վասն այնորիկ զխ. (40) ամ յանապատ սրբեց զնոսա: Եւ ապա հրամաեց մտանել յերկիրն աւետոց:

From manuscript M1254

---

[^34]: պատճառաւ p.m. in marg. B is grammatically preferable.
[^35]: Note the orthography.
[^36]: In the manuscript here, the Question and the Answer are erroneously metathesized and small supralinear բ and ա indicate that this is to be corrected.

23. QUESTIONS AND ANSWERS FROM HOLY BOOKS

30A/ / fol 157v / Հարց: Ընդէ՞ր բամբասեցին զՄովսէս Ահարոն եւ Մարիամ:[37]
Պատասխանի: Վասն այնր, զի կին էառ եթովպացի:

30B/ Հարց: Եւ Ահարոն ընդէ՞ր ոչ պատուհասեցաւ, այլ Մարիամ:
Պատասխանի: Վասն զի ոչ ունէր իշխանութիւն Մարիամ, զի[38] կին մարդ էր:

30C/ Հարց: Եւ Ահարոն ընդէ՞ր ոչ {պատուհասեցաւ}[39] յառաջեր ի ծովն թմբկաւն, այլ քոյրն:
Պատասխանի: Վասն զի Մարիամ կոյս էր, եւ թմբուկն աւրինակ էր կուսութեան:

Ms M1654 resumes:

31/ Հարց: Եւ ի ցամաքն ընդէ՞ր ոչ սատակեց զփարաւոն, այլ ի ծովն:
Պատասխանի: Վասն զՀ. (70) ամ զիսրայէլացոց զճնունդն ջրահեղցոյց[40] արար:
Վասն այնորիկ նովին ջրովն եւ ինքն սատակեցաւ:

32/ Հարց: Խոզն ի սկզբանէ՞ էր պիղծ, եթէ՞ Մովսէս ասաց զնա պիղծ:
<Պատասխանի>: Վասն զի, զոր ինչ ունէին եգիպտացիքն, զայն պեղծ համարեցաւ, եւ զոր ոչն ունէին, զայնոսիկ հրամեց ուտել:

33/ Հարց: Վէմն, որ երթայր զհետ յԻսրայէլի, կենդանի՞ էր, եթէ՞ անշունչ:
Պատասխանի: Այո, կենդանի էր, վասն զի վէմն էր ինքն Քրիստոս:

34/ Հարց: Եւ զհետ Իսրայէլի զիա՞րդ երթայր. տանէի՞ն, եթէ՞ ինքն երթայր:
Պատասխանի: Ոչ տանէին, այլ ինքն երթայր:

From M1254:

34A/ / fol 158v / Հարց: Մինչ Դաւիթ զԳողիաթ եհար, Սաւուղ ճանաչէ՞ր զԴօիթ, թէ ոչ:
Պատասխանի: Այոյ, ճանաչէր, վասն զի յառաջագոյն երգէր ի վերայ Սաւուղայ քնարօն:

M1654 resumes:

---

37. The question and answer are transposed in this section and this is marked in the manuscript. Compare the preceding n. 36.
38. զի above line, p.m.
39. This is a corrupt dittography from §30B, and is not translated.
40. Sic!

35/ Հարց: / fol 193r/ Ընդէ՞ր ոչ էթող Աստուած Դաւթի շինել զտաճարն, մինչ նա սուրբ էր, քան զՍողոմոն:
Պատասխանի: Վասն պատերազմացն չհրամաեցաւ Դաւթի:
36/ Հարց: Եւ զՍողոմոնի զաւուրսն ընդէ՞ր լիացոյց եւ խաղաղացոյց:
Պատասխանի: Վասն շինե[լ]ոյ զտաճարն:
37/ Հարց: Եւ Սողոմոնի [յ]անցանացն եղե՞ւ թողութիւն, թէ՞ ոչ:
Պատասխանի: <Ո>չ եղեւ թողութիւն:

From manuscript M1254:

37A/ / fol 158r / Հարց: Դաւտայ դուստերքն վասն պոռնկութեա՞ն խորհրդոյն ենջեցին ընդ հայրս իւրեանց, եթէ՞ այլ պատճառաւ:
Պատասխանի: Ոչ եթէ այլ պատճառաւ, այլ վասն ազգին իւրեանց. առ ի թողուլ նոցա զաւակ ի վերայ երկրի:
37B Հարց: Թողութիւն գտի՞ն, եթէ՞ ոչ:
Պատասխանի: Ոչ գտին թողութիւն:
37C/ Հարց: Եւ Սողոմանի յանցանացն եղե՞ւ թողութիւն, եթէ՞ ոչ:
Պատասխանի: Ոչ ընկալաւ թողութիւն:
37D/ Հարց: Եզեկիէլ<ի> տեսիլն զոսկերսն ցամաքեց. տեսի՞լ էր, եթէ՞ յարութիւն:
Պատասխանի: Տեսիլ եւ յարութիւն:

M1654 resumes:

38/ Հարց: Յունան ի Տեառնէ առաքեցաւ ի Նինվէ. ընդէ՞ր եղեւ փախստական յԱստուծոյ:
<Պատասխանի>: Վասն զի գիտէր զԱստուծոյ մարդասիրութիւնն, որ խափանելոց էր զմարգարէութիւն նորա:
39/ Հարց: Յովհաննէս ի ծնունդս կանայջի՞նչ պատճառ անուանեցաւ մեծ:
Պատասխանի: Վասն զի յորովայնէ երկրպագեց Քրիստոսի, զոր ոչ այլ ոք ի ծնունդս կանաց արար:
40/ Հարց: Եւ փոքրիկն յարքայութեանն մեծ ո՞վ է:
Պատասխանի: Ինքն Բանն Աստուած, որ եկն եւ վասն մեր փո/ fol 193v /քրկացաւ, զի զմեզ մեծս արասցէ:
41/ Հարց: Հրեշտակն, որ ասէին. «Ո՞վ է սա, որ դիմել գա յԵդովմա».

ի կուսէ՞ ծնընդեանն չին տեղեկ, եթէ՞ ի Հօրէ
Պատասխանի: Ի կուսէ ծնընդեանն միայն չին տեղեկ:
42/ Հարց: Սատանա մինչեւ ցո՞յր վայր ոչ գիտաց զՈրդի Աստուծոյ՝ ի մկրտութեա՞նն, եթէ՞ ի փորձութեանն, թէ՞ ի խաչելութեանն:

Պատասխանի: Հանապազ կայր ի կասկածի, բայց ի խաշելութեանն, յորժամ ի ձեռս Հաւր աւանդեց զհոգին, յայնժամն ապա զիտաց, եթէ Աստուած էր եւ Որդի Աստուծոյ:

43/ Հարց: Ի զալրստէն Տեառն անցանէ՞ երկիրս, եթէ՞ նորոգի:
Պատասխանի: Ոչ եթէ անցանէ, այլ նորոգի. ոչ եթէ վասն մեղաւորացն, այլ վասն արդարոցն, զի երեսնաւոր լինելզց են, որպէս եւ ասաց Քրիստոս եւ կարգեց երեսնաւոր զերկիրս. եւ Կ.աւր (60) զդր///

From M1254:

43/ fol 158r / continued/ . . . զի երեսնաւոր լինելզց են, որպէս եւ ասաց Քրիստոս եւ կարգեաց զերեսնաւոր զերկիրս եւ վաթսունաւոր զդրախտն, եւ հարիւրաւոր ի վերինն Երուսաղէմ:

44/ Հարց: Ի սրբոցն կա՞յ ոք ի դրախտին, եթէ՞ յունայն է ի մարդոյ:
Պատասխանի: Երկուք եղին, որ յանցեանն եւ երկուք մտին, որ առաքեցանն՝ Ենովք եւ Եղիայ:

45/ Հարց: Յորժամ Ենովք փոխեցաւ, եւե՞ս Ադամ զԵնովքայ փոխումն, եթէ՞ ոչ, կենդանի՞ էր, եթէ՞ ոչ:
Պատասխանի: Այոյ, կեն/ 158v /դանի էր Ադամ, զի այն, որ էր զրեալ, է վասն նորա. եթէ զոր աւրինակ փոխեցաւ Եղիայ եւ եւես զնայ Եղիսէ, է նոյն աւրինակ՝ փոխեցաւ Ենովք, եւ եւես զնայ Ադամ:

46/ Հարց: Եւ զի՞նչ էր պատճառն, որ եւես Ենովք Ադամայ:[41]
Պատասխանի: Վասն յանդիմանութեան մեղանց իւրոց եւ վասն յուսոյ կենաց իւրոց, զի ի կարծիս կայր եւ երկիւղի հանապազ, եթէ յուրոց[42] ծնընդոցն այլ ոք ոչ մտանէ յառաջին ժառանգութիւնն. վասն այնորիկ եւես աչաւք իւրովք զԵնովք՝ իւ ի դրախտն փոխեալ:

47/ Հարց: Վասն զի՞նչ պատճառի Աստուած փութապէս յանդիմանեաց զԿայէն:
Պատասխանի: Յաղագս յԱդամայ, զի յորժամ եհարց Ադամ զԿայէն, թէ. «Ո՞ւր է Աբէլ զեղբայր քո»,[43] նայ խափեալ[44] եթէ՝ ընդունելի եղեւ պատարագ նորա եւ փոխեցաւ ի դրախտն: Վասն

---

41. The oblique case is strange here.
42. Odd orthography of իւրոց.
43. Gen 4:9.
44. Reading as խաբեալ.

յայնորիկ յարագ յանդիմանեաց զնայ Աստուած, զի իմացի
Ադամ զանաւրէնութիւնն, զոր գործեաց Կայեն։
48/ Հարց։ Զի՞նչ էր սուրն, որ էսպան զԿայէն Աբէլ։
Պատասխանի։ Գալախազ էր։
49/ Հարց։ Քան յանցումն յանցեա՞լ Կայեն։
Պատասխանի։ Եաւթն վրէժն հատոյ<գ>[45] նմայ Աստուած։
50/ Հարց։ Եւ Ղամեքայ քանի՞ յուզեցան պատիժքն վասն սպանելոյ
նորա զԿայէն եւ գործին որդոյ նորա։
Պատասխանի։ Եաւթանասնեկին եաւթնյուզեցան պատուհասքն։
51/ Հարց։ Եւ վասն է՞ր յուզեցան ի նմանէ անչափ պատուհասքն։
Պատասխանի։ Վասն զի դատաստանաւն զանձ[46] արար
եւ ինքն դատապարտեաց զԿայեն, վասն այնորիկ առաւել
դատապարտեցաւ։
52/ Հարց։ Այն, որ ասաց Աստուած ցաւազակն. «Այսաւր ընդ իս իցես
ի դրախտին», նոյնժամա՞յն տարաւ զնայ ի դրախտն, եթէ՞ յետոյ է
տանելոց։
Պատասխանի։ Այսաւր զհազարսն նշանակէ եւ յետոյ տանելոց
է, զի հոգին եւ մարմինն ի միասին են ընդունելոց զհատուցումն
բարեաց եւ չարեաց, որպէս եւ գրեալ է, եթէ մի անգամ խաւսեցաւ
Աստուած եւ երկուք պայս լուաք։
53/ Հարց։ Զի՞նչ էր արծաթն, որ եառուն Յուդայի կամ ուստի՞ էր։
Պատասխանի։ Ոմանք ասեն, թէ այն արծաթն է, որ Աբրահամ
զայրն ի Քեբրոն զնեաց, եւ այլք ասեն, թէ այն արծաթն[47] է, որ ի
Եգիպտոսն[48] Յովսէփայ առին եղբայրք նորա,[49] բայց մեզ գիտելի
էր, եթէ ի ժամանակին դահեկանն արծաթի էր, որ ունէր տասն
դրամ, եւ առեալ ի տաճարին արծաթոյն, եառուն նմայ երեսուն
արծաթի, որ բաւական եղեւ ընդ ամենայն Գ-Ճ. (300) դրամ։
54/ Հարց։ Զի՞նչ է այն, որ ասէ յՕետարանն վասն Յուդայի, եթէ
յետ պատառոյն, ապայ եմուտ ի նայ <ս<ատանայ։[50] Եթէ ունէ՞ր
իշխանութիւն սատանայ մտանել ի նայ։

---

45. Emendation of հատոյն, which is corrupt by haplography.
46. Note the orthographic variant.
47. ն above line p.m.
48. The physical reading is difficult.
49. Apparently, a wrong case-ending. The preposition ի does not occur with the genitive. On the preceding word, the strange use of -ը may be observed. This has been noted quite often in medieval texts.
50. Emending the corrupt reading of the manuscript: տատանայ.

23. QUESTIONS AND ANSWERS FROM HOLY BOOKS 267

<Պատասխանի>: Եթէ կարացեալ էր սատանա ունել իշխանութիւն, յառաջագոյն եւ յայլ ընտրեալսն էր մտեալ, բայց յորժամ նայ զինքն արար անաւթ// ի սատանայի,[51] յայնժամ ապայ եմուտ ի նայ սատանայ:

55/ Հարց: Զի՞նչ պատճառ էր, որ ի Թափուրական լեռն գերիսն միայն եհան զաշակերտ<ս>ն[52] զՊետրոս եւ զՈհաննէ<ս>[53]{ր} եւ[54] զԱկոբոս՝ գորդին Զեբեդեայ, որպէս / fol 159r / զԱւետարանն ասէ. «Զայլսն ոչ տարաւ ընդ իւր ի վեր»:
Պատասխանի: Ոչ եթէ ընտրութիւն արար ի մէ<ջ>[55] նոցա եւ սոցայ, բայց վասն Յուդայի ոչ տարաւ զայլսն զամենայն, զի ոչ արար արժանի զնայ այնմ ահաւոր եւ սոսկալի տեսլեանն, որպէս եւ չեր իսկ արժանի:

M1654 195r resumes: From this point its text is used:

վասն զի գիտէր զնորա զանզեղջականլի եւ զանագորոն զմիտսն, զի եթէ զայլսն եւս ընդ իւր տարել զմետասանսն ի լեռն, եւ զնա միայն թողեալ, նա յաղտեղի[56] բերանայպաց էր լեալ յաղագս իւրր չարութեանն: Վասն այնորիկ ամենատէրն զպատճառսն էբարձ ի միջոյ:

56/ Հարց: Ի խաչելութեանն Տեառն յարեան բազումք ի ննջեցելոց սրբոց, դարձեալ մեռա՞ն, եթէ՞ կենդանի փոխեցան:
Պատասխանի: Յաւուր ուրբաթուն յարեան, եւ յետ յարութեանն նորա մտին ի քաղաքն սուրբ, որպէս ասէ աւետարանագիրն, զի մի առ աչաւք համարեսցեն զեղեալսն եւ դարձ<ա>լ ննջեցին, այլ ումանք ասեն, եթէ կենդանիք են մնացին եւ յանմահութեանն են ընդ Ենովքա եւ ընդ Եղիայի:

§§57 and 58 are not in M1654 and are given here according to M1254:

---

51. The case ending is anomalous; see n. 49.
52. Emended from the singular.
53. The manuscript has, corruptly, զՈհաննէր.
54. The copyist here caused confusion. He erred in the last letter of the name Ոհաննէս "John" and he wrote եւ twice.
55. Emending the corrupt reading of the manuscript: մէն.
56. Read as: աղտեղի "filthy."

57/ Հարց: Զի՞նչ էր բանն, զոր ասաց Զաքարիայ ի վերայ հրէական ազգի, եթէ՛ ծանիցեն քանանացիքն գխաշինս պահեստի⁵⁷ իմոյ, զի բան Տեառն է:
Պատասխանի: Վասն զի {քանանացոցն ազգն}⁵⁸ հրէական ազգն ի քանանացոց աշխարհին էին բնակեալ եւ զնոցա զկուտադեալ եւ զարիւնարբայ⁵⁹ զբարսն ի յանձինս իւրեանց էին ստացեալ, եւ զորոց զբարսն ստացան, զնոցին եւ զանուն ժառանգեցին, վասն այնորիկ անուանեցան քանանացիք:

58/ Հարց: Եւ ո՞վ էին խաշինքն պահեստի իմոյ:
Պատասխանի: Խաշինք զտաքեալսն անուանեաց, որպէս ինքն ասաց, եթէ՛ առաքեմ զձեզ իբրեւ գոչխարս ի մէջ գայլոց:

M1654 resumes:

59/ Հարց: Յերկրէ, որ առ/ fol 195v /աւել բարի գործեն, քան զքրիստոնեայք, կորընչի՞ն, թէ՞ ոչ:
Պատասխանի: Զայդ եւ Տէրն իսկ ասաց, եթէ. «Որ ոչ հաւատա Որդո, բարկութիւնն Աստուծոյ մնա ի վերայ նորա»: Եւ դարձեալ ասէ, թէ. «Որ ոչ ծնցի ի ջրո եւ ի հոգո, ոչ կարէ մտանել յարքայութիւնն Աստուծոյ»: Այլ դու մի քննել զանքննելին եւ մի հետազաւտել զդատաստան նորա:

60/ Հարց: Իցէ՞ ծանաւթութիւն յարքաութեանն Աստուծոյ, եթէ՞ ոչ:
Պատասխանի: Այո, կարի առաւել ծանաւթութիւն ունին, ոչ միայն յիւրոց յազգականսն, եւ այլ եւ առ ամենայն արդարսն, որպէս եւ ի Թափառական լերինն, որ⁶⁰ ծանեն առաքեալքն զՄովսէս եւ զԵղիա:

61/ Հարց: Եւ ի դժոխքն⁶¹ ունի՞ն ծանաւթութիւն, թէ՞ ոչ:
Պատասխանի: Զայդ եւ Յոհան Ոսկեբերանն վկայէ, թէ՛ կարի ան/ fol 196r /հնարին տանջանս է⁶² մեղաւորաց, որք զիւրոց անձինս միայն տեսանեն ի տանջանսն:

62/ Հարց: Ծերն եւ երիտասարդն որպիսի՞ հասակաւ յառնեն ի մեռելոց ի յարութեանն. երիտասա՞րդք, եթէ՞ ծերք:

---

57. ա is written over g, p.m.
58. These two words are a dittography and a corruption, perhaps in two distinct stages. They are not translated.
59. This appears to be a variant spelling of արիւնարբու "bloodthirsty."
60. For variation of որ / ուր, see Stone and Hillel, "Index," no. 407.
61. Observe once more the strange case usage.
62. The accusative of տանջանս and the singular of է are both odd from the perspective of normative Ancient Armenian grammar.

Պատասխանի: Երիտասարդք են յառնելոց ամենեքեան, վասն զի ծերն ոչ կարէ ստանալ ժառանկութիւն, այլ ամենեքեան այնպէս լինին, որպէս զԱդամ, որ ի դրախտին էր, եւ որպէս Քրիստոս, որ ի վերայ երկրի:

63/ Հարց: Իցէ՞ ճաշակումն յարքայութեանն երկնից:
Պատասխանի: Զայդ Պաւղոս վկայէ, թէ՛ ոչ է արքայութիւնն Աստուծոյ կերակուր եւ ըմբելի, այլ արդարութիւն եւ խաղաղութիւն, եւ խնդութիւն ի Հոգին Սուրբ:

64/ Հարց: Խաչն, որ ընդ յամբս գալոցէ, ա՞յս է, որ ի յերկրիս է, եթէ՛ այն, որ ընդ իւր տար/ fol 196v /ալ, որպէս ասէ Յոհան Ոսկէբերանն:
Պատասխանի: Մի խաչ էր, որ յերկինս եւ յերկրի, այլ զոր Յոհան ասէ, եթէ՛ առել ընդ իւր տարաւ ի վեր. ոչ եթէ զխաչն տարաւ, այլ գշարշարանս խաչին եւ ազեստն յարեն թաթաւել, որպէս եւ երկնային գաւրքն վկաեն:

65/ Հարց: Լուսաւորք եւ աստեղք ի յարութեանն բանին ի միջոր, եթէ՛ ոչ:
Պատասխանի: Ոչ բառնին, այլ առաւել պատիւ են ընդունելոց, որպէս եւ վկայէ Յեսայի մարգարէ, թէ. «Եղիցի լոյս լուսնին իբրեւ զլոյս արեգականն, եւ լոյս արեգականն եւթնապատիկ եղիցի»: Այլ խաւարումն վասն այնորիկ կոչէ գիրք, զի ար աստուածային լուսովն նոցային եւագել գտանի, որպէս եւ արեգականբն ճրագն:

66/ Հարց: Ձո/ fol 197r /րք մնա՞ն, եթէ՛ գամաքին յետ յարութեանն:
Պատասխանի: Յաւիտենից ջուրքն ոչ գամաքին, վասն զի նոյն երկիրս ի վերայ չրի է հաստատէ[ա]լ, այլ տեսանելի ջուրքս գամաքին, որպէս եւ գրել է, թէ. «Յամաքի ծով, հիանան արարածք ամենայն»:

67/ Հարց: Հրեշտակ[63] եւ մարդիք արդարք ունի՞ն փառաբանութիւն յարքայութեանն,[64] եթէ՛ ոչ:
Պատասխանի: Այո, մեծ փառաբանութիւն եւ գովութիւն յայնժամ ելանելոց է յարքայութեանն, զի եթէ երկրաւոր թագաւորս յորժամ զաւրաց իւրոց պարզեւ եւ մեծութիւնս շնորհեն, բազում գովութիւն եւ պատիւ ընդունին ի գորացն: Որչափ եւս առաւել, որ Տէրն է ամենեցուն, եւ զամենեսեան զհրեշտակս եւ զարդարս պասկելոցէ, եւ խառնո<ւ>րդս[65] առել/ fol 197v /ոցէ ընդ միմեանս, որպէս փառաբանութիւն պարտ է մատուցանել Աստուծոյ:

---

63. This is a plur. with the loss of the plur. ending -ք, as happens sometimes in words ending in -կ. See Stone and Hillel, "Index," no. 333.

64. A locative case would be expected.

65. Orthographic correction.

68/ Հարց: Ադամ յաղագս պատուիրանազանցութեա՞ն եկեր զպտուղն, եթէ՞ յաղագս կնոջն ողորմելոյ:
Պատասխանի: Ադամ ոչ է պարտեալ եւ ոչ է յանցեալ ընդ պատուիրանաւն, որպէս Պաւղոս վկայէ, եթէ՛ Ադամ ոչ պարտեւ, այլ կինն պարտեցաւ եւ յանցեւ: Եւ ճաշակեց Ադամ վասն կնոջն ողորմելոյ,
եւ Քրիստոս նմա եւ մեզ ողորմեցաւ եւ ողորմի, եւ ինքն արհնեալ յաւիտեանս. ամէն:

Apparatus

   Lemma   M1654   A
   Variant   M1254   B

1/ հրեշտակ B | փառաւորէր B
2/ յանցեւ B
3/ երկիրդի] անկան] անկանիցին B | երկիրդին bis B | յանդադար B | ի3°] om B
4/ պատկեր Աստուծոյ B | էր] են B | անձնիշխանութեան B
5/ յԱդամայ B | լուաւ B
6/ յարտաքոյ B | դրախտին] om B
7/ դրախտն] այլք] այլ եւ B | գիտաց] կարաց գիտել B | յԱդամայ B
8/ ոչն] կնոջն B : this is the correct reading | բարբառովն B |
9/ 2°] ոչ ունէր իշխանութիւն մտանել B
10/ միջն] միջոյ B : preferable
11/ յԱդամ B
12/ եկն] երեկ B
13/ զինչ պատճառի] յինչ պատճառս B | բարի B
14/ պատճառ B
15/ inc.] հարց B | Մաթուսադա --- շատ] Մաթուսադար ընդէ՞ր եղեւ յերկայնակեաց առաւել քան B | մարդիք B | առաջինութեան : preferable B | իւրոյ B
16/ յառաջինութիւնն յեւնվքայ B | ոչ ճաշակեցաւ] ոչ ինչ ճաշակեցաւ ի յերկրաւորացս
17/ Նոյ B | հինկ B
18/ պատճառաւ B | ժամանակս] + ա` կուսութեամբ B | վասն] om B | երկեաւ] ժամանակին B + նոյն B | զի] թէ B | ծնունդն] ծնունդքն + զնոյն : (ն3° s.m.*) նախանձ բերեն զանձինս իւրոց B
19/ inc.] եւ B | առ հրաման] ∞ B | շինել B
20/ ամ] p.m. ամաց s.m. B | զտապանն B | Նո] om B | Զճ. (600)] վեց հարիւր B

23. QUESTIONS AND ANSWERS FROM HOLY BOOKS

21/ քառասուն
22/ լերինն] լեառն B | յԱզափ Մասիս B
23/ վասն է՞ր] ընդէ՞ր B | գործի B | անիծիւք B | Աստուած] om B
24/ պատասխանի B|պատճառի 1°]պատճառաւ B|միւս B|պատճառի 2°] պատճառաւ B | անհոգացեալ է անձնակամակութիւն իւրեանց B : անձնակամակութիւն means 'presumption'
25/ ըսկիզբն B | յԱդամայ
26/ թագուցին B
27/ զերկուսեանն B
28/ զինչ] եւ զինչ B | խափերութեամբ B | մինչ B | վաստակսն B | ծառայութեան B | յեզիպտացոցն B
29/ inc] + եւ B | աշխատեալ B | յաղուսարկութիւնն B
30/ թաւալեալ] թաւթափեալ B | զժողովուրդն B | վասն 2°] om B | յայնորիկ B | յանապատն B
31/ հարց: եւ (ւ above line) ի ցամաքն ընդէր B | զՀ] զի եաւթնասուն B[66] | զիսրայէլացւոցն B | Չքեղձոյց B
32/ պեղծ bis B | [պատասխանի]] This word is found in B + Մովսէս ասաց զնայ պեղծ B
34/ երթայր] գնայր B | ոչ] + եթէ above line p.m. B
36/ էթող] թողացոյց B | չիրամայեաց B | Դաւթայ B | շինելոյ
37/ շինելոյ B | Սողոմանի B | եղեւ] ընկալաւ B
38/ Յունան] Յովնան B | Նինուէ | Աստուծոյ B | մարդասիրութիւնն] բարերարութիւնն B
39/ կանաց] կանանց B | յանուանեցաւ B | զոր] որ B | կանանց B
40/ յարքայութեան B
41/ ով է] + սայ թագաւոր փառաց եւ B : omitted from A by haplography | կուսեն տեղեակք B | Հայրէ | տեղեակ B
42/ զՈրդի] զՔրիստոս Որդի B | կասկածի] + եւ երկուդի B | յայնժամ | ապա] + սատանայ գիտեաց B
43/ զալրստեանն | երկիր B | անցանէ] + երկիր B | մեղօրացն | արդարոց B զերեսնաւոր B | here M1654 breaks off and it resumes in §55
55/ զանգխշանալի | զայլն B | եւս] + էր | գնայ B | թողեալ—լեալ] om B : hmt | ի միջոյ երկարձ B
56/ ի սրբոցն ննջեցելոցն B | յուրբաթուն | համարեսցեն] կարծեսցեն B | կենդանիք մնացին
57–58 omitted by M1654

---

66. For the variant q- /զի see Stone and Hillel, "Index," no. 251.

59/ յերկրի B | բարեզործք են B | զքրիստոնեայսն | բարկութիւն B | թէ] om B | ոչ կարէ մտանել] ոչ մտանէ B | քններ B | հետազուտել B
60/ յարքայութիւն B | առ իւրեանց B | ազզականսն | եւ1°] առ եւ B | այլ] + եւ առ B | որպէս եւ] որպէս B | ծանեան B
61/ դժոխս B | որ B | զանձինս + իւրեանց B | տանձանս B
62/ յառնեն] առնեն B | մեռելոց յարութեան B | երիտասարք[դ]ք թէ B | յամենեքեանB|ժառանզութիւն]+եւտղայնչունիկատարելութիւն B | ամենեքայն B | երկրի] երկրի էր B
63/ յարքայութեան յերկնից B | յարքայութիւնն B | ընդելի B | ի] է B
64/ խաշն] եւ խաշն B | ամպա B | ի յերկրիս] յերկինս է B | զզեստ B | յարեան B | թալթափեալ B
65/ յարութեան B | բառնան B | միջոյ B | բառնին] + ի միջոյ2° B | պատուեն B | Եսայի B | մարգարէ - թէ B | արեգական bis B | եաւթնապատիկ B | կոչի B | նուազեալ B | որպէս եւ] որպէս B | ճրազ B
66/ զրել է] զրեալ է B | էթէ] թէ B |
67/ Հրեշտակք B | յարքայութեան B | թէ B | յերկրաւոր B | մեծութիւն B | զոհութիւն B | զաւրազն | միմեանս | առնելցզ B
68/ պատուիրանազանցութեան B | կնոչն B | պարտեաւ B | պարտեցաւ] պարտեաւ B | յանցեաւ B | ճաշակեազ B | եմայ ողորմեցաւ / եւ մեզ] ∞ B | ողորմեցաւ] + եւ B | ողորմեցզի B | եւ ինքն—յաւիտեանս] om B

Translation

Title/ Questions and Answers from the Holy Books.
[W]hile angels and humans had not yot been created, who glorified the Divinity?
Answer: The Father was glorified by the Son, and the Son by the Father, and the Holy Spirit by them. They were glorifying one another.

2/ Question: Why did Satan transgress?
Answer: Because he thought to become like the Most High.[67]

3/ Question: Were the angels always in that same fear,[68] lest they fall?
Answer: Yes, they were always in that same fear. On account of that they were ceaselessly glorifying.

4/ Question: In what way was man called the image of God when he was not like His image?

---

67. See Isa 14:13–14.
68. That is, in fear of the same.

23. QUESTIONS AND ANSWERS FROM HOLY BOOKS 273

Answer: Man was called the image of God on account of (his) free will.[69]

5/ Question: Did Satan know (of) how many trees God commanded Adam to eat?
Answer: He knew for that (reason), that he heard the speech spoken by the Lord to Adam.[70] For that (reason) he spoke with the woman.[71]

6/ Question: Were Adam and the woman created inside the garden or were they created outside (it)?
Answer: They were created outside (it), because it written that "He put there the man whom He created."[72]

7/ Question: How long did Adam remain in the garden, for some books say a lot and others, not one day?[73]
Answer: Because in the garden there was no day and no night but it was always light, therefore no one knew the limits of Adam's life.[74]

8/ Question: Did the serpent speak with human speech with the wo<man>, or with its own speech?
Answer: The serpent desired (to speak) with this human speech; for that reason, Satan entered into it and caused it to speak with human speech.[75]

9/ Question: Did Satan have the authority to enter the serpent, or not?
Answer: He did have, because God gave permission to enter (the serpent) for the sake of testing man.

From manuscript M1254:

9A/ Question: What is Adam's leathern garment?
Answer: The leather is on account of its thickness and is with opposition to the body which we received.[76]

---

69. Or: autonomy. See Stone, *Traditions*, index s.v. "free will." See Gen 1:26.
70. That is, Gen 2:16–17.
71. Because she had not been directly commanded by God.
72. Quoting Gen 2:8, 15. Eve's creation is mentioned in Gen 2:22–23.
73. Observe the learned character of the formulation of this question. For various views on this issue, see Stone, *Traditions*, 34–36, 75–76, et al. This topic was subject of lively debate in the fifth–eleventh centuries.
74. This idea is found in Mxit'ar Ayrivanec'i but not before; Stone, *Traditions*, 153.
75. This is based on the idea of demonic possession: Satan possessed the serpent; see Stone, *Traditions*, 177–210. A description of Jonah in the whale using its faculties to pray, phenomenologically resembling Satan's possession of the serpent, is to be found in De Jona 18 and 21. There, in 18:3, the whale is even described as a musical instrument on which Jonah played, as is the serpent in some Adam texts.
76. The meaning of this second phrase is unclear, though the thickness of leather may be contrasted with the thinness of human skin.

M1654 resumes:

10/ Question: Does the flaming sword still guard the garden, or not?[77]
Answer: The sword was removed by means of the cross from the midst, and the way to the tree of life was opened for us.[78]

11/ Question: If Adam had not transgressed, would he always have remained in the garden or not?
Answer: Yes. Like a king[79] he would have moved from palace to palace.[80]

12/ Question: Did Cain repent or not?
Answer: He surely repented, since the flood came on his account and he was saved from the flood.[81]

13/ Question: For which reason did Cain kill Abel?
Answer: Because his own works were evil and his brother's, good.[82]

14/ Question: And for which reason did Lamech kill Cain?
Answer: Because of the dishonor of his family.[83]

15/ Question: Why did Methuselah live longer than other humans?
Answer: It is on account of his father Enoch's virtue.

16/ Question: And what was Enoch's virtue?
Answer: That he did not taste of the fruit of this world.[84]

17/ Question: How many years did Noah live in virginity?
Answer: five hundred years.[85]

---

77. Gen 3:24.
78. Cf. 4 Ezra 8.52.
79. Literally, "a crown."
80. Presumably, this means he would have had multiple residences in the garden.
81. That is, had he not repented, he would not have been saved from the flood. The view that Cain survived the flood, however, is unusual. This conflicts with the legend to which §14 refers.
82. See History of the Forefathers, Adam §§4–5. There it is the character of the offerings, and a concomittant moral dimension.
83. Lamech's story is discussed by A. Bereznyak in the excursus in Stone, *Angels and Heroes*, 92–93. This is, of course, the Cainite Lamech, see Gen 4:18–19, 23–24.
84. Armenian conceptions of Enoch are considered by Annette Y. Reed "Enoch in the Armenian Apocrypha," in *The Armenian Apocalyptic Tradition: A Comparative Perspective*, ed. Kevork B. Bardakjian and Sergio LaPorta, SVTP 25 (Leiden: Brill, 2014), 149–87; Michael E. Stone, "Some Texts on Enoch in the Armenian Tradition," in *Gazing on the Deep: Ancient Near Eastern and other Studies in Honor of Tzvi Abusch*, ed. Jeffery Stackert, Barbara N. Porter, and David P. Wright (Bethesda: CDL, 2010), 517–30. See further in Lipscomb, *Armenian Adam Literature*, 62–68 where the story of Enoch's refraining from eating fruit is studied in detail.
85. Gen 5:32. That verse reads, "After Noah was five hundred years old, Noah became

23. QUESTIONS AND ANSWERS FROM HOLY BOOKS   275

18/ Question: And for what reason did he live for so long?[86]
Answer: Because he feared the evil offspring of that time, lest his offspring also be evil.

19/ Question: When did he take[87] his wife?
Answer: When he received a command to build the ark.

20/ Question: And for how many years did Noah build the ark?
Answer: For six hundred years.[88]

21/ Question: And for how many days did the flood come?
Answer: forty days.[89]

22/ Question: And where did they put the ark?
Answer: In the mountain of Sararad,[90] in great Mazis.[91]

23/ Question: And why did Noah curse his son's son and not his own son who transgressed?[92]
Answer: Because God had blessed the first-born. For that reason, he could not expel God's blessing with a curse.[93]

24/ Question: Did they build the Tower for the reason of climbing to heaven,[94] or for some other need?

---

the father of Shem, Ham, and Japheth." It is, therefore, not a far reach for our Christian author to make the assertion put forward here.

86. That is, in virginity, before begetting children.

87. That is, marry.

88. Gen 7:6 says that the flood took place in Noah's six-hundredth year, and that is the basis of the inference in this section that the building took a hundred years.

89. Gen 7:4, 12, 17.

90. See P'awstos Buzand 3:10, who has "Sararat," and the discussion in Nina G. Garsoïan, *The Epic Histories Attributed to P'awstos Buzand (Buzandaran Patmut'iwnk')*, Harvard Armenian Texts and Studies 8 (Cambridge: Harvard University Press, 1989), 252–53. See further discussion in Michael E. Stone and Aram Topchyan, *Studies in the History of the Jews in Armenia* (Oxford: Oxford University Press, forthcoming), where the extensive bibliography on the identification of Mt. Ararat is discussed.

91. The higher of Masis's two peaks. On the mountain's identification, see Michael E. Stone, Aryeh Amihai, and Vered Hillel, *Noah and His Book(s)*, EJL 28 (Atlanta: Society of Biblical Literature, 2010), 307–11 and Stone and Topchyan, *Studies in the History of the Jews in Armenia*.

92. See Gen 9:25. Ham, the father of Canaan sinned (Gen 9:22) but his son, Canaan, received the curse. See Step'anos Siwnec'i, *Commentary on Genesis* 1.8; Stone and Topchyan, *Studies in the History of the Jews in Armenia*, forthcoming.

93. This is odd, since Ham was not Noah's firstborn son (see Gen 10:1), nor was Canaan Ham's firstborn (Gen 10:6).

94. The Bible, in Gen 11:4 does not provide a reason, but simply that they they built, "a Tower with its top in heavens." So our text's question is exegetically reasonable.

<Answer:> They built for two reasons. The first, because of that,[95] if again a flood will take place again; and the second, other reason, because they were most indifferent.[96]

25/ Question: Was the beginning of eating meat from Adam?
Answer: Not from Adam, but from Noah was it commanded to be eaten. Likewise, wine.[97]

26/ Question: Which idea[98] was it that (brought) Moses's parents to hide him?
Answer: Because the redemption of Israel was going to take place through him.

27/ Question: Did God give Moses a book or a commandment?[99]
Answer: Both, a book and a commandment.

28/ Question: Why did God command the people to plunder the Egyptians of their treasures by a ruse, while the Lord himself commanded all of them to work honest labor?
Answer: It is not that he[100] plundered (them), but they served the Egyptians for four hundred years of bitter and hard service.[101] He ordered (them) to take that wage.

29/ Question: Why did he not command Moses to take?[102]
Answer: Because he had not labored in the clay and in the bricklaying.

30/ Question: Why did he keep the people in the desert for forty years?
Answer: Because due to the Egyptian sin,[103] the people were topsy-turvy. For that reason, he purified them in the desert for forty years. And then he commanded (them) to enter the promised land.[104]

---

95. See Concerning the Tower 1 and 2 (IV.1 and IV.2) for this reason.
96. The exact import is unclear.
97. This is evident from the commandment concerning blood that was first given to Noah (Gen 9:4–5) and from Noah's planting of the vine (Gen 9:20–21). The planting of the vine is taken to show that the drinking of wine was from that point on, though it was not an explicit divine commandment.
98. Or "plan, mystery."
99. That is, an oral commandment.
100. That is, Israel.
101. Exod 3:21–22. This reason is also advanced in a number of Jewish Hellenistic and Rabbinic sources as well as by Patristic authors: see Ginzberg, *Legends of the Jews*, 5:436. Of course, the four hundred years are taken from Gen 15:13.
102. That is, the wage.
103. That means, the sin that they learned from the Egyptians or in Egypt.
104. See Deut 1:8, 31:7, etc.

23. QUESTIONS AND ANSWERS FROM HOLY BOOKS

From M1254:

30A/ Question: Why did Aaron and Miriam speak ill against Moses?
Because of that, that he took[105] an Ethiopian woman (wife).

30B/ Question: And why was Aaron not punished, but (only) Miriam?[106]
Answer: Because Miriam did not have authority, because she was a woman.[107]

30C/ Question: And why did Aaron not go first into the sea with a drum, but his sister?[108]
Answer: Because Miriam was a virgin and the drum was a symbol of virginity.

Ms M1654 resumes:

31/ Question: And why did he not slaughter Pharaoh on dry land, but in the sea?[109]
Answer: Because for seventy years he had the Israelite offspring drowned.[110] On account of that, he himself was slaughtered by the same water.

32/ Question: Was the pig originally unclean, or did Moses proclaim it unclean?
<Answer>: Because whatever the Egyptians ate, that was reckoned unclean. And that which they did not eat, that he commanded (the Israelites) to eat.[111]

33/ The rock that went after Israel, was it alive or inanimate?[112]
Answer: Yes, it was alive, because the rock was Christ Himself.[113]

34/ Question: And how did it go after Israel? Did they carry (it) or did it go of itself?
Answer: They did not carry it, but it went of itself.

---

105. That is, married. This is related in Num 12:1.
106. Num 12:8–10.
107. Quite how this answer responds to the question is unclear.
108. In fact, Exod 15:20 does not say that Miriam actually entered the sea, but that she sang and danced.
109. Exod 15:19, Deut 11:4.
110. Exod 1:22. The detail of seventy years is not biblical. Here it is not specified that the drowned children were boys.
111. The answer is implied, but not explicit.
112. The rock of Exod 17:6 was assumed to be the same as that of Num 20:8, 10 and to have traveled in the desert with the Israelites.
113. 1 Cor 10:4 is the direct source of this text.

From M1254:

34A/ Question: While David smote Goliath, did Saul know David or not?
Answer: Yes, he knew (him) because formerly he had sung over Saul with the lyre.

M1654 resumes:

35/ Question: Why did God <not> permit David to build the Temple, since[114] he was holier than Solomon?
Answer: Because of (his) wars, David was not commanded.[115]

36/ Question: Why did he fill[116] Solomon's days and make (them) peaceful?
Answer: On account of the building of the Temple.[117]

37/ Question: And was there forgiveness of Solomon's sins, or not?[118]
Answer: There was no forgiveness.

From M1254:

37A/ Question: Did Lot's daughters sleep with their father because of promiscuous thoughts, or for some other reason?
Answer: Not for any other reason but for their family, so as to leave their offspring upon the earth.[119]

37B/ Question: Did they find forgiveness or not?
Answer: They did not find forgiveness.[120]

---

114. Literally: while. See 1 Kgs 5:3.
115. 2 Sam 7:5; 1 Chr 22:8.
116. That is, extend: picking up the biblical turn of phrase "full of days." Oddly it is to David that the phrase is applied in 1 Chr 23:1; 29:6.
117. Cf. 1 Chr 22:5, which also struggles with the question of why Solomon, and not David, built the Temple.
118. The question of Solomon's sins and repentance received a different answer in Armenian Solomon apocrypha: see Michael E. Stone, "The Penitence of Solomon," *JTS* 29 (1978): 1–19 and Stone, *Biblical Heroes*. For a range of attitudes towards Solomon in the Armenian tradition, see Shahé Ananyan, "La Figure de Salomon et les livres sapienteaux dans la tradition arménienne," *REArm* 34 (2012): 29–39. On Solomon in general see Torijano, *Solomon the Esoteric King*. Solomon's penitence is studied by Lorenzo DiTommaso, "The Penitence of Solomon (*De penitentia Salomonis*)," in DiTommaso, Henze, and Adler, *The Embroidered Bible*, 371–452.
119. See Gen 19:30–36.
120. This point is not described in Genesis.

37C/ Question: And Soloman,[121] was there forgiveness for one of his sins, or not?

Answer: He did not receive forgiveness.[122]

37D/ Question: Did Ezekiel's vision dry up the bones; was it a vision or a resurrection?

Answer: A vision and a resurrection.

M1654 resumes:

38/ Question: (If) Jonah was sent to Nineveh by the Lord, why did he flee from God?

<Answer>: Because he knew God's love of humans which would obstruct his prophecy.[123]

39/ Question: For what sort of reason was John, born of woman,[124] called "greatest?"

Answer: Because from the womb he worshipped Christ, which no one else born of women did.

40/ Question: And which infant is great in the kingdom?

Answer: The Word God himself, who came, became small for our sake, for he will make us great.[125]

41/ Question: The angels who were saying, "Who is this who comes from the direction of Edom,"[126] were they not informed that He was born from a virgin or from the Father?

Answer: They were not informed only about the birth from a virgin.

42/ Question: Up to which place did Satan not know the Son of God—His baptism, or His temptation, or His crucifixion?

Answer: He (Satan) was always in doubt, but in the crucifixion, when He (Christ) yielded up his spirit (soul) to the hands of the Father, then he realized that He was God and Son of God.[127]

43/ Question: Will this earth pass away at the Lord's coming, or will it be renewed?

---

121. Apparently, Solomon.
122. This repeats §37.
123. See Stone, *Angels*, 266. This is the Story of Nineveh an[d of Jo]nah.
124. Literally: "women." This is based on Matt 11:11 and Luke 7:28.
125. The source of this material is unclear.
126. Isa 63:1, taken as a Messianic prophecy both by Jews and Christians. The exegesis implied is unclear. Could it be taking "Edom" as "Adam," which means "man"?
127. Cf Matt 27:54; Mark 15:39; the centurion there plays the role here attributed to Satan.

Answer: It will not pass away but be renewed, not for the sake of the wicked but for the sake of the righteous. For they are going to become thirty-fold[128] as Christ also said [end of photograph.]

From M1254:

43 continued / for they are going to become thirty-fold, as Christ also said. And he arranged this earth (to be) thirty-fold and the garden to be sixty-fold,[129] and it is to be a hundred-fold in the supernal Jerusalem.

44/ Question: Is anyone of the saints in the garden or is it bereft of humans?
Answer: Two who sinned went forth (from the garden),[130] and two who were sent entered: Enoch and Elijah.

45/ Question: When Enoch was transferred did Adam see Enoch's transferral or not? Was he (Adam) living or not?
Answer: Yes, Adam was living. For that which had been written[131] is concerning him, that just as Elijah was transferred and Elisha saw him,[132] in the same fashion Enoch was transferred and Adam saw him.

46/ Question: And what was the reason that Adam saw Enoch?
Answer: On account of reproach for his[133] sins and on account of hope of his own life. For he was always mindful and fearful that no one else of their descendants would enter into the first heritage.[134] On account of this he saw with his own eyes concerning Enoch having been transferred to the garden.

47/ Question: On account of which reason did God quickly rebuke Cain?
Answer: On account of Adam. For, when Adam asked Cain, "Where is Abel your brother?"[135] he was mistaken, (thinking) that his offering was acceptable and that he[136] had been transferred to the garden. On account of that God quickly rebuked him, so that Adam might apprehend the lawless deed that Cain had done.

48/ Question: What is the sharp object with which Cain killed Abel?

---

128. Thus, taking it from երեսուն and see Matt 13:8, 23.
129. Based on Mark 4:8. The idea of the eschatological renewal of the earth and the heavens derives from the prophet Isaiah (Isa 65:17. 66:22) and is widespread.
130. That is, Adam and Eve.
131. If this is a reference to a literary source, it remains unidentified.
132. 2 Kgs (4 Kgdms) 2:11–12.
133. That is, Adam's.
134. That is, the garden of Eden.
135. Gen 4:9, but in that verse it is God who asks Cain.
136. He (Adam) was mistaken ... his (Abel's) ... he (Abel)... . ... him (Cain).

23. QUESTIONS AND ANSWERS FROM HOLY BOOKS

Answer: It was flint.[137]

49/ Question: How many transgressions did Cain do?
Answer: Seven vengeances God gave back to him.[138]

50/ Question: How many punishments were required of Lamech on account of his killing Cain and his son's son?[139]
Answer: Seven-fold seven punishments were required.[140]

51/ Question: Why were so many[141] punishments required of him?
Answer: Because he transgressed the judgment and he himself convicted Cain, because of that he was found to be guiltier.[142]

52/ Question: That which God said to the bandit, "This day you will be with me in the garden,"[143] at that very time did He bring him to the garden, or would he bring (him there) afterwards?
Answer: "This day" symbolizes the millennia,[144] and afterwards he will bring (him). For body and soul are together to receive the recompense of good and evil deeds,[145] just as has been written, that "God spoke one time and you heard this twice."[146]

53/ Question: What was the silver that they gave to Judah and whence did it come?[147]
Answer: Some say that it is that silver with which Abraham bought the cave in Hebron; and others say,[148] "That (is) the silver that the brothers

---

137. This is a common idea in Armenian texts: see, for example, Abel and Cain §§26–33, and Lipscomb, *Armenian Adam Books*, 148–50, 163–65.
138. That Cain committed seven sins is inferred from the seven vengeances mentioned in Gen 4:15, 24.
139. That is, his grandson. See Bereznyak, "Appendix," Angels and Heroes, 92–93.
140. Gen 4:24. The text in Arm Genesis also says եւթանասնեկին եւթն, as here.
141. Thus I interpret անշափ as a variant spelling of այնշափ. It could also be read as written to be "innumerable, without measure."
142. This is based on Gen 4:23–24, where Lamech says he killed a man and that Cain will be avenged seven-fold.
143. Luke 23:43. God, that is Christ.
144. Literally, thousands.
145. This is a widespread theme: see Pseudo-Ezekiel "The Blind and the Lame" in *The Apocryphal Ezekiel*, ed. Michael E. Stone, Benjamin G. Wright, and David Satran, EJL 18 (Atlanta: Society of Biblical Literature, 2000), 9–16 (E. Chazon) and 61–69 (M. Bregman). It also occurs in Questions of St. Gregory §§14–24, 40–41: see Stone, "Questions of St. Gregory," 141–72.
146. Ps 62(61):11. "Once" is just the soul, but "twice" indicates soul and body.
147. See Matt 26:15.
148. This is an additional strong marker of a learned text.

received in Egypt for Joseph {to him}."[149] But it was to be known[150] to us that, at that time, there was a silver drachma that was worth ten drams. And having taken of the temple silver, they gave him thirty silver pieces, which was altogether three hundred drams.[151]

54/ Question: What is that that the Gospel says concerning Judah, that after the morsel (of bread),[152] then <S>atan entered him. Did Satan have authority to enter him?
<Answer>: If Satan had been able to have authority, he would have entered previously and into other elect ones. But when he made himself a receptacle for Satan, then indeed Satan entered into him.[153]

55/ Question: What is the reason that to Mt. Tabor he brought only the three (apostles), Peter and John and James son of Zebedee, as the gospels say? "He did not take the others up with him."[154]
Answer: It is not that he made a selection between these and those, but on account of Judah he did not take all the others, for he did not make him worthy of that fearsome and tremendous vision. And indeed, he was not worthy

M1654 195r resumes. From this point on its text is used:

because he knew his (Judah's) unrepentant and perfidious mind. For if he had taken the eleven others with him to the mountain, and left him alone, then he would have become filthily desirous on account of his wickedness. For this reason, the Lord of all removed this cause.[155]

56/ Question: At the crucifixion of the Lord, many of the sleeping saints arose: did they die again or were they transferred alive?
Answer: They arose on Friday, and after His resurrection they entered

---

149. The location of the cave is confused; see above p. 104 and n. 181 and Stone, *Step'anos Siwnec'i*, 9–10. However, the idea that the money the brothers received for the sale of Joseph is an anticipation of Judas's thirty pieces of silver is found in the Armenian Joseph apocrypha. See, e.g., in Stone, *Angels and Heroes*, Memorial of Patriarchs §62 and n. 293 on p. 113; Third Story of Joseph §16.

150. A common formula in school exegesis; see Stone, *Step'anos Siwnec'i*, forthcoming.

151. The source of this explanation is still to be uncovered.

152. John 13:27.

153. See the discussion of spirit possession in n. 86 above.

154. See Matt 17:1, Mark 9:2, and Luke 9:28. The gospels do not explain why he took just these three apostles.

155. Literally: excuses or reasons from their midst, i.e., from there.

23. QUESTIONS AND ANSWERS FROM HOLY BOOKS 283

the holy city, just as the Gospel book says.[156] For they shall not reckon the things that have happened by their eyes,[157] and they shall fall asleep again. But certain people say that they remain alive and are in immortality with Enoch and Elijah.

§§57 and 58 are not in M1654 and are given here according to M1254:

57/ Question: What was the word that Zechariah said over the Jewish people, that "the Canaanites will know the sheep of my keeping, for it is the word of the Lord"?[158]
Answer: Because the Jewish people were living in the land of the Canaanites and[159] they accepted their furious and bloodthirsty ways into themselves and their ways settled on them. And they inherited the name of those whose way they had accepted; on account of that they were called "Canaanites."[160]

58/ Question: And who were the "sheep of my keeping"?
Answer: He named the Apostles, "sheep" as he himself said, "I send you like sheep in the midst of wolves."[161]

M1654 resumes:

59/ Question: Will those who do more good deeds than the Christians perish from the earth or not?"
Answer: As the Lord indeed said, "The one who does not believe in the Son, God's anger abides upon him."[162] And again he says, "Whoever is not born of water and the spirit, cannot enter the kingdom of God.[163] But

---

156. Matt 27:52–53.
157. That is, by appearances.
158. Zech 11:11. The exegesis is of the Armenian text of Zechariah which here follows the LXX. The LXX vary quite considerably from the MT and read: καὶ γνώσονται οἱ Χαναναῖοι τὰ πρόβατα τὰ φυλασσόμενα, διότι λόγος κυρίου ἐστίν.
159. The image is unusual. Close in sentiment, with drinking blood as a punishment, is Rev 16:6 "because they shed the blood of saints and prophets, you have given them blood to drink. It is what they deserve!" This differs, for here it is God who threatens to drink the blood.
160. The author is interpreting the "Canaanites" of Zechariah's verse as the Jewish people. This interpretation is somewhat unclear as it stands.
161. Matt 10:16.
162. John 3:18.
163. John 3:5.

you, do not investigate the uninvestigable and do not study closely his judgment."[164]

60/ Question: Will there be acquaintance[165] in the kingdom of God, or not?
Answer: Yes, people (will) have much more acquaintance, not only of their own relatives, but also of all the righteous, as on Mt. Tabor, where the disciples made acquaintance of Moses and Elijah.[166]

61/ Question: And in Hell, do people have acquaintance or not?
Answer: This too, John Chrysostom witnesses, that there are extremely difficult tortures for sinners, who only see themselves in the tortures.

62/ Question: Old and young people, at which sort of age do they arise from the dead in the resurrection, young or old?
Answer: All are going to rise up young, because an old person cannot receive an inheritance,[167] but all will be thus—like Adam who was in the garden and like Christ who was on the earth.[168]

63/ Question: Will there be food in the kingdom of heaven?
Answer: Paul witnesses to this, that there is no eating and drinking (in) the kingdom of God, but righteousness and peace and joy in the Holy Spirit.[169]

64/ Question: The cross which is going to come in clouds, is this the one that is in heaven, or (is it) that which he carried with him, as John Chrysostom says?[170]

---

164. In its phrasing, this is reminiscent of Arm 4 Ezra 4.10 and 4.21: compare also Sir 3:21–22. It is interesting that the author having quoted verses that explicitly say that there is no redemption except through Christ, then adds this lapidary sentence and creates, despite the explicit Gospel verses, an ambiguity about the answer to this question. The question is itself is rather unconventional as well.

165. That is, of other or additional people.

166. See the description of the Transfiguration: Matt 17:3, Mark 9:4, Luke 9:30, 33. See §55 above.

167. Eternal life or reward is called an inheritance, particularly in the NT Epistles: See Eph 1:11, 14, 18; Col 1:12. 3:24; 1 Pet 1:4; as well as Acts 20:32.

168. Both are said to be like thirty-year-old men in various sources. See, e.g., Aṙakʻel Siwnecʻi's *Adamgirkʻ* (transl. Michael E. Stone), 212–13 who says Adam was created aged thirty and that Christ died at the same age. See further, p. 49 n. 16 above.

169. Rom 14:17.

170. The expression "come with the clouds" derives from Dan 7:13 where it refers to the "one like a human being" or "son of Man." This is applied to Jesus in very well-known verses in Matt 24:30 and 26:64 with parallels in Mark and Luke. The cross derives from Matt 24:30 which refers to "the sign of the Son of Man" appearing in the heavens, for which the proof-text is the expression referred to in the preceding sentences. One wonders whether there is an iconographic background to the question.

Answer: There was one cross, which is in heaven and on earth, but as for what John said, that he took and carried (it) with him upwards, it does not mean that he carried the cross, but the sufferings of the cross and the blood-spattered garment, just as the heavenly hosts also witness.[171]

65/ Question: In the resurrection, will the luminaries and stars be taken away, or not?

Answer: They are not taken away, but they will receive more honor[172] as the prophet Isaiah witnesses, "The light of the moon will become like the light of the sun, and the light of the sun will become sevenfold."[173] But Scripture calls (it) darkness on account of that, near the divine light they are found to be lesser, like a candle near the sun.[174]

66/ Question: After the resurrection, do the waters remain or are they dried up?

Answer: The eternal waters are not dried up, because this very earth is founded upon waters,[175] but the visible waters are dried up, as it is written, "The sea is dried up and all the creations are amazed."[176]

67/ Question: Do angels and righteous humans have praise in the kingdom, or not?[177]

Answer: Yes. Great praise and laudation is going to issue forth[178] at that time to the kingdom. For when these earthly kings bestow gifts and dignities on their forces, they receive much praise and honor from the forces. In the measure that the Lord is more than all and he will crown all the angels and righteous, and he is going to make them a mixture with one another, in that measure it is necessary to offer praise to God.[179]

68/ Question: Did Adam eat the fruit because of transgression of commandment, or because of pity on the woman.[180]

Answer: Adam was not deceived and did not transgress the commandment, as Paul witnesses: "And Adam was not deceived, but the woman

---

171. The source is unknown.
172. That is, glory, brilliance.
173. Isa 30:26.
174. This may refer to Isa 13:10; cf. Isa 42:6.
175. See Ps 136(135):6.
176. Isa 51:10. It is notable how dependent the author is on Isaiah for these cosmic aspects of eschatology. The drying up of the sea is found as Sign 2 in Signs of the Judgment; see Stone, *Signs of the Judgement*, 24–25, 34–35, 44–45.
177. That is, do they praise God.
178. Or, perhaps, rise/climb up.
179. Apparently this refers to the angels taking the prayers of the saints to God; Rev 8:1–3. This idea, of course, is older; for an example, see 3 Bar. 11.
180. Or: the wife.

was deceived and transgressed."[181] And Adam ate (the fruit) on account of pity for his wife.[182]

And Christ has had mercy and has mercy on him and us. And He is blessed forever. Amen.

23.2. Manuscript M1405, the Short Recension

In this text, which omits the tags "Question" and "Answer," except for Question 1, I have introduced indicators of them for clarity's sake: Հ and Q, Պ and A in the text and in the translation.

Text

M1405/ 1/ Հարց: Մինչ ոչ էին ստեղծեալ հրեշտակ[183] եւ մարդիկ, qԱստուած ո՞վ փառաւորէ: Պատասխանի: Հայր յՈրդոյ, եւ Որդի ի Հօրէ, եւ Սուրբ Հոգին ի նոցունց փառաւորէին:

2/ <Հ.>: Զի՞նչ յանցեաւ սատանայ: <Պ.>: Խորհեցաւ լինել նման բարձրելոյն:

3/ <Հ.>: Հրեշտակք կա՞ն ի նոյն երկիւղին, եթէ՞ ոչ: <Պ.>: Այո՛, կան:

4/ <Հ.>: Մարդն պատկեր Աստուծոյ ի՞ւ կոչեցաւ, յորժամ ոչ նման պատկերի նորա: <Պ.>: Մարդն պատկեր Աստուծոյ վասն անճշխանութեանն կոչեցաւ:

6/ <Հ.>: Ադամ եւ կինն ի դրախտի՞ն ստեղծան, եթէ՞ արտաքոյ: <Պ.>: Արդաքոյ ստեղծան, զի գրեալ է, թէ. «Եդ անդ զմարդն, զոր ստեղծ»:

8/ <Հ.>: Օձն մարդկային բարբառո՞վ[184] խօսեցաւ ընդ կնոջն: Սատանայ ունէ՞ր իշխանութիւնն մտանել ի յօձն, որ եմուտ: <Պ.>: Ոչ ունէր իշխանութիւնն մտանել, զի թոյլ ետ Աստուած յաղագս փորձելոյ զմարդն:

9A/ <Հ.>: Արդ, զի՞նչ է մաշկեղէն հանդերձն Ադամայ: <Պ.>: Մաշկեղէնն յաղագս թանձրամած եւ {ընդդեմ<ա>մարտ}[185] մարմնոյն, որ մեք ստեղծաք:

---

181. 1 Tim 2:14.

182. This view first appears in the Armenian sources in the tenth century, notably in Grigor Narekacʻi, and again in later centuries; See Stone, *Traditions*, 59, 67, 111–12, etc.

183. For the loss of -ք in such contexts, as also in մարդիկ here, see Stone and Hillel, "Index," no. 333.

184. Observe the unusual orthography.

185. ընդ on line; դեմ<ա>մարդ above line p.m. It seems to be corrupt, perhaps for ընդդեմամարտ "opposite."

23. QUESTIONS AND ANSWERS FROM HOLY BOOKS 287

10/ <Հ.>: Բոցեղէն սուրն[186] դեռ եւս պահէ՞ զդրախտն, եթէ՞ ոչ: <Պ.>: Ի ձեռն խաչին բարձաւ ի միջոյ եւ բացաւ մեզ ճանապարհի ծառոյն կենաց:

11/ <Հ.>: Եթէ Ադամ չեր յանցեալ, ի դրախտին կա՞յր հանապազ, թէ՞ ոչ: <Պ.>: Այո՛, փոխելոց էր որպէս թագաւոր յապարանաց յապարանս:

12/ Ապաշխար<u>հ</u>եաց[187] ստոյգ, զի վասն նորա ապրեցաւ Նոյ:

14/ <Հ.>: Ղա{դա}մէք[188] զի՞նչ պատճառի եսպան զԿային: <Պ.>: Արդ՝ վասն նախատանաց ազգին իւրեանց:

15–16/ <Հ.>: Մաթուսաղա երկար ապրեցաւ վասն առաքինութեանն հօրն Ենոքայ: Եւ զի՞նչ էր առաքինութիւնն Ենոքայ: <Պ.>: Ի պտղոյ աշխարհիս ոչ ճաշակեաց:

17/ <Պ.>: Նոյ Շ. (500) ամ կուսութեամբ եկաց, զի երկնչէր զի մի ծնունդ իւր չար լիցի:[189]

20–21/ <Պ.>: Նոյ Ճ. (100) ամ տապանն շինեաց. ջրհեղեղն Խ. (40) օր եկաւ:

24/ Չի աշտարակն[190] Բ. (2) պատճառի շինեցին՝ ա. վասն ջրհեղեղին, բ. վասն անյոգ լինելոյ:

25/ <Հ.>: Միս եւ զինի ուտելոյ Ադամա՞յ եղեւ: <Պ.>. Ոչ, Նոյէ հրամայեցաւ:

26/ Մովսէս վասն այն թագուցին, զի ի ձեռն նորա լինելոց էր փրկութիւնն Իսրայելի:

27/ <Հ.>: Մովսէսի Աստուած զի՞ր ետ, թէ՞ պատուիրանս: <Պ.>: Յերկոսեան ետ:

30A/ <Հ.>: Ահարոն եւ Մարիան բամբասեցին զՄովսէս,[191] զի էառ կին եթովպացի:

30B/ Ահարոն ընդէ՞ր ոչ պատուհասեցաւ, այլ Մարիամ: <Պ.>: Վասն զի կինն ոչ ունի իշխանութիւնն ի վերա մարդոյ:

30C/ <Հ.>: Ընդէ՞ր Մարիամ յառաջէր ի ծովս թմբկաւ: <Պ.>: Վասն զի Մարիամու թմբուկն օրինակէր կուսութիւնն[192] իւր:

31/ <Հ.>: Եւ ի ցամաքի ընդէ՞ր ոչ սատակեաց փարաւոն, այլ ի ծովս:

---

186. դ below line p.m.
187. Othographic error; the h is superfluous.
188. Corrupt dittography of դա.
189. լիցի in marg. p.m.
190. For this variant of զ-/զի, see Stone and Hillel, "Index," no. 251.
191. Observe the varied orthographies of "Moses" in §§26–30A.
192. A genitive would be expected.

<Պ.>: Վասն զի Հ. (70) ամ իսրայէլացոց ձնունդ ջրիեղձ արար, վասն որոյն ջրով ստտակեաց:

32/ <Հ.>: Խոզն ի սկզբնէ˚ էր պիղձ, եթէ˚ Մովսէս ասաց զնա պիղձ: <Պ.>: Ջե{կ}զիպտացիք¹⁹³ ունէին. Մովսէս զնա ասաց պիղձ ընդ հնոյն, յորժամ<ժամ> էհան ի միջոյ նոցա, հրամայեաց չուտել:

33/ <Հ.>: Վէմս, որ երթայր զհետ Իսրայէլի, կենդանի˚ էր, թէ˚ անշունչ: <Պ.>: Այո˚, կենդանի էր, զի որպէս ասէ, եւ վէմս էր ինքն Քրիստոս:

34/ <Հ.>: Եւ զհետ Իսրայէլի զիա˚րդ զնայր˚ տանէի˚ն, թէ˚ ինքն երթայր:

37A/ <Հ.>: Ղովտա դստերքն¹⁹⁴ թողութիւնն գտի˚ն: <Պ.>: Չգտին թողութիւնն / fol 147r /

37/ [Հ.]: Սողոմոնի յանցանացն թողութիւնն եղե˚լ, թէ˚ ոչ: <Պ.>: Չեղեւ թողութիւնն:

39/ [Հ.]: Յոհաննէս ի ձնունդս կանանց մեծ զի˚նչ պատճառի անուանեցաւ: <Պ.>: Վասն զի յորովայնէ երկիր պագ Քրիստոսի, զոր ոչ այլ ոք ի ձնունդ կանանց արար:

41–42/ <Հ.>: Հրեշտակք, որք ասէին «Ո˚վ է սա որ դիմեալ....», մի˚ թէ ոչ զիտէին: <Պ.>: Ի Հօրէ զիտէին, ի կուսէ ձնընդեանն միայն չէին տեղեակ.: [Հ.]: Սատանայ միշտ կասկածի˚ կա˚յր մինչ ի խաչելութիւնն: <Պ.>: Յերբ աւանդեաց հոգին, զիտաց:

43/ <Հ.>: Ի գալստեան Տեառն անցանի˚ երկիրս, եթէ˚ նորոգի: <Պ.>: [Ն]որոգի վասն արդարոց Լ. (30)-աւոր, դրախտն Ադամայ Կ. (60)-աւոր. վերինն Երուսաղէմ՝ Ճ. (100)-աւոր:

44/ <Հ.>: Բ˚. (2) ելին ի դրախտէն եւ Բ˚. մտին դրախտն: <Պ.> Ենոյբ¹⁹⁵ եւ Եղիա:

45/ <Պ.> Ադամ դեռ ևս կենդանի էր ի փոխմանն Ենոյբայ:

52/ <Հ.>: Աւազակին, որ ասաց Աստուած. «Այսոր ընդ իս իցես ի դրախտն», տարա˚ւ, թէ˚ ոչ: [Պ]: Այսօրն Ռ. (1,000) նշանակէ, յետոյ տանելոց է: Հատուցումս մի անգամ լինի վերջի[ն]¹⁹⁶ արդարոց եւ մեղաւորաց. միանգամ խոսեցաւ Աստուած եւ երկուս:

55/ <Հ.>: Զի˚նչ է պատճառն, որ ի Թափորական լեառն Պետրոս, Յովհաննէս, Յակոբոս միայն տարաւ: <Պ.>: Ոչ եթէ ընդրութիւնն արար ի մէջ նոցա եւ ոցա, վասն զի զիտեր անգոշանալի միտսն Յուդայի, զի չէր արժանի այնմ տեսլեան եւ թէ մետասանն տանիւր, բերանաբաց լինէին, վասն այնորիկ պատճառն եբարձ . . . :

---

193. The initial զ- is anomalous.
194. Othographic error of կզ for զ.
195. Observe the strange spelling of "Enoch."
196. ն covered by paper patch.

56/ <Հ.>: Ի խաչելութեանն Քրիստոսի բազում ննչեցեալք յարեան. <կ>ենդանի[197] մնացին, թէ ոչ: <Պ.>: <Իսկ>ույն[198] յարեան, զի մի առ աշօր կարծեցեն, դարձեալ ննչեցին:

61A/ <Հ.>: Արդարքն ունի՞ն և ծանօթութիւնն ընդ միմեանս[199] ի դժոխն: <Պ.>: Ոչ:

69/ <Հ.>: Մեծն ի մարգարէն[200] Յեսայի սղոցեցաւ ի Մնասէ արքայէ:

Translation

1/ Question: Until the angels and humans had been created, who glorified God?
Answer: The Father glorified the Son, the Son (was glorified) by the Father, and the Holy Spirit by them.

2/ <Q>: How did Satan transgress? <A>: He thought to become like the Most High.

3/ <Q>: Are the angels in that same fear or not? <A>: Yes, they are.

4/ <Q>: In what way was the man called the image of God, when he is not like His image? <A>: The man was called image of God because of his free-will (autonomy).[201]

6/ <Q>: Were Adam and the woman created in the garden or outside (it)? <A>: They were created outside (it), for it is written, "He put there the man whom he created."[202]

8/ <Q>: The serpent spoke with the woman with human speech. Did Satan have authority to enter the serpent, which he entered.[203] <A>: He did not have authority to enter (it), for God gave permission[204] for the sake of testing the man.

9A/ <Q>: Now, what is Adam's leather garment? <A>: The leather was on ac-

---

197. The text has, corruptly, դենդանի.
198. Apparently Իսկ was omitted.
199. Observe the orthography.
200. One would expect a plural of a partitive ablative, literally "The greatest of the prophets."
201. A standard explanation, found in early Armenian exegesis from the fifth century on: see Stone, *Traditions*, 19–20, etc. and index, s.v. "free-will."
202. Gen 2:8, 15 Eve is not mentioned in this verse, but her creation is mentioned in Gen 2:22.
203. This question combines two questions of the long recension, §§8 and 9. Moreover, it is composed of their answers, and their questions are not preserved.
204. That is, for him to enter.

count of its thick garment and <opposed> to the human body which we created.[205]

10/ <Q>: Does the flaming sword still guard the garden, or not? <A>: It was removed by the Cross and the way to the tree of life was opened to us.

11/ <Q>: If Adam had not sinned, would he always have remained in the garden, or not? Yes, he would have moved like a king from palace to palace.

12/ <A>: He[206] surely repented since Noah was saved on his account.

14/ <Q>: For what reason did Lamech kill Cain: <A>: Now, on account of the dishonor of their family.

15–16/ <Q>: Methuselah lived a long time because of the virtue of his father Enoch.: <Q>: And what was Enoch's virtue? <A>: He did not taste of the fruit of this world.

17/[207] <A>: Noah lived five hundred years in virginity, for he feared lest his offspring be wicked.

20–21/ <A>: Noah built the ark during one hundred years. The flood came for forty days.

24/ <A>: For they built the Tower for two reasons: (a) on account of the flood; (b) on account of being without worry.[208]

25/ <Q>: Did Adam have meat and wine to consume?[209] <A>: No. That was commanded by Noah.

26/[210] <A>: They hid Moses because of this, that through him the redemption of Israel was going to take place.

27/ <Q>: Did God give Moses a book[211] or commandments? <A>: He gave both.

30A/ <Q>: Aaron and Miriam spoke ill of Moses for he took an Ethiopian wife.[212]

30B/ Why was Aaron not punished, but (only) Miriam? <A>: Because the woman does not have the authority over a man.

30C/ <Q>: Why was Miriam first into the sea with a drum? <A>: Because Miriam's drum was a symbol of her virginity.

---

205. M1254 has սաացաք "we received," which makes better sense here.
206. Apparently Adam. No question corresponds to this answer,
207. This and the next items are answers, from which the questions are missing.
208. They thought that by its height the Tower would save them from any future Flood that their sins would bring upon them.
209. Or: Was the consumption of meat and wine from Adam?
210. Answer without a question.
211. Or: writing.
212. See the excursus on pp. 122–34 above.

31/ <Q>: And why did he not slaughter Pharaoh on dry land, but in the sea? <A>: Because for seventy years he had the Israelite offspring drowned. On account of that he slaughtered (him) with water.

32/ <Q>: Was the pig unclean from the beginning, or did Moses declare it unclean. <A>: The Egyptians used to eat (it). Moses declared it unclean, with the old.[213] When he brought (them) forth from their midst, he commanded (them) not to eat (it).

33/ <Q>: The rock that went after Israel, was it alive or inanimate? <A>: Yes, it was alive, for as it says, the rock was Christ himself.[214]

34/ <Q>: And how did it follow the Israelites? Did they carry (it) or did it go of itself?[215]

37A/ <Q>: Did the daughters of Lot find forgiveness? <A>: They did not find forgiveness.

37/ <Q>: Was there forgiveness for Solomon's transgressions? There was no forgiveness.

39/ <Q>: For what reason was Yohannēs[216] called greatest of those born of women? <A>: Because he worshipped Christ from the womb, which no one else born of women did.

41–42/ <Q>: The angels who were saying, "Who is this who is coming …?"[217] Was it that they did not know? <A>: They knew (it)[218] from the Father,. <Q>: Were they uninformed only of the virgin birth? <A>: Satan always was doubtful until the crucifixion. When he (Christ) gave up his soul, he (Satan) knew.[219]

43/ <Q>: In the coming of the Lord, does this earth pass away or is it renewed? <A>: It is renewed on account of the righteous thirty-fold; the garden of Adam (will be) sixty-fold; the heavenly Jerusalem, one hundred-fold.

44/ <Q>: Two went forth from the garden; and two entered the garden. <A> Enoch and Elijah.[220]

45/[221] <Q>: Was Adam still alive at the transfer of Enoch?

52/ <Q>: The bandit of whom God said, "Today you (will be) with me in

---

213. Meaning uncertain: perhaps, "old covenant."
214. 1 Cor 10:4.
215. The answer is lost.
216. That is, John the Baptist.
217. Isa 63:1.
218. The virgin birth.
219. That is Satan apprehended the incarnation and crucifixion, and perhaps the descensus ad infernos is also implied here.
220. The two who exited the Garden were, of course, Adam and Eve.
221. Question without an answer.

the garden,"²²²—was he taken or not? <A>: "Today" symbolizes one thousand;²²³ afterwards he will be taken. The last recompense is to take place at one time for the righteous and the sinners. God spoke one time and two.²²⁴

55/ <Q>: What is the reason he brought only Peter, John, and James to the Taborite mountain. <A>: It was not that he made the selection between these and those,²²⁵ (but) because he knew the unrepentant intent of Judah, for he was not worthy of that vision. And if he brought the eleven, he (Judah) would be most desirous. For that reason, he took....²²⁶

56/ <Q>: In²²⁷ the crucifixion of Christ, many who had fallen asleep, arose: did they remain alive or not? <A>: ... arose so that they might not perish at the sight, they fell asleep again.

61A/ <Q>: Do the righteous recognize one another in Hell:²²⁸ <A>: No!

69/ <Q>: Was the greatest prophet Isaiah sawn by King Manasseh?²²⁹

---

222. Luke 23:43.

223. That is, "one thousand years, a millennium." This is a chiliastic response drawing on a common exegesis of Ps 90(89):4: "For a thousand years in thy sight are but as yesterday when it is past." This was taken to mean that a millennium was God's day.

224. God will declare a double judgement at one fell swoop, on righteous and on the sinners.

225. That is, between those he did not take up the mountain and those that he did.

226. The end of the sentence was omitted, but it must have said that for that reason he took only the three apostles with him.

227. That is, at the time of.

228. One might suspect a confusion of դրախտ "garden" and դժոխք "Hell."

229. This is apparently an additional question not to be found in the other recension. The story of Isaiah being sawn into two is well known.

24. Three Tales: Solomon, Noah, and Satan

Introductory Remarks

M2188 is a miscellany of the fifteenth century.[1] The texts that are preserved on fols 265r–266v consist of short narrative tales, mostly featuring biblical figures. Here we publish three tales—about Solomon, Noah, and Satan. As distinct from most of the Armenian apocryphal biblical stories published in this series, these tales relate to imaginary incidents in which these biblical figures play a central role. The same heroes are also prominent in biblical retellings, but the three documents published in this section of the book have relatively little, either in wording or in content, that ties them specifically to the Bible or its text. This, combined with the anthropomorphic roles played by animals, gives them a general character resembling the popular literary and oral tales collected by Srabyan, Łanalanyan, and Žamkočʻyan in their respective collections.[2] We are, in these instances, in the world of fables and folk tales.

The Solomon tale is the eighth short Solomon text which we have published to date in these volumes of Armenian apocryphal texts.[3] Of those already published, No. 7 Solomon and the Bubu Bird is in a similar genre to the fable published here.[4] The Noah story here is overwhelmingly aetiological. The tale of Satan's crown is strongly reminiscent of the tale of Michael the Archangel who steals back the heavenly garment Satan had taken when he

---

1. *General Catalogue* 7:365–372. The texts presented here are described on col. 272.
2. See Armenuhi Srapyan, *Medieval Armenian Tales* (Հայ միջնադարեան գրույցներ) (Erevan: Academy of Sciences, 1969); Aram Łanalanian. *Traditional History* (Աւանդապատում) (Erevan: Academy of Sciences, 1969). Compare also the recent work Anušavan Žamkočʻyan, *The Bible and Armenian Oral Tradition* (Աստուածաշունչը եւ հայ բանաւոր աւանդոյթը), Ajemian Series 15 (Erevan: Erevan State University, 2012).
3. Another Solomon fragment has been noted in in M4618 on fol 131v; see "Adam Fragment," above.
4. Indeed, it is also printed by Srapyan, *Medieval Armenian Tales*, 318–19.

fell. That tale exists in Greek (unpublished), Bulgarian and, apparently, other languages.[5]

The Armenian of these text is much influenced by dialects and has many late forms, chief of which are signaled in the annotations.

24.1. Solomon Text 8[6]

Text

/ 265r / 1/ Իմաստնացեալն յԱստուծոյ Սողոմոն խնդրեաց յԱստուծոյ թէ. «Հրամա՛ն տուր ինձ, որ Գ. (3) ամիս, զինչ որ կենդանի կայ, ես կեր[ա]կրեմ»։ Եկն հրեշտակն, ասաց, թէ. «Չես բաւ‹ա›կան,[7] որ Գ. (3) օր կերակրես»։

2/ Եւ հրաման ետ Աստուած, զի բազում կերակուրս՝ ի մտոյ, ի հացոյ, ի խոտոյ, ի հնդոյ, մինչեւ մեծամեծ բլրնի եղիր։ Եւ հրամանքն[8] Աստուծոյ արձակեցաւ եւ ի գալ կենդանեացն կերակրիլ։ Եւ յանկարծակի էլեալ ի ծովէն ձուկ մի՝ եւ ի յԳ. (3) ժամն կերաւ[9] զամէնն, զինչ պատրաստեալ էր Սողոմոն։

3/ Եւ հիացաւ եւ ասէր, թէ. «Ա՛յ իմ ողորմած Աստուած, այս ի՞նչ կենդանի էր»։ Եւ ասաց հրեշտակն, թէ. «Ձուկ մի կայ ի ծովն, որ կերակուր է Լեւիաթանին եւ Գ. (3) ի յասկից[10] նորա է կերակուր։ Եւ այլ կենդանիքն անօթի դարձան։

Translation

1/ Solomon, having received wisdom from God, asked of God, "Command me that for three months I eat whatever animal there is." The angel came, he said, "You are unable to eat (that) for three days."

---

5. The Greek text of this tale is being edited by Emmanouela Grypeou and the present writer. On the Bulgarian text, see Anissava Miltenova, "The Apocryphon about the Struggle of the Archangel Michael with Satanail, in Two Redactions," *Starobŭlgarska* 9 (1981): 98–113; Miltenova, "An Unknown Redaction of the Apocryphon about the Struggle of the Archangel Michael with Satanail," in *Literary Study and Folklore* (Sofia, 1983), 121–27 (Bulgarian).

6. For texts 1–7, see Stone, *Biblical Heroes*, 143–67

7. Emending բաւկան of the text.

8. This noun has a pluralizing ք k' but in context is singular. Odd uses of this ending are frequent in late texts.

9. A Middle Armenian form.

10. A Middle Armenian form, see Karst, *Historische Grammatik*, 240.

2/ And God gave a command, "Put much food—of meat, of bread, of grass, of seed, until (it makes) great hills." And God's command was sent forth and when the animals came to be eaten, suddenly a fish came forth from the sea and in three hours devoured everything that Solomon had prepared.

3/ And he[11] was amazed and said, "O, my merciful God, what animal was this?" And the angel said, "There is a fish in the sea which is food for Leviathan and three of these are his food and the other living creatures[12] are famished."

24.2. Noah

Text

1/ Յորժամ Նոյ ի տապանն էր, աս[ա]ցե[ա]լ են,[13] թէ տապանն ծակեցաւ, եւ ասաց Նոյ, թէ. «Ի կենդանեացդ, ով որ կալնու զծակն, յորժամ ի դուրս ելանենք,[14] զորն ի կենդանացս ուզէ, / fol 265v / ես իրեն կերակուր տամ»: Եւ օձն կալաւ զծակն:

2/ Եւ յորժամ ելան ի տապանէն, ասաց Նոյ. «Խնդրեա՛յ, զորն կու խնդրես»: Եւ օձն որկեց զզորեհին եւ ասաց, թէ. «Տէ՛ս, թէ որու արիւն անուշ է եւ ինձ ասա՛յ»: Եւ գնաց զամէն կենդանեացն տեսաւ եւ գիտաց, զի մարդոյն շլեցն արիւն անուշ է: Եւ յորժամ գայր խապար բերել,

3/ ծիծառն ազգն հալէ եւ ասաց, թէ. «Ես եւ դուն եղբայր ենք, ինձ ասա՛յ, թէ ո՞րն է անուշ»: Եւ նայ ասաց, թէ. «Մարդոյն շլեցն»: Եւ ասաց, թէ. «Չլեզուտ ի բերանս ած, որ տեսնում, թէ ըղորդ ես: Եւ կտրեց զլեզուն ի տակն, եւ հասեալ օձին ասաց. «Չի՞նչ է», եւ սկսաւ դրել:

4/ Եւ գիտացեալ օձին եւ փախեաւ ծիծեառն, եւ օձն գիտ<ա>մտել՝ խած զազգին եւ կտրեցաւ, եւ մնաց ազ<ի> ծիծռռանն: Խոռ եւ սատակեալ օձն այն եղեւ լու[15] եւ այն է, որ խայթէ զմարդն, վասն խոստման Նոյի:

---

11. Solomon.
12. That is, of the sea.
13. If this is one word it is some sort of adjective. The last four letters, if separated off, could be read as եղեն =եղեն "were, became," but then աաց remains without interpretation.
14. Late form.
15. This word is corrected clumsily and illegible.

Translation

1/ When Noah was in the ark they said that the ark had a hole. And Noah said, "The one of you animals who blocks the hole, when we go forth, I (will) give it that which it desires of the animals to eat." And the snake blocked the hole.

2/ And when they went forth from the ark, Noah said, "Ask for that which you seek." And the snake sent the wasp and said, "See whose blood is sweetest, and tell me." And it went and saw all the animals. And it ascertained then that the blood of humans' neck is sweet. And when it came it brought information.

3/ The swallow is a clever bird and it said, "I and you[16] are brothers. Say to me, which is sweetest." And it[17] said, "The neck of humans." And it said, "Put your tongue into my mouth so that I may see whether you are right." And he cut the tongue in its under part.[18] And when the snake arrived, he said, "Which is it?"[19] And it began to fly off.[20]

4/ And the snake realized (what had happened) and the swallow fled and the snake went after it. It bit the tail and cut off the tail and the tail of the swallow remained worthless.[21] and the serpent having slaughtered that, it became flea[22] and that is what bites humans, on account of Noah's promise.[23]

24.3. Satan

Text

/ 265v–266r / 1/ Յորժամ անկաւ սատանայ յերկնից, եւ մնաց թագն ի գլուխն, եւ եկեալ Գաբրիէլ խաբեաց զսատանայ եւ ասաց. «Էջ

---

16. "You" here is apparently the wasp.

17. The wasp.

18. Is this an aetiological tale about the origin of the snake's forked tongue? Yet, the text seems to be saying that the snake only arrived after this incident.

19. What is sweetest.

20. Here the narrative line is unclear.

21. Apparently a dialect word, listed in Riggs dictionary 1845 of nonclassical words, accessed in Nairi dictionaries site on 12 December 2019.

22. Overwritten sign and neither under- nor overwriting is legible.

23. The story seems at least to have two aetiologies behind it: first, the forked tongue of the snake, and second, the wasps biting humans. However, in both instances (§§3–4), the last step of the action is unclear in the text.

յատակս ծովուն, եւ ձուկ մի կայ ի ծովն, եւ²⁴ ի բերան նորա ծաղիկ մի կայ: Ա՛ռ եւ կե՛ր, եւ այլ ի քո տեղն պիտի փոխիս»:

2/ Եւ եդիր սատանայ զթագն ի յեզր ծովուն եւ իջաւ ի ծովն, եւ առեալ զթագն Գաբրիէլ եւ փախեաւ յերկինքն:²⁵ Եւ հասեալ Սատայէլի հետեւէ՝ խած զոտիցն լերբանքն եւ անկաւ ի վայր: Եւ ասաց Գաբրիէլ. «զՀայր /fol 266r/ մեր, որ յերկինքն»: Եւ անկաւ սատանայ, եւ մնաց լերբնուցն միսն ի բերանն սատանայի. եւ այն է պատճառ, որ մարդոյն լերբանքն խոռ է:

Translation

1/ When Satan fell from heaven, a crown remained on his head. And Gabriel came and deceived Satan, and he said, "Descend to the foundations of the sea.

And there is a fish in the sea and there is a flower in its mouth. Take and eat it and you will be transferred again to your (former) place."

2/ And Satan put the crown on the sea shore and descended in the sea. And Gabriel took the crown and fled to heaven. And Satan, realizing (this), he ascended after (him) and he bit the soles of his feet; he fell down. And Gabriel said the Lord's Prayer. And Satan fell and the flesh of the soles remained in Satan's mouth. And that is the reason that human soles hollowed.[26]

---

24. Above line p.m.
25. Here, once more, to loss of the pluralizing meaning of -ք, is evident.
26. The story is thus an aetiology of the arch of the human foot. The narrative framework, however, is provided by the folktale of an angel retrieving an accoutrement stolen from heaven by Satan. See pp. 293–94.

Bibliography

Catalogues of the Manuscripts in the Matenadaran, Erevan

Short Catalogue

Eganyan, O., A. Zeyt'unyan, and P'. Ant'abyan. *Catalogue of Manuscripts of the Maštoc' Matenadaran* (Ցուցակ ձեռագրաց Մաշտոցի անուան Մատենադարանի). Vols. 1, 2. Erevan: Academy of Sciences, 1965–1966.
Malxasyan, Armen, *Catalogue of Manuscripts of the Maštoc' Matenadaran* (Ցուցակ ձեռագրաց Մաշտոցի անուան Մատենադարանի). Vol. 3. Erevan: Erevan State University Press, 2007.

General Catalogue

K'eōškerean, K., A. Suk'iasean, and Y. K'eosēean. *General Catalogue of Armenian Manuscripts of the Maštoc' Matenadaran* (Մայր ցուցակ հայերէն ձեռագրաց Մաշտոցի անուան Մատենադարանի). Vol. 4. Erevan: Nairi, 2008.
Tēr Vardanyan, Gēorg. *General Catalogue of Armenian Manuscripts of the Maštoc' Matenadaran* (Մայր ցուցակ հայերէն ձեռագրաց Մաշտոցի անուան Մատենադարանի). Vol. 7. Erevan: Nairi, 2012.
Tēr Vardanyan, Gēorg. *General Catalogue of Armenian Manuscripts of the Maštoc' Matenadaran* (Մայր ցուցակ հայերէն ձեռագրաց Մաշտոցի անուան Մատենադարանի). Vol. 9. Erevan: Nairi, 2017.

Other Works Cited

Agat'angełos. *History of the Armenians* (Պատմութիւն հայոց). Łoukasean Library 15. Tbilisi: Ałanean, 1914.
Albrecht, Felix, and Arthur Manukyan. *Epiphanius von Salamis: Über die Zwölf Steine im hohepriesterlichen Brustschild (De Duodecim Gemmis Rationalis)*. Gorgias Eastern Christian Studies 37. Piscataway, NJ: Gorgias, 2014.
Alexander, Paul Julius. *The Oracle of Baalbek: The Tiburtine Sibyl in Greek Dress*. Washington: Dumbarton Oaks, 1967.
Alishan, L. *Ancient and Pagan Religion of the Armenians* (Հին հաւատք կամ հեթանոսական կրօնք հայոց). Venice: Mekhitarist, 1910.
Ananyan, Shahé. "La Figure de Salomon et les livres sapienteaux dans la tradition arménienne." *REArm* 34 (2012): 29–39.

Anasyan, H. S. *Armenian Bibliology, 5–18th Centuries* (Հայկական մատենագիտութիւն (Ե.-ԺԲ. դդ.)), vol. 1. Erevan: Academy of Sciences, 1959.
Anonymous. *Armenian Classical Authors* (Մատենագիրք հայոց, Ժ. դար). Vol. 5.1. Antelias: Armenian Catholicossate of Cilicia, 2005.
Awetikʻean, G., X. Siwrmēlean, and M. Awkʻerean. *New Dictionary of the Armenian Language* (Նոր բառգիրք հայկազեան լեզուի). 2 vols. Venice: St. Lazzaro, 1837.
Bar-Ilan, Meir, "Magic Seals on the Body among Jews in the First Centuries C.E." *Tarbiz* 57 (1988): 37–50. (Hebrew)
Bardakjian, Kevork B., and Sergio LaPorta. *The Armenian Apocalyptic Tradition: A Comparative Perspective*. SVTP 25. Leiden: Brill, 2014.
Baronian, Sukias, and Frederik C. Conybeare, *Catalogue of the Armenian Manuscripts in the Bodleian Library*. Oxford: Clarendon, 1918.
Bauckham, R., James R. Davila, and Alexander Panayotov. *Old Testament Pseudepigrapha: More Noncanonical Scriptures*. Grand Rapids: Eerdmans, 2013.
Beer, Bernhard, *Leben Abrahams nach Auffassung der jüdischen Sagen*. Leipzig: Oskar Leiner, 1859.
Bezold, Carl. *Die Schatzhöhle, Syrisch und Deutsch herausgegeben*. Leipzig: Hinrichs, 1888.
Bobokhyan, A., Alexandra Gilibert, and Pavel Hnila, eds. *The Vishap on the Borderline of Fairy Tale and Reality* (Վիշապը հեքիաթի եվ իրականության սահմանին). Erevan: Institute of Archeology, 2019.
Bogharian, N. *Yovhannēs Tʻlkurancʻi: Poems* (Յովհաննէս Թլկուրանցի, Տաղեր). Jerusalem: St. James, 1958.
Brock, Sebastian P. "Clothing Metaphors as a Means of Theological Expression in Syriac Tradition." Pages 11–38 in *Typus, Symbol, Allegorie bei den östlichen Vätern und ihren Parallelen im Mittelalter: Internationales Kolloquium, Eichstatt 1981*. Edited by Margot Schmidt in collaboration with C. F. Geyer. Regensburg: Pustet, 1982.
———. "The Queen of Sheba's Questions to Solomon: A Syriac Version." *Le Muséon* 92 (1979): 331–45.
———. "Some Syriac Legends concerning Moses." *JJS* 33 (1982): 237–55.
Burchard, Christoph. *A Minor Edition of the Armenian Version of Joseph and Aseneth*. HUAS 10. Leuven: Peeters, 2010.
Chabot, Jean-Baptiste. *Chronique de Michel le Syrien, patriarche Jacobite d'Antioche (1166–1199)*. Paris: Leroux, 1899–1910. Repr., Brussels: Culture et Civilisation, 1963.
Chadwick, Henry. *Early Christian Thought and the Classical Tradition: Studies in Justin, Clement, and Origen*. Oxford: Clarendon, 1966.
Charles, Robert H. *The Book of Jubilees or the Little Genesis*. London: Black, 1902.
Charlesworth, James H., ed. *The Old Testament Pseudepigrapha*. 2 vols. Garden City, NY: Doubleday, 1983–1985.
Clements, Ruth A. "A Shelter amid the Flood: Noah's Ark in Early Jewish and Christian Art." Pages 277–99 in *Noah and His Books*. Edited by Michael E. Stone, Aryeh Amihay, and Vered Hillel. EJL 28. Atlanta: Society of Biblical Literature, 2010.
Collins, John J. *Daniel: A Commentary on the Book of Daniel*. Hermeneia. Minneapolis: Fortress, 1993.
———. *Daniel, with an Introduction to Apocalyptic Literature*. FOTL 20. Grand Rapids: Eerdmans, 1984.
———. *Seers, Sibyls and Sages in Hellenistic-Roman Judaism*. JSJSupp 54. Leiden: Brill, 1997.

———. *The Sibylline Oracles of Egyptian Judaism*. SBLDS 13. Missoula, MT: Scholars Press, 1974.
Conybeare, Frederick C. "An Old Armenian Version of Josephus." *JTS* 9 (1908): 577–83.
Conybeare, Frederick C., J. Rendel Harris, and Agnes Lewis Smith. *The Story of Aḥiḳar from the Aramaic, Syriac, Arabic, Armenian, Ethiopic, Old Turkish, Greek and Slavonic Versions*. Cambridge: Cambridge University Press, 1913.
Cox, Claude. *Armenian Job: Reconstructed Greek Text, Critical Edition of the Armenian with English Translation*. HUAS 8. Leuven: Peeters, 2006.
Cowe, S. Peter. *The Armenian Version of Daniel*, UPATS 9. Atlanta: Scholars Press, 1992.
———. "The Reception of the Book of Daniel in Late Antique and Medieval Armenian Society." Pages 81–125 in *The Armenian Apocalyptic Tradition: A Comparative Perspective*. Edited by Kevork Bardakjian and Sergio La Porta. Leiden: Brill, 2014.
Crouzel, Henri. *Origen*. Edinburgh: T&T Clark, 1989.
DiTommaso, Lorenzo. "The Penitence of Solomon (*De Paenitentia Salomonis*)." Pages 371–452 in *The Embroidered Bible: Studies in Biblical Apocrypha and Pseudepigrapha in Honour of Michael E. Stone*. Edited by Lorenzo DiTommaso, Matthias Henze, and William Adler. SVTP 26. Leiden: Brill, 2018.
Dowsett, Charles J. F. *The History of the Caucasian Albanians by Movses Dasxurancʻi*. London Oriental Series 8. London: Oxford University Press, 1961.
Ervine, Roberta R. "Antecedents and Parallels to Some Questions and Answers on Genesis in Vanakan Vardapet's Book of Questions." *Le Muséon* 113 (2000): 417–28.
Eshel, Esther. "The Imago Mundi of the Genesis Apocryphon." Pages 111–31 in *Heavenly Tablets: Interpretation, Identity and Tradition in Ancient Judaism*. Edited by Lynn LiDonnici and Andrea Lieber. JSJSup 119. Leiden: Brill, 2007.
Eshel, Esther, and Michael E. Stone. "The Eschatological Holy Tongue in Light of a Fragment from Qumran." *Tarbiz* 62 (1993): 169–77. (Hebrew)
Feldman, Louis H., *Flavius Josephus: Judean Antiquities 1–4*. Leiden: Brill, 2000.
Feydit, Frédéric. *Amulettes de l'Arménie chrétienne*. Bibliothèque arménienne de la Fondation Calouste Gulbenkian. Venice: St. Lazare, 1986.
Garitte, G. "Le texte arménien de l'invention des Trois Enfants de Babylone." *Le Muséon* 74 (1961): 91–108.
———. "L'Invention géorgienne des Trois Enfants de Babylone." *Le Muséon* 72 (1959): 69–100.
Garsoïan, Nina G. *The Epic Histories Attributed to Pʻawstos Buzand (Buzandaran Patmutʻiwnkʻ)*. HATS 8. Cambridge: Harvard University Press, 1989.
Geffcken, Johannes. *Die Oracula Sibyllina*. Leipzig: Hinrichs, 1902.
Ginzberg, Louis. *The Legends of the Jews*. 7 vols. Philadelphia: Jewish Publication Society, 1909–1938.
Greenfield, Jonas C., Michael E. Stone, and Esther Eshel. *The Aramaic Levi Document: Edition, Translation, Commentary*. SVTP 19. Leiden: Brill, 2004.
Gruen, Erich S. "Artapanus." Pages 675–85 in vol. 1 of *Outside the Bible: Ancient Jewish Writings Related to Scripture*. Edited by Louis H. Feldman, James L. Kugel, and Lawrence H. Schiffman. 3 vols. Philadelphia: Jewish Publication Society, 2013.
Hartman, Louis F., and Alexander A. Di Lella. *The Book of Daniel*. AB 23. Garden City, NY: Doubleday, 1978.
Haase, Felix. "Die armenischen Rezensionen der syrischen Chronik Michael des Grossen." *Oriens Christianus* NS 5 (1915): 60–82, 271–84.

Harutʻyunyan, Sargis. *Armenian Incantations and Folk Prayers* (Հայ հմայական եւ ժողովրդական աղօթքներ). Erevan: Erevan State University Press, 2006.

Henze, Matthias. "Nebuchadnezzar's Madness (Daniel 4) in Syriac Literature." Pages 559–71 in *The Book of Daniel: Composition and Reception*. Edited by John J. Collins and Peter W. Flint. Leiden: Brill, 2001.

Hilkens, Andy. "Language, Literacy and Historical Apologetics: Hippolytus of Rome's Lists of Literate Peoples in the Syriac Tradition." *Journal of Eastern Christian Studies* 72 (2020): 1–32.

———. "'Sons of Magog' or 'Thorgmians'?: The Description of the Turks (Book XIV) in Michael's Chronicle and Its Armenian Adaptations." Pages 401–14 in *Syriac Encounters: Papers from the Sixth North American Symposium, Duke University, 26–29 June 2011*. Edited by Maria Doerfler, Emanuel Fiano, and Kyle Smith. Eastern Christian Studies 20. Leuven: Peeters, 2015.

Himmelfarb, Martha. *Tours of Hell: An Apocalyptic Form in Jewish and Christian Literature*. Philadelphia: University of Pennsylvania, 1983.

Hollander, Harm W., and Marinus de Jonge. *Testaments of the Twelve Patriarchs: A Commentary*. SVTP 8. Leiden: Brill, 1985.

Issaverdens, James. *The Uncanonical Writings of the Old Testament Found in the Armenian MSS. of the Library of St. Lazarus*. 2nd ed. Venice: Mechitarist, 1934.

James, Montague R. *The Biblical Antiquities of Philo*. London: Society for Promoting Christian Knowledge, 1917. Repr. with prolegomenon by L. Feldman, New York: Ktav, 1971.

Jamkochian, see Žamkočʻean.

Karst, Josef. *Historische Grammatik des Kilikisch-Armenischen*. Strassburg: Trübner, 1901.

Kohler, Kaufman, and Isaac Broydé. "Nations and Languages, The Seventy." *Jewish Encyclopedia* 9:188–90.

Kraft, Robert A. "Moses and Ethiopia: Old Scripturesque Traditions behind Josephus, *Ant.* 2.238–253." Pages 602–16 in *The Embroidered Bible: Studies in the Biblical Apocrypha and Pseudepigrapha in Honour of Michael E. Stone*. Edited by Lorenzo DiTommaso, Matthias Henze, and William Adler. SVTP 26; Leiden: Brill, 2018.

Łanalanyan, Aram, *Traditional History* (Ավանդապատում). Erevan: Academy of Sciences, 1969.

Levene, Abraham. *The Early Syrian Fathers on Genesis from a Syriac Ms. on the Pentateuch in the Mignana Collection*. London: Taylor's Foreign Press, 1951.

Lewy, Hans. *The Armenian Text with a Critical Introduction*. Part 1 of *The Pseudo-Philonic De Jona*. Studies and Documents 7. London: Christophers, 1936.

Lipscomb, W. Lowndes. *The Armenian Apocryphal Adam Literature*. UPATS 8. Atlanta: Scholars Press, 1990.

———. "A Tradition from the Book of Jubilees in Armenian." *JJS* 29 (1978): 149–63.

Loeff, Yoav. "Four Texts from the Oldest Known Armenian Amulet Scroll: Matenadaran 115 (1428) with Introduction, Translation." MA thesis, Hebrew University of Jerusalem, 2002.

Mansfeld, Jaap. "Doxography of Ancient Philosophy." *Standford Encyclopedia of Philosophy*, 2004 (substantively revised 2020). Online: https://plato.stanford.edu/entries/doxography-ancient/.

Martirosean, A. A., *The Story and Counsels of Xikar the Wise*, 2 vols. Erevan: Academy of Sciences, 1969. (Armenian)

Mécérïan, Jean. "Introduction à l'étude des Synaxaires arméniens." Pages 99–188 in *Bulletin Arménologique. Melanges de l'Université de St. Joseph* 40. Beirut: Imprimerie Catholique, 1953.

Michael the Syrian: See Sawalaneanc', T.

Milikowsky, Chaim. *Seder Olam: A Critical Edition* (סדר עולם : מהדורה מדעית). Jerusalem: Yad Ben-Zvi, 2013.

Miltenova, Anissava. "The Apocryphon about the Struggle of the Archangel Michael with Satanail in Two Redactions." *Starobŭlgarska* 9 (1981): 98–113. (Bulgarian)

———. *South Slavonic Apocryphal Collections*. Sofia: Iztok-Zapad, 2018.

———. "An Unknown Redaction of the Apocryphon about the Struggle of the Archangel Michael with Satanail." Pages 121–28 in *Literary Study and Folklore*. Sofia, 1983. (Bulgarian)

Minov, Sergey. "The Cave of Treasures and the Formation of Syriac Christian Identity in Late Antique Mesopotamia: Between Tradition and Innovation." Pages 165–77 in *Between Personal and Institutional Religion: Self, Doctrine, and Practice in Late Antique Eastern Christianity*. Edited by Brouria Bitton-Ashkelony and Lorenzo Perrone. Cultural Encounters in Late Antiquity and the Middle Ages 15. Tournhout: Brepols; 2013.

Muradyan, Gohar, *Echoes of Ancient Greek Myths in Mediaeval Armenian Literature* (Հին հունական առասպելների արձագանքները հայ միջնադարյան մատենագրության մեջ). Erevan: Nairi, 2014.

Muradyan, Gohar, and Aram Topchyan. "Pseudo-Philo, On Samson and On Jonah." Pages 750–803 in vol. 1 of *Outside the Bible: Ancient Jewish Writings Related to Scripture*. Edited by Louis H. Feldman, James L. Kugel, and Lawrence H. Schiffman. 3 vols. Philadelphia: Jewish Publication Society, 2013.

Murray, Robert. *Symbols of Church and Kingdom: A Study in Early Syriac Tradition*. Cambridge: Cambridge University Press, 1975.

Nickelsburg, George W. E. "The Bible Rewritten and Expanded." Pages 149–52 in *Jewish Writings of the Second Temple Period*. Edited by Michael E. Stone. Compendia rerum judaicum ad Novem Testamentum 2.2. Philadelphia: Fortress; Assen: Van Gorcum, 1984.

Orlov, Andrei. "Moses' Heavenly Counterpart in the Book of Jubilees and the Exagoge of Ezekiel the Tragedian." *Biblica* 88 (2007): 153–73.

———. "The Face as the Heavenly Counterpart of the Visionary in the Slavonic Ladder of Jacob." Pages 59–76 in vol. 2 of *Of Scribes and Sages: Early Jewish Interpretation and Transmission of Scripture*. Edited by Craig A. Evans. 2 vols. Studies in Scripture in Early Judaism and Christianity 9. London: T&T Clark, 2004.

Parke, Herbert W. *Sibyls and Sibylline Prophecy in Classical Antiquity*. London: Routledge, 1988.

Paz, Yakir. "From Scribes to Scholars Rabbinic Biblical Exegesis in Light of the Homeric Commentaries." PhD diss., Hebrew University of Jerusalem, 2014.

Rajak, Tessa. "Moses in Ethiopia: Legend and Literature." Pages 257–72 in *The Jewish Dialogue with Greece and Rome: Studies in Cultural and Social Interaction*. By Tessa Rajak. Arbeiten zur Geschichte des antiken Judentums und des Urchristentums 48. Leiden: Brill, 2000.

Reed, Annette Y. "Enoch in the Armenian Apocrypha." Pages 149–87 in *The Armenian*

Apocalyptic Tradition: A Comparative Perspective. Edited by Kevork B. Bardakjian and Sergio La Porta. SVTP 25. Leiden: Brill, 2014.

Rubin, Milka. "The Language of Creation or the Primordial Language: A Case of Cultural Polemics in Antiquity." *JJS* 49 (1998): 306–33.

Runnalls, Donna. "Moses' Ethiopian Campaign." *JSJ* 14 (1983): 135–56.

Russell, James R. *Armenian and Iranian Studies*. HATS 9. Cambridge: Harvard University Press and Armenian Heritage Press, 2004.

———. *Zoroastrianism in Armenia*. Harvard Iranian Series 5. Cambridge: Harvard University, Department of Near Eastern Languages and Civilizations, 1987.

Sanjian, Avedis K. *Colophons of Armenian Manuscripts 1301–1480*. HATS 2. Cambridge: Harvard University Press, 1969.

Sarghissian, Barsegh. *Grand Catalogue des manuscrits arméniens de la bibliothèque des PP. Mekhitaristes de Saint-Lazare*. Venice: Mekhitarist, 1914. (Armenian)

Satran, David. *Biblical Prophets in Byzantine Palestine: Reassesing the Lives of the Prophets*. SVTP 11. Leiden: Brill, 1995.

Sawalaneancʻ, Tigran, ed. *Rev. Michael the Syrian Patriarch: The Chronography* (Տեառն Միքայէլի պատրիարքի Ասորւոյ Ժամանակագրութիւն). Jerusalem: St. James, 1870.

———. *Chronography of Rev. Michael, Patriarch of the Syrians* (Ժամանակագրութիւն տեառն Միքայէլի Ասորւոց պատրիարքի). Jerusalem: St. James, 1871.

Schermann, Theodor. *Prophetarum Vitae Fabulosae Indices Apostolorum Discipulorumque Domini Dorotheo Epiphanio Hippolyto Aliisque Vindicata*. Leipzig: Teubner, 1907.

Schmidt, Andrea B. "The Armenian Versions I and II of Michael the Syrian." *Hugoye* 16 (2013): 93–128.

———. "Die zweifache armenische Rezension der syrischen Chronik Michaels des Grossen." *Le Muséon* 109 (1996): 300–319.

Schwemer, Anna Maria. 1995. *Studien zu den frühjüdischen Prophetenlegenden Vitae Prophetarum: Einleitung, Übersetzung und Kommentar*. Texte und Studien zum Antiken Judentum 49, 50. 2 vols. Tübingen: Mohr Siebeck.

Scott, James M. "The Division of the Earth in Jubilees 8:11–9:15 and Early Christian Chronography." Pages 295–319 in *Studies in the Book of Jubilees*. Edited by Matthias Albani, Jörg Frey, and Armin Lange. Tübingen: Mohr Siebeck, 1997.

Serjuni, A. H. "St. Ephraem's 'On the Seven Vahangs(?) of Joseph.'" *Sion* 47 (1973): 26–37, 137. (Armenian)

Shinan, Avigdor. "Moses and the Ethiopian Woman: Sources of a Story in the Chronicle of Moses." *Scripta Hierosolymitana* 27 (1978): 66–78.

Speyer, Wolfgang. *Die literarische Fälschung im heidnischen und christlichen Altertum: Ein Versuch ihrer Deutung*. Munich: Beck, 1971.

Srapyan, Armenuhi. *Medieval Armenian Tales* (Հայ միջնադարեան գրոյցներ). Erevan: Academy, 1969.

Stone, Michael E. *Adam and Eve in the Armenian Traditions, Fifth through Seventeenth Centuries*. EJL 38. Atlanta: Society of Biblical Literature, 2013.

———. *Adamgirkʻ: The Adam Book of Aŕakʻel of Siwnikʻ*. Oxford: Oxford University Press, 2007.

———. *Ancient Judaism: New Visions and Views*. Grand Rapids: Eerdmans, 2011.

———. *Apocrypha, Pseudepigrapha and Armenian Studies: Collected Papers*. 3 vols. OLA 144–145, 253. Leuven: Peeters, 2006–2017.

———."The Armenian Apocryphal Literature: Translation and Creation." Pages 611–46 in *Il Caucaso: Cerniera fra culture dal Mediterraneo alla Persia (Secoli IV–XI)*. Settimane di studio dal centro italiano de studi sull'alto medioevo 43. Spoleto: Presso la Sede del Centro, 1996.

———. *Armenian Apocrypha Relating to Abraham*. EJL 37. Atlanta: Society of Biblical Literature, 2012.

———. *Armenian Apocrypha Relating to Adam and Eve*. SVTP 14. Leiden: Brill, 1996.

———. *Armenian Apocrypha Relating to Angels and Heroes*. EJL 45. Atlanta: SBL Press, 2016.

———. *Armenian Apocrypha Relating to Biblical Heroes*. EJL 49; Atlanta: SBL Press, 2019.

———. *Armenian Apocrypha Relating to Patriarchs and Prophets*. Jerusalem: Israel Academy of Sciences, 1982.

———. "Armenian Canon Lists II: The Stichometry of Anania of Shirak (c. 615–c. 690 C.E.)." *HTR* 68 (1975): 253–60.

———. "The Armenian Embroidered Bible." *JSP* 29 (2019): 3–11.

———. "The Armenian Embroidered Bible." Pages 380–91 in *Levon Khachikian Centenary: Proceedings of the International Armenological Dedicated to the 100th Anniversary of of Academician Levon Khachikian's Birth (28–30 June, 2018)*. Edited by Gēorg Ter-Vardanian, with Gohar Muradyan. Erevan: Matenadaran, 2019. (Armenian)

———. "An Armenian Epitome of Epiphanius' *de Gemmis*." *HTR* 82 (1982): 467–76.

———. "The Armenian Questions of St. Gregory: A Text Descended from 4 Ezra: Edition of Recension I." *Le Muséon* 131 (2018): 141–72.

———. "An Armenian Tradition Relating to the Death of the Three Companions of Daniel." *Le Muséon* 86 (1973): 111–23.

———. "Biblical Text and Armenian Retelling." *JSAS* 26 (2017): 82–87.

———. "The Bones of Adam and Eve." Pages 241–45 in *For a Later Generation: The Transformation of Tradition in Israel, Early Judaism, and Early Christianity*. Edited by Randal A. Argall, Beverly A. Bow, and Rodney A. Werline. Harrisburg, PA: Trinity Press International, 2000.

———. "The Death of Adam: An Armenian Adam Book." *HTR* 59 (1966): 283–91.

———. *Fourth Ezra: A Commentary on the Book of Fourth Ezra*. Hermeneia. Minneapolis: Fortress, 1990.

———. "Further Angelological Texts." Pages 427–35 in vol. 1 of *Apocrypha, Pseudepigrapha and Armenian Studies: Collected Papers*. OLA 144. Leuven: Peeters, 2006.

———, with additional annotations by Shlomi Efrati, *The Genesis Commentary by Step'anos of Siwnik'*. CSCO 695. Leuven: Peeters, forthcoming.

———. "Hidden in Crannies in Noah's Ark." Pages 333–57 in *Festschrift in Honor of Levon Ter Petrossian's 75th Anniversary*. Erevan: Matenadaran, 2021.

———. "Lists of Revealed Things in the Apocalyptic Literature." Pages 414–54 in *Magnalia Dei, the Mighty Acts of God: Essays on the Bible and Archaeology in Memory of G. Ernest Wright*. Edited by Frank M. Cross, Werner E. Lemke, and Patrick D. Miller. New York: Doubleday, 1976.

———. "The Months of the Hebrews." *Le Muséon* 101 (1988): 5–12.

———. "A New Edition and Translation of the Questions of Ezra." Pages 293–316 in *Solving Riddles and Untying Knots: Biblical, Epigraphic, and Semitic Studies in Honor of Jonas C. Greenfield*. Edited by Ziony Zevit, Seymour Gitin, and Michael Sokoloff. Winona Lake, IN: Eisenbrauns, 1995.

———. *Noncanonical Books and Traditions*. (Պարականոն գիրքեր եւ աւանդութիւններ). Erevan: Matenadaran, 2015.

———. "A Note on Daniel I.3." *ABR* 7 (1959): 67–71.

———. *The Penitence of Adam*. CSCO 429–430; SerArm 13–14. Leuven: Peeters, 1981.

———. "The Penitence of Solomon." *JTS* 29 (1978): 1–19.

———. "Sadayēl's Fall from Heaven." Volume in honor of Z. Aleksidze. Forthcoming

———. *Selected Studies in Pseudepigrapha and Apocrypha: With Special Reference to the Armenian Tradition*. SVTP 9. Leiden: Brill, 1991.

———. *Signs of the Judgement, Onomastica Sacra, and the Generations from Adam*. UPATS 3. Chico, CA: Scholars Press, 1981.

———. "Some Armenian Angelological and Uranographical Texts." *Le Muséon* 105 (1992): 147–57.

———. "Some Further Armenian Angelological Texts." Pages 427–35 in *Apocrypha, Pseudepigrapha and Armenian Studies: Collected Papers*. By Michael E. Stone. Leuven: Peeters, 2006.

———. "Some Texts on Enoch in the Armenian Tradition." Pages 517–30 in *Gazing on the Deep: Ancient Near Eastern and Other Studies in Honor of Tzvi Abusch*. Edited by Jeffrey Stackert, Barbara N. Porter and David P. Wright. Bethesda, MD: CDL, 2010.

———. "Three Apocryphal Fragments from Armenian Manuscripts." Pages 939–46 in *A Teacher for All Generations: Essays in Honor of James C. Vanderkam*. Edited by Eric F. Mason et al. Leiden: Brill, 2012.

———. "Two Armenian Manuscripts and the Historia Sacra." Pages 21–36 in *Apocryphes arméniens: Transmission, traduction, création, iconographie; Actes du colloque international sur la littérature apocryphe en langue arménienne, Genève, 18–20 septembre, 1997*. Edited by Valentina Calzolari Bouvier, Jean-Daniel Kaestli, and Bernard Outtier. Lausanne: Zèbre, 1999.

———. "Two Stories about the Ark of the Covenant." Pages 253–66 in *Sion, mère des églises: Mélanges liturgiques offerts au Père Charles Athanase Renoux*. Edited by M. D. Findikyan, Daniel Galadza, and André Lossky. Münster: Aschendorff, 2016.

———. "Warum Naphthali? Eine Diskussion im Internet." *Judaica: Beiträge zum Verständnis des Judentums* 45 (1998): 188–91.

Stone, Michael E., Aryeh Amihai, and Vered Hillel. *Noah and His Book(s)*. EJL 28. Atlanta: Society of Biblical Literature, 2010.

Stone, Michael E. and Roberta E. Ervine. *The Armenian Texts of Epiphanius of Salamis De mensuris et ponderibus*. CSCO 583; CSCO Subsidia 105. Leuven: Peeters, 2000.

Stone, Michael E., and E. Eshel. "The Eschatological Holy Tongue in Light of a Fragment from Qumran." *Tarbiz* 62 (1993): 169–77. (Hebrew)

Stone, Michael E., J. C. Greenfield, and E. Eshel. *The Aramaic Levi Document: Edition, Translation, Commentary*. SVTP 19. Leiden: Brill, 2004.

Stone, Michael E., and Vered Hillel. *The Armenian Version of the Testaments of the Twelve Patriarchs: Edition, Apparatus, Translation and Commentary*. HUAS 11. Leuven: Peeters, 2012.

Stone, Michael E. and Vered Hillel, "Index of Variants." Pages 421–46 in *The Armenian Version of the Testaments of the Twelve Patriarchs: Edition, Apparatus, Translation and Commentary*. HUAS 11. Leuven: Peeters, 2012.

Stone, Michael E., and M. E. Shirinian. *Pseudo-Zeno: Anonymous Philosophical Treatise*. Philosophia Antiqua 83. Leiden: Brill, 2000.

Stone, Michael E., and John Strugnell. *The Books of Elijah*, Parts 1 and 2. SBLTT 5. Missoula, MT: Scholars Press, 1979.

Stone, Michael E., and Aram Topchyan. *Studies in the History of the Jews in Armenia*. Oxford: Oxford University Press, forthcoming.

Stone, Michael E., and Edda Vardanyan, "Jacob and the Man at the Ford of Jabbok: A Biblical Subject in the Vine Scroll Frieze of the Church of the Holy Cross atAłt'amar." In *Armenia through the Lens of Time: Multidisciplinary Studies in Honour of Theo Maarten van Lint*. Edited by Frederico Alpi, Robin Meyer, Irene Tinti, and David Zakarian. Leiden: Brill, forthcoming.

Stone, Michael E., Benjamin G. Wright, and David Satran. *The Apocryphal Ezekiel*. EJL 18. Atlanta: Society of Biblical Literature, 2000.

Suciu, Alin. "The Sermo Asceticus of Stephen the Theban in Sahidic Coptic." *JTS* 69 (2018): 628–73.

Tat'ewac'i, Grigor. *Book of Questions* (Գիրք Հարցմանց). Constantinople, 1729. Repr. Jerusalem: St. James Press, 1993.

———. *Book of Sermons Called Summer Volume* (Գիրք քարոզութեան, որ կոչի Ամառան հատոր). Constantinople, 1741. Repr., Jerusalem: St. James, 1998.

Thomson, Robert W. *The Armenian Adaption of the Ecclesiastical History of Socrates Scholasticus: Commonly Known as "the Shorter Socrates."* HUAS 3. Leuven: Peeters, 2001.

———. *The Teaching of St. Gregory*. Rev. ed. Avant 1. New Rochelle: St. Nersess Armenian Seminary, 2001.

Thomson, Robert W., James Howard–Johnston, and Tim Greenwood. *The Armenian History Attributed to Sebeos*. Translated Texts for Historians 31. Liverpool: Liverpool University Press, 1999.

Torijano Morales, Pablo. *Solomon the Esoteric King: From King to Magnus, Development of a Tradition*. JSJSup 72. Leiden: Brill, 2002.

Wevers, John William. *Genesis: Septuaginta*. Vetus Testamentum Graece 1. Göttingen: Vandenhoeck & Ruprecht, 1974.

Williams, Frank. *The Panarion of Epiphanius of Salamis: Books II and III (Sects 47–80 De Fide)*. Nag Hammadi and Manichaean Studies 36. Brill: Leiden, 1994.

Wright, G. Ernest. "Art: Sinai." *IDB* 4:376.

Wutz, Franz Xavier. *Onomastica Sacra: Untersuchungen zum Liber Interpretationis Nominum Hebraeorum des Hl. Hieronymus*. TU 41/2. Leipzig: Hinrichs, 1915.

Xač'ikyan, L., Y. Kēosēeyan, and M. Papazian. *Commentary of Genesis by Eghishe*. Erevan: Magharat, 2004. (Armenian)

Yovsēp'ianc', Sargis. *Uncanonical Books of the Old Testament* (Անկանոն գիրք Հին Կտակարանաց). Venice: Mekhitarist, 1896.

Žamkoč'ean, Anushavan. *The Bible and Armenian Oral Tradition* (Աստուածաշունչը եւ հայ բանաւոր աւանդոյթը). Ajemian Series 15. Erevan: Erevan State University, 2012.

Zeyt'unyan, A. *The Book of Genesis* (Գիրք Ծննդոց). Monuments of Ancient Armenian Translations. Erevan: Academy of Sciences, 1985.

Zohrabean, J., ed. *The Scriptures of the Old and New Testaments*. Venice: Mekhitarist, 1805.

Index of Subjects

Aaron
    bewailed thirty days, 148
    buried on mountain, 148
    death of, 148
    and Miriam calumniate Moses, 147, 148, 277, 290
    and Miriam, God rebukes, 147
    Moses's brother, priest, 121, 123, 142, 149, 150, 162, 163
    and sons, ordained priests, 147
Abednego, 215
Abel
    begetting of, 49
    murder of, 49
Abełmaoul, place, 168
Abgar V, king, son of Nabopolassar, 214
Abimelech, king, 79, 103, 106
Ableman, Oren, xi
Abraham, 52, 53, 59, 69, 80, 96, 97, 98, 105, 106, 108, 142, 163, 204, 210, 242, 243
    astronomer, 76
    death of, 79
    and Lot, separation of, 103
    name changed, 101
    possessions of, 103
    promise to, 98
    prophecy to, 100
    recognition of God, 75, 76
    traditions, 245
    trial of by fire, 96
    two brothers of, 103
Abram (Abraham), 101
abyss, 14
Adam, 13, 41, 210, 274
    and Eve, created outside Eden, 273, 289
    ate fruit from pity of Eve, 285–286
    brilliant countenance of, 148
    crown of, 157
    feared his descendants would sin, 280
    form of, 157
    in the garden, time unknown, 273
    language of, 65
    language of, questions and answers about, 59, 64
    leather garment of, 273
    luminous, 155
    repented, 290
    saw Enoch's transferal, 280. 291
    sin of, inadvertent, 42
    sleep of, 43
adamant, 163
Adamē, place, 97
Adler, William, 278
Adoniel, angel, 18, 21
Adullamite, 114
adultery, 114
Aeneid, work, 252
aetiologies, 295
Africa, 68
Agatʻangełos, 233
    Teaching of St. Gregory, work, 71
Ahab, King, 186, 190
Ahiqar, 3, 53, 233
Albani, Matthias, 68
Albrecht, Felix, 9
Alexander, Paul Julius, 252
Alexandria, School of, 256
Alishan, Łevont, 12
altar, 108
    Abraham builds, 97
    three, Abraham builds, 97
Amalekites, 147, 152, 162
Amat-horn, daughter of Job, 209
Amēlasad, overseer of three youths, 216

Amihai, Aryeh, 48, 275
Ammon, birth of, 103
Ammonites, 103
Amram, father of Moses and Aaron, 143, 210
amulet rolls, 29
Anania Širakac'i, texts by, 9
Anania(h), 32, 242, 244, 245,
    appointed overseer, 243
    called Sedrak, 230
    son of Jehoiakim, 214
Ananian(e)s
    blessing in fiery furnace, 232
    name for three young men, 230, 232
Ananyan, Shahé, 278
Anasyan, Hakob, 53
Anayel, angel, 18, 21
Ancient of Days, God, 235
angel(s), 15, 21, 23, 28, 99, 101, 103, 108, 236, 295
    apotropaic text concerning, 27
    classes of, 15, 19, 21
    classes of, order, 16, 22
    in danger of hubris, 289
    descends, 231
    encounters Hagar, 99
    fallen, 17
    glorify God, 272
    hosts of, twelve, 27
    image of, 30
    invocation of, 29
    Jacob's countenance like, 111
    names, orthography of, 16
    names, protective use of, 37
    nine classes of, 15, 17, 19, 20, 24, 27
    not informed of virgin birth, 279, 291
    of presence, 34
    protects Lot, 102
    seven classes of, 21
    tenth class of, 15, 17
    three, appear to Abraham, 100
    two, at Lot's house, 102
    wrestles with Jacob, 110
angelic ceremony, 205
Anton
    presbyter of monastery, 235
    steals relics, 235

Apollo, Temple of, 252, 254
Apostles called sheep, 283
apotropaic texts, 26
Aquila, 101
Arab (language), 65
Araboth Moab, place, 151
Arak'el Siwnec'i, *Adamgirk'*, work, 9
Arakelyan, Ani, xi, 5, 156
Aram, 96
Aram (Achan, Haran), death of, 96
Aran (Haran), person, 104
Ararat, Mt., 50
arch of foot, aetiology of, 297
archangels, 29
    class of, 21, 23, 28
archistrategos, 162
Arevshatyan, Sen, xi
Aristotle, 251
ark, 52, 57, 58, 62
    building, six hundred years, 275
    of the covenant, 143
    dimensions, 48
    door of, 49
    four-cornered, resembled a box, 48
    hole in, 295,
    reason it was built by Noah, 49
Armenian Pseudepigrapha, 221, 238
    in erotapokritic form, 256
    of Solomon, 278
    technique of composition, 166, 199
arms outstretched, in prayer, 195
Artashes, 233, 235
asceticism, Christian, 243
Asia, 68
Asp'aneh, chief eunuch, 230, 231
Assyrians, 198
astrologers, 142
Atticus, king, 218, 233
authorial practice, 111
Azaria(h), 242, 244
    appointed treasurer, 243
    called Misak', 230
    son of Jehoiakim, 214
    takes Mishael's head 233
Azariēl, angel, 35
Azotus (Ashdod), place, 190

INDEX OF SUBJECTS

Babylon, 12, 56, 58, 63, 193, 222, 230, 234, 247
Bałdat, ruler of Sawkʻites, 208
Balthasar, King, 233
Bar-Ilan, Meir, 35
Baraguel, Barakʻiel, 18, 21
Bardakjian, Kevork B., 274
Barhebraeus, 101
barley, 106
Baronian, S., 29
Baruch, 3, work, 256
Bathuel, 104
beard, pulling of, 144, 182
bears, 169
beastiality, 113
beasts, Daniel's vision of, 235
Beer, Bernhard, 76
Bel. *See* Bēl
Bēl
    name of a god, 215
    statue of, 231, 244
Bel and the Dragon, work, 215
Bēl, Hamite, 56, 57, 58
    hunter, 57, 58
Belteshazzar, Baltasar, 215
Benjamin, 116, 117
    birth of, 112
Benjamin, tribe, 152
Bereznyak, Asya, 256, 274, 281
Bethel
    altar set up at, 112
    place, 108, 165, 168, 169, 191
Bezalel b. Uri b. Hur, built Tabernacle, 147
Bezold, Carl, 65
Bible, 11, 13
biblical epitome, 80
Biblical Paraphrases, work, 70
Bilhah, 109, 112
birds, come to Abraham, 99
births, multiple, 62, 188
Blokland, Dina, xi
blood, sweet, of human neck, 296
Bobokhanyan, A., 12
Book and commandment, God gave Moses, 276, 290
Book of the Watchers, 256
booty, 98

bread and wine, 98
Bregman, Marc, 281
brick, 56, 57, 58, 62, 71
Brock, Sebastian P., 58, 78, 129, 130
Broydé, Isaac, 71
Burchard, Christoph, 242
burning bush, 145
butler, Pharaoh's, 115

Cain
    birth of, 49
    killed Abel for envy, 274
    killed Abel with flint, 281
    repented, 274
    seven transgressions of, 281
    survived the flood, 274
calf, 100
Calne (Kʻałanē), plain of, 56, 58, 63
calves, heifers, two golden, 168
Calzolari Bouvier, Valentina, 220
Canaan, land, 96, 103
Canaanites, 112, 116, 157
    thirty-two kings of, 162
Čařĕndir (Collection of Homilies), work, 166
carob tree, 77
catch-phrase citations, 80
cave, 192
    Jonah buried in, 192
centurion, 279
Chabot, J.-B., 130
Chadwick, Henry, 24
Chaldean (language), 65
Chaldeans, wise men and magicians of, 232
Chanethothes, assassin, 123, 126, 131, 132
Charles, Robert H., 69
Charlesworth, James H., 252
Chazon, Esther, 281
Chedorlaomer, king, 98
Chenephres, King of Memphis, 122, 123,
Cherubs, 17, 21, 24, 28, 33
Christ, 158
    created material being, 6
    prophecy of, 254
circumcision, 100, 112, 123
Clements, Ruth A., 48

cloud, 246
    black, mixed with fire, 181, 196, 197
    luminous, 146
coffin
    silver, 234
    golden, of Daniel, 218
cold, as punishment, 13
Collins, John J., 58, 215, 245, 251, 253
commandment and book, God gave
    Moses, 276
Concerning the Ark of God, work, 246
conversion, of Gentiles, 187
Conybeare, F. C., 3, 29, 128
cosmogonic views, 3
countenances
    angelic, of three youths, 216
    resplendent, 243
Cowe, S. Peter, 221, 224
Cox, Claude, 199
creation
    artistry of, 5
    from nothing, 5
    through wisdom, 3, 4
cross
    of four types of wood, 27
    invocation of, 254
    nature of, 284–285
    removes flaming sword, 274
Crouzel, Henri, 25
crown, cast down, 182
cupbearer, Pharaoh's, 115, 116
cures, by Jew, 234
Cushite woman, Moses marries, 122
Cyrus, King, 218, 233

Daguel, Dakuel, angel, 18, 21
Dan, place, 165, 168
Daniel
    and three youths honored, 233
    and three youths, into fiery furnace, 231
    and three youths, refrain from king's food, 216
    beloved of God, angels, humans, 218
    buried in Babylon, 237
    called Baldasar, 230
    cast into lions' den, 236
    court tales of, 245
    Epitome of, work, 211
    interprets dream, 232, 233
    in lions' den, 222
    LXX, 238
    means judgement, 215
    physiognomic description of, 237
    prophet, 235
    retelling of, 154
    takes Anania(h)'s head, 234
    texts from hagiographic literature, 221
    uncle of three young men, 230
    uncle of three youths, son of Jehoiakim, 214
    wisdom of, 231
Dara, place, 231
Darius, King, 233, 235
darkness, 157, 285
    thick, 12, 13
David
    forbidden to build Temple, 278
    King, sons of, 229
    meaning Psalms, 217
David of T'oxat', merchant, 45
Day, daughter of Job, 209
death
    sad news of, 181
    description of, 13
Deborah, 112
    oak of, 186, 187, 190
deer, 127, 147
    deer hunt, 143
    hunting serpents, 123
demon(s), 12, 14, 15, 35, 37
demonic possession, 273
desert, 157
dew
    drops in furnace, 246
    produces cold wind, 246
diacritical marks, 156
dialogic-dispute form, 256
Dinah, 109, 111
Dionysius of Telmaḥre, Chronicle, 129
directions
    four, 6
    six, 7

INDEX OF SUBJECTS

DiTommaso, Lorenzo, 124, 252, 278
doctors (learned), 66
Doerfler, Maria, 130
Dominions, angelic class, 17, 21, 23, 28
Dotayin, place, 113
dove, 50, 51
Dowsett, Charles J.F., 69
doxographic collection, 251
dragon, 12, 195
    Daniel kills, 237
dream interpretation, 233
drum, symbol of virginity, 277
Duraʻ, toponym, Armenian forms of, 224

earth, 5
    creation of, 5
    creation of, material beings from, 6
    made of wind and water, 7
    in midst of heavens, 7
    to be renewed manyfold, 280, 291
earthquake, 181, 183, 196
Easter chronology, 152
Eber, person, 65
Eden, Enoch, and Elijah in, 280, 291
Edessa, 214
Edom, is Esau, 112
Edomites, 105
educated in Egyptian wisdom, Joseph, 122
Egypt, 12, 97, 113, 117, 122, 145
    darkness of, 12
    plagues of, 100
    quakes in, 152
Eleazar, 145
Ełēazar, of Damascus, 99
Eleazar, confusion with name, 145
elements, 5–6
    creation of, 5
    four, 5, 6
    four, mixture of, 5
    four, positions of, 6
    role of in cosmogony, 6
Eli, 164–66
    death of, 165
    identified with Ahaiah and Selōm, 165
    vision of two heifers, 165
Elijah, 168, 169, 186, 187, 190, 283, 284

Eliphaz, king of Teman, 208
Elisha, 166, 167, 168, 169, 199
    ploughing, 168
    saw Elijah's transferral, 280
Elpia, land, 68
Enoch, 283
    did not eat fruit, 274
    virtue, 274
Enosh, 65
Ephraim, 117
    blessing of, 118
Ephron the Hittite, 104
Epistle, God gave to Adam, 3
Er, son of Judah, 114
erotapokritic writings, 46, 59, 66, 153
erpotapokritic dialogues, 256
Ervine, Roberta R., 9, 54, 256
Esau, 105, 106, 107, 108, 110, 111, 152, 188, 192, 210
    called Edom and Sēir, 112
    reconciled with Jacob, 111
    reddish, hunter, 105
    sons of, 80
eschaton, visible waters dried up, 285
Eshel, Esther, 65, 69, 168
Ethiopia, Ethiopians, 123, 152, 195
    and India confused, 152
    Queen of, 125
Europe, 68
Eusebius, 127
Eve, 289
    attitude to, 41
    creation of, 41
    inadvertent sin of, 41, 42
    obedient to head, 43
    shares rib, 43
ewes, lambed thrice yearly, 109
exile
    Assyrian, 214
    Babylonian, 214
    due to sins, 245
eyes, vision and not light, 158
Ezekiel, prophet, 279

face, shining, 155
false prophets are Sodomites, 102

family heads or princes, seventy/seventy-two, 56, 57, 61, 68
famine, 97, 106
fast(s), 182, 196, 197, 243
    Daniel and three young men, 233
    forty days, 137, 151
    forty days, three, 146
Father (God), 25, 63
Feldman, Louis H., 122, 124, 192
Feydit, Frédéric, 19, 26, 29, 32, 33, 34, 36, 37
Fiano, Emanuel, 130
fiery flames, from Jonah's mouth, 196
Findikyan, M. Daniel, 190
finger of God, wrote tablets, 146
fire, 5, 6, 183
    Christ's form, 253
    column of, 146
    connected with Nimrod, 69
    from heaven, 99
    heavens made of, 6
    in furnace, extinguished, 247
    like dew, 231
    punishment by, 14
    unquenchable, 8
    worship of, 69, 96
fish, devouring, 295
Flint, Peter W., 58
Flood
    chronology of, 50
    forty days, 275
Floods, Two, 56, 62
folk tales, 293
Form and Structure of Noah's Ark 8, 62
forty days, Joshua stands for, 161
four hundred men, Esau's, 111
fourth man, brilliant, in furnace, 232
fragrance
    of Eden, 50
    of Jacob, 107
    sweet, 66
free will, 273
Frik, 4
Frey, Jörg, 68
furnace, 244

Gabriel
    angel, 18, 21, 33, 37, 144
    deceives Satan, 297
Galadza, Daniel, 190
Ganges, River, 152
garden of Eden, 13
    beauty and glory of, 42, 44
    search for, 57, 58, 62
Garitte, Gerard, 218, 222, 223, 238
Garsoïan, Nina G., 275
gazelles, 132
Geffken, Johannes, 253
geomancer, 254
Gersam, 145
Gilibert, Alexandra, 12
Ginzberg, Louis, 76, 187, 276
gloom, of Adam, 158
God
    appears to Job, 209
    creator of all, 245
    glorification of, 289
    intervention of, 246
    mercy of, 181
    name of, Daniel mentions, 236
    permitted Satan's possession of serpent, 273
    power of, 66, 195
    revelations by, to pagans, 253
    rewards three youths, 217
    told Adam that Cain had killed Abel, 280
Gog and Magog, 53
Gomorra, 97
    destruction of, 101
Goshen, land of, 117
Gospel, 12
gourd vine, 184
Greek ideas, in cosmogony, 5
Greek traditions, in Armenian culture, 252
Greenfield, Jonas C., 168
Greenwood, Tim, 218
Grigor Narekac'i, 286
Grigor Tat'ewac'i, 6, 42–45, 48
    Book of Questions, work, 256
Grigor Xlat'ec'i Cerenc', 159
groaning, 13

INDEX OF SUBJECTS 315

Gruen, Erich S., 122
Grypeou, Emmanouela, 294

Haase, Felix, 130
Habakkuk, 166
    story, 236
    food for reapers, 236
    prophet, 236
    translated to lions' den, 236
Hades, 114
Hagar, Abraham's concubine, 99, 105
hail, of stones, 13
Ham, 275
Hamites, thirty-two languages of, 70
Hamor and Shechem, confusion of, 104
Hamor, Hittite, sold cave to Abraham, 104
Haran, place, 96, 108
Harris, J. Rendall, 3
Harutʻyunyan, Sargis, 19, 26, 29
Hayk, 56, 57, 244
heaven, creation of, 5
heavenly table, 217
heavens
    fiery, 6, 7
    height of, 7
    number of, 5
    of earth and water, 6
    sphere of, divided into two, 7
Hebrew children, 143, 145
Hebrews, 152
Hell, 10
    created by God, 11
    description of, 13
    grave called, 13
    name of, 11
    no acquaintance in, 284, 292
    outside this world, 13
    texts concerning, 8
    thick darkness, 12
    tortures of, 53
Hellad, Greece, 193
hendiadys, 233
Henze, Matthias, 58, 124, 278
Hermopolis
    construction of, 131
    Moses founded, 123
Herod, 36

hexameter, 253
Hezekiah, King, 229
hierarchy, earthly, 27
high priest, 168
High Priesthood, angelic, 21
Hilkens, Andy, 65, 130
Hillel, Vered, 48, 93, 142, 146, 172, 271, 275, 286, 287
Himmelfarb, M., 9
hinds. *See* deer
Hirah, 114
Hittite wives of Esau, 108
Hittites, 104
Hnila, Pavel, 12
Hollander, Harm, 142
Holy Spirit, 25, 63, 178, 180, 236
honey, wild, 77
Hosea, Joshua's former name, 161
Howard-Johnson, James, 218
Hṙakʻēl, angel over mountains, 34
humans, multiplication of, 67

ibis(es)
    sacred, habitat of, 127
    attack serpents, 123
idolatry, 168
idols, 76
    broken, 77
    Laban's, 110
Ignatios of Amida, scribe, 45
image of God is free will, 272
India, 128
    river of, 195
infanticide, 143
intelligible, attribute, 66, 157
Inventio of of the relics of the three young men, 217, 221–22, 235, 238
invocation, by Moses, 121
Isaac, 53, 79, 103, 105–7, 142, 163, 210, 242, 243
    blindness of, 107
    death of, 112
    prayers of, 105
Isaiah, 285
    sawn in two by Manasseh, 292
Iscah, Lot's daughter, 96
Isfahan (Šoš), 222, 235

Ishmael, 79, 99, 163
  daughter of marries Esau, 108
  sons of, 80
  twelve peoples from, 99
Ishmaelites, 113
Ishodad of Merv, 130
Israel, Israelites, 105, 151, 168, 198
  buried Egyptian masters, 152
  in desert for 40 years, 146
  plundered Egyptians of wages owed, 276
Issaverdens, Jacques, 193, 198

Jabbok, stream, 111
Jacob, 34, 105, 106, 108, 111, 116, 117, 118, 142, 163, 210, 242, 243
  agreement with Laban, 110
  anger of, 112
  blesses sons, 118
  change of name, 110
  disguised, 107
  father of Joseph, Mary's husband, 211
  favored Joseph, 112
  gifts of, to Esau, 111
  interred in Canaan, 118
  Joseph's garment sent to, 113
  reconciled with Esau, 111
  smooth, 105
  wages of, 108, 109
  wrestles with angel, 110
Jacob of Edessa, 133
Jaffa, place, 194
James son of Zebedee, 282
James, Montague Rhodes, 192
Jannes and Jambres, 130, 131, 133, 134
Japheth, 49, 275
Japhetites, fifteen languages of, 70
Jehoiakim, King of Judah, 214, 229
Jericho, 150, 169
Jerome, 187
Jerusalem, 23, 168, 190, 191, 192, 230, 235, 242
  heavenly, 291
  overthrown, 186, 192
Jews, 105, 234
  called Canaanites, 283
  language of, 65

Jezebel, 186, 190
Joakim, first, in Daniel, 211
Job, 199, 210
  all creation revealed to, 209
  Book of, 166
  Book of, Armenian, expansion in, 207, 210
  brothers and sisters of, 209
  faithful in losses, 206, 207
  formerly Yobab, 204
  good deeds of, 204
  grandson of Esau, 204
  image of Adam, 210
  king, 204
  offers sacrifices for his children, 204
  response to friends, 209
  restoration of, 209
  saw great-grandchildren, 210
  sixth generation from Abraham, 210
  wife of rebukes him, 207, 208
  wife of remains faithful, 208
Jobab son of Zerah, king of Edom, 204
Jochebed, 143
  daughter of Levi, 142–43
  Moses's mother, 142
John Chrysostom, 284
John Damascenus, writings of, 251
John, apostle, 282
John the Baptist
  food of, 75, 77
  worshipped Christ from the womb, 279, 291
Jonah, 62, 170
  Book of, 12
  buried in cave, 186, 187
  commanded by Holy Spirit, 178. 180
  fifth birth of, 186, 190
  fled not to be false prophet, 279
  four births of, 178
  four mothers or births of, 190
  gives sign, 186
  gloomy, 184, 197
  God reproaches, 197, 198
  and his mother go to Tyre, 186
  instructs the people of Nineveh, 185
  lied, 185
  people of Nineveh comfort, 185

INDEX OF SUBJECTS

prophet, 180, 181, 190, 192, 193, 196
rebuked, 184
resurrected by God, 186
returns home, 185
shining face of, 196
slept in storm, 194
texts, list of, 170
of tribe of Asher, 187
Jonah 1, work, 142, 170, 172
Jonge, Marinus de, 142
Jordan, River, 150
 splitting of, 162, 169
Joseph, 115, 117, 118, 242
 in Armenian pseudepigrapha, 242
 bowl of, 117
 dreams of, 113
 flowery robe of, 112
 imprisoned, 115
 imprisons brothers, 116
 interprets dreams, 115, 116
 Jacob favored, 112
 and Potiphar's wife, 115
 set over Egypt, 116
 sojourn in Egypt, 118
 taxes collected by, 118
 type of Christ, 113, 242
Joseph and Asenath, 242
Josephus, 123–25, 127
 Jewish War, Armenian version of, 128
 Syriac summary of, 129
Joshua
 attends Moses on Sinai, 161
 biography of, 159
 Moses ordains, 161
 son of Nun, 3, 148, 149
 texts, nine, 159
 type of Christ, 161
 virgin, 161
Judah, 23, 113, 114
 kingship given to, 142
Judah, apostle, perfidious and unworthy, 282, 291
Judah, tribe, 152, 229
Judean Hills, 190
Jupiter Capitolinus, 253

Kʻsantʻi, 145
 Moses kills, 122, 126, 132
Karst, Josef Dan, 230, 294
Kassia, daughter of Job, 209
Kenaz, judge, 188, 192
 cave of, 186, 187, 192
Keturah, 105
King of Nineveh, lament of, 182
kingdom of God
 acquaintance in, 284
 praise by angels and righteous in, 285
kingdom of heaven, no eating or drinking in, 284
kings, five, 98
Kirakos Arewelcʻi, 218
Kiriath Jearim, place, 177, 190
knowledge, rational, 216
Kohath, 142, 210
Kohler, Kaufmann, 71
Kraft, Robert A., 124
Kr̄etios, angel over the luminaries, 37
Kugel, James L., 122

Laban, 107, 108
 agreement with Jacob, 110
ladder, vision of, 108
Lamech (Cainite)
 killed Cain, 274, 290
 suffered forty-nine punishments, 281
 traditions of, 256
Lamur, Shemite, 56, 57
Łanalanyan, Aram, 293
land
 division of, 162
 promises of, omitted, 80, 100
Lange, Armin, 68
language(s)
 confusion of, 52, 63, 66, 70
 eschatological, 66
 heavenly, 65
 new, 152
 seventy-two, 66
 taught to three youths, 216
 twelve, 69
LaPorta, Sergio, 274
laws and books, ancestral, 245
Leah, 108, 109

learned (scholastic) works and writing, 66, 79, 80, 103, 106, 112, 255
leather cloak, 168, 169, 179, 289–90
left side, 43
legumes, 216, 230, 231, 243
lecanomancy, 117
lentil, 105, 106
Levene, Abraham, 65
Levi, 142, 210
Levites, 147, 152
Leviathan, food of, 295
levirate marriage, 114
Levite origin of Moses and Aaron, 142
Lewy, Hans, 171
LiDonnici, Lynn, 69
Lieber, Andrea, 69
lightning, 183
Limbo, text concerning, 8
Lint, Th. M. van, xi
lions, famished for seven days, 236
lions' den, Daniel freed from, 237
Lipscomb, W. Lowndes, 41, 274, 281
list(s)
    apocryphal traditions in, 255
    examples of, 255
    of familial relations, 183
literate peoples, twelve, 75
liturgy, angelic, heavenly, 27, 37
locusts, 77
Loeff, Yoav, 11
Lord's Prayer, 297
Lossky, André, 190
Lot, 96, 97, 102, 103
    captured, 98
    daughter's incest, for offspring, 278
    daughters, not forgiven, 278, 291
    mocked, 102
    wife and daughters of, 102
    wife, pillar of salt, 102
luminaries and stars, eschatological enhancement of, 285
luminosity, 158
luminous faces, 148
Luza, Luz, place, 112
Lybia, 68

3 Maccabees, work, 221
Machpelah, cave of, 103, 104, 106, 118
magi, 235
magical manuscripts, texts, 26, 29
magicians, execution of, 233
Mahanaim, place, 111
Malxutʻa, Christian
    disguised as Jew, 234
    learns of relics, 234
Mamre
    oaks of, 97
    place, 112
man, image of God means free will, 289
Manasseh, 117
    blessing of, 118
mandrakes, 109
manna, 146
Mansfeld, Jaap, 251
Manukyan, Arthur, 9
Mari, Moses's adoptive mother, 122, 126, 131, 132, 145
Mari. See Mari,
Martirosean, A. A., 3
martyrological sentiments, 245
Mary, Virgin, 211
Mashtots Matenadaran. See Matenadaran
Masis, Mt., Ark stops on, 50
Matenadaran, xi
Maurice, king of Greeks, 218
Mazis, Great, Ark stops on, 275
meat, Noah started eating of, 290, 276
Mécérian, Jean, 159
mediator, 180
Melchizedek, 23, 53
    oracular function, 105
    priest, 98
Melkʻol (Phikʻol), 106
Melkʻisn, angel over waters, 34
Melkʻos
    blesses Christ, 35
    over water, 34
Menologium, 159
Meribah, place, 150
Meroë, named by Cambyses, 124
Merris
    buried in Meroë, 123, 131

INDEX OF SUBJECTS

Moses's adoptive mother, 122, 123, 126, 129, 130, 132
Meshach, 215
Mesopotamia, 56, 215, 244
Methuselah, longevity of, 274, 290
Michael
  angel, 18, 21, 33
  archangel, 150, 293
Michael the Syrian, *Chronography*, 130, 134, 220
Midian, 125, 145
  Moses flees to, 122
Milchah, 96
Milikowsky, Ch., 145
millennia, meaning of "this day," 281
Miltenova, Anissava, 294
Minēl, angel, 37
Minov, Sergei, 65
miracle attends martyrdom of three youths, 218
miracles, 234
Miriam
  criticizes Moses, 127
  dies, reason for, 149
  drum of, symbol of virginity, 290
  entered sea first, 277
  handmaiden of Pharaoh's daughter, 143
  leprosy of, 147
  Moses mourns, 149
  Moses's sister, 143
  punished, because woman, 277
  virgin and prophet, 149, 277
Mishael, 242, 244
  appointed chief scribe, 243
  called Abednego, 230
  decapitated, 233
  son of Jehoiakim, 214
Moab, birth of, 103
Moabites, 103
Moses, 6, 25, 62, 121, 180, 210, 284
  arms high, 162
  birth and hiding of, 143
  birth of, 142
  bringer of oracles, 146
  burns tongue, 144
  called god, 142
  called Hermes, received divine honors, 122
  connected with worship of ibises, 123
  countenance of, 153, 216
  countenance of, brilliant like Adam, 148, 157
  cruciform seal, 152
  death of, 150
  delayed mission to Egypt, 145
  education, Egyptian, 145
  in Egypt, Syriac sources of, 129
  Egyptian general, 121, 122, 123, 145
  Ethiopian campaign, 121, 122, 123, 131,
  face of, aroused fear, 157
  fled to Arabia, 123
  fought At'iupas, King of the Philistines, 131
  four births of, 151, 178
  grave of, hidden, reason for, 150
  Greek teachers of, 145
  handsome, 144
  hidden, redemption of Israel, 276, 290
  intelligible light of, 157
  invocation by, 152, 236
  knew Lord face to face, 151, 157
  marries Cushite woman, 147
  marries Sippora, 134
  marries Tharbis, 124
  medieval Jewish portrayal of, 125
  miracles happened to, 157
  name for Pentateuch, 79, 80, 106, 112
  no beard, 149
  ordains Eleazar priest, 148
  people calumniate, 149
  proto-prophet, 142
  pulls Pharaoh's beard, 144
  received God's command, 146
  reformed Egyptian administration, 122
  refuses to return to Egypt, 133
  shoes of, 161
  smites rock, 149, 150
  son of rock, 151
  speech impediment, 145
  submitted to test, 144

Moses, *continued*
   ten years' war against Ethiopia, 145, 147
   wetnurse of, 143
   wrote Job, 210
Moses and Aaron, sources of, 125–27, 134
Movsēs Xorenac'i, 56
Mt. Hor, 148
mule, miscegenation of, 96
Muradyan, Gohar, xi, 171, 245, 252
Murray, Robert, 58
musical instruments, 244
Mxit'ar Ayrivanec'i, 6, 234, 273
Mxit'ar, Rev., 45
myrrh (storax), 113

Nabupolassar, king, father of Nebuchadnezzar, 214
Nahor, 69, 96, 104
   eight sons of, 104
name
   God's, power of, 236
   of angel, 35
Naphtali, 188
naphtha and oil, inflammable agents, 246
narrative elements forestalling Questions, 256–57
Natanayēl, over children, 35
Nebo, Mount, 150
      Moses dies on, 148
Nebuchadnezzar, 230, 231, 232, 237, 242, 244,
   dream of, 232
   praises God, 247
Nebuzradran, 214
Nep'rovt. *See* Nimrod
Nersēs, craftsman of the Ark, 49
New Testament Apocrypha, 221
Nickelsburg, George W. E., 238
Nimrod
   casts Abraham into fire, 96
   hunter, 62, 69
Nineveh, 178, 179, 180, 181, 186, 187, 190, 191, 193, 195, 279
   penitence of, 196, 197, 198
   rejoicing of, 184
   three days to repent, 180

Ninevehites
   honor Jonah, 197
   sinned, 178
   wish to accompany Jonah, 185, 198
Ninos, Nineveh named after, 193, 194,
Noah, 295
   built Ark in 100 years, 290
   curses Canaan and not Ham, 275
   longevity of, 275
   mocked, 49
   virgin for 500 years, 49, 274, 290
Noyem Zara, Noah's wife, 50

odor, ill, 12
Og, King, 147
omens, 192
Onan, son of Judah, 114
one thousand, symbolized, 291–292
onomastic explanations, 214, 215
Or (Hur), 162
ordination, 142
Origen, 24
   On First Principles 1.1.8, 25
   opposition to, 19
Orlov, A. A., 34
Ōsit, place, 210
Othniel, judge, 188, 192

Parke, Herbert W., 251
patience, virtue of, 199
Paul, 14
Paz, Yakir, 256
penitence, 182, 183
Peoples of the Sons of Noah, work, 68
peoples
   dispersed, twelve, 68
   seventy-two, 71
Peor, idols of, 150
Perez, 115
Persians, sea of, 195
Peter, apostle, 282
Phanuel, angel, 18, 22
Pharan, place, 77
Pharaoh, 115, 116, 142, 143, 144, 146, 150
   drowned because he drowned boys, 146, 152, 277, 291
   daughter of saw Moses's ark, 143

INDEX OF SUBJECTS

daughter of adopts Moses, 144
Philo
    Questions on Exodus, 256
    Questions on Genesis, 256
pig unclean because Egyptians ate it, 277, 291
Pirkei deRabbi Eliezer, work, 187
pitch, 48, 56, 57, 58, 62, 71
plagues, ten, 146
Plato, 251
Pollak, Yuval, xi
Porter, Barbara N., 274
possessed, as lyre, 273
Potiphar, eunuch, 113
Powers, angelic class, 17, 21, 23, 28
prayer, thrice daily to Jerusalem, 235
Prayers of Azariah and of Three Young Men, work, 221, 238, 247
pride, causes Satan's fall, 16
priests' deception, 237
primogeniture, 105–7
Princedoms, angelic class, 17, 23
princes, 181
Principalities, angelic class, 17, 21
prison, called Hell, 12
promise, God's to Jacob, 108
prophecy, 100
    interpretation of, 100
prophet, false, 178
prostitute, 114
proto-prophet (Moses), 160
proto-martyr, 160
Proverbs, 210
ps.-Zeno, *Philosophical Treatise*, 6
Pseudo-Dionysius, Heavenly Hierarchy, 15

quail, 146
Queen of Ethiopia
    honored by Moses, 147
    in desert wandering, 148
    Moses captures, 148
Questions and Answers from Holy Books
    work, 53
    manuscripts of, 256
    texts, 256
    polemical use of, 256
questions in Jewish literature, 256

Questions of Ezra, work, 256
Questions of St. Gregory, work, 8, 9, 256
Questions of the Queen, work, 78, 256

Ra'osa, Syriac name of Moses's adoptive mother, 129, 130, 131
Rabbis and Homeric scholarship, 256
Rachel, 34, 108, 109, 110
    barren, 109
    death of, 112
    steals idols, 110
Raguel, 123, 124, 145, 210
    Moses marries daughter of, 123
Rajak, Tessa, 124
Ṙak'el, oak of, 198
rape, 111
Raphael, Rayphael, angel, 18, 21, 34
raven(s), 50
    Abraham story of, 76,
Rebecca, 104, 105, 108, 112
    barren, 105
    favors Jacob, 107
Red Sea, splitting of, 100, 146
Reed, Annette Y., 274
Rehoboam, Eli prophesied concerning, 165
responses, ten, 42
resurrected, will be like Adam in Eden, 284
resurrection, 157
Reu, 69
Reuben
    son of Leah, 109, 113, 116
    kills Shechemites, 112
Reuben, tribe, 168
rib, character of, 42
Riggs, Elias, 296
righteous
    non-Christians, fate of, 283
    light of, 157
ring, of king, 235
rock
    destroys statue, 232
    cries out, 186, 192
    in the desert was Christ, 277, 291
Rulers, angelic class, 21, 28
Runnalls, Donna, 124

Russell, J. R., 12

Saba, Ethiopian capital, 124
Sabbath, 235
Sabeans, 205
sacrifice, Abraham's, 99
saints
    arose on Friday after Christ's resurrection, 282
    resurrected, 283, 292
Sałamanos, angel, 36
Salathiel,
    father of Zerubbabel, 33
    angel, 33
Samaria, woman of, 169
Samuel Anec'i, 6
Sanctus prayer, 23, 32
Sanjian, A. K., 50
Saragiēl, 35
Sarah, 96, 99, 101, 103
    angel, 34
    death of, 104
    deceit by, 97
    laughs, 100
    name changed, 101
    received 1,000 silver pieces, 103
Sarak'iel, over births, 35
Sarankas, River, 195
Sarara, land, 186, 192
Sararad, Mt., Ark stopped at, 275
Sarghissian, Basile, 222
Sarra (Sarah), 101
Sasanians, 218
Satan, 13, 14, 34, 42, 204, 205, 206, 207
    crown of, 293, 297
    entered Judah, 282
    fall of, 16, 18
    heard God's words to Adam, 273
    hubris of, 289
    humiliates Job, 207
    possessed serpent, 273, 289
    reason for transgression by, 272
    tries Job's faith, 205, 207
    uncertain about of Son of God, 279, 291
Satran, David, 192, 236, 281
Saul, knew David, 278

Sawalaneanc', T., 131, 220
Schermann, Theodor, 165, 187, 190
Schiffman, Lawrence H., 122
Schmidt, Andrea B., 130
Schwemer, Anna Maria, 190
Scott, James M., 68
seal, 235
Sedrach, 215
Sefer Ha-Yashar, 124
Sēir, 111
Sēir is Esau, 112
semantron, summons animals to Ark, 50
Semē, place, 97
Semiramis, 193
Seraphs, 17, 21, 23, 24, 28, 33, 37
Serjuni (Kahavedjian), A. H., 242
Sermon (Preaching) of Jonah in Nineveh, work, 181
Sermon Concerning the Three Young Men, work, 238
Sermon, as title, 26
serpents, infest route, 123
seven foundations, 163
seven sons and seven daughters, Job's, 204
Seven "Vanangs" of Joseph, work, 242
seventh/seventy-two, variation of, 61
seventy-two
    family heads, 71
    languages and peoples, 68
Seventy-Two Languages, work, 61
Shamiram, 193
Sheba, Queen of, 253
Shechem and Hamor, confusion of, 104
Shechem, son of Hamor, 111
Shelah, son of Judah, 114, 115
Shem, 49, 275
Shemites, twenty-five languages, 70
shepherds, 23
    quarrel, 97
Shiloh, city, 165
Shinan, Avigdor, 124, 125
shining face(s), 148, 196, 216
    of Moses, 149
Shirin, queen, wife of Xosrov Parviz, 218, 219
Shirinian, M. E., 6
Short Story of Elijah, work, 251

Shtrubel, Anita, xi
Shua
    daughter of Hirah, 114
    identification of, 114
Sibyl, 251
    Cumaean, 252
    Egyptian, Sabba, 253
Sibylline Books, of Rome, 253
Sibylline Oracles, Jewish and Christian, 251
Sibyls, connection to cross, 253
sign(s), 146
    fifteen, 53
    hint at Christ, 187
    and miracles, 151
    Jonah gives, 192
Sihon, King, 147
silver drachma worth ten drams, 282
silver
    given to Judah
    that given by Abraham, 281
    that received for Joseph, 282
    thirty pieces of, 113
Simeon, 116, 117
    kills Shechemites, 112
Simēon Abarancʻi, *Pahlavuni House* 2, 4
Sippora, Moses's wife, 124
Smith, Agnes Lewis, 3
Smith, Kyle, 130
snake blocks hole in Ark, 295
snakes, 148
Sodom, 97, 193
    destruction of, 101
    king of, 98
sodomy, 113
Sokʻayēl, angel, 36
Solomon, 53, 75, 217, 279, 295
    and the Bubu Bird, work, 293
    Eli prophesied concerning, 165
    sins of not forgiven, 278, 279, 291
    Solomon texts, 165, 293
    texts about, 75
    versified Job, 210
    wisdom saying of, 78
    wise, 294
    wives lead astray, 165
    Writings of, 3

Son (divine), 25, 63, 232
    comes with clouds, 235
    Word identified with angel, 231
sons of prophets, 169
Sophar, monarch of Mineans, 208
Šoš (Isfahan), 222, 235
sound, seven physiological instruments of, 61
speakers with God, 242
Speyer, Wolfgang, 245
splitting, drying up of Tigris and Euphrates, 219
Srapyan, Armenuhi, 46, 293
St. Gregory, story of, 233
stade, 57, 58
statue of metals, 232
Stephen the Theban, *Sermo Asceticus*, work, 66
Stephen, protomartyr, 216
Stone, Michael E., passim
stone, standing, anointed, 108
stoning, 114
stork(s), 127, 132, 147
Story of Daniel, work, 154
Story of Father Abraham, work, 3
Story of Nineveh, work, 171, 183, 191
Story of Noah, work, 61, 70
Story of Terah and of Father Abraham, work, 76
Strugnell, John, 9
Suciu, Alain, 66
Sukʻayēl, 36
Sun and moon, stand still, 162
Sunday, 152
Susana, story of, 211, 221, 230
Susanna, name midrash, 215
swallow, bird, 296
sweetness, of God, 66
sword
    flaming, 274
    flaming, removed by Cross, 290
    two-edged, 11
Synaxarium, Armenian, 218, 222
Syriac, role of, 65
Syrians, 198

T'ad, person, placed in Babylon, 69
t'an, 236
T'esbi, Ethiopian queen, 122, 126, 127, 132, 133, 145
T'ovbeni, angel, 37
T'ulkuran, place, 210
Tabernacle, likeness of heavens, 147, 147
tables, two, stone, 53, 146
Tablets, glory of, enhanced, 157
Tabor, Mount, 155, 158, 284
Tabula Gentium, 61, 71
Tamar, 114
Tamrazyan, Hrachea, xi
Tarsus (Tarshish), 178, 179, 194
teeth, gnashing of, 13
Temple made without hands, 36
Temple, heavenly, 21
Ter-Ghevondyan, Vahan, xi
Ter-Vardanyan, Gēorg, xi, 45
Terah, 96
Terah, idol-maker, 76, 77
Terian, Abraham, xi, 15
Tesbi or Tharbis, daughter of king, 133
Testaments of the Twelve Patriarchs, work, 242
Tharbis
    daughter of Ethiopian king, 124, 128, 129, 132
    falls in love with Moses, 134
The Story of Jonah and Nineveh, work, 191
The Three Hebrews, work, 216
Theodor Ber Koni, *Scholia*, 129
theophany, 162
there, meaning: the world to come, 182
Thermouthis, Moses's adoptive mother, 123, 131, 132
Third Story of Joseph, work, 242, 282
thirty days mourning, 151
thirty years, 49, 155
Thomson, R. W., 67, 71, 218
three apostles on Mt. Tabor, 282, 291
three hundred and eighteen, warriors, 98
three young men, 238, 242
three youths
    learn Chaldean writing and wisdom, 230, 242
    bound to a plank, 246
    cast into furnace, 238, 246
    countenances of, 230, 231
    education of, 243
    praise God, 246–247
    refuse king's food, 230
    refuse to worship statue, 244
    eat divine food, 217
    high appointments of, 217
    instructed in Chaldean learning, 215, 216
    relics of, honored, 217
Throne of God, 34
Thrones, angelic class, 15, 17, 21, 24, 28
thunder, 102
Thursday, 152
tongues, confusion of, 71, 72
Topchyan, Aram, xi, 50, 171, 275
Torah, giving of, omitted, 121
Torijano Morales, Pablo, 78, 278
Tower of Babel, 52, 53, 59, 62
    building for forty years, 56, 57, 58, 63
    building of, purpose of, 61
    built for fear of new flood, 276, 290
    height of, 56, 57, 58, 62, 64, 67, 71, 72
Transfiguration, 155, 158
Translators, Seventy-Two, 54
trial, ordeal, 245
Trinity, 231
Twelve Literate Nations, work, 68, 69
Tyre, 190

Uriel, 18, 21, 33
Ushakova, Maria, xi

Van, city, 45
Vanakan *vardapet* Taušec'i, *Book of Questions*, 256
Vardan Arewelc'i, 130
Vardan, *Commentary on Genesis*, 79
Vardanyan, Edda, 35, 144, 182
veil, Moses's, 149, 158
Vergil, 251, 252
višap, 12
vision
    of dry bones, nature of, 279
    four meanings of word, 214

intelligible, 66
Vita of Daniel, work, 237
Vita of Jonah, work, 171, 172, 186, 187, 188, 189, 190, 191, 192, 198
Vitae Prophetarum, work, 165
Vitae Prophetarum, Armenian, work, 166
Vřam, King of Persians, 234

wandering in desert, for purification, 276
wasp, 296
water, 5, 6
weapons, 152
well, filled with stones, 106
Wevers, John William, 101
whale, dragon of fish Jonah, 195
whipping, 99
Williams, Frank, 25
wind, 5, 6
    regulation of, 7
    scatters the Tower, 66
    weighing of, 7
wine, Noah started consumption of, 276
wisdom
    of God's spirit fills three youths, 216
    divine, 216
    of three youths, 217
Word God became infant, 279
world, divided into three, 68
worm
    beseech from wood, 186, 192
    unsleeping, 8, 53, 193
Wright, Benjamin G., 281

Wright, David P., 274
Wutz, Franz Xavier, 101, 215

Xosrov, king of Persians, 218

Yeshu', Syrian physician, 131
Yespanēs, chief eunuch, 215
Yovhannēs T'lkuranc'i, 148
Yoviēl, over sleep, 35
Yovsēp'eanc', S., 41, 166, 170, 186, 187, 189–93, 196
Yusuf and Zuleika, Story of, work, 242

Zacharias, 23
Žamkoč'yan, A., 293
Zareh, 210
Zarephath, place, 190
Zarephath, widow of, 186, 187
Zaros, King of Ethiopia, 131
Zeboiim, place, 97
Zechariah, prophet, 283
Zephaniah, 166
Zerah (Zara), 115
Zeyt'unyan, Antranik, 101
ziggurat, 62
Zilpah, 109
Zippora, 147
Zit'ayel, angel, 33
Zoar, place, 97, 102
Zohrabean, J., 199
Zoroastrians, 69

Index of Ancient Sources

Hebrew Bible

Genesis
1:1	6
1:2	6
1:3–5	7
1:21	12
1:22	67
1:28	67
2:4	7
2:8	273, 289
2:15	289
2:16–17	273
2:22	289
2:22–23	273
2:5	6
3:9	50
3:23	13
3:24	274
4:9	265, 280
4:10	101
4:15	281
4:18–19	274
4:23–24	274, 281
4:24	281
5:32	49, 274
6:9	49
6:14	48
6:15	48
6:16	48
7:4	275
7:6	49, 275
7:11	51
7:12	275
7:17	62, 275
7:19	50
7:24	50, 62
8:5–6	50
8:8–11	51
8:9	50
8:12	51
8:13	51
9:4–5	275
9:13–16	62
9:20–21	275
9:22	275
9:25	275
10	61, 71
10:1	275
10:6	275
10:9	63
10:10	56, 63
11:1	71
11:3	56, 57, 58, 62
11:3–4	71
11:4	62, 275
11:7	63
11:7–9	71
11:26–27	96
11:27	96
11:28	96
11:31	96
12:1, 4	96
12:5	96
12:10	97
12:13	97

Genesis, continued			
12:15	97	19:5	102
12:17	97	19:7–8	102
12:18–20	97	19:9b–11	102
13:7	97	19:11	102
13:7–12	97	19:12	102
13:14–15	97	19:13–14	102
14:1–3	97	19:16–17	102
14:4	98	19:23	102
14:8–10	98	19:26	102
14:1–2	97	19:30	102
14:12	98	19:30–36	103, 278
14:14–16	98	19:37–38	103
14:18–20	98	20:1	103
14:21–24	98	20:1–2	103
14:24	98	20:2–3	103
15:1	98	20:4–12	103
15:1–3	99	20:6	103
15:4	99	20:14	103
15:9–11	99	20:16	103
15:9–16	100	21:1–2	103
15:13	100, 118	21:21	77
15:14	100	22:1	96
15:17	99	22:23	104
15:24–25	118	23	104
16:2	99	23:16	103, 104
16:4–6	99	23:2–19	104
16:5	99	23:34–35	108
16:10	99	24:1–8	104
16:6–9	99	24:10	104
17:4–5	101	24:12–14	104
17:5	101	24:15–25	104
17:10–13	100	24:22	104
17:14	100	24:28–33	104
17:15	101	24:30	104
18:2	100	24:33–45	105
18:6–8	100	24:58–59	105
18:9–16	100	24:63–65	105
18:10	101	24:67	105
18:13	100	25:1–4	105
18:14	101	25:5–6	106
18:16–17	101	25:8	163
18:20	101	25:9–10	106
18:21	101	25:12–15	99
18:32–33	101	25:17	163
19:1	102	25:22	105
19:3	102	25:22–23	105
		25:25–27	105

25:29–33	106	30:25	109
25:32	105	30:25–36	109
26:1–11	106	30:37–42	109
26:12	106	31:7	109
26:15	106	31:19	110
26:16	106	31:24	110
26:18–22	106	31:30	110
26:26	106	31:32	110
26:26–31	106	31:34–35	110
26:27	106	31:44–49	110
27:1	107	31:50	110
27:3–4	107	32:7–11	110
27:7	107	32:8	111
27:9–13	107	32:17–18	111
27:14–17	107	32:20	22
27:19–22	107	32:24–25	110
27:26–30a	107	32:26–28	110
27:29	107	32:29–30	110
27:29–30a	107	32:31	110
27:31	107	33:4	111
27:33	107	33:9	104
27:35	107	33:11	111
27:37	107	33:12–14	111
27:38	107	33:14–17	111
27:39	107	33:16	111
27:40	107	33:18	111
27:41–43	107	34:1–2	111
28:8–9	112	34:3–4	112
28:9	108	34:25–29	112
28:11	108	34:30	112
28:18–19	108	35:1	112
29:1–10	108	35:5	112
29:4	109	35:6	112
29:15–18	108	35:11	112
29:17	108	35:16–18	112
29:23–25	108	35:22	112
29:26–27	108	35:27–28	112
29:28	108	35:29	163
29:30	109	35:6	191
29:32–35	109	35:8	187
30:7	109	36:2–3	112
30:9	109	36:11	192
30:14	109	36:11, 15	188
30:15–16	109	36:12	152
30:16–17	109	36:33	204
30:17	109	37:2	113
30:22–24	109	37:5–8	113

Genesis, continued			
37:9–10	113	44:3	117
37:12–36	113	44:3–11	117
37:14	113	44:22	117
37:14–22	113	45:4	117
37:25–28	113	45:28	117
37:30	92	46:29	117
37:31–33	114	46:29–32	117
37:35	114	46:29–34	117
38:1	114	47:1–6	117
38:2	114	47:13–19	118
38:11	114	47:22	118
38:11–20	114	47:28	118
38:18	92	47:29	118
38:23	114	48:1	118
38:24	114	48:3	112
38:24–26	115	48:5–20	118
38:27–30	115	49:1	118
38:28	115	49:5–7	142
39:1	115	49:33	163
39:4	115	50:20	118
39:11–18	115	Exodus	
39:22	115	1:22	143, 277
40:1–14	115	2:2	143
40:14	115	2:3	143
40:16–23	115	2:5	143
40:23–41:1	115	2:6	143
41:1	93	2:6–9	143
41:1–7	116	2:10	144
41:8	116	2:11	145
41:9–12	116	2:15	145
41:14–17	116	2:20	144
41:34	116	2:22	145
41:38–44	116	3:1	161
41:45	117	3:2–4:17	145
41:47–49	116	3:5	161
41:50–52	117	3:21–22	275
41:55–57	116	4:10	145
42:1–14	116	4:11	146
42:18–34	117	4:14–16	146
42:22	116	4:16	150
42:24	116	4:28–31	146
42:25	116	5:1	146
42:36–38	117	6:20	143
43:9–11	117	6:22	145
43:15–22	117	7:1	142, 150
43:32	117	7:3	151
		13:1	118

14:15	162	20:12	114
14:15–22	152	Numbers	
14:21	219	3:5–49	147
14:21–22	162, 169	8:5–26	147
14:22	12	10:12	77
14:23–28	152	12:1	122, 124, 133, 277
14:29	12	12:1–4	147
14:30	152	12:8	157
14:31	146	12:8–10	277
15:1	152	12:9–10	147
15:19	277	20:2–8	149
15:20	277	20:2–13	150
17:1–7	150	20:11	150
17:6	277	20:22–28	148
17:8–13	147, 162	20:23–28	147
17:10–13	162	20:24	149
17:12	162	20:29	148
18:4	145	21:12	150
19:9	161	21:16	150
24:12	146	25:59	143
24:13	161	26:59	142
24:18	137	27:12–14	150
25:9	147	27:14	150
28:1	142, 147	27:15–23	148
28:9	147	27:18–23	161
29	142	33:38	148
29:1	147	Deuteronomy	
29:9	147	1:2	161
29:20–21	147	1:8	275
31:3	216	1:38	161
31:8	156	3:28	161
31:18	146	4:34	151
31:35	216	6:22	151
32:1	161	8:2–3	146
32:15–16	146	8:15–16	146
32:26–28	147	9:9	137
33:11	157, 161	9:18	137
33:20–24	151	11:4	277
33:22–23	157	22:22	114
34:3	161	31:7	148, 161
34:28	137, 161	31:7	275
34:29–30	216	32:8	66, 71
34:29–35	149, 154	32:48–52	149, 150
35:31	216	32:50	163
40:12–16	147	32:51	150
Leviticus		33:8–11	142
8	142, 147	34:1	148

332 ARMENIAN APOCRYPHA FROM ADAM TO DANIEL

Deuteronomy, *continued*		17:9	191
34:1–5	150	17:19–22	188
34:4	149	19	167
34:6	150	19:12	167
34:7	148	19:20	168
34:8	151	Second Kings	
34:9	161	2:8	169
34:9–10	151	2:11–12	280
34:10	157	2:14	169
34:10–11	151	2:15	169
Joshua		2:16	169
3:7	162, 163	2:19–22	169
3:15	169	2:23	169
3:15–17	219	3:24	169
3:16–17	162, 169, 219	4:1	169
4:23	162	17:5–6	214
5	162	24:13–15	214
5:13–14	162	25:1–8	242
5:14	162	25:11	214
6:5	163	Isaiah	
8:18	162	6:3	23, 32, 37
8:26	162	10:9	56, 63
10:11	162	14:12	18
10:12–14	162	14:13–14	272
12:9–24	162	15:2	182
12:24	162	30:26	285
13:7–19:51	162	42:6	285
18:1	165	50:6	182
24:22	118	51:10	285
24:29	163	53:6	17
Judges		63:1	279, 291
2:8	163	65:17	280
2:10	163	66:22	280
First Samuel		66:24	8, 14, 193, 194
1:9	165	Jeremiah	
4:15	165	39:9	214
4:18	165	50:6	17
5:1–7:2	190	Ezekiel	
Second Samuel		18:33	194
7:5	278	33:11	194
19:19	179	Amos	
First Kings		6:2	56, 63
2:8, 13, 14	179	Jonah	
5:3	278	1:2	178
12:14	165	1:3	178
12:28	165	1:4	179
17:8–24	187	1:5	194

INDEX OF ANCIENT SOURCES 333

1:5c	179	2:2, 23	33
1:6	179	Zechariah	
1:6b	195	1:12	23
1:7	179	11:11	283
1:8	194	Psalms	
1:9b	195	2:8	23
1:10	179	16(15):10	13
1:10–11	195	21:6 (20:7)	213, 217
1:12	179	24(23):8	23
1:12a	195	28(27):1	13
1:13–14	179	45:5(44:7)	24
1:14	195	62(61):11	281
1:15	179, 195	66(65):6	162
1:16	195	72(71):19	24
1:17	180, 195	90(89):4	291, 292
2	170, 171	110(109):4	23
2:1	177	115:17 (113:17)	13
2:1–9	195	119(118):176	17
2:2	188	135(134):13	72
2:6	188	136(135):6	285
2:9	188	145(144):13	23
2:10	180, 195	Proverbs	
2:29	151	8:17	217
3	178	Job	
3:1–2	180	1:2–3	204
3:3	196	1:4	204
3:4	178, 196	1:5	204
3:6	181	1:6–7	20
3:6a	180	1:11	205
3:7–9	181, 182	1:12–15	205
3:10	184	1:15	205
4:1–2	175	1:16	205, 206
4:2	178, 191, 197	1:17	206
4:2–3	194	1:18–19	206
4:3	184	1:19	206
4:4	197	1:21	206
4:5–6	197	1:22–2:1	206
4:6	184	2:2	206
4:8	185	2:3	207
4:9	197	2:4	207
4:9–10	184	2:5–6	207
4:10	197	2:7	207
4:11	184, 198	2:8	207
Habakkuk		2:9	208
2:11	192	2:11	208
Haggai		2:12–13	208
1:1, 12, 14	33	2:21b	208

Job, continued		2:2–19	232
3:6b	209	2:10–11	233
19:8	148	2:12	233
38	209	2:13	233
38–41	209	2:16	233
38:1–2	209	2:31–34	232
42:10	209	2:34–35	232
42:1–6	209	2:47	232
42:11	209	2:48	233
42:12	209	3:1	231
42:13–14	209	3:5	232, 244
42:16	209	3:6	244
42:16–17	210	3:8–12	244
Job, Arm		3:10	244
1:6–7	205	3:12	245
LXX 2:9	202	3:12–19	231
1:12	205	3:13	244
1:22	206	3:13–14	244
2:8	207	3:15	244, 245
2:9	208	3:19	244
2:10	208	3:21	246
2:12–13	202	3:21–22	246
3:2–3	209	3:24–5	247
Esther		3:25	231, 232, 246
2:23	115	3:26	247
5:14	115	3:28	246
Daniel		3:28–29	245
1:1–6	242	Greek 3:88	246
1:3	215, 230	4:37	245
1:4	215, 230	6:4–6	235
1:5	216, 230, 242	6:9	236
1:6	230	6:10	235, 236
1:7	215	6:12	236
1:8	216	6:14	236
1:8–13	243	6:16	236
1:10	230, 238	6:17	236
1:10–13	243	6:19–30	237
1:11–15	216	6:20	237
1:12	216, 230, 243	6:24	237
1:12–14	231	6:26–27	245
1:14–16	243	7	235
1:15	216, 231	7:10	27
1:17	215, 216, 231	7:13	284
1:17–20	243	9:8	245
1:19	217	10:11	213
1:19–20	217	10:11–19	218
2:1–4	233	10:19	213

INDEX OF ANCIENT SOURCES

12:3	148, 216	Mark	
12:13	218	4:8	280
14:31–32	237	9:2	282
Dan, Arm 1:11	216	9:4	284
Ezra		15:39	279
3:8	33	Luke	
5:2	33	2:14	23
9:7	245	3:4	35
Nehemiah		7:28	279
9:2	245	9:28	282
9:26–30	245	9:30	284
12:1	33	9:33	284
First Chronicles		23:43	281, 292
3:15	230	John	
3:17	33	1:23	35
7:27	161	3:5	283
22:5	278	3:18	283
22:8	278	8:12	35
23:1	278	11:52	66
29:6	278	12:46	35
Second Chronicles		13:27	282
36:20	214	Acts	
		6:15	216
New Testament		7:58–60	160
Matthew		20:32	284
1:12	12, 13, 33	Romans	
1:16	211	11:10	14
3:3	35	14:17	284
3:4	77	1 Corinthians	
5:14	35	10:4	277, 291
10:16	283	2 Corinthians	
11:11	279	5:1	36
13:8	280	Ephesians	
13:23	280	1:11	284
17:3	284	1:18	284
17:1	282	Colossians	
22:13	12, 13	1:12	284
24:30	284	3:24	284
25:30	12, 13	1 Timothy	
25:34	217	2:14	285
26:15	113, 281	Hebrews	
26:64	284	4:12	11
27:3	113	9:11	36
27:9	113	11:7	96
27:52–53	283	1 Peter	
27:54	279	1:4	284
		2:25	17

Jude		3 Bar. 11	285
9	150	4 Ezra (2 Esd)	
Revelations		5:5	12
7:9	66	1:5	36
8:1–3	285	3:28–36	243
16:6	283	7:97	36, 148, 155
18:5	101	7:106	180
		7:125	35, 148, 155
APOCRYPHA		8:52	274
		10:25	148, 155
Bel and the Dragon		13:5	36
14:2, 6	244	14:1	188
14:31, 33–39	236	4 Ezra Arm	
Jdt 8:26	96	4:10	284
1 Macc 2:52	96	4:21	284
3 Macc 6:6	231	Hist. Rech. 2:8	57
Pr Azar		Jos. Asen. 56:17	50
1	232	Jub.	
4–9	245	4:33	49, 50
23	246	8:10–9:15	68
23–27	246	31:9–20	142
24	244	36:10	62
26	231	LAB	
26–27	246	12	155
27	246	19:16	150
Sir 3:21–22	284	25–28	192
Sir 49:51	118	25–29	188
Wis 18:16	11	26:8	246
		LAE 49:3	62
PSEUDEPIGRAPHA		Odes Sol. 15:2	148
		Pr. Man. 3	236
ALD 4–5	142	Sib. Or.	
Apoc. Ab. 1–3	76	5.257	253
1 En.		6.26–28	253
38:4	155	Syr. Men. 2:309	155
40:4	7	T. Job	
41:4	7	1:1	204
60:12	7	1:6	204
62:10	148	9–10	204
63:11	148	T. Jos. 3:4	216, 243
102:1	62	T. Levi	
2 En.		2:3	168
65:11	148	8:1–100	142
66:7	148	Vita of Elisha 1–3	166
69:1	148, 155	Vita of Habakkuk	236
A 65:11	155		
A 66:7	155		
1 Bar. 1:1–2	214		

INDEX OF ANCIENT SOURCES

Dead Sea Scrolls

1QapGen ar 2.23	58
1QapGen ar 20.21–34	97
1QH 11:3–4	155
4Q464	65

Jewish Greek Sources

Artapanus, Fg. 3.7–18	122, 123, 124, 125, 129
Josephus, *A.J.*	
1.70–71	62
2.9.2	142
2.9.6–7	144
2.238–253	122
Philo, *Moses*	
1.5	144
1.5–7	145

Armenian Pseudepigraphical Sources

Abel and Cain 26–33	281
Armenian Life of Moses	66
Brief History of Joshua 5	161
11	162
13	162
24	162
27–28	162
41	162
58	162
Chronography of Philo of Tikor, MH	
165	255
906.57	255
Concerning the Good Tidings of Seth 29–33, 38c	49
Concerning the Tower 4	51
Death of Adam 14	155
Elisha 3	199
Good Tidings of Seth 33	50
Grigor Magistros in MH 16.letter 17	254
History of Adam and His Grandsons 1–12	49
History of the Forefathers, Adam 4–5	274
History of the Forefathers	
41	56, 62
42–43	65
Hours of the Day and Night Nviii	246
Jonah 1	
2	190
6	186
Joshua b. Nun Text 9 6	147
Memorial of the Patriarchs 62	282
Moses and Aaron 34	236
Names of Gems	54
Names, Works, and Deaths of Holy Prophets	252
12	236
17	187
Of Moses and Aaron 1	160
Pʻawstos Buzand 3.10	275
Philo of Tekor, Chronography	
057	66
101–105	68
Ps.–Philo, de Iona	
18, 21	273
18.3	273
Ques. Ezra	
A 20	155
A3, A16, B11–12	12, 13
Ques. Greg.	
14–24	281
32–34	243
40–41	281
42	155
Sebēos chap. 13	218
Seder Olam 5	145
Sodomites 30	47
Stepʻanos Siwnecʻi, *Commentary on Genesis*	
2.1.31–33	97
2.2.46	96
2.2.56–60	108
2.2.59–60	104
9–10	282
1.8	275
Story of Nineveh	
2	178
3	178
11	180
16	180
19	184
21	184
Story of Noah 9	53
Story of the Ark of the Covenant 32	246
Third Story of Joseph 25, 93	199

Other Armenian Authors and Works

Aṙakʿel Siwnecʿi, *Adamgirkʿ*
1.24.69	36
2, 69, 116, 124–60	12
2.1.5	155
3.5.3	155

Agatʿangełos
274	3
276	4
297	66

Movsēs Xorenacʿi
1.10–11	244
2.26–33	214

Simēon Aparancʿi, *Epic on the Pahlavuni House* 2 — 2

Vardan Arewelcʿi M1267, 5r — 151

Yačapatum Čaṙkʿ
3	5
33	4

Ancient Christian Patristic and Parabiblical Sources

Cave of Treasures
1:29	65
18:13	58

Apoc. Sedr. 7:5–6	148
Ephrem, *Hymns of Paradise* 23, 2–3	58
Ephrem on Gen 4:8	58
Epiphanius, *Panarion* 64.3–4	25
Eusebius, *Praep. ev.* 9.27.7–18	122
George Synkellos, *Chronography* 139	128
Michael the Syrian, *Chronography* 14	65

Onomastica Sacra
Ona IV 22	215
Ona V 153	215

Palaea Historica
69	144
70	127, 128, 129
168	236

Rabbinic and Other Hebrew Sources

b. B. Bat. 15a	210
b. Sanh. 39a	150

b. Soṭah
12b	142
13b	150
14a	150

m. Soṭah 1.9	150
m. Tehillim 22	187
m. Tanḥuma 8	191
m. Lekaḥ Ṭob Exod. 32.19	161
Mekh. R. Shimʿon on Exod 3.8	146
Pirkei deRabbi Eliezer 10.1	191
Seder Olam Rabba 6	137

Sipre Deut.
305	148
357.28	150

Sipre Num. 32	150
Tanḥ Beshallaḥ 2.3	150
m. Tanḥ. Exod 8.2	144
Tanḥ Lek Leka 2.2	76
m. Tanḥ. Vayakhel l 4.9	142

Tg. Ps.-J.
Exod 1:15	142
Num 12.1	124

y. Soṭah 5.6	210
y. Sukkah 5.1	187
Yalqut Shimʿoni 167	124

Midrash Rabba

Deut. Rab. 9.5	150

Exod. Rab.
1.18	142
1.26	144
20.19	150

Gen. Rab.
8.13	150
38.28	96
99.13	187

Num. Rab. 10.17	150

Index of Manuscripts

Armenian Patriarchate of Jerusalem

J393, 176
J631, 176
J652, xi xii, 148, 151, 157, 159
J669, 176
J730, 176
J652, xi xii, 148, 151, 157, 159
J1761, 145
J2558, xii, 145, 147, 157

Erevan, Maštoc' Matenadaran

M43, 145
M59, 205
M101, xi, xii, 175, 178, 204
M268, 20
M503, 176
M533, 172
M537, 20
M605, 20
M682, xi, 15
M706, 176
M724, xi, xii, 218, 219
M843, 176
M1134, xi, xii, 207
M1495, 137, 139
M1500, xi, xii, 143, 145, 146, 150, 156, 157, 176
M2168, xi, xii, 58, 79, 91
M2242, xi, xii, 24, 38
M2245, xi, xii, 1, 176
M2679, 20
M3854, 58
M4231, 58
M4618, xi, xii 7, 20, 58, 59, 61, 91, 144, 147–51, 154, 157–59, 167, 180

M5531, xi, xii, 171
M5571, xi, xii, 24, 38
M5607, xi, xii, 197, 224–27
M5933, xi, xii, 137
M6092, xi, xii, 58, 59, 73, 74, 77, 79, 101, 175, 178
M6340, xi, xii, 58, 109, 114
M6349, 58
M8093, 176
M8239, 176
M8494, 20
M9100, xi, xii, 58, 123
M10561, 145
M10986, xi, xii, 128, 143, 146

Istanbul, Armenian Patriarchate

Galata 54, 58, 126

London, British Library

Egerton 708, xii, 58, 123

Paris, Bibliothèque Nationale de France

P121, 20
BnF 128, 128

Venice, Mekhitarist Fathers

V176, 172
V280/10, 150, 151
V570, 219
V927, 4
V1260/1095, 150, 158
V1957, xii

www.ingramcontent.com/pod-product-compliance
Lightning Source LLC
Chambersburg PA
CBHW050855300426
44111CB00010B/1258